COVENANT MARRIAGE
*in*
COMPARATIVE PERSPECTIVE

## RELIGION, MARRIAGE, AND FAMILY

*Series Editors*

Don S. Browning
John Witte, Jr.

# COVENANT MARRIAGE
## *in*
# COMPARATIVE PERSPECTIVE

*Edited by*

John Witte, Jr., *&* Eliza Ellison

WILLIAM B. EERDMANS PUBLISHING COMPANY

GRAND RAPIDS, MICHIGAN / CAMBRIDGE, U.K.

Wm. B. Eerdmans Publishing Co.
255 Jefferson Ave. S.E., Grand Rapids, Michigan 49503 /
P.O. Box 163, Cambridge CB3 9PU U.K.

Printed in the United States of America

10  09  08  07  06  05      7  6  5  4  3  2  1

ISBN-10  0-8028-2993-7
ISBN-13  978-0-8028-2993-1

www.eerdmans.com

# Contents

*Series Foreword*

The Religion, Marriage, and Family series has a complex history. It is also the product of some synergism. The books in the first phase evolved from a research project located at the University of Chicago and supported by a generous grant from the Division of Religion of the Lilly Endowment. The books in this new phase of the series will come from more recent research projects located in the Center for the Study of Law and Religion in the School of Law of Emory University.

This second phase of the series will include books from two of this Center's projects, both supported by generous grants from The Pew Charitable Trusts and Emory University. The first project was called Sex, Marriage, and Family in the Religions of the Book and began with an Emory University faculty seminar in 2001. The second project was called The Child in Law, Religion, and Society and also was initiated by a semester-long Emory faculty seminar that met during the autumn of 2003.

Although the first phase of the Religion, Marriage, and Family series primarily examined Christian perspectives on the family, it also included books on theological views of children. In this second phase, family in the broad sense is still in the picture but an even greater emphasis on children will be evident. The Chicago projects and the Emory projects have enjoyed a profitable synergistic relationship. Legal historian John Witte, director of the two Emory projects, worked with practical theologian Don Browning on the Chicago initiatives. Later, Browning worked with Witte on the research at Emory. Historian Martin Marty joined Witte and Browning and led the 2003 seminar on childhood.

Some of the coming books in the Religion, Marriage, and Family series will be written or edited by Emory faculty members who participated in the two seminars of 2001 and 2003. But authors in this new phase also will come from other universities and academic settings. They will be scholars, however, who have been in conversation with the Emory projects.

This series intends to go beyond the sentimentality, political manipulation, and ungrounded assertions that characterize so much of the contemporary debate over marriage, family, and children. In all cases, they will be books probing the depth of resources in Christianity and the other Abrahamic religions for understanding, renewing, and in some respects redefining current views of marriage, family, and children. The series will continue its investigation of parenthood and children, work and family, responsible fatherhood and motherhood, and equality in the family. It will study the responsibility of the major professions such as law, medicine, and education in promoting and protecting sound families and healthy children. It will analyze the respective roles of church, market, state, legislature, and court in supporting marriages, families, children, and parents.

The editors of this series hope to develop a thoughtful and accessible new literature for colleges, seminaries, churches, other religious institutions, and probing laypersons. In this post-9/11 era, we are all learning that issues pertaining to families, marriage, and children are not just idiosyncratic preoccupations of the United States; they have become worldwide concerns as modernization, globalization, changing values, emerging poverty, changing gender roles, and colliding religious traditions are disrupting families and challenging us to think anew about what it means to be husbands, wives, parents, and children.

In the book *Covenant Marriage in Comparative Perspective,* editors John Witte and Eliza Ellison have brought together a powerful interdisciplinary team of scholars to examine the very old, yet very new, concept of covenant as it applies to marriage. It is old because covenant was a dominant metaphor for marriage throughout the histories of Judaism, Christianity, and Islam. The interaction of the idea of covenant with the concepts of contract in law, creation in theology, and nature in science made up the core of our inherited understandings of marriage.

Many commentators believe that marriage is in a state of crisis today. It is not just the sociological realities of divorce, nonmarital births, increasing cohabitation, and the possibility of same-sex unions that are thought to threaten marriage. It is also the new difficulties modern societies are having in defining marriage. Signs of this struggle are the new efforts to revive an understanding of covenant marriage. But in the present situation, the concept is not used only by church, synagogue, and mosque; it is being used by secular law and the state. Three states — Louisiana, Arkansas, and Arizona — offer their citizens the option of a kind of super marriage called covenant marriage. The essays in this collection provide probing analyses of what the idea of covenant has meant in the Abrahamic religions in the past. They also give us analyses and evaluations of what covenant might mean in the future as both a concept in law and a guiding image of marriage in religion.

DON S. BROWNING *and* JOHN WITTE, JR.

# Acknowledgments

This volume is one of a series of new volumes to emerge from the project on "Sex, Marriage, and Family & the Religions of the Book," undertaken by the Center for the Study of Law and Religion at Emory University. The project seeks to take stock of the dramatic transformation of marriage and family life in the world today and to craft enduring solutions to the many new problems it has occasioned. The project is interdisciplinary in methodology: it seeks to bring the ancient wisdom of religious traditions and the modern sciences of law, health, public policy, the social sciences, and humanities into greater conversation and common purpose. The project is interreligious in inspiration: it seeks to understand the lore, law, and life of marriage and family within Judaism, Christianity, and Islam both in their genesis and in their exodus, in their origins and in their diasporas. The project is international in orientation: it seeks to place current American debates over sex, marriage, and family within an emerging global conversation.

This combination of interdisciplinary, interreligious, and international inquiry featured in our project as a whole is at the heart of the methodology of this volume. The doctrine of covenant has reemerged in a number of contemporary Jewish, Catholic, Protestant, Orthodox, and Islamic circles around the world as a common trope to map and measure the higher spiritual dimensions of marriage. The doctrine of covenant has also reemerged separately in a number of recent American states as a convenient means of strengthening marital formation and dissolution requirements both domestically and internationally. This volume brings together leading jurists, ethicists, historians, and theologians from each of these religious traditions and beyond in an effort to integrate and elaborate this covenant theology and law of marriage. We wish to thank our contributors for sharing their special talents with us in crafting these fresh and powerful contributions to the emerging literature on covenant marriage.

We wish to express our deep gratitude to our friends at The Pew Charitable Trusts in Philadelphia for their generous support of our Center for the Study of Law and Religion at Emory University. We are particularly grateful to Pew's President Rebecca Rimel and program officers Luis Lugo, Susan Billington Harper, and Diane Winston for masterminding the creation of this Center, along with sister Centers at ten other American research universities — a bold and visionary act of philanthropy that is helping to transform the study of religion in the American academy. And, we wish to thank our Emory colleagues, former Provost Rebecca Chopp, former Provost and Dean Howard O. Hunter, and Deans Russell Richey, Robert Paul, and Thomas Arthur for generously supporting the establishment of this Center at Emory University.

We also wish to express our deep gratitude to our Emory Center colleagues, April Bogle, Anita Mann, Amy Wheeler, and Janice Wiggins, for their extraordinary work on our project on "Sex, Marriage, and Family & the Religions of the Book." Over the past three years, these colleagues have worked with us to create a dozen major public forums, an international conference in 2003 with 80 speakers and 750 participants, scores of new journal, electronic, and video publications, all to culminate in more than thirty new books on various issues of "Sex, Marriage, and the Family." They are also working with us on administering a new Center project on "The Child in Law, Religion, and Society" that will yield a dozen new public forums and two dozen new volumes over the next three years. For her editorial and production work on this volume in particular, we would like to thank the Center's Associate Editor, Amy Wheeler, ably assisted by Matthew Titus and Laurie-Ann Fallon.

We owe a special word of appreciation and admiration to Don S. Browning, Robert W. Woodruff Visiting Professor of Interdisciplinary Religious Studies at Emory University, and Alexander Campbell Professor of Ethics and the Social Sciences, Emeritus, at the University of Chicago, who joined us in the leadership of this project and who authorized the publication of this volume in the Religion, Marriage, and Family Series that he established.

Finally, we wish to thank Jon Pott and his colleagues at Wm. B. Eerdmans Publishing Company for taking on this manuscript and working so assiduously to see to its timely publication.

JOHN WITTE, JR.
ELIZA ELLISON
*Emory University*

# Contributors

**Azizah Y. al-Hibri,** J.D., Ph.D., is Professor of Law at the T. C. Williams School of Law, University of Richmond, and Founder and President of KARAMAH: Muslim Women Lawyers for Human Rights.

**Margaret F. Brinig,** J.D., Ph.D., is William G. Hammond Distinguished Professor of Law and Associate Dean for Faculty Development at the College of Law, University of Iowa.

**Michael J. Broyde,** J.D., is Professor of Law and Projects Director of the Center for the Study of Law and Religion at Emory University School of Law.

**Eliza Ellison,** M.T.S., Ph.D. candidate, is Senior Editor and Director of Fellowships of the Center for the Study of Law and Religion at Emory University.

**Stanley Samuel Harakas,** Ph.D., is the Archbishop Iakovos Professor of Orthodox Theology, Emeritus, at Holy Cross Greek Orthodox School of Theology in Brookline, Massachusetts.

**Peter Hay,** J.D., is L.Q.C. Lamar Professor of Law at Emory University School of Law.

**James Turner Johnson,** Ph.D., is Professor of Religion at Rutgers–The State University of New Jersey.

**Michael G. Lawler,** Ph.D., is Amelia B. and Emil G. Graff Professor of Catholic Theological Studies and Director of the Center for Marriage and Family at Creighton University.

**Richard C. Martin,** Ph.D., is Professor of Religion at Emory University.

**Joel A. Nichols,** J.D. and M.Div., is Assistant Professor of Law at Pepperdine University.

**Steven L. Nock,** Ph.D., is Professor of Sociology and Director of the Marriage Matters Project at the University of Virginia.

**David Novak,** Ph.D., holds the J. Richard and Dorothy Shiff Chair of Jewish Studies at the University of Toronto.

**Katherine Shaw Spaht,** J.D., is Jules F. and Frances L. Landry Professor of Law at Louisiana State University Law Center.

**Max L. Stackhouse,** Ph.D., is the Rimmer and Ruth de Vries Professor of Reformed Theology at Princeton Theological Seminary, and Director of the Kuyper Center for Public Theology.

**John Witte, Jr.,** J.D., is Jonas Robitscher Professor of Law and Director of the Center for the Study of Law and Religion at Emory University.

# Introduction

*John Witte, Jr., and Joel A. Nichols*

## Covenant Marriage v. Contract Marriage

On August 15, 1997, the State of Louisiana put in place the nation's first modern covenant marriage law.[1] The law creates a two-tiered system of marriage. Couples may choose a contract marriage, with minimal formalities of formation and attendant rights to no-fault divorce. Or couples may choose a covenant marriage, with more stringent formation and dissolution rules. The licensing costs for either form of marriage are the same. But in order to form a covenant marriage, the parties must receive detailed counseling about marriage from a religious official or professional marriage counselor, and then swear an oath, pledging "full knowledge of the nature, purposes, and responsibilities of marriage" and promising "to love, honor, and care for one another as husband and wife for the rest of our lives." Divorce is allowed such covenanted couples only on grounds of serious fault (adultery, capital felony, malicious desertion, and/or physical or sexual abuse of the spouse or one of the children) or after two years of separation. Separation

---

1. See chapters herein by Katherine Shaw Spaht and by Margaret Brinig and Steven Nock. It is important to note that covenant marriage laws, of various sorts, were commonplace in colonial New England, building in part on the Puritan covenantal theology described in the chapters herein by James T. Johnson and Max L. Stackhouse. See also George Eliot Howard, *A History of Matrimonial Institutions,* 3 vols. (Chicago, 1904), vol. 3; Edmund S. Morgan, *The Puritan Family: Religion and Domestic Relations in Seventeenth-Century New England,* revised ed. (New York: Harper and Row, 1966).

---

This introduction is excerpted, in part, from an article by the two authors, "Marriage As More Than a Mere Contract," in *The Ethics of Contract,* ed. Robin Lovin (forthcoming), and from Joel A. Nichols, "Louisiana's Covenant Marriage Law: A First Step toward a More Robust Pluralism in Marriage and Divorce Law," *Emory Law Journal* 47 (1998): 929-1001.

from bed and board is allowed on any of these grounds, as well as on proof of habitual intemperance, cruel treatment, or outrages of the other spouse. Comparable covenant marriage statutes are now in place in Arizona and Arkansas as well. Twenty-seven other states either have under consideration or have considered covenant marriage alternatives to contract marriage.[2]

These new covenant marriage laws are designed, in part, to help offset the corrosive effects of America's experiment with a private contractual model of marriage. Historically, in America, marriages were presumptively permanent commitments, and marriage formation and dissolution were serious public events. Marriage formation required the consent of parents and peers, the procurement of a state certificate, the publication of banns, and a public ceremony and celebration after a period of waiting and discernment. Marriage dissolution required public hearings, proof of serious fault by one party, alimony payments to the innocent dependent spouse, and ongoing support payments for minor children.[3]

In the last third of the twentieth century, many of these traditional rules gave way to a private contractual model of marriage grounded in new cultural and constitutional norms of sexual liberty and privacy. In virtually all states, marriage formation rules were simplified to require only the acquisition of a license from the state registry followed by solemnization before a licensed official — without banns, with little or no waiting, with no public celebration, without notification of others. Marriage dissolution rules were simplified through the introduction of unilateral no-fault divorce. New streamlined and inexpensive marital dissolution procedures aimed to release miserable couples from the shackles of unwanted marriages and to relieve swollen court dockets from the prospects of protracted litigation. Either the husband or the wife could now file a simple suit for divorce. No fault by either party would need to be proved — or staged. Courts would dissolve the union, often make a one-time division of marital property, and give each party a clean break to start life anew.[4]

This private contractual model of marriage leaves little conceptual room for the higher dimensions of marriage and little constructive role for parties other than the couple themselves to play in the process of its formation and dissolution. The strong presumption today is that an individual who has reached the age of consent has free entrance into marital contracts, free exercise of marital relationships, and free exit from marital bonds. The legal advantages that

2. See detailed citations in chapter herein by Peter Hay.

3. For a comprehensive survey of these earlier American marriage laws, see Chester G. Vernier, *American Family Law*, 5 vols. (Stanford, Calif.: Stanford University Press, 1931-38).

4. See chapters by Spaht, Brinig and Nock, and Hay herein.

still attach to the status of marriage — social welfare benefits, tax breaks, zoning protections, evidentiary privileges, life insurance and inheritance rights, probate priorities, and more — continue to make marriage more attractive than simple cohabitation, at least for couples with children or with plans to be together for the long-term. But the growing reality today is that marriage is "just a piece of paper" to be drawn up and torn up as the parties see fit.[5]

America's experiment with the private contractual model of marriage has failed on many counts and accounts — with children and women bearing the primary costs.[6] From 1969 to 1994, the national divorce rate rose to over 50 percent, with nearly two-thirds of divorces involving minor children. In the same period, a quarter of all children were raised in single-parent households. One-third of all children were born to single mothers. Two-thirds of all African-American children were raised without a father. Mother-only homes had less than a third of the median income of homes with a regular male present, and four times the rates of foreclosure and eviction. Children from broken homes proved two to three times more likely to have behavioral and learning problems as teenagers than children from two-parent homes. More than two-thirds of juveniles and young adults convicted of major felonies from 1970 to 1995 came from single- or no-parent homes.[7]

Covenant marriage laws have been one of several legal responses to these mounting social and psychological costs of America's experiment with easy-in/easy-out marriage. Covenant marriage laws capture the traditional ideal that marriage is more than just a piece of paper, more than just a transient private contract. The foundation of covenant marriage is a pledge of permanent sacri-

---

5. Katherine Anderson, Don Browning, and Brian Boyer, eds., *Marriage: Just a Piece of Paper?* (Grand Rapids: Eerdmans, 2002).

6. David Blankenhorn, *Fatherless America: Confronting Our Most Urgent Social Problem* (New York: Basic, 1995); Don S. Browning, *Marriage and Modernization* (Grand Rapids: Eerdmans, 2003); Katherine Shaw Spaht, "For the Sake of the Children: Recapturing the Meaning of Marriage," *Notre Dame Law Review* 73 (1998): 1547-49; Linda J. Waite, *Does Divorce Make People Happy? Findings from a Study of Unhappy Marriages* (New York: Institute for American Values, 2002); Judith Wallerstein and Sandra Blakeslee *Second Chances: Men, Women, and Children a Decade After Divorce,* fifteenth ann. ed. (Boston: Houghton Mifflin, 2004); Judith Wallerstein, Julia Lewis, and Sandra Blakeslee, *The Unexpected Legacy of Divorce* (New York: Hyperion, 2000); Barbara Dafoe Whitehead, *The Divorce Culture* (New York: Alfred A. Knopf, 1997).

7. See detailed sources and discussion in Joel A. Nichols, "Louisiana's Covenant Marriage Law: A First Step toward a More Robust Pluralism in Marriage and Divorce Law," *Emory Law Journal* 47 (1998): 920. More recent studies, some with more encouraging recent statistics, include Mary Ann Mason, Arlene Skolnick, Stephen D. Sugarman, *All Our Families: New Policies for a New Century* (New York: Oxford University Press, 1998); Milton C. Regan Jr., *Alone Together: Law and the Meanings of Marriage* (New York: Oxford University Press, 1999); Steven M. Tipton and John Witte Jr., eds., *Family Transformed* (Washington, D.C.: Georgetown University Press, 2005).

JOHN WITTE, JR., AND JOEL A. NICHOLS

fice — "to love, care, and honor one another as husband and wife for the rest of our lives." The formation of covenant marriage is a public and deliberative event — requiring a waiting period, and at least the consent of the couples' parents or guardians and the counseling of therapists or clerics, and by implication the communities whom those third parties represent. The dissolution of covenant marriage comes only upon betrayal of the fundamental goods of this institution — through adultery, abuse, desertion, or capital felony — or after a suitable period of careful deliberation.

Covenant marriage laws reflect the historical lesson that rules governing marital formation and marital dissolution must be balanced in their stringency — and that separation must be maintained as a release valve. Stern rules of marital dissolution require stern rules of marital formation. Loose formation rules demand loose dissolution rules. To fix the modern problem of transient marriages requires reforms at both ends of the marital process, insists Katherine Shaw Spaht, one of the principal drafters of Louisiana's covenant marriage law.[8] Today, more than twenty states have bills under discussion seeking to tighten or abolish the rules of no-fault divorce, without corresponding attention to the rules of marital formation and separation. Such efforts, standing alone, are misguided. The cause of escalating marital breakdown is not only no-fault divorce, as is so often said, but also no-faith marriage.

Covenant marriage laws allow prospective marital couples to contract out[9] of the state's laws of marriage contract by choosing a covenant marriage. Couples who consider covenant marriage must fully apprise themselves of the costs and benefits of protracting the process of marital formation and waiving their rights to no-fault divorce. But the choice of marital form is theirs. Having this choice encourages inaptly matched couples to discover their incompatibility before marriage, rather than after it. If one engaged party wants a contract marriage and the other a covenant marriage, the disparity in prospective commitment will, for many couples, be too plain to ignore. Couples will delay their wedding until their mutual commitment has deepened, or cancel their wedding if their respective commitments remain disparate. Better to prepare well for a marriage than to rush into it. Better to cancel a wedding than to divorce shortly after it. Such is the the-

8. See chapter by Spaht herein.

9. In his chapter herein, Michael Broyde argues that, in allowing private parties to opt out of the state's contract marriage regime, covenant marriage statutes had important antecedents in the New York Jewish Divorce Law of 1983. That 1983 law, revised in 1992, required New York state courts, when adjudicating divorce cases between two Orthodox Jewish parties, to postpone their civil judgment of divorce until a religious divorce had been granted by appropriate rabbinic authority. Broyde elaborates this thesis in his *Marriage, Divorce, and the Abandoned Wife in Jewish Law* (New York: Ktav, 2001).

ory of the new covenant marriage laws. The early indication, according to Margaret Brinig and Stephen Nock, is that the theory is working, even though the number of new covenant marriages remains relatively small.[10]

These covenant marriage laws seek to respect both the virtues of marriage contracts and the values of enduring marriages. These laws have been attacked as an undue encroachment on sexual liberty and on the rights of women and children; as a "Trojan horse" designed to smuggle biblical principles into American law; as an improper delegation of state responsibilities to religious officials; and as a reversion to the days of staged and spurious charges of marital fault which no-fault laws had sought to overcome. But, given the religiously neutral language of these laws, their explicit protections of both voluntary entrance and exit from the covenant union, their insistence that religious counselors be restricted in the marriage counseling they can offer on behalf of the state, and the overriding commitment of these laws to both parties' freedom of contract, such constitutional objections seem largely unavailing.[11]

The greater vulnerability of covenant marriages lies not in constitutional challenges but in individual evasions. A spouse can escape a covenant marriage simply by moving to and filing for divorce in any of the forty-seven American states without covenant marriage options, or in any number of foreign countries. As Peter Hay shows, current conflict of laws rules, both domestic and international, do not favor the enforcement of covenant marriage laws over the contract marriage laws of the forum state where the divorce case is litigated. And the trend in many noncovenant states and many foreign nations in the past decade has been to weaken, rather than strengthen, traditional forms and norms of marriage.[12] These unfavorable conflicts rules, though not yet strongly tested through litigation, underscore the reality that covenant marriage laws are an important, but only a partial, legal response to the fallout of the modern revolution of marriage and divorce.

## Marriage As More Than a Mere Contract

### Common Law Teachings

Covenant marriage laws are not only a new form of social engineering, designed to counter the rise of privatized marriage and no-fault divorce. They are also a

---

10. See chapters by Spaht and by Brinig and Nock herein.
11. See these and other objections raised and answered in Spaht and in Brinig and Nock.
12. See detailed analysis and sources in chapter by Hay herein.

new forum for the expression of traditional common law teachings that marriage is "more than a mere contract." In the American common law tradition, marriage has long been regarded as a natural if not a spiritual estate, a useful if not an essential association, a pillar if not the foundation of civil society. Marriage has required more than the general rules of private contract — of offer and acceptance, consideration and rescission, reformation and remedy. It has drawn to itself special rules and rituals of betrothal and espousal, of registration and consecration, of consent and celebration. It has also provided the basis for a long series of special rights and duties of husband and wife, parent and child, that are respected at both public and private law. As the American jurist Joseph Story put it in 1834,

> Marriage is treated by all civilized societies as a peculiar and favored contract. It is in its origin a contract of natural law. . . . It is the parent, and not the child of society; the source of civility and a sort of seminary of the republic. In civil society it becomes a civil contract, regulated and prescribed by law, and endowed with civil consequences. In most civilized countries, acting under a sense of the force of sacred obligations, it has had the sanctions of religion superadded. It then becomes a religious, as well as a natural and civil contract; . . . it is a great mistake to suppose that because it is the one, therefore it may not be the other.[13]

Chancellor James Kent, one of the great early systematizers of the American common law, wrote this about the spiritual and social utility of the marriage contract:

> The primary and most important of the domestic relations is that of husband and wife. It has its foundations in nature, and is the only lawful relation by which Providence has permitted the continuance of the human race. In every age it has had a propitious influence on the moral improvement and happiness of mankind. It is one of the chief foundations of social order. We may justly place to the credit of the institution of marriage a great share of the blessings which flow from the refinement of manners, the education of children, the sense of justice, and cultivation of the liberal arts.[14]

13. Joseph Story, *Commentaries on the Conflict of Laws, Foreign and Domestic, in Regard to Contracts, Rights, and Remedies, and Especially in Regard to Marriages, Divorces, Wills, Successions, and Judgments* (Boston: Hilliard, Gray, and Company, 1834), p. 100 (sec. 108). In his second edition, Story added this note to the quoted passage: "It appears to me something more than a mere contract. It is rather to be deemed an institution of society founded upon the consent and contract of the parties; and in this view it has some peculiarities in its nature, character, operation, and extent of operation, different from what belongs to ordinary contracts."

14. James Kent, *Commentaries on American Law*, twelfth ed., ed. Oliver Wendell Holmes Jr., 2 vols. (Boston: Little, Brown, and Company, 1896), 2:76.

W. C. Rogers, a leading jurist at the end of the nineteenth century, opened his oft-reprinted treatise on the law of domestic relations with a veritable homily on marriage:

> In a sense it is a consummation of the Divine to "multiply and replenish the earth." It is the state of existence ordained by the Creator, who has fashioned man and woman expressly for the society and enjoyment incident to mutual companionship. This Divine plan is supported and promoted by natural instinct, as it were, on the part of both for the society of each other. It is the highest state of existence, . . . the only stable substructure of our social, civil, and religious institutions. Religion, government, morals, progress, enlightened learning, and domestic happiness must all fall into most certain and inevitable decay when the married state ceases to be recognized or respected. Accordingly, we have in this state of man and woman the most essential foundation of religion, social purity, and domestic happiness.[15]

Likewise, the United States Supreme Court spoke repeatedly of marriage as "more than a mere contract," "a Godly ordinance," "a sacred obligation."[16] In *Murphy v. Ramsey* (1885), one of a series of Supreme Court cases upholding the constitutionality of anti-polygamy laws, Justice Field declared for the Court,

> For, certainly, no legislation can be supposed more wholesome and necessary in the founding of a free, self-governing commonwealth . . . than that which seeks to establish it on the basis of the idea of the family, as consisting in and springing from the union for life of one man and one woman in the holy estate of matrimony; the sure foundation of all that is stable and noble in our civilization; the best guarantee of that reverent morality which is the source of all beneficent progress in social and political improvement.[17]

The Court elaborated these sentiments in *Maynard v. Hill* (1888), a case upholding a new state law on divorce, and holding that marriage was not simply a "contract" for purposes of interpreting the prohibition in Article I sec. 10 of the United States Constitution: "No State shall . . . pass any . . . Law impairing the Obligation of Contracts." After rehearsing at length the theological and common law authorities of the day, Justice Field declared for the Court,

---

15. W. C. Rogers, *A Treatise on the Law of Domestic Relations* (Chicago: T. H. Flood, 1891), sec. 2 (p. 2).

16. *Maynard v. Hill*, 125 U.S. 190, 210-11 (1888); *Reynolds v. United States*, 98 U.S. 145, 165 (1879); *Murphy v. Ramsey*, 114 U.S. 15, 45 (1885); *Davis v. Beason*, 133 U.S. 333, 341-42 (1890).

17. *Murphy v. Ramsey*, 114 U.S. at 45.

[W]hilst marriage is often termed a civil contract . . . it is something more than a mere contract. The consent of the parties is of course essential to its existence, but when the contract to marry is executed by marriage, a relation between the parties is created which they cannot change. Other contracts may be modified, restricted, or enlarged, or entirely released upon the consent of the parties. Not so with marriage. The relation once formed, the law steps in and holds the parties to various obligations and liabilities. It is an institution, in the maintenance of which in its purity the public is deeply interested, for it is the foundation of the family and society, without which there would be neither civilization nor progress.[18]

## Religious Teachings

These traditional common law teachings that marriage is both a contract and something more were rooted in ancient Christian teachings, which in turn had antecedents and analogues in ancient Jewish and Islamic teachings. Jewish, Christian, and Islamic traditions alike have long taught that marriage is a contract — called the *ketubah* in Judaism, the *pactum* or *sponsalia* in Christianity, the *kitab* in Islam. But these traditions have also long taught that marriage is more than a mere contract — more than simply a private bargain to be formed, maintained, and dissolved as the two marital parties see fit. For all three traditions, marriage is an institution that is both private and public, individual and social, temporal and transcendent in quality. Its origin, nature, and purpose lie beyond and beneath the terms of the marriage contract itself.

Some of these parallel teachings on marriage are parts and products of broader parallels among Judaism, Christianity, and Islam. Each of these Abrahamic traditions is a religion of revelation, founded on the eternal command to love one God, oneself, and one's neighbors. Each tradition recognizes a canonical text as its highest authority — the Torah, the Bible, and the Qur'an. Each designates a class of officials to preserve and propagate its faith, and embraces an expanding body of authoritative interpretations and applications of its canon. Each has a refined legal structure — the Halacha, the canon law, and the Shari'a — that has translated its enduring principles of faith into evolving precepts of works. Each has sought to imbue its religious, ethical, and legal norms into the daily lives of individuals and communities. Each tradition has developed its own internal system of legal procedures and structures for the enforcement of these norms, which historically have and still can serve as both prototypes and complements to secular legal systems.

18. *Maynard v. Hill,* 125 U.S. at 210-11 (1888).

The chapters herein by David Novak, Michael Broyde, Michael Lawler, Stanley Harakas, James Johnson, Max Stackhouse, Azizah al-Hibri, and Richard Martin analyze and illustrate these ancient religious teachings on marriage and their continued relevance for the Jewish, Christian, and Islamic traditions today as well as for the secular legal systems of which these communities are a part.

### Marriage As Contract

It is important to recognize that, while all three traditions have long taught that marriage is more than a contract, they have also insisted that marriage is not less than a contract.

Nearly two millennia ago, Jewish rabbis created the *ketubah,* the premarital contract in which the husband and the wife spelled out the terms and conditions of their relationship before, during, and after marriage, and the rights and duties of husband, wife, and child in the event of marital dissolution. The Talmudic rabbis regarded these marriage contracts as essential protections for wives and children who were otherwise subject to the unilateral right of divorce granted to men by the Mosaic law. While the terms of the *ketubah* could be privately contracted, both the couple's families and the rabbinic authorities were often actively involved in their formation and enforcement. Moreover, the Talmud provided elaborate liturgies for their celebration of the signing of the *ketubah* and the wedding that followed.[19]

More than a millennium and a half ago, Christian theologians adopted the marriage pact or bond.[20] These contracts forged a new relationship between husband and wife and their respective families. They adopted and adapted a number of the marital and familial rights and duties set out in the household codes of the New Testament and the apostolic church constitutions as well as in Jewish, Greek, Roman, and patristic writings.[21] The early rules governing these marriage contracts, as well as related contracts respecting dowries and other marital property, were later systematized and elaborated by Christian jurists and theologians — in the eighth and ninth centuries by Eastern Orthodox, in the twelfth and thirteen centuries by Catholics, in the sixteenth and seventeenth centuries by Protestants.

---

19. See chapters by David Novak and Michael Broyde herein.

20. See Philip L. Reynolds and John Witte, Jr., eds., *To Have and to Hold: Marrying and Its Formation in Western Christendom, 400-1600* (Cambridge/New York: Cambridge University Press, forthcoming 2006).

21. Eph. 5:21–6:9; Col. 3:18–4:1; 1 Tim. 2:8-15; 5:1-2; 6:1-2; Titus 2:1-10; 3:1; 1 Peter 2:11–3:12. See sources and discussion in David Balch and Carolyn Osiek, *Families in the New Testament World: Household and House Churches* (Louisville: Westminster John Knox, 1997); Don S. Browning et al., *From Culture Wars to Common Ground,* 2nd ed. (Louisville: Westminster John Knox, 1997).

More than a millennium ago, Muslim jurists and theologians developed the *kitab,* a special form of contract *('aqd)* that a devout Muslim was religiously bound to uphold in imitation and implementation of the Prophet's example and teaching. The *kitab* ideally established a distinctive relationship of "affection, tranquility, and mercy" between husband and wife. It defined their respective rights, duties, and identities vis-à-vis each other, their parents and children, and the broader communities of which they were part. The signing of the *kitab* was a solemn religious event involving a cleric who instructed the couple on their marital rights and duties as set out in the Qur'an. While the Qur'an and Hadith set out basic norms of marriage life and liturgy, it was particularly the Shari'a, the religious laws developed in the centuries after the Prophet, that crystallized much of this tradition of marital contracts, with ample variation among the Islamic schools of jurisprudence.[22]

While these marriage contracts differed markedly within and among these three Abrahamic traditions, several broad features were common.

First, Jewish, Christian, and Islamic traditions alike made provision for two contracts — betrothals or future promises to marry and spousals or present promises to marry — with a mandatory waiting period between them, at least in Jewish and Christian circles. The point of this waiting period was to allow couples to weigh the depth and durability of their mutual love. It was also to invite others to weigh in on the maturity and compatibility of the couple, to offer them counsel and commodities, and to prepare for the celebration of their union and their life together thereafter.

Second, all three traditions insisted that marriage depended in its essence on the mutual consent of the man and the woman. Even if the man and woman were represented by parents or guardians during the contract negotiation, their own consent was essential to the validity of their marriage. Jewish and Muslim jurists came to this insight early in the development of their law of marriage contracts. The Catholic tradition reached this insight canonically only in the twelfth century, after which it was absorbed in Orthodox and later in Protestant teachings. All three traditions continued to tolerate the practice of arranged marriages and child marriages, particularly when those were politically or commercially advantageous. But the theory was that both the young man and the young woman reserved the right to dissent from the arrangement upon reaching the age of consent.

Third, while all three traditions taught that every person of the age of con-

---

22. See chapter by Azizah al-Hibri herein, and additional sources and discussion in Abdullahi A. An-Na'im, ed., *Islamic Family in a Changing World: A Global Resource Book* (London: Zed Books, 2002).

sent was free to choose a marital partner, persons were not free to choose just any-one. God and nature set a first limit to the freedom of marital contract. Parties could not marry those who were related to them by blood or by marriage — by bonds of consanguinity and affinity, as these relations were called in Scripture. Custom and culture set a second limit. The parties had to be of suitable piety and modesty, of comparable social and economic status, and ideally (and, in some communities, indispensably) of the same faith. The general law of contracts set a third limit. Both parties had to have the capacity and freedom to enter contracts, and had to follow proper contractual forms and ceremonies. Parents and guardians set a fourth limit. A valid marriage (at least for minors) required the consent of both sets of parents or guardians — and sometimes as well the consent of po-litical and/or spiritual authorities who stood *in loco parentis.*

Fourth, all three traditions often accompanied marriage promises with elaborate exchanges of property, which sometimes gave rise to their own mari-tal property contracts. The prospective husband gave to his fiancée (and, some-times to her father or family as well) a betrothal gift, sometimes a very elaborate and expensive gift. In some cultures, husbands followed this by giving a wed-ding gift to the wife. The wife, in turn, usually brought into the marriage her dowry, which was at minimum her basic living articles, sometimes a great deal more. These property exchanges were not an absolute condition to the validity of a marriage. But breach of a contract to deliver property in consideration of marriage could often result in dissolution at least of the engagement contract.

Fifth, all three traditions eventually developed a marriage liturgy — al-though whether and when this liturgy became mandatory for the validity of a marriage differed markedly within and among these traditions. In the Jewish tradition, the Talmud provided detailed liturgies and prayers for both the be-trothal and the marriage, building in part on prototypes in the book of Tobit. In the Jewish tradition, weddings were essential community events, presided over by the rabbi, and involving the entire local community.[23] The Christian tradition celebrated wedding liturgies of some sort from the start, but the earli-est surviving marriage liturgies are from the eighth century.[24] Particularly among the Eastern Orthodox, as Stanley Harakas shows, these liturgies became extraordinary visual and verbal symphonies of prayers, blessings, oaths, and rituals, including the Eucharist. These liturgies grew more slowly in the Chris-tian West, not becoming mandatory among Catholics until 1563, and subject to

23. See chapter by Novak herein. See also Kenneth W. Stevenson, *Nuptial Blessing: A Study of Christian Marriage Rites* (New York: Oxford University Press, 1982), pp. 3-8.

24. Stevenson, *Nuptial Blessing*, pp. 33-122, with samples in Mark Searle and Kenneth W. Stevenson, *Documents of the Marriage Liturgy* (Collegeville, Minn.: Liturgical Press, 1992), pp. 3ff.

wide and perennial variation and disputation among Protestants. The Islamic tradition mandated an engagement ceremony, which was a private, religious occasion involving the couple, their families, a cleric, and two or more witnesses. It began with readings from the Qur'an and marital instruction followed by final negotiation of the terms of the marriage contract, and execution and attestation by the parties. The wedding was a separate and joyous celebration, entirely secular in nature and significance, and optional.[25]

Finally, all three traditions gave husband and wife standing before their religious tribunals to press for the vindication of their marital rights. The rights to support, protection, sexual intercourse, and care for the couple's children were the most commonly litigated claims in all three traditions. But any number of other conjugal rights stipulated in the marriage contract or guaranteed by general religious law could be litigated. Included in all three traditions was the right of the parties to seek dissolution of the marriage on discovery of an absolute impediment to its validity (such as incest) or on grounds of a fundamental breach of the marriage commitment (such as adultery). In the Christian tradition, discovery of an absolute impediment resulted in an annulment of the engagement or marriage; proof of adultery or other fundamental breach resulted in divorce with the right to remarry. Orthodox and Protestant tribunals provided for either annulment or divorce; Catholics recognized only annulment and separation. The Jewish and Muslim traditions generally treated all such dissolutions through the procedures of divorce or through simple judicial declarations that the unions were contracted in error and thus void.

### Marriage As More Than Contract

The insistence on a marriage liturgy, with its solemn rituals, prayers, blessings, and oaths, is one important indication that, for Jews, Christians, and Muslims, marriage was more than a simple bilateral contract.[26] It was also a fundamental public institution and religious practice. Other media complemented the liturgies in reflecting these higher dimensions of marriage — the beautiful artwork, iconography, and religious language of the marriage contracts themselves; the elaborate rituals and etiquette of courtship, consent, and communal involvement in establishing the new marital household; the impressive production of poems, household manuals, and books of etiquette detailing the proper norms and habits of love, marriage, and parentage of a faithful religious believer. All these media, and the ample theological writings on them, helped to confirm

25. See chapter by al-Hibri herein.
26. These liturgies are emphasized especially in the chapters by Novak, Harakas, Johnson, and Stackhouse herein.

and celebrate the deeper origin, nature, and purpose of marriage in Judaism, Christianity, and Islam.

First, all three traditions recognized that marriage has its ultimate origin in the creation and commandments of God. The Jewish and Christian traditions shared the teaching of Genesis that, already in Paradise, God had brought the first man and the first woman together, and commanded them to "be fruitful and multiply" (Gen. 1:28). God had created them as social creatures, naturally inclined and attracted to each other. God had given them the physical capacity to join together and to beget children. God had commanded them to love, help, and nurture each other and to inculcate in each other and in their children the love of God, neighbor, and self. "Therefore a man leaves his father and mother and cleaves to his wife, and the two become one flesh," Genesis concludes (2:24). Both the Jewish tradition and the Christian tradition eventually built on this primeval commandment, and its later biblical echoes, many of the basic norms of heterosexual monogamous marriage and sexual ethics.[27]

The Muslim tradition rooted marriage not only in the teachings of the Qur'an but also in the example of Mohammed.[28] The Qur'an speaks of marriage as a "solemn covenant" *(mithaqan)* (4:20), indeed a form of worship *('ibadat)* and religious observance enjoined upon each Muslim as a way of keeping faith with the tradition of Islam. In the Hadith, the Prophet provided that "marriage is my *Sunnah,* so the one who turns away from my *Sunnah,* turns away from me."[29] Also in the Hadith, the Prophet set out in great detail the principles of proper marriage for a Muslim that were elaborated in later books of Islamic law and etiquette.[30] A number of these teachings emulated, if not echoed, Jewish and Christian rules — the requirement of monogamy notably excepted.

Second, all three traditions recognized that marriage is by nature a multi-dimensional institution, whose formation, maintenance, and dissolution involve a variety of parties besides the couple themselves. Yes, marriage is a contract, formed by the mutual consent of the marital couple, and subject to their wills and preferences. But in all three traditions, marriage is also a spiritual association, subject to the creed, code, cult, and canons of the religious community. Marriage

---

27. See chapters by Novak, Lawler, and Johnson herein. See illustrative texts from all three traditions in Kristen E. Kwam et al., eds., *Eve and Adam: Jewish, Christian, and Muslim Readings on Genesis and Gender* (Bloomington: Indiana University Press, 1999).

28. Both David Novak and Richard Martin emphasize that Mohammed's role as exemplar of marriage for Muslims was very different from the non-exemplary roles of Moses (who married a foreigner) or Abraham (a perennial polygamist) for Jews, or of Christ and Paul (both bachelors) for Christians.

29. Quoted in chapter by al-Hibri herein at n. 68.

30. See chapter by Richard Martin herein.

is a social estate, subject to special laws of property and association, and to the expectations and exactions of the local community. Marriage is an economic institution, involving the creation and merger of properties, and triggering obligations of mutual care, nurture, and sacrifice between husband and wife, parent and child. And marriage is a ritual institution, formed through liturgical prayers, oaths, and blessings, and functioning thereafter as a vital site of religious instruction, piety, and worship alongside the synagogue, church, or mosque.

Third, all three traditions recognized that marriage has inherent goods that lie beyond the preferences of the couple, or the terms of their marriage contract. Fundamental to all three traditions is the ideal of marriage as the divinely sanctioned means of perpetuating the faith — not only by the couple maintaining their own household rites as vital sites of confessional identity, but also by the couple's procreation and teaching of children who will form the next *Schul*, the next church, the next *Umma*. Hence the emphasis in all three traditions of avoiding marriage with a nonbeliever.

The emphasis on the procreation and nurture of children in the faith and the corresponding prohibition on interreligious marriage were particularly prominent themes in biblical and diaspora Judaism. These rules were not only fundamental safeguards against assimilation into (an often hostile) gentile culture. They were also essential conditions for the Jewish community to continue to flourish and grow despite its aversion to proselytism.[31] These same emphases on procreation and against intermarriage also emerged among some later Christian and Islamic communities, particularly when they were placed in minority contexts. Think of Catholics in nineteenth-century America, and Muslims and Orthodox in twentieth-century America.

The Christian tradition devised more elaborate lists of the inherent goods and goals of marriage, beyond the good of producing the next generation of the faithful. Among the most famous formulations was St. Augustine's fifth-century discourse on the marital goods of *fides, proles, et sacramentum*.[32] Marriage, said Augustine, is an institution of *fides* — faith, trust, and love between husband and wife, and between parent and child, that goes beyond the faith demanded of any other temporal relationship. Marriage is a source of *proles* — children who carry on the family name and tradition, perpetuate the human

---

31. See chapters by Novak and Broyde herein, and also chapters by Novak, Broyde, and Jocelyn Hellig in *Sharing the Book: Religious Perspectives on the Rights and Wrongs of Proselytism*, ed. John Witte Jr. and Richard C. Martin (Maryknoll, N.Y.: Orbis, 1999), pp. 17-78.

32. See detailed sources and citations for this and the next four paragraphs on the "goods of marriage" in John Witte Jr., "The Goods and Goals of Marriage," in *Marriage, Health, and the Professions*, ed. John Wall, Don S. Browning, William J. Doherty, and Stephen Post (Grand Rapids: Eerdmans, 2002), p. 49.

species, and fill God's church with the next generation of saints. And marriage is a form of *sacramentum* — a symbolic expression of Christ's love for his church, even a channel of God's grace to sanctify the couple, their children, and the broader community. This trilogy of marital goods became axiomatic in later medieval Catholic theology, and remains at the core of Catholic marriage teaching to this day.

An overlapping formulation, drawn from Roman law and patristic lore, was captured by the early-seventh-century encyclopedist, St. Isidore of Seville. Marriage, Isidore argued, provides husbands and wives with the following goods: (1) mutual love and support; (2) mutual procreation and nurture of children; and (3) mutual protection from sexual sin and temptation. This formula of marital goods denied the sacramentality of marriage, even while confirming its divine origins. It also placed greater emphasis on the virtues of marital love and the need for protection from sexual sin. This was a popular formulation of marital goods among both Orthodox and Protestant Christians.

The Christian tradition, building on Graeco-Roman sources, also emphasized the broader social goods of marriage — teaching that marriage is good not only for the couple and their children, but also for the broader civic communities of which they are a part. Ancient Greek philosophers and Roman Stoics called marriage "the foundation of the republic," "the private font of public virtue." The Church Fathers called marital and familial love "the seedbed of the city," "the force that welds society together." Catholics called the family "a domestic church," "a kind of school of deeper humanity." Protestants called the household a "little church," a "little state," a "little seminary," a "little commonwealth." At the core of all these metaphors is a perennial Western ideal that stable marriages and families are essential to the survival, flourishing, and happiness of the greater commonwealths of church, state, and civil society. And a breakdown of marriage and the family will eventually have devastating consequences on these larger social institutions.

Much the same emphasis on the individual and social goods of marriage can be found in the Islamic tradition, as Richard Martin documents. Among the most famous formulations was that developed by the great eleventh-century medieval jurist and theologian, Abu Hamid al-Ghazali, who listed as marital goods: (1) procreation; (2) proper satisfaction of natural sexual desires; (3) love and companionship; (4) efficient ordering of the household; and (5) disciplining oneself.[33] The parallels between al-Ghazali's list of marital

---

33. See chapter by Martin herein. There are striking parallels in the five goods of marriage listed by seventeenth-century Calvinist Richard Baxter, discussed in the chapter by Johnson herein.

goods formulated in the eleventh century, and those developed in the next century by Catholic writers like Aquinas and Jewish writers like Maimonides, suggest that these traditions may well have cross-fertilized each other.

## Marriage As Covenant

"Covenant" is emerging in Western law, theology, and ethics today as a common trope to capture some of these higher dimensions of marriage.[34] It is also emerging as a common term to connect the interreligious dialogue among Jews, Christians, and Muslims and the interdisciplinary dialogue among jurists, theologians, and ethicists about marriage. The connections between these layers of dialogue about marriage and covenant are still developing; indeed, one of the aims of this volume is to spell out and encourage some of these connections more explicitly. But it is no coincidence that the covenant marriage movement in American law has been orchestrated, in ample part, by proponents of a covenantal theology and ethics of marriage.

Covenant (*berit* in Hebrew; *diatheke* in Greek; *foedus* in Latin; *mithaquan* in Arabic) is an ancient and religiously laden term that reaches far beyond the realm of marriage. Michael Lawler's definition of covenant and distillation of recent covenant scholarship is worth quoting at some length:

> Scholars agree that the term [covenant] is either derived from, or is closely related to, the Akkadian *biritu,* which means to bind together. *Berit,* or covenant, at root, means to bind together, but it connotes more. The parties bound together are originally free and unbound, and they agree to be bound in a relationship that both limits and guarantees their freedom in accord with the terms of the covenant. It matters not whether the covenant is between equals *(bnai berit)* or between a superior and a subordinate *(ba'alei berit);* both parties are equally bound by the terms of the covenant. The standard term for making a covenant, *likhrot berit,* literally to cut a covenant, derives from an ancient ritual of covenant-making in which an animal was cut in half, the covenanting parties walked between the two halves, and the halves were then bound together. The unitive symbolism of this rite is further underscored by the sacred, sacrificial meal which commonly accompanied the covenant and invoked God as its witness (cf. Exodus 24:1-12).

Daniel Elazar comments that "it is significant that cutting [dividing]

---

34. See several examples in the chapter by Brinig and Nock herein; see also William Johnson Everett, *Religion, Federalism, and the Struggle for Public Life* (New York: Oxford University Press, 1997).

and binding are the principal elements in the terminology and early practice of covenant-making since a covenant both divides and binds, that is to say, it clarifies and institutionalizes both the distinction between or separate identities of the partners and their linkage." Covenants constitute two or more distinct parties in a relationship of mutual dialogue and justice, to which they are *morally* as well as *legally* bound. The covenant partners are to be faithful to the covenant; they are to be *lumen fidelitatis gentium,* a light of faithfulness to the nations. As the notion of covenant was adapted in cultural settings beyond the ancient Near East, *berit* successively gave way to the Greek *diatheke,* the Latin *foedus,* more technical than *testamentum,* the old English *troth,* and the modern English sacred promise, oath, and even contract, though this latter results in the loss of the essential moral overtones of covenant.[35]

*Covenant* in this rich sense is a common scriptural term for Jews, Christians, and Muslims alike. It appears 286 times in the Hebrew Bible (as *berit*), 24 more times in the New Testament (as *diatheke* or *foedus*), 26 times in the Qur'an (as *mitaq* and its variations). *Covenant* has multiple meanings and purposes in these three sacred Scriptures. But it is used most importantly and most frequently to describe the special relationship between Yahweh and Israel, God and his elect, Allah and his chosen ones.

In each of these three Scriptures, covenant is also occasionally used to describe marriage. In the Hebrew Bible, Yahweh's special covenantal relationship with Israel is analogized to the special relationship between husband and wife. Israel's disobedience to Yahweh, in turn, particularly its proclivity to worship false gods, is frequently described as a form of playing the harlot. Idolatry, like adultery, can lead to divorce, and Yahweh threatens this many times, even while calling his chosen to reconciliation. This image comes through repeatedly in the writings of the Prophets: Hosea (2:2-23), Isaiah (1:21-22; 54:5-8; 57:3-10; 61:10-11; 62:4-5), Jeremiah (2:2-3; 3:1-5, 6-25; 13:27; 23:10; 31:32), and Ezekiel (16:1-63; 23:1-49).[36]

The Hebrew Bible also speaks about marriage as a covenant in its own right (Prov. 2:17; Mal. 2:14-16). The Prophet Malachi's formulation is the fullest:

---

35. See chapter by Lawler herein at note 5, quoting in part Daniel J. Elazar, *Covenant and Polity in Biblical Israel: Biblical Foundations and Jewish Expressions* (New Brunswick, N.J.: Transaction, 1995), p. 65. See also Daniel J. Elazar, *Covenant and Commonwealth: From Christian Separatism through the Protestant Reformation* (New Brunswick, N.J.: Transaction, 1996).

36. See analysis in the chapter by Lawler herein and the detailed study in Gordon P. Hugenberger, *Marriage As Covenant: A Study of Biblical Law and Ethics Governing Marriage Developed from the Perspective of Malachi* (Leiden: Brill, 1994).

You cover the LORD's altar with tears, with weeping and groaning because he no longer regards the offering or accepts it with favor at your hand. You ask, "Why does he not?" Because the LORD was witness to the covenant between you and the wife of your youth, to whom you have been faithless, though she is your companion and your wife by covenant. Has not the one God made and sustained for us the spirit of life? And what does he desire? Godly offspring. So take heed to yourselves, and let none be faithless to the wife of his youth. "For I hate divorce, says the LORD the God of Israel, and covering one's garment with violence, says the LORD of hosts. So take heed to yourselves and do not be faithless." (Mal. 2:13-16).

The Qur'an has comparable verses about marriage as a "solemn covenant" *(mithaqan ghalithan)* which cannot be easily broken:

But if you decide to take one wife in place of another, even if you have given the latter a quintal for dowry, take not the least amount of it back; would you take it by slander and a manifest wrong? And how could you take it when you have gone into one another, and they have taken from you a solemn covenant? (4:20-21).

Jews, Christians, and Muslims alike have long used these kinds of scriptural verses to speak of marriage, inter alia, as a covenant and to encourage the procreation of children and to discourage the practice of divorce in direct application of these verses. This comes through in many theological, pastoral, and liturgical texts already in the first millennium of the common era.[37] What has not been common in these three traditions until more recently is to link explicitly the divine covenant between God and humanity and the marital covenant of husband and wife — in effect to make God a third party to the marriage covenant, and in turn to make marriage a forum for the expression of the divine-human covenant. What has also not been common until recently is to develop a theology and jurisprudence of covenant marriage, a way of describing the higher dimensions of marriage in concrete covenantal terms, and linking those terms to the concrete contractual terms of marriage that all three traditions have long had in place.

In the Jewish and Muslim traditions, the development of a covenant model

---

37. See examples in the chapters by Novak, Lawler, Harakas, al-Hibri, Martin, and Johnson herein. See also Max L. Stackhouse, *Covenant and Commitments: Faith, Family, and Economic Life* (Louisville: Westminster John Knox, 1997); Paul F. Palmer, "Christian Marriage: Contract or Covenant," *Theological Studies* 33 (1972): 617-65; William Johnson Everett, *Blessed Be the Bond: Christian Perspectives on Marriage and Family* (Philadelphia: Fortress, 1985).

of marriage is very recent, indeed. Two of the leading proponents of these ideas are contributors to this volume. In his chapter herein, and in a brilliant book-length study, David Novak lays out a compelling case for a Jewish theology and law of covenant marriage.[38] In her chapter herein, and in a bold new book in the making, Azizah al-Hibri makes the same case for covenant marriage in the Islamic tradition. What makes Novak's and al-Hibri's efforts so promising is their insistence on grounding their covenantal models of marriage in long-neglected texts of the Bible and Qur'an respectively, and rereading and rethinking their own traditions in light of these original canonical texts. What makes their efforts so edifying for a comparative volume like this is their openness to seeing analogies, sometimes even antecedents, in the covenantal law and lore of other religious traditions besides their own.

There is a long-standing tradition of covenant marriage in the Christian tradition. The emerging scholarly consensus is that John Calvin, the sixteenth-century Protestant reformer of Geneva, was the first to develop a detailed covenant model of marriage in place of the prevailing Catholic sacramental theology and canon law of marriage.[39] Much of Calvin's general covenant theology was not new. Calvin expounded the traditional biblical idea of a divine covenant or agreement between God and humanity. He followed conventional Christian teachings in distinguishing two interlocking biblical covenants: (1) the covenant of works whereby the chosen people of Israel, through obedience to God's law, are promised eternal salvation and blessing; and (2) the covenant of grace whereby the elect, through faith in Christ's incarnation and atonement, are promised eternal salvation and beatitude. The covenant of works was created in Abraham, confirmed in Moses, and consummated with the promulgation and acceptance of the Torah. The covenant of grace was created in Christ, confirmed in the gospel, and consummated with the confession and conversion of the Christian. These traditional teachings on the covenant were common among Catholics, Orthodox, and Protestants.

Calvin went beyond the tradition, however, by using the doctrine of covenant to describe not only the vertical relationships between God and humanity but also the horizontal relationships between husband and wife. Just as God draws the elect believer into a covenant relationship with him, Calvin argued,

---

38. David Novak, *Covenantal Rights: A Study in Jewish Political Theory* (Princeton, N.J.: Princeton University Press, 2000).

39. See chapters by Lawler, Martin, and Stackhouse herein. See elaboration of this thesis in John Witte, Jr., *From Sacrament to Contract: Marriage, Religion, and Law in the Western Tradition* (Louisville: Westminster John Knox, 1997), chap. 3, and in John Witte, Jr., and Robert M. Kingdon, *Sex, Marriage, and Family in John Calvin's Geneva*, vol. 1: *Courtship, Engagement, and Marriage* (Grand Rapids: Eerdmans, 2005).

so God draws husband and wife into a covenant relationship with each other. Just as God expects constant faith and good works in our relationship with him, so he expects connubial faithfulness and sacrificial works in our relationship with our spouses. "God is the founder of marriage," Calvin wrote. "When a marriage takes place between a man and a woman, God presides and requires a mutual pledge from both. Hence Solomon in Proverbs 2:17 calls marriage the covenant of God, for it is superior to all human contracts. So also Malachi [2:14] declares that God is as it were the stipulator [of marriage] who by his authority joins the man to the woman, and sanctions the marriage."[40]

God participates in the formation of the covenant of marriage through his chosen agents on earth, Calvin believed. The couple's parents, as God's "lieutenants" for children, instruct the young couple in the mores and morals of Christian marriage and give their consent to the union. Two witnesses, as "God's priests to their peers," testify to the sincerity and solemnity of the couple's promises and attest to the marriage event. The minister, holding "God's spiritual power of the Word," blesses the union and admonishes the couple and the community of their respective biblical duties and rights. The magistrate, holding "God's temporal power of the sword," registers the parties, ensures the legality of their union, and protects them in their conjoined persons and properties. This involvement of parents, peers, ministers, and magistrates in the formation of marriage was not an idle or dispensable ceremony. These four parties represented different dimensions of God's involvement in the marriage covenant, and they were thus essential to the legitimacy of the marriage itself. To omit any such party in the formation of the marriage was, in effect, to omit God from the marriage covenant. On this foundation, Calvin worked out in great detail a covenantal theology of the origin, nature, and purpose of marriage and a covenantal law of marital formation, maintenance, and dissolution, spousal rights, roles, and responsibilities, and more. This was the first comprehensive covenantal model of marriage in the Christian tradition, and it informed the policies of the Genevan church and state alike.

Calvin may have developed the first covenantal model of marriage, but by no means the last. An analogous covenantal model of marriage emerged from the hand of contemporary Zurich reformer Heinrich Bullinger, whose work was tremendously influential both on the Continent and in England. By the later sixteenth century, as James Johnson and Max Stackhouse carefully document, the writings of Calvin and Bullinger, separately and together, catalyzed a veritable industry of Protestant covenant theology, jurisprudence, and ethics.

---

40. Calvin, *Lect. Mal.* 2:14. See further discussion in chapters by Lawler, Stackhouse, and Martin herein.

These writings on covenant, which crested in seventeenth- and eighteenth-century England and New England, provided a detailed integrated understanding not only of marriage per se, but also of the place of marriage in church, state, and broader society.[41] In the last two centuries, covenantal language has also become prominent in Protestant marriage and wedding liturgies. Indeed, today, Stackhouse and Johnson conclude, Protestant liturgies more than Protestant theologies are strongholds for covenant marriage lore.

In the Catholic tradition, Michael Lawler shows, the Council of Trent closed the door firmly on covenant marriage language in 1563. In its decree *Tametsi,* the Council declared canonical the pervasive medieval teaching that marriage is a sacrament. Heretical Protestant teachings on marriage, including the teaching on covenant marriage, could henceforth have no place in the Catholic tradition. Four centuries later, however, the Second Vatican Council reopened this door, using the language of covenant as an organizing idiom to describe the origins, nature, and purpose of marriage. In *Gaudium et Spes,* one of the Council's most influential documents, the Vatican Fathers put it thus:

> The intimate partnership of married life and love has been established by the Creator and qualified by His laws. It is rooted in the marriage covenant of irrevocable personal consent. . . . [A] man and a woman, who by the marriage covenant of conjugal love "are no longer two but one flesh" (Mt. 19:6), render mutual help and service to each other through an intimate union of their persons and of their actions. Through this union they experience the meaning of their oneness and attain to it with growing perfection day by day. As a mutual gift of two persons, this intimate union, as well as the good of children, imposes total fidelity on the spouses, and argues for an unbreakable oneness between them. Christ the Lord abundantly blessed this many-faceted love, welling up as it does from the fountain of divine love and structured as it is on the model of His union with the Church. For as God of old made himself present to His people through a covenant of love and fidelity, so now the Savior of men and the Spouse of the Church comes into the lives of married Christians through the sacrament of matrimony.[42]

In the Orthodox Christian tradition, Stanley Harakas shows, the term *covenant marriage* is foreign. Yet the rich understandings of marriage in the Ortho-

---

41. See sources and discussion in David A. Weir, *Early New England: A Covenanted Society* (Grand Rapids: Eerdmans, 2005); Colloquium, "Creativity and Responsibility: Covenant, Contract, and the Resolution of Disputes," *Emory Law Journal* 36 (1987): 533.

42. Second Vatican Council, *Gaudium et Spes,* para. 48, in *The Documents of Vatican II,* gen. ed. Walter M. Abbott, translation ed. Joseph Gallagher (London: G. Chapman, 1966).

dox tradition also have resonance with some aspects of covenantal approaches to the marital union in traditional Protestantism and modern Catholicism.

## Summary and Conclusions

The Jewish, Christian, and Muslim traditions have long taught that marriage is a contract. Marriage is predicated on the mutual consent of the man and the woman. It is recorded in written instruments. It is celebrated in formal rituals. It triggers exchanges of property. It creates a new legal entity, the marital household, with a complex of new rights and duties between husband and wife, parent and child, couple and state. It grants husband and wife alike the right to press lawsuits to vindicate their marital rights. Contract is the backbone of marriage. It gives marriage its legal structure, stature, and strength.

The Jewish, Christian, and Muslim traditions have also long taught, however, that marriage is more than a mere contract. Marriage is also one of the great mediators of individuality and community, revelation and reason, tradition and modernity. It is at once a harbor of the self and a harbinger of the community, a symbol of divine love and a structure of reasoned consent, an enduring ancient mystery and a constantly modern invention. Marriage is rooted in primeval commands and prophetic examples. It is reflected in religious, ceremonial, social, economic, political, and cultural norms and forms. It is at once private and public, contractual and spiritual, voluntary and natural, psychological and civilizational in origin, nature, and function.

While the teachings of marriage as contract and marriage as covenant coexist in all three traditions, they are not without tensions. Michael Broyde shows that a contractual model of marriage dominated Judaism in the first millennium of the common era and a covenantal model of marriage dominated it in the second millennium — which has led many contemporary Jews in Israel and in America to a fundamentally "schizophrenic" attitude toward marriage. Azizah al-Hibri and Richard Martin document clearly that a private (and pervasively patriarchal) contractual perspective dominates much historical and contemporary Islamic law, even though the Qur'an and Hadith, as well as medieval literature and jurisprudence, command and celebrate a communal and more egalitarian covenant of marriage. Stanley Harakas and Michael Lawler show that marriage has always proceeded on "two trajectories" in the Orthodox and Catholic traditions — a negative theology that deprecates marriage as a material and carnal institution that obstructs true service of God, and a positive theology that celebrates marriage as a sublime symbol if not sacrament of Christ's relationship with his church, God's relationship with his elect. James

Johnson and Max Stackhouse point to a growing tension between the traditional covenant theologies of marriage taught by both Protestant churches and states and the modern contract theories of marriage that have captured not only Western states but a growing number of Protestant churches as well.

While the Jewish, Christian, and Muslim traditions have found ways to reconcile the contractual and covenantal dimensions of marriage, American law today juxtaposes them. In all but three states, parties who wish to marry must choose the state's contract marriage option. Contract marriage has minimal rules of formation and dissolution and hundreds of built-in state and federal rights and duties for the couple and their children. Couples may add rights and duties beyond those defined by the state's contract marriage law. These can be set out in prenuptial contracts negotiated between the parties, or they can be set out in the religious laws and customs of the community of which these marital parties are voluntary members. But, even here, the contractual dimensions of marriage are preferred. Private prenuptial contracts will be enforced by state courts. Religious laws of marriage and divorce will not be enforced — even if the couple's prenuptial contract stipulates that religious law should govern their contract in the event of dispute. New York's *get* statute — which allows an Orthodox Jewish couple to divorce only if their rabbis first give them a Jewish divorce — is a rare and remarkable exception to the usual rules. State courts usually will not enforce religious laws of marriage and divorce, particularly if those religious laws differ from state laws. Religious authorities are thus largely powerless to enforce their religious rulings on marriage against one of their members who sues in state court. They may apply spiritual pressure and sanctions to get a party to comply with their internal religious norms — even shun or excommunicate that party for defying their authority. But if the party persists in the civil suit, the state court will enforce its own state marriage and divorce laws, not those of the religious community. Religious norms and forms of marriage and divorce are subordinate to the state's contract laws of marriage.

This is not altogether true in Louisiana, Arkansas, and Arizona today. In these three states, parties who wish to marry may choose either contract marriage or covenant marriage. The contract marriage option in these three states is largely the same as that available in any other state. The covenant marriage option, however, is unique in that it tightens marital formation and dissolution rules considerably. In particular, covenant marriage requires parties to involve third party counselors, including the parties' own religious authorities if they are licensed to be counselors. It also requires parties to waive their rights to unilateral no-fault divorce and to accept rules of marital dissolution that are closer to the grounds and procedures traditionally recognized by Jewish, Christian, and Muslim authorities.

Covenant marriage laws thus go further than contract marriage laws in reflecting and protecting some of the higher dimensions of marriage. Covenant marriage statutes serve a particularly valuable teaching function — instructing the community on the higher regard that the state has for marriage, instructing the couple of the higher rigor that marriage has for them, instructing religious communities that marriage is more than a mere contract.

It is the state authorities, however, not the religious authorities, who enforce covenant marriages in these three states. As with contract marriage, so with covenant marriage, parties may supplement the rights and duties set out by state law with voluntarily chosen or religiously mandated norms. But the same limitations on the enforceability of these supplementary norms by religious authorities will apply in these three covenant marriage states as prevail in contract marriage states. State formulations of what marriage entails in the individual case will still trump countervailing religious formulations — even if the state is interpreting the meaning of a "covenant" marriage.

Moreover, outside of Louisiana, Arkansas, and Arizona, the state will not even recognize a covenant marriage, only a contract marriage. As we have noted, an estranged spouse can thus escape a covenant marriage simply by moving to and filing for divorce in any American state or any foreign country without covenant marriage options. Current conflict of laws rules, both domestic and international, do not favor the enforcement of covenant marriage laws over the contract marriage laws of the state where the divorce case is litigated. In addition, in many noncovenant states and foreign nations the trend in the past decade has been to weaken, rather than strengthen, traditional forms and norms of marriage. Such realities emphasize the fact that covenant marriage laws are an important, but not a complete, legal response to the problems surrounding marriage and divorce in America today.

A fuller legal response requires additional strategies of reform and engagement, particularly on the part of religious communities. The first step is for America's religious communities to get their legal and theological houses on marriage and the family in order. Too many religious communities in America today, Christian churches notably among them, are losing the capacity to engage the hard legal, political, and social issues of our day with doctrinal rigor, moral clarity, and canonical authenticity. In centuries past, the Jewish, Christian, and Muslim traditions alike produced massive codes of religious law and discipline that covered many areas of private and public life, including domestic life. They instituted sophisticated tribunals for the equitable enforcement of these laws. They produced exquisite works of theology and jurisprudence that worked out the precepts of proper domestic living in great detail. Some of that sophisticated legal work still goes on among some religious communities today.

Some religious jurists and ethicists still take up some of these questions. But the legal structure and sophistication of modern American religious communities as a whole is a pale shadow of what went on before. And their marital norms and habits have increasingly become simple variations on the cultural status quo.

American religious communities must think more seriously about restoring and reforming their own bodies of religious law on marriage, divorce, and sexuality, instead of simply acquiescing in state laws and culture. American states, in turn, must think more seriously about granting greater deference to the marital laws and customs of legitimate religious and cultural groups that cannot accept a marriage law of the common denominator or denomination. Other sophisticated legal cultures — England, India, and South Africa — grant semi-autonomy to Catholic, Hindu, Jewish, Muslim, and other groups to conduct their subjects' domestic affairs in accordance with their own laws and customs, with the state setting only minimum conditions and limits. It might well be time for America likewise to translate its growing cultural pluralism into a more concrete legal pluralism on marriage and family life.

# 1 Jewish Marriage: Nature, Covenant, and Contract

*David Novak*

## The Institution of Marriage: General, Specific, and Particular

At the beginning of his comprehensive treatment of the institution of Jewish marriage, the great twelfth-century jurist and theologian Maimonides represents the fact of Jewish marriage as a novum in human history. And, even though Maimonides is writing centuries after the biblical and early rabbinic texts had been written and edited, he nonetheless gives the institution of Jewish marriage presented and prescribed in these texts unsurpassed conceptual clarity. Aside from some of his own individual opinions about marriage, which need not concern us here, Maimonides brings a conceptual clarity to the original biblical and rabbinic sources they did not give themselves. As the Talmud mentions about an earlier sage, Maimonides here is not to be looked upon as a source of the tradition as much as one who brilliantly ordered its normative content.[1] About marriage he writes:

> Before the giving of the Torah, a man would meet a woman in the marketplace. If both he and she wanted him to marry [*leesa*] her, he would then bring her into his home and have sexual intercourse with her privately. She then became a wife to him. — When the Torah was given, Israel was commanded that if a man wanted to marry a woman, he should first acquire conjugal rights over her [*yiqah otah*] in the presence of witnesses; thereafter she becomes a wife to him.[2]

1. *Babylonian Talmud,* 20 vols. (Vilna: Romm, 1898) [hereafter "B."]: Pesahim 105b.
2. *Mishneh Torah,* 12 vols., ed. S. Frankel (B'nai Brak: Shabse Frankel, 2001) [hereafter "MT"]: Marriage, 1.1.

All translations, unless otherwise noted, are by the author.

In this discussion of marriage, Maimonides is representing marriage generically and then specifically. He structures his discussion here with the Aristotelian logic he typically employs in many of his other discussions, even though the social phenomena under discussion are constructed by the Jewish tradition: more prescriptively regarding Jewish marriage; more speculatively regarding marriage in general. He is talking *to* Jews directly; only *about* Gentiles indirectly.

In the generic sense, marriage is an agreement between two parties: one male and the other female. These two parties freely enter into this agreement, which is meant to be a permanent mutual relationship (although the rabbinic source Maimonides most likely drew upon mentions the right of mutual divorce).[3] It presupposes prior rights and duties on both sides (such as who may or may not marry whom); it entails subsequent rights and duties on both sides (such as what one is required to either give to or take from the other). This relationship is consummated by an act of sexual intercourse, conducted in private, but whose occurrence is assumed to be a matter of public knowledge thereafter. By implication, then, a sexless marriage, especially if so by design, is considered to be an oxymoron.[4] Therefore, we can even confirm or deny the validity of a sexual relationship that its members wish to have publicly validated; not all sexual relationships can or should be given official status. Love, on the other hand, although no doubt necessary for the existential vitality of a marriage, is something that could hardly be ascertained by any public criterion. Most would agree that marital love is a reality, indeed the most important reality in a marriage, yet it is something known only by the couple themselves. Its privacy is its essence. (In Jewish or "covenantal" marriage, as we shall later see, marital love, whether present or absent, is something also known to the God before whom the covenantal marriage is initiated and endures.[5])

Jewish marriage, however, is what has been prescribed for Jews specifically after their acceptance of the Torah at Mount Sinai. In rabbinic teaching, this is the covenantal event that separated the Jews from the rest of the peoples of the world and gave them their unique identity.[6] Jewish marriage, though, is still part of the genus *marriage* (called *nisu'in*, literally denoting the man "carrying the woman into his domicile"). It is still a free mutual agreement between a male and a female party.[7] Thus Maimonides does not claim that Judaism in-

---

3. See *Palestinian Talmud,* Venice reprint ed. (New York: n.p., 1948) [hereafter "Y."]: Kiddushin 1.1/58c.

4. See *Palestinian Talmud* 58c re Gen. 20:3.

5. Y. Berakhot 9.1/12d re Gen. 1:26.

6. B. Keritot 9a.

7. B. Kiddushin 2b.

vented the institution of marriage per se. What Judaism did was to further specify marriage as a basic institution of Judaism for the Jewish people. To be sure, Jews are to assume that Judaism has elevated the institution of marriage in the divinely ordained cosmic order, but it has done so without changing marriage's generic character.[8]

The specific difference instituted by Judaism lies in the public character of the initiation of a Jewish marriage. Whereas in this view of marriage in general, the public significance of a marriage is assumed *after* its consummation, in this view of Jewish marriage specifically, the public significance of a marriage must be ascertained *before* its consummation. Thus what we see is that in marriage in general the community merely *confirms* the marital event *post factum*, whereas in Jewish marriage the community *determines* the marital event *ab initio*. In fact, the presence of the witnesses at the event initiating a Jewish marriage (what we would today call the "wedding ceremony"), representing as they do the whole covenanted community, should be first ascertained in order for the initiation of marriage freely performed by the man and freely accepted by the woman to be officially recognized as valid.[9] One could indeed say that in Judaism marriage itself is a duty owed the community by those able to reproduce its members; hence the priority of the community is emphasized by the recognized presence of its official representatives.[10] In general marriage, conversely, the couple have a right to the community's recognition of what they themselves have created — provided, however, they have not violated minimal moral restrictions of who may marry and who may not.

When Maimonides speaks of the time before the giving of the Torah, he means the time when, according to Jewish tradition, the Jewish people lived under a universal law, one binding on all humankind and taken to be affirmed by most of humankind. Judaism, then, is the post-Sinaitic religion of the Jewish people, yet the Jewish people's beginning occurs over several centuries before the revelation at Sinai when God elects Abraham and his clan to be a people singularly related to God in an everlasting covenant. Even after Abraham's election but before the revelation of the Torah at Sinai, the Jewish people had been living according to a law binding on all the rest of humankind.[11] As such, they

---

8. See MT: Marriage, 1.4 based on *Sifre:* Devarim 260 re: Deut. 23:18, ed. Finkelstein, p. 283. See B. Yevamot 61b; also, B. Yevamot 22a; B. Sanhedrin 59a.

9. B. Kiddushin 65b and Tosafot of Rabbi Isaac the Elder thereon.

10. Thus, for example, a Gentile who fathered children before his conversion to Judaism is required to father Jewish children after his conversion, unless his gentile children converted along with him. See B. Yevamot 62a; MT: Marriage, 15.6.

11. See David Novak, *The Image of the Non-Jew in Judaism* (New York: Edwin Mellen, 1983), pp. 257-73.

were marrying like everybody else, or like everybody else is supposed to be married even now.

Though other peoples may very well have further specified marriage in general as did the Jews, Jewish recognition of a non-Jewish marriage, either their own before Sinai or those of Gentiles even after Sinai, need only recognize the fact of marriage according to these minimal universal standards. Further specifications are the business only of the specifying communities themselves, be they Jewish or gentile. (The question of intermarriage between Jews and Gentiles shall be dealt with later.) Thus these cultural specifications can be called into question only when they attempt to displace the generic definition of marriage instead of improving upon it. In other words, the notion of universal marriage is not so much a cross-cultural description of an empirically evident commonality as it is a philosophical construction of the very conditions that need to be fulfilled in order for any marriage to be recognized as such by anyone who is rational and morally earnest, whoever he or she happens to be. Such recognition is to be made not only by those who are inside the confines of the particular traditional community in which the marriage took place, but even by outsiders. It is both a view from somewhere and a view from anywhere. Therefore, there is to be a universal definition of marriage that is necessary everywhere, even if it is sufficient nowhere to either describe or prescribe what a marriage is in its specific cultural concreteness. Marriage everywhere is meant to be much more than this minimal universal standard imagined by Judaism, but it is not meant to be less than it anywhere.

In his work where he enumerates and defines the 613 commandments later rabbinic tradition considered to be biblical (that is, God-given, as distinct from God-authorized/human-made rabbinic commandments), Maimonides designates two commandments that pertain to marriage per se. He juxtaposes these commandments one to the other. About the first commandment pertaining to marriage, he writes,

> The Torah has commanded us to procreate and to intend the continuation of the [human] species, as God Himself, may he be exalted, stated, "be fruitful and multiply" (Genesis 1:28) . . . but women are not obligated for this commandment as the Rabbis said, "the man is commanded to procreate, but not the woman."[12]

About the second commandment, he writes, "The Torah commanded us to consummate the sacred marriage *(qiddushin)*. . . . Indeed, it has already been

---

12. *Sefer ha-Mitsvot:* positive commandment, no. 212.

explained that the commandment of marriage is biblically ordained."[13] The contrast between these two passages is striking. The first passage is talking about what could be considered universal or "natural" marriage; the second is talking about specifically Jewish marriage, whose sanctity is mandated by revelation over and above its natural necessity. This type of marriage is best termed "covenantal."

Finally, there are aspects of marriage that could be considered contractual, that is, rights and duties mutually pertaining to the male and female parties to the marriage and which are negotiated and concluded by these parties themselves to operate among themselves. These contractual arrangements are meant to be a supplement to those rights and duties considered to be both natural and covenantal. As it turns out, these contractual arrangements, at least when they are formal and put in writing (and thus enabling redress to the public institution of the court in disputed cases), all pertain to the financial aspects of a marriage. Here Jewish law gives the widest leeway to couples to work out their own financial agreement, even if that agreement contradicts what covenantal law has stipulated for most (but not all) married couples. In other words, financial benefits of marriage that either the Torah or the rabbis stipulate on behalf of most married people can be waived by some people who are convinced that they can work out a better, more beneficial, agreement for themselves. Like all valid contracts, such privately initiated agreements receive public sanction when witnessed, and especially when also put into an official written document (called a *shtar* in rabbinic Hebrew).

Nevertheless, even when Jewish tradition clearly borrows certain financial criteria involved in Jewish marriage from earlier or contemporary non-Jewish law, it is unconcerned about how the Gentiles have worked out the financial criteria of *their* own marriages, be it in their statutes or even more so in their contracts. Jews were only concerned if one of their marital contracts attempted to override Jewish law (for example, an explicit contract between the parties not to observe the rules pertaining to stipulated periods of sexual abstinence) or natural law (for example, an explicit contract between the parties for what some today call an "open marriage," that is, an agreement between the parties to tolerate adultery committed by either side).[14]

In summary, then, the conceptual structure put forth here consists of the interaction of three elements: (1) natural or general; (2) covenantal or specific;

13. *Sefer ha-Mitsvot:* positive commandment, no. 213.
14. The general principle in the *Mishnah* [hereafter "M."] is, "Whoever contracts *[ha-matneh]* contrary to what is written in the Torah, his contract *[tna']* is null and void" (M. Baba Metsia 7.11; B. Kiddushin 19b and parallels).

and (3) contractual or particular. It is now for us to see in some greater detail how they operate in Jewish marriage as presented in the early rabbinic sources, especially in their well-known attempt to see the norms they formulate and the social institutions they construct as rooted in the Bible in one way or another.


## Jewish Marriage: The First Step

The best way to see how these three elements interact in Jewish marriage is to look at the basic Jewish marriage ceremony as it is presented in the Talmud. By commenting on the various aspects of that initiating ritual and their order, we can see what rabbinic tradition intended Jewish marriage to be.

In Talmudic times, the initiation of marriage took place in two separate events: one, the designation of the marriage; two, the consummation of the marriage. The first event is when the man designates a woman to be his wife. This usually involves his freely giving her an article whose minimal worth is evident to all and, simultaneously, her free acceptance of that instrument of transference. The transaction must take place before at least two bona-fide Jewish witnesses. This event and the relationship it creates is called *erusin,* which is usually translated into English as "betrothal."[15] Nevertheless, that translation must be qualified so that it is understood *erusin* is less than what we normally call a "marriage," but more than what we normally call an "engagement."

*Erusin* is more than our notion of "engagement" because the betrothed woman can be convicted of adultery or be divorced on grounds of adultery if she has sexual relations with any other man.[16] (If she had relations with her betrothed, however, they are guilty of the much less serious sin of fornication, extra-marital sex being much more strictly proscribed than pre-marital sex.[17]) But *erusin* is less than our notion of "marriage" because the couple are not yet to live together, certainly not conjugally. The bride-to-be remains in her parents' home. The groom-to-be is supposed to be preparing the home into which he will, usually after a one-year interval, "carry" his bride, thereby creating their joint domicile. It is this event and the relationship that it entails which is also called *qiddushin.* This is a sacrament, which is a relationship initiated and conducted before God in the presence of the representatives of the covenanted

---

15. See B. Sanhedrin 59a re Deut. 33:4, where the Torah is considered to be Israel's betrothed (*m'orasah*). The actual etymology of the word *erusin,* though, is uncertain.

16. Deut. 22:23 and *Sifre: Devarim* 242, p. 272.

17. M. Ketubot 1.5; B. Kerubot 12a; also, Y. Pesahim 10.1/37b. Most marital rights and duties only begin after the couple is living together in a common domicile. See B. Yevamot 22b re Lev. 21:2; B. Sanhedrin 28b.

community.[18] It is this relationship that Maimonides, bespeaking the tradition, locates as the heart of what makes specifically Jewish marriage distinct from marriage in general.

The *Mishnah* mentions that a man may initiate *erusin* by an act of publicly witnessed intercourse with his betrothed.[19] That seems to have been a somewhat standard procedure in early rabbinic times. But, even then, that did not mean the couple engaged in the act of sexual intercourse in actual view of two witnesses (something, by the way, required to ascertain adultery).[20] Instead, it meant that the couple's sequestration *for the sake of engaging in sexual intercourse* was attested to by two witnesses, who also heard the man utter the betrothal formula, which in this case was, "Be consecrated to me by this act of intercourse."[21] Nevertheless, even when this really did take place, it seems the couple would then have to separate until the marriage was legally consummated.[22] That legal consummation would occur when the bride was taken by the groom into his house or the house he had provided for his wife, both being called *huppah*.[23]

Despite the legality of this procedure, Rav, the Babylonian authority of the second century C.E., punished anyone who initiated his or her marriage this way, his reason no doubt being that this practice inevitably involves lewd associations by those present, thus compromising the very sanctity of marriage itself.[24] This prohibition is mentioned in connection with Rav's prohibition of initiating a marriage in the marketplace and his prohibition of initiating a marriage without formal premarital arrangements *(shidukhei)*. In other words, the sanctity of marriage is compromised by initiating it in an atmosphere of voyeurism, in a commercial atmosphere, or in an informal atmosphere. That kind of intercourse, publicly heard even if not publicly seen, looks too much like forbidden fornication.[25]

Nevertheless, the earlier practice of initiating marriage by an act of sexual intercourse does reflect the fact that marriage must be initiated by a man with a

18. See B. Kiddushin 2b, where marriage is considered to be as if the woman had been dedicated to the temple *(ke-heqdesh)*. Hence a violation of marriage is like a violation of what is dedicated to God. See B. Meilah 18a-b re Chron. 5:25.

19. M. Kiddushin 1.1.

20. Cf. B. Makkot 7a.

21. *Tosefta*: Kiddushin 1.3; Saul Lieberman, *Tosefta Kifshuta: Nashim* (New York: Jewish Theological Seminary of America, 1973), pp. 914-15; also, MT: Marriage, 3.5, and Vidal of Tolosa, *Magid Mishneh* thereon re B. Gittin 25b.

22. Cf. B. Kiddushin 22a and Tosafot, s.v. "she-lo" (the view of Rabbenu Tam).

23. See M. Sotah 8.7; B. Sukkah 25b.

24. B. Kiddushin 12b.

25. See B. Niddah 17a; MT: Marriage, 3.21-22; 14.16.

willing woman, which is what marital sex is supposed to be. By initiating the marriage, the man is beginning to fulfill the marital commandment: "Be fruitful and multiply by filling the earth and subduing it *[ve-kivshuah]*" (Gen. 1:28). According to the majority of the rabbis, the actual commandment to marry and make a family devolves on a man but not on a woman.[26] It is the man who must act as his duty; the woman may let him so act with her as her right. But a greater right assumes desire behind it; hence it is assumed that a woman's desire to be married is greater than that of a man.[27] Therefore, it could be said that a woman does not need to be commanded to marry as does a man. As such, at the core of marriage itself, a woman has more rights than a man; a man has more duties than a woman. The rabbis were quite sensitive to these needs of women and legislated accordingly.[28] This recognition of the differences between male and female nature is taken by the rabbis to be indicated by the creation narrative itself, thus making it pre-covenantal.[29] The covenantal innovation does not supplant nature but improves upon it by truly socializing human sexuality in the sanctity of the covenant between God and Israel that Jewish marriage is supposed to reflect. Indeed, in rabbinic teaching, Song of Songs was included in the biblical canon not so much to compare God's love for Israel to that between a man and a woman but, rather, to show a man and a woman how their love can be an imitation of God's love for their people and their people's love for God in the covenant.[30]

There is some uncertainty as to when the Talmud meant the ceremonial aspects of the event of *erusin* to begin — that is, the betrothal benediction *(birkat erusin)* — either before or after the actual transaction of *erusin*.[31] (Today, that benediction is always recited before the transaction in traditional ceremonies.) The benedictory formula for betrothal is stipulated in the Talmud as follows:

> Blessed art Thou O' Lord our God, king of the universe, who has sanctified us by His commandments, and has commanded us concerning forbidden sexual relations *[ha'arayot]*, forbidding [sexual relations] with [our] betrothed *[he'arusot]*, and permitting [sexual relations] with those to whom we

---

26. M. Yevamot 6.6; B. Yevamot 65b. Cf. Y. Yevamot 6.6/7d. Re sexual rights and duties in marriage, see D. M. Feldman, *Birth Control in Jewish Law* (New York: New York University Press, 1968), pp. 60-80.

27. B. Yevamot 118b and parallels.

28. See, e.g., B. Gittin 49b; Y. Gittin 65b; B. Kiddushin 30b re Jer. 29:6.

29. B. Yevamot 65b and Y. Yevamot 6.6/7d re Gen. 1:28.

30. See *Shir ha-Shirim Rabbah* 1.11 re Cant. 1:1 (the view of Rabbi Akiba); also, David Novak, *Jewish Social Ethics* (New York: Oxford University Press, 1992), pp. 94-98.

31. See MT: Marriage, 3.23. Cf. note of Abraham ben David of Posquieres (Ravad) thereon.

are fully married *[ha-nesu'ot]* by means of the bridal dwelling *[huppah]* and its sanctity *[ve-qiddushin]*. . . . Blessed art Thou O' Lord our God, who sanctifies His people Israel by means of the bridal dwelling and its sanctity *[huppah ve-qiddushin]*.[32]

We have just seen the difference between betrothal and actual marriage *(nisu'in)* and what it means in fact. The transition from *erusin* to *nisu'in* turns a merely formal legal relationship into an existential one, where two bodies can intimately act as "one flesh" (Gen. 2:24) and where their two hearts can "seal themselves" (Song 8:6) on each other.[33] The formal legal relationship is the necessary precondition in order for the existential relationship to be sanctified *eros*.

We now need to examine this preliminary moral relationship more carefully, especially the sexual prohibitions it presupposes. Indeed, in talmudic logic, one infers the positive from the negative, so that is the place to begin a reflection on sexual morality and its logical relation to marriage.[34] (It might be called a "ground clearing," borrowing a phrase from a modern philosopher.) Although the number of persons with whom a Jew may not have sexual relations is greater than those considered forbidden to Gentiles, nonetheless the major area of prohibition is identical.[35] That being the case, the Talmud sees this basic area of sexual prohibition as having emerged from the Torah's view of creation, a view which is only confirmed but not fundamentally initiated by the revelation of the Torah to Israel. In fact, one sees examples of these generally prohibited sexual practices in Genesis, which, according to the canonical sequence, totally precedes the revelation at Sinai. So, the accounts in Genesis that assume, either explicitly or implicitly, the prohibitions of incest (9:20-27; 19:30-35), homosexuality (9:20-27; 19:5), adultery (39:6-20), bestiality (2:18-24), and rape (6:4; 12:10-20; 20:2-11; 34:1-31), all of these accounts involve the Hebrews before they became the people of Israel at Sinai.[36] That is, they concern the Hebrews when their moral-legal status was the same as the universal moral-legal status of all the other peoples. Interestingly enough, all of these accounts describe egregious violations of these prohibitions.

These prohibitions are seen in the words by which Scripture describes the initiation of marriage as a morally compelling human reality in the conclusion

32. B. Ketubot 7b.
33. Cf. B. Sanhedrin 28b.
34. B. Nedarim 11a and parallels.
35. B. Sanhedrin 57b re Lev. 18:6.
36. See D. Novak, *Natural Law in Judaism* (Cambridge: Cambridge University Press, 1998), pp. 27-61.

of the creation account in Genesis 2:24, namely, "Therefore a man *[ish]* shall leave his father and his mother, by cleaving to his wife *[b'ishto]*, and they shall then become one flesh *[le-vasar ehad]*." The Talmud interprets this verse not so much as what humans actually do (although there is certainly intercultural evidence to that fact), but, rather, what humans ought to do. It is what they should know about what they ought to do even before Genesis was written, or even if they have never read Genesis at all. In other words, from the following interpretation it does not seem that the basic sexual prohibitions are being presented *de novo* in this text. As the Talmud puts it in another context, "what is being upheld in the present is what was already accepted in the past."[37] The past being upheld in this text is the primordial past of human origins.

> Rabbi Akiba says "his father" [means the prohibition of] his stepmother; "his mother" [means the prohibition of] his own mother. "Cleaving" [means the prohibition of] another male; "to his wife" [means the prohibition of] the wife of his fellow man. "They shall then become one flesh" [means limiting intercourse to one] with whom they can become one flesh, thus excluding either domesticated or wild animals with which they cannot become one flesh.[38]

Even the prohibition of rape is implied in this interpretation of Genesis 2:24. Proscribing the violation of the rights of a man over a woman, rights that also entail his duty to protect her from violence, applies not only to some other woman's husband, but in the case of many minors it also applies to their fathers and brothers, as one sees in the story of the rape of Dinah (especially in Genesis 34:25-31). Rape, then, violates the legitimate relationship not only between a woman and her husband, but also between a daughter and her father and a sister and her brothers. This is very much akin to the crime of kidnapping.[39]

The forbidden sexual unions considered to be universal, just mentioned above, are also explicitly forbidden to Israel in Leviticus 18:1-24, with a few additions. The Pentateuch itself, however, is not too clear about what in the rabbinic period came to be the most serious sexual prohibition of all: the prohibition of marriage between a Jew and a Gentile. That is probably because the forbidden sexual unions of Genesis and then Leviticus are almost always private matters, difficult to detect in public, whereas a *marriage* between a Jew and

---

37. B. Shabbat 88a re Est. 9:26.

38. B. Sanhedrin 58a. For the prohibition of inter-female sexuality, see *Sifra*: Aharei-Mot, ed. Weiss, p. 86a; *Vayiqra Rabbah* 23.9; Maimonides, *Commentary on the Mishnah*: Sanhedrin 7.4 and MT: Forbidden Intercourse, 21.8; B. Yevamot 76a.

39. Cf. B. Sanhedrin 86a re Exod. 20:13.

a Gentile is by definition public.[40] Furthermore, aside from the fact that Moses, who brought the Law of God to the people, seems to have been married to a gentile woman, the most explicit prohibition of what we now call "intermarriage" is, "You shall not marry [tithatten] them; your daughter you shall not give [in marriage] to his son, and his daughter you shall not take [in marriage] for your son" (Deut. 7:3).[41] Yet this prohibition is explicitly connected to the prohibition of having any covenantal relationship with the Canaanite nations because of their blatant idolatry and its attendant sexual practices. (The inner relation of idolatry with sexual license is a ubiquitous biblical trope.) Also, such marriages would give legitimacy to Canaanite claims on the land of Israel since marriage in that early period inevitably involved claims on landed property, thus bringing into question absolute Israelite sovereignty in the land of Israel in the present (it only being "the land of Canaan" before Joshua's conquest of the land immediately after the death of Moses).

Even the Talmud has to admit that according to biblical law, strictly speaking, the Deuteronomic prohibition is limited to the Canaanites.[42] Moreover, by the time the rabbis came on the historical scene, it was assumed that the Canaanite nations were no longer intact.[43] Therefore, there are some attempts to connect the general prohibition of a Jew marrying *any* Gentile to several verses in the Pentateuch, but in such a way as to strongly suggest that the actual source of this general prohibition lies elsewhere.[44]

The actual source of this general prohibition surely lies with Ezra and the innovations that he decreed upon the return of the Jewish people to the land of Israel some seventy years or so after the exile from Jerusalem at the hands of the Babylonians in 586 B.C.E. (Thus "Judeans" or "Jews" are all of "Israel" still left intact.) The reconstitution of the Jewish people, with the Mosaic Torah now as their national constitution, and with a public authority it did not seem to have in the pre-exilic times of the first temple, also led to a tighter definition of what qualified as a valid Jewish marriage and what did not. Thus Ezra is horrified when the leaders of those who are returning to the land of Israel inform him that the people, even the Aaronide priests and the Levites,

> have not separated themselves from the nations of other lands [me'ammei ha'aratsot] with their abominations . . . for they have taken for themselves and for their sons [wives] from their [the other nations'] daughters and as-

40. See Deut. 27:20-23.
41. B. Sanhedrin 82a.
42. B. Kiddushin 68b.
43. M. Yadayim 4.4.
44. B. Kiddushin 68b-69a.

similated *[ve-hit'arvu]* the holy seed *[zera ha-qodesh]* with the nations of other lands; indeed major and minor officials have been the first to commit this sacrilege *[ma'al]*. (Ezra 9:1-2)

It is also quite likely that the definition of Jewish identity, both national and familial (the nation itself taken to be an amalgam of proper Jewish families), needed to be tightened in the face of Samaritan attempts to blur distinctions between the Jews and themselves at this time (Ezra 4:1-6).[45] An earlier biblical text, describing the time between the exile of the ten tribes of northern Israel by the Assyrians in 721 B.C.E. and the return of the Jews (that is, the larger tribe of Judah and the much smaller tribe of Benjamin), casts aspersions on the validity of the conversion to the worship of the Lord God of Israel of the Gentiles who came into Samaria to replace the exiled Israelites (2 Kings 17:24-41). So, carrying this distinction between Jews and Samaritans to its logical conclusion, which is meant to make an absolute differentiation between the two communities, the Talmud ends all Jewish ambivalence toward the Samaritans by insisting that subsequent evidence of official (albeit esoteric) Samaritan idolatry proves retroactively that the Samaritans never really converted to the religion of the Torah at all.[46] Hence they are as different from the Jews as are all the other Gentiles, even though it is also admitted that some of the rabbis did accept some religious commonality between Jews and Samaritans at one time.[47] All this is important to note since in the time of Ezra, intermarriage with the peoples who had come to occupy the land of Israel during the absence of the Jews, especially the peoples who eventually came to be known as "Samaritans" (later in the Talmud called "Kutheans"), would be a ready opportunity for many Jews. Would that not be so since these new neighbors were most anxious to legitimize their presence in the land by intermarrying with its older inhabitants now returned home?

At first glance, though, it looks like Ezra was just reiterating the prohibitions of the Pentateuch itself, which have been violated by the Jews from their leadership on down to ordinary folk, probably abetted by the absence of any national authority during the Exile. Indeed, the sin of intermarriage, like its treatment in the Pentateuch, is connected in the passage above with "their abominations" *(ke-to'avoteihem)*, namely, the idolatry long seen to be gentile in essence: *their* despised social practices being correlate to *their* despicable gods. Nonetheless, there is a difference between the situation of the Pentateuch and

45. See B. Kiddushin 70b re Jer. 30:25.
46. B. Hullin 6a re Prov. 23:2.
47. B. Hullin 4a. See T. Zevahim 13.1; Y. Pesahim 1.1/27b.

its contemporaries and that of Ezra and his contemporaries. One notices that in the enumeration of the forbidden nations (v. 1), more than the usual Canaanite ones are listed. Now also included are "the Ammonite, the Moabite, the Egyptian, and the Amorite." Thus it seems that the world is now divided into two main groupings: Israel who worships the Lord God, and all the other nations who worship gods whom Israel regards to be false. It is not just Israel versus the seven or so Canaanite nations, with everyone else having a theological-political neutrality as it were. Now the lines of division are much more strictly theological, with no Gentiles being taken to be any better or any worse, at least as regards Jews intermarrying with them.[48]

Furthermore, at this great juncture in Jewish history, Israel has not really returned to its specific tribal patrimony, since only the tribe of Judah — who are now "the Jews" — has returned back intact to the land. All the old nations, with the great exception of the Jews (but minus the other "lost" tribes of Israel), seem to have lost their clear national identity. So, there is no longer the possibility that intermarriage with members of nearby nations will confuse Jewish tribal claims on the land of Israel itself.[49] Moreover, whereas in pre-exilic times it seems that gentile women came into the Israelite community, leaving their old national identity behind simply by virtue of their having married an Israelite man, now it is assumed that gentile women are still Gentiles.[50] Accordingly, the leaders of the nation, in some sort of parliamentary assembly, solemnly covenant themselves "to remove all the women and their children . . . and it shall be done as divine law [ve-kha-torah]" (Ezra 10:3). Thus Ezra publicly confirms this solemn covenantal commitment by stating, "But now do acknowledge [tenu todah] the Lord God of your fathers and do his will by separating yourselves [ve-hibbadlu] from the peoples of the earth and from the foreign women" (Ezra 10:11). Whether at this time women who had formally converted to Judaism prior to their marriage to Jewish men were exempt from this harsh decree, indeed whether there was formal conversion at all at this time, both are hard to

48. See B. Kiddushin 68b re Deut. 7:4 (according to Rabbi Simeon).
49. In the pre-exilic period, even intertribal marriages were discouraged. See Num. 36:1-10; B. Baba Batra 120a.
50. Despite talmudic suggestion to the contrary (B. Yevamot 47b and Ruth Rabbah 2.17, 23, 25 re Ruth 1:11-17), it does not seem that Ruth (the ancestress of King David, no less!) underwent any formal conversion to the Israelite religion. If marriage brought one into the Israelite community, that would explain why the levirate claims of her deceased Israelite husband's clan on her are valid (Ruth 4:1-11), which would not be the case had she been considered a total foreigner at the time she married him in her native Moab. It also seems that Boaz's blessing for Ruth for her coming to the God of Israel (Ruth 2:12) refers back to her first marriage, when she seems to have become an Israelitess ipso facto. See, also, B. Yevamot 69a and parallels re Deut. 23:4.

discern from these post-exilic biblical texts. Also, the exact status of children born to Jewish mothers and gentile fathers remained questionable until late in the Talmudic period.[51]

The upshot of this innovation of Ezra and his assembly is the firm establishment of the principle of matrilineal descent in Judaism, namely, that a child's communal religious identity is determined through his or her mother rather than his or her father. Thus the Talmud connects this to (without really basing it on) the biblical words, "for he will turn your son away from Me" (Deut. 7:4), meaning, "Your son who comes from a Jewess is called *your son,* but your son who comes from a gentile woman is not called 'your son' but, rather, *her son.*"[52] Even though Jewish women married to gentile men, and the children born of such unions, are both still considered to be fully Jewish, the marriage itself is not recognized to be a Jewish marriage. It seems that the rabbis viewed the cultural assimilation of a child born to a gentile mother to be immediate, whereas the cultural assimilation of a child born to a Jewish mother and a gentile father would probably take another generation or so.[53] And, the Talmud records rabbinic decrees designed to prevent such unions from ever taking place, such as forbidding even any casual nonmarital sexual relations between Jews and Gentiles, and even going so far as to forbid the drinking of wine with Gentiles because this might lower one's sexual inhibitions and lead one to "their daughters."[54] (The mention of "daughters" rather than "sons," even though intermarriage is proscribed for Jewish women as well as for Jewish men, no doubt reflects the social situation which, until quite recently, made illicit sexual liaisons easier for men than for women because of the more public lives of most men and the more domestic lives of most women.[55])

The new post-exilic emphasis on marriage as a strictly intercovenantal reality during the period of Ezra comes out in the one explicit mention in the Bible about marriage itself as a covenant. It comes from Malachi, the last of the literary prophets, who some in the rabbinic tradition even identify with Ezra:

> Have we not one father? Did not one God create us? Why does a man betray his brother to profane the covenant of our fathers? . . . [F]or Judah, the holy one *[qodesh]* whom the Lord loves, has married the daughter of a strange god. . . . For the Lord witnesses what is between you and the wife of your

51. See B. Yevamot 45a.

52. B. Kiddushin 68b.

53. See B. Kiddushin 68b, Tosafot, s.v. "binekha."

54. B. Avodah Zarah 36b.

55. See B. Sukkah 30a re Ps. 45:14; also, *Tanhuma*: Vayishlah 12 re Gen. 34:1, ed. Buber, pp. 85b-86a.

youth whom you have betrayed; yet she is your companion *[haverttekha]* and your covenanted wife *[eshet britekha]*. (Mal. 2:10-11, 14)

The great medieval exegete David Kimhi puts this indicting passage in its proper historical context.[56] The prophet is particularly concerned with the fact that many Jews, especially many leaders of the people (their "role models," as we would say today), had married non-Jewish women, thus betraying their Jewish wives. At that time, polygamy was widely practiced by Jews, especially by upper-class men who could afford to support multiple wives. Or, perhaps, the prophet is even speaking against Jewish men who had avoided marrying any Jewish wife at all. Calling the betrayed wife "your covenanted wife" makes any intermarriage not just an ordinary sin but a major covenantal violation. Marriage is now seen as an instantiation of the master covenant between God and Israel made at Sinai. And, the official text of the Mosaic Torah has now been determined by Ezra to be the constitution of the newly regenerated nation (Mal. 3:22).

The purpose of Jewish marriage, which largely explains its various specific norms, is to maintain and perpetuate the covenanted community. Thus "the one father" is not God the cosmic creator, but Jacob/Israel whose name the covenanted people bear. And the "one God who created us" is not God as cosmic creator, but God as the One who created Israel by electing her to be his unique covenanted partner. Thus the difference between natural/universal marriage and uniquely Jewish marriage is that Jewish marriage intends more than the mere perpetuation of the human species. Rather, Jewish marriage is for the sake of maintaining and perpetuating the covenant of Sinai. That is best accomplished in a family-centered community.

After viewing all these sexual prohibitions, one could easily draw an erroneous conclusion about sexuality in the Jewish tradition, namely, that the "puritanical" Jewish tradition would like to get rid of as much sexual activity as possible, thus getting as close to zero as possible, without, of course, eliminating normal procreation needed for national survival. On the contrary: like the Sabbath, whose many prohibitions make no sense unless they are taken to be for the sake of concentrating and intensifying one's experience of the holiness of the day itself by being freed from as many distractions as possible, so, too, the many sexual prohibitions are for the sake of concentrating and intensifying one's erotic marital experience by being freed from as many distractions as possible. "To sanctify" *(qadesh)*, which is the word used to designate most specifically how a Jewish marriage is created, means to "set apart." That is why the betrothal benediction ends by praising God "who sanctifies His people Israel."

56. Radaq on Mal. 2:10.

Marriage, like the Sabbath, is an event of covenantal intimacy between God and the female and male members of his truly elect community — what the rabbis liked to call "the congregation of Israel" *(keneset yisra'el).*[57]

In fact, the intimacy of Israel's experience of the Sabbath (also called "sacred") with God is compared to the intimacy between husband and wife, both of which are to be freed from as many distracting intrusions as possible.[58] Finally, although certain Jewish groups in the last days of the second temple had advocated celibacy (obviously, though, not for all Jews), the rabbinic tradition regarded the commandment to marry and have a family to be without exception.[59] In fact, regular sexual activity between spouses is advocated even when the likelihood of conception resulting from it is very remote.[60]

Both the natural and covenantal aspects of the positive celebration of marital sexuality shall be discussed later when we get to the third step in Jewish marriage: the celebration of its consummation.

## Jewish Marriage: The Second Step

Sometime after the betrothal but before the full consummation of the marriage, the marriage document is drawn up, witnessed, and then given to the bride. This document is called the *ketubah* or *ketubat ishah* (literally, "the woman's document"). There was usually a one-year hiatus between the betrothal and the marriage itself. But, before the marriage's consummation, the woman is supposed to have her *ketubah* in hand as her right.[61] Her *ketubah* is very much her social and economic protection.[62]

In ancient times, when marriage between Jews, including its financial arrangements, was totally under the control of Jewish authorities, the *ketubah* had a very important social-economic function. It dealt with the rights a woman had regarding property she brought into the marriage, her rights to support from her husband, and her rights to payment from her husband's estate in the event of the termination of the marriage as a result of death or divorce.[63] In the event of

---

57. See, e.g., *Tanhuma: Ki Tissa* 9 on Exod. 31:18 re Cant. 4:11.

58. *Shemot Rabbah* 25.15 and *Devarim Rabbah* 1.18 re Exod. 31:17.

59. B. Yevamot 63b re Gen. 9:6-7. See also B. Baba Batra 60b.

60. B. Yevamot 62b; B. Betsah 36b-37a and Rashi, s.v. "eet leih."

61. M. Ketubot 4.7. The by-now classic study of the *ketubah* is that of Louis M. Epstein, *The Jewish Marriage Contract* (New York: Jewish Theological Seminary of America, 1927).

62. B. Baba Kama 89a.

63. See, e.g., B. Ketubot 58b. For a listing of these rights, culling from various talmudic sources, see MT: Marriage, 12.2.

being widowed or divorced, a woman became a creditor of her late husband or her former husband, thus having the right to sue his heirs or him for nonpayment of the *ketubah* settlement. The *ketubah* basically stipulated a woman's specific rights in marriage, which are her lawful claims upon her husband and his corresponding duties to her. It is obvious, then, that the *ketubah* lifted a woman from the level of chattel in a marriage to a level where she now had considerable power over her husband as a result of the claims she could now make upon him and his estate, claims that rivaled the claims he already could make upon her. Although the emphasis of male-female differences so prevalent in Judaism would surely prevent any simple equation of women and men in their most intense area of interrelation — marriage — we see nonetheless how the *ketubah* created a proportional equality, that is, an approximate distribution of both rights and duties among the male and female partners in the marriage so that either partner might benefit from the other and neither partner might exploit the other.

Moreover, according to biblical law a man divorces his wife of his own free will, but a woman does not divorce her husband.[64] One could easily infer from the one biblical text prescribing how and why one is to divorce his wife (Deut. 24:1) that a man could do so with total caprice and full impunity. By stipulating a man's duties to his wife, which involve attention to both her monetary and her personal needs, however, the institution of the *ketubah* enables a woman to sue for divorce in court because of her husband's noncompliance with his stipulated obligations to her. Here the *ketubah* largely explicates the obligations of support, financial and also sexual, obligations assumed to be originally mandated by the Bible (Exod. 21:10). If a woman is successful in her suit, the court would be essentially acting on her behalf by forcing her husband to divorce her, even when his requisite "free will" here is a legal fiction.[65] Thus the *ketubah* stipulates a man's responsibilities *after* the termination of the marriage but, also, his responsibilities *during* the marriage, responsibilities he can no longer ignore with impunity in the present, just as he cannot ignore his post-marital obligations in the future.

The Talmud queries whether the *ketubah* with the rights and duties it codifies is of biblical or rabbinic origin.[66] If its origin is biblical, that origin is seen to be based on the biblical institution of *mohar*, which was originally the price the Torah deemed proper for a male to pay to the father of a virginal unbetrothed minor whom he had seduced (Exod. 22:16-17). By considerable extension, this is now seen by some to be the price anyone has to pay the woman he has aban-

64. M. Yevamot 14.1; T. Ketubot 12.3.
65. M. Ketubot 5.6; 7.9-10; M. Arakhin 5.6; M. Gittin 9.8.
66. B. Ketubot 10a.

doned either by death or by divorce. But the purpose of this specific biblical institution of *mohar* is to punish the sinner with a fine *(qenas)*. Should the institution of the *ketubah*, which the rabbis "based" *(samkhu)* on Scripture (but which is not explicitly biblical), be traced back to what is obviously the original biblical reason here, namely, that "the sinner not profit [that is, pay for his sin]"?[67] But this seems counterintuitive. Is a man's commitment to the marital relationship meant to be a financial penalty imposed upon him? Is an ordinary bridegroom really the same as the debauched seducer of a childish virgin? If this is the only biblical basis for the institution of the *ketubah*, then it seems we ought to be wary of trying to make a specific biblical connection at all. So, what we see from this Talmudic dilemma in general is the fact that looking at the Bible alone, we do not get enough basis for truly enhancing the status of women.[68] A more radical justification of the institution of the *ketubah* is called for.

So, the Talmud seems to be more inclined to see the institution of the *ketubah* to be a rabbinic enactment *(taqqanah)*.[69] Designating this institution to be rabbi-made law, the Talmud thereby frees the justification of this institution from being tied to an analogy to a rather unattractive case dealt with in biblical law, where the purpose of the law is essentially punitive.[70] Furthermore, this freeing of the justification of the institution of the *ketubah* from being tied to a specific biblical text enables the Talmud to discover a more general and a more humane reason for it. Also, whereas the reason *(ta'ama)* for a biblical law is to be inferred *from* a specific text, the reason *for* a rabbinic enactment is always supposed to be made explicit by the human beings who enacted it.[71] Thus biblical reasons being divine thoughts are only *implicit* and thus subsequently inferred *from* the biblical text; rabbinic reasons being human thoughts are *explicit* and are already assumed *by* the rabbinic text.[72] As such, the latter can be reinterpreted, even radically reinterpreted, when socially necessary.

Here the reason for the rabbinic enactment of the *ketubah* is assumed to be, "so that it not be easy *[qalah]* for him to get rid of her *[le-hotsi'ah]*."[73] Of

---

67. See B. Baba Kama 38b-39a.

68. Thus the fourteenth-century exegete, Menahem ha-Meiri, boldly stated that were there only marriage as constituted by biblical law alone, where women have very few marital rights, no woman would remain Jewish (*Beit ha-Behirah:* Kiddushin, ed. Sofer, p. 8). For post-Talmudic developments in the expansion of a woman's marital rights, see Z. W. Falk, *Jewish Matrimonial Law in the Middle Ages* (London: Oxford University Press, 1966).

69. B. Ketubot 10a and Tosafot, s.v. "amar."

70. M. Ketubot 3.1.

71. See B. Gittin 14a.

72. See B. Avodah Zarah 35a. Cf. B. Baba Batra 173b.

73. B. Ketubot 11a.

course, one could see this too as a penalty. Does it not say to the man in effect: "divorce will cost you"? By not being tied down to the exact sum of the biblical fine employed in the earlier view where the *ketubah* is biblically based, however, the rabbis were enabled to freely stipulate the amount of post-marital payment that would really benefit the woman in their own time and place. Looking at the *ketubah* this way shows "what the Rabbis accomplished *[ho'ilu]* by their enactment," which is what the Talmud sometimes asks about the positive benefit of a rabbinic enactment for those for whom it was made in the first place.[74] So, we can see the original purpose of the *ketubah* to be an empowerment of women by protecting them from being capriciously divorced, and, if they are divorced or widowed, a means of preventing them from being left in poverty. That is why it is better to see this institution as rabbinic rather than biblical. As for its importance, one can see this in the rabbinic ruling that a woman has minimal *ketubah* rights by virtue of rabbinic stipulation even when the *ketubah* was not written out for her.[75]

Whatever parallels the *ketubah* has had in non-Jewish societies and their legal systems, it is considered to be a completely Jewish institution. It basically represents a covenantal responsibility of the normative Jewish community toward Jewish women, a responsibility it lays upon the Jewish men whom it permits to marry these women.[76] And, even though the majority of the rabbis saw the strict duty to marry and make a family to devolve on men rather than women, nevertheless, it was also recognized that almost all women desire marriage and children for themselves, as we have seen. As such, women have a basic right to marry, and their exercise of this right is to be promoted by the legal system. Moreover, this right is not only *to* marry but, as a sequitur, to be treated fairly *within* marriage.

Because of this essentially covenantal character of Jewish marriage, one should not look upon the *ketubah* as a contract in essence. Instead, the *ketubah* applies the stipulations of the Torah itself, the reasons for which we infer to be the fulfillment of a Jewish woman's marital rights. And it then applies the enactments of the rabbis, whose reason is explicated to be for a wife's rightful welfare.[77] Nevertheless, there are some important contractual aspects added to the *ketubah*. They are contractual because they can be negotiated between the par-

74. B. Ketubot 10a. Cf. B. Baba Metsia 17b.

75. M. Ketubot 4.7.

76. Hence it is assumed that all Jewish marriages have been initiated with the tacit acceptance of the right of the community, in the persons of its rabbis, to annul any marriage retroactively for significant cause (B. Gittin 33a and Tosafot, s.v. "kol"). See David Novak, *Halakhah in a Theological Dimension* (Chico, Calif.: Scholars Press, 1985), 29-44.

77. M. Ketubot 4.8-12.

ties themselves. In other words, like a contract but unlike a covenant (in the biblical sense), there are some areas of the marital relationship that are left for the couple to make their own rules for themselves. One of these rights is the woman's right to be supported by her husband. That right is correlated with her duty to turn over to her husband whatever she might earn or find.[78]

In ancient times, when few free women had regular employment outside the home, this arrangement definitely benefited most women. Usually, a husband's support of his wife far outweighed whatever a wife could possibly obtain by herself outside the home. But the Talmud does recognize that there might be exceptions, that there might be women who would rather depend on their own earnings even if that means forgoing the financial support of their husbands. As such, the view the Talmud subsequently accepted as normative opinion is that a couple can make their own contractual conditions *(tn'ai)* in their financial relationship.[79] But, this right to waive financial claims and correlative financial duties through negotiation, and concluded by mutual agreement, is confined to the area of domestic economy alone.

Of the three marital rights of a woman mentioned in Exodus 21:10 — food, clothing, and regular sexual intercourse — the first two can be the subject of financial negotiations between the couple. By mutual consent, each of the parties can waive his or her financial obligations to the other. But, when it comes to regular sexual intercourse, a woman or a man may not waive this right as a condition of their marriage. It is considered to be a personal right that is inalienable, even by the original bearer of that right.[80] In fact, if such a condition were to be publicly made before the initiation of the marriage at betrothal, the marriage would be annulled automatically. And, if regular intercourse is denied by either party to the other after the time when the couple is allowed to fully live together as husband and wife, then the offended party has the right to petition the court for redress of grievance.[81] That means the court requires the offending party to perform his or her marital duties. But, if there is no compliance with this court order, the woman is to be divorced by her husband or the husband is to be forced by the court to divorce his wife.

Of course, in this latter situation, if no complaint is filed by an offended party, then the continuation of the marriage is, in effect, the private business of the couple willing to live in such a nonsexual union. Here we see how a private agreement, subsequently contracted between husband and wife, can be opera-

78. B. Ketubot 58b; 107b.
79. B. Kiddushin 19b.
80. Y. Kiddushin 1.3/59c; B. Kiddushin 19b and Rashi, s.v. "be-dvar mamon."
81. M. Ketubot 5.6-7; M. Nedarim 11.12.

tive in a Jewish marriage *de facto.* Unlike a contracted financial agreement, however, which must be made in public as part of the *ketubah* negotiations, such a personal, intimate agreement between the couple themselves can only be private. To negotiate it in public would be to admit that a woman or a man can waive what is considered a personal (or physical) right, which is assumed to be an inalienable right, one that cannot be waived *de jure.* In other words, whereas we *own* property that can be bought and sold, we *are* our bodies and cannot, therefore, be alienated or alienate ourselves from them.

## Jewish Marriage: The Third Step

The Talmud text we examined earlier, which presented the benediction that is uttered at the occasion of betrothal *(erusin),* then continues with a discussion of the ceremonial celebration of the consummation of the marriage *(nisu'in).* This legal consummation (the actual sexual consummation taking place some-time thereafter) took place in what is called "the house of grooms" *(beit hatanim),* which might mean either the house of the groom himself into which he "carries" his bride to live together with her, or some sort of wedding hall.[82] In either case, though, the celebration seems to have been at the groom's ex-pense, perhaps to show his wife and the world that he is able to both support her and entertain her in public.[83] Seven days of wedding celebration are held, and the "wedding benediction" *(birkat hatanim)* is repeated each day, provided there are ten men present for a quorum and that among them there are some new guests each day.[84] Most likely, this benediction was recited each day at a festive meal when wine was drunk in celebration of the event.[85] Although this benediction is designated in the singular, it consists, nonetheless, of several parts, the exact number of which is debated in the Talmud's ensuing discussion. The original version of this multifaceted benediction is as follows:

> Blessed art Thou O' Lord our God, king of the universe, who has created ev-erything for his glory; and created human beings *[ha'adam];* created in His image, in the likeness of His image *[tavnito],* and who has ordained for him [the man] what has been built for the perpetuity of humankind *[binyan adei ad];* blessed art Thou O' Lord, who forms *[yotser]* human beings. Surely make the barren one [Zion] rejoice and be gladdened by the happy gathering

82. B. Ketubot 7b.
83. T. Ketubot 1.1; Y. Ketubot 1.1/24d; B. Ketubot 2a.
84. B. Ketubot 7b.
85. See B. Sukkah 25b; also, B. Pesahim 109a re Ps. 104:15.

of her children in her midst; blessed art Thou O' Lord, who has Zion rejoice in her children. Do make the loving and beloved companions [re'im ha'ahuvim] happy [with one another] as you made your [human] creatures happy in the Garden of Eden originally [mi-qedem]; blessed art Thou O' Lord, who makes the groom and bride happy. Blessed art Thou O' Lord our God, king of the universe, who has created joy and happiness [simhah], groom and bride, mirth, song, gladness, and delight, love, harmony [ahvah], peace [shalom] and companionship [re'ut]. O Lord our God, may there quickly be heard in the cities of Judah and the precincts of Jerusalem the sound of joy and the voice of happiness, the voice of the groom and the voice of the bride, the voice of grooms from their bridal chamber [huppatam], and youngsters arising from songful celebration. Blessed art Thou O' Lord, who makes the groom be happy with his bride.[86]

This long passage, indeed one of the longest single prayers presented in the Talmud, represents the most complete theology of Jewish marriage in an original rabbinic source. Parsing it will tell us much about the key motifs in this original theological statement of marriage. Like any communal prayer, which is a prayer through which "we" rather than just "I" speak, it is as much a third-person statement to the faith community as it is a second-person address to God. It is uttered *within* the community's covenantal relationship with God as well as uttered as a didactic description *about* the meaning of that covenantal relationship with God. (That is perhaps why in liturgical Hebrew, God is spoken *about* as much in the third person "He" as God is spoken *to* in the second person "Thou.")

The first three clauses refer to nature. The first clause, "who has created everything for his glory," refers to nature in general of which human nature is a part, albeit the highest part in biblical-rabbinic theology.[87] What is the link between human nature and the nature of the rest of the world, especially the animal world whose creation immediately precedes the creation of human beings in the biblical account, and with which humans do have the most in common in the evolutionary chain? The answer is sexuality, especially sexuality as the medium through which procreation takes place: the survival and perpetuation of the species. This species instinct is in close relation with the individual instinct of self-preservation. Without that natural substratum, the social institution of marriage which builds upon it would have no connection to the physical world, in this case what we now call the "biosphere." Humans might well have

---

86. B. Ketubot 7b-8a.
87. See, e.g., M. Sanhedrin 4.5.

souls that are "breathed" into them directly by God, but they are just as much "dust from the ground" (Gen. 2:7), like all other living things.[88]

This first declaration of natural sexuality implies that no creature should be neutered. The Bible prohibits the castration of animals (Lev. 22:24). Following this line, it is important to note how every human being is considered to have a right to a sexual relationship with some other (but never all or even most) human beings, and that legal technicalities should not place an insuperable barrier to the exercise of that right. This comes out in the following discussion in the *Mishnah* (the substratum of the Talmud):

> Someone who is half slave and half free . . . the Shammaites say to the Hillelites [about the latter's ruling that leaves such a person in sexual limbo] . . . you have not rectified *[lo tiqqanttem]* his situation: [by your criteria] it is impossible for him to marry a slave woman because he is already half free; it is impossible for him to marry a free woman because he is half slave. Should he be sexually nullified *[yibbatel]*? But wasn't the world created in order to procreate *[le-piryah ve-rivyah]*, as it is written: "He did not create it to be a void but, rather, He formed it to be a dwelling *[la-shevet]*" (Isaiah 45:18)?[89]

The text concludes with the Hillelites being persuaded by the Shammaite theory, and then agreeing that in practice the good of human society *(tiqqun ha'olam)* requires the one who owns the "slave half" of this bifurcated person to emancipate his share in this unfortunate human life so that the man can lead a normal human life.[90]

That natural normality is the physical and social capacity of humans to start and maintain human community, whose origin and center is the domestic relationship between and among spouses and children: what is properly called "family" *(mishpahah)*. Thus the general biological drive to procreate, and the specifically human drive to constitute a community through speech, beginning with the initiation of a family in a mutually free, explicitly agreed upon situation, these two drives come together in this opening celebration of creation in the marriage ceremony itself.

The next two clauses are considered two sides of the same coin, as it were. The first clause speaks of the creation of man *(adam)*. Now, even though the term *adam* usually means a human being, its use here is seen by Rashi, the great medieval Bible and Talmud exegete, to refer to the first man (Adam).[91] Then

---

88. See B. Sanhedrin 38a.

89. M. Gittin 4.5.

90. B. Gittin 43b; Y. Gittin 4.5/46a.

91. B. Ketubot 8a, s.v. "sameah." There Rashi alludes to the passage in the Talmud

the second clause, referring to what has been built from him, is seen to refer to the creation of woman who "from the man *[ish]* was taken" (Gen. 2:23). This implies, of course, the superiority of man over woman. One could instead, however, follow the Talmudic teaching that the first human being was ambisexual, and that the creation of two sexually distinct persons — woman and man — is the bifurcation of this originally ambisexual creature. Following this teaching enables us both to better avoid charges of male chauvinism in the constitution of Jewish marriage and to better explain the celebration of sexual attraction leading into marriage and conscientiously sustained and developed within it. This attraction is thus the two halves of the previously unified body, each seeking his or her lost half.[92]

The next clause speaks of the covenant between "the loving and beloved companions." The relationship is covenantal because it is unconditional, and because it is without any built-in termination provisions. That is the case even if the marriage was initiated with a conditional betrothal *(ten'ai be-qiddushin)* such as "be consecrated unto me on condition that I am X."[93] The verification or falsification of such a condition of betrothal must be made before the marriage is actually consummated since afterward there are no conditions which, if not fulfilled, could annul the marriage anymore.[94] In fact, a couple who are living together in any sort of ongoing union having some public recognition (they somehow or other are known as "a couple") are considered married *ex post facto*, even though their marriage started improperly *ab initio*. The public representation of their union as being more than an ephemeral liaison *(zenut)* makes it a marriage *de facto*.[95] This means that the very life arrangement they have incurred upon themselves entails the obligations of marriage, even if that might well not have been their original intention, as evidenced by the informality with which the relationship was initiated. So, if such a couple desire to end their relationship and thereby be free of charges of adultery should they take up with someone else, they must obtain an official Jewish divorce *(get)*.[96] And, just

---

(B. Berakhot 61a re Gen. 2:22) where a Rabbi imagines that God himself personally arranged the wedding *(shushbin)* of Adam and Eve.

92. B. Berakhot 6a and B. Eruvin 8a. See Louis Ginzberg, *The Legends of the Jews,* vol. 5 (Philadelphia: Jewish Publication Society of America, 1925), pp. 86-91, nn. 36-48.

93. See, e.g., M. Kiddushin 2.3.

94. B. Yevamot 107a. Cf. Tosafot, s.v. "Beit Shammai."

95. B. Ketubot 72b-73a.

96. B. Gittin 81a-b. For the ramifications of this principle for the modern situation of many Jews who have not married in a traditional manner, see David Novak, "The Marital Status of Jews Married under Non-Jewish Auspices," *Jewish Law Association Studies* I, ed. B. S. Jackson (Chico, Calif.: Scholars Press, 1985), pp. 61-77.

as a couple who began their marriage without official blessing are frowned upon, so are a couple who begin their marriage with the definite notion that they will be ending it after a time.[97]

Referring to the now fully married couple as "loving companions" gets us back to the whole question of how love can possibly be ascertained in marriage or in any human relationship. It also raises the question of how love can be commanded. Is love not an emotion and are not emotions basically involuntary? Yet the Bible presents the commandment, "You shall love your neighbor as yourself" (Lev. 19:18), and Rabbi Akiba (the most famous of the rabbis of the Talmud) famously designates this commandment to be the most wide-reaching precept *(kellal gadol)* in the entire Torah.[98] It would seem, however, that in biblical-rabbinic anthropology, love is commanded because love is basically an act. Love is benefiting the other person by one's personal attention and being benefited by that other person's personal response. Optimally the feeling of love, which is one's desire to be with and act with the beloved, should precede its actualization in deeds.[99] Yet that is a desideratum, not an absolute precondition.

Like the practice of the other commandments of the Torah, *to love* (as distinct from feeling affectionate) frequently means that one is to act even before one can intend his or her action to be what he or she truly desires. To feel love is to desire, and desire is transitive, not intransitive; transactional, not narcissistic. Desire, as distinct from lust, definitely intends the presence of another person. Thus, there are several interpretations of the commandment of neighbor-love in the Talmud. (The word "neighbor" *[re'a]* here is the translation of the same Hebrew word translated as "companion" in the English representation of the nuptial benediction presented above.) Among them is the following interpretation: "It is forbidden *[asur]* for a man to betrothe a woman until he sees her [first] lest he find something disgusting *[dvar meguneh]* about her and she become disgusting to him; yet the Torah says 'You shall love your neighbor as yourself.'"[100]

When one looks at this dictum carefully, it does not speak romantically about having to "fall in love" before marrying someone. It is more minimal

97. That is why the Talmud and its commentators are clearly embarrassed by the story of the great sage, Rav (indeed, the very authority who made several decrees, as we have seen, designed to elevate the initiation of marriage from any semblance of fornication), who advertised for a wife "for a day" (B. Yoma 18b).

98. Y. Nedarim 9.4/4c; *Beresheet Rabbah* 24.7, ed. Theodor-Albeck, p. 237.

99. See G. A. Anderson, *A Time to Mourn, A Time to Dance: The Expression of Grief and Joy in Israelite Religion* (University Park, Pa.: Pennsylvania State University Press, 1991), pp. 19-27.

100. B. Kiddushin 41a. See, also, B. Niddah 17a re Lev. 19:18.

and, I think, more realistic. It seems to be saying that before betrothing a woman (which in those days was usually long before a young man was going to actually live with this woman as his wife), a man should at least be sure that this woman is someone he *could come to love*, both in action and in feeling. Moreover, the same rabbi (the Babylonian sage, Rav) who interpreted the commandment of neighbor-love to refer to the husband's love of his wife also prohibited the marrying off of a minor girl by her father (who in biblical law has this right), reasoning that a marriage should be initiated only when the young woman is truly able to say, "X is whom I want *(ani rotsah)!*"[101] In other words, neither a man nor a woman should marry or have to marry anyone whom they know they could not possibly love. Like Israel at Mount Sinai, who promised "we shall do" (Exod. 24:7) before we shall "fully agree" (literally, "hear"), the man and the woman need to act before they can feel the full meaning of what they are doing together.[102] At present, all they need to know is that such a growth into love is not out of the question for either of them now.

In the clause about "the loving companions," there is already mention of the theme of the last two clauses, which is the return to Zion. That motif is eschatological, meaning the anticipation of a messianic event: the rebuilding of the temple, the third and last temple, which, unlike the previous two, will stand forever.[103] This eschatological emphasis bespeaks the covenantal significance of the marriage celebration itself. The wedding is meant to be the social consummation of the process from betrothal to marriage. The wedding is also meant to reflect the covenantal marriage initiated at Sinai between God and the people Israel. But how can one man and one woman, and even their families and community along with them, fully celebrate the consummation of their covenant when the master covenant of Sinai is not yet consummated?[104] The covenant, after all, is meant to affirm God's full kingship over Israel and over the whole world with Israel, but that has clearly not yet taken place. How could it have taken place when the temple, considered to be the center of the universe *(axis mundi)*, still lies in ruins?[105] If the celebration of any covenant of marriage is complete, does that not strongly imply that those celebrating it here and now have made their own joy in the present greater than the joy yet to come in the

101. B. Kiddushin 41a.

102. B. Shabbat 88a re Cant. 2:3.

103. See, e.g., *Shir ha-Shirim Rabbah* 4.31 on Cant. 4:6 re Ezek. 39:2.

104. See *Shemot Rabbah* 15.30 on Exod. 12:2 re Isa. 54:5, where the initiation of the covenant at the Exodus is taken to be God's betrothal *(erusin)* of Israel, and the messianic event is taken to be the true consummation *(nisu'in)* thereof. Cf. B. Sanhedrin 22b re Isa. 54:5.

105. For Jerusalem's cosmic centrality because of the temple's cosmic centrality, see B. Yoma 54b.

messianic future? For that reason, then, the wedding ceremony concludes not so much with the satisfaction of a past human accomplishment but, rather, with the anticipation of a future divine accomplishment. That can only be the object of hope. But hope is not certitude and, as such, it always contains a strong dose of anxiety.[106] That is why some commentators explain the practice of shattering a glass at the wedding celebration, mentioned in the Talmud, to be a dramatic way of calling the attention of all the celebrants, especially the exuberant bride and groom, to the fact that the temple in Jerusalem is still in ruins, still not rebuilt.[107] The symbolism here of shattering what is most fragile is certainly frightening. Because the covenant itself has not been fully consummated with its Lord, because creation itself is not yet fully reconciled with its Creator, the complete joy of the lesser covenant of marriage, the lesser creation of the marriage bed, cannot — indeed, must not — be fully satisfied. It still needs continuing hope for a future beyond the horizon of ordinary expectation.

106. See B. Berakhot 4a re Ps. 27:13-14.

107. B. Berakhot 30b-31a. See Tosafot, s.v. "aitai," and Rabbenu Jonah Gerondi on *Alfasi: Berakhot*, chap. 5, ed. Vilna, 21a-b. For other practices designed to remind Jews of the destruction of the temple, especially at times of joy, see T. Sotah 15.10; B. Baba Batra 60b.

## 2  The Covenant-Contract Dialectic in Jewish Marriage and Divorce Law

*Michael J. Broyde*

It is an ancient question whether and to what extent Jewish marriage and divorce law is essentially covenantal or contractual. The answer has changed over time, varies according to different authorities, and is still in flux today.

On the one hand, the Jewish tradition is replete with references to the sacred nature of marriage. The Talmud recounts that a person is not complete until he or she marries, and is not even called a person until two are united.[1] Furthermore, the classical sources recount the profound divine hand in the creation of marriage. One Talmudic source goes so far as to state, "Forty days prior to birth, the Holy One, Blessed be He, announces that so-and-so should marry so-and-so."[2] Marriages appear to be holy relationships that embrace and are embraced by the Divine. For example, the earliest commentaries on the Bible posit that God performed the wedding ceremony between Adam and Eve.[3] Indeed, the blessings recited at a Jewish wedding recount that it is God who "commanded us with regard to forbidden relationships, forbade [merely] betrothed women to us, and permitted wives [to husbands] through the Jewish wedding ceremony."[4]

But the incorporation of godliness, sanctity, and covenant into the union is but one facet of marriage of the Jewish tradition. The tradition also presents the countervailing model of marriage as a private contract. Central to this model is the rabbinic tradition of the *ketubah,* the premarital contract to which the couple agrees that spells out the terms and conditions of both the marriage and its termi-

---

1. Babylonian Talmud (hereafter referred to as "BT"), *Yevamot* 63a. Translations throughout are by the author unless otherwise noted

2. BT *Sotah* 2a.

3. Louis Ginzberg, *The Legends of the Jews* (New York: Jewish Publication Society, 1968), p. 68.

4. See, e.g., Rabbi Nosson Scherman, ed., *The Complete Artscroll Siddur,* Rabbinical Council of America Edition (New York: Mesorah Publications, 1995), pp. 202-3.

nation. This tradition, discussed in dozens of pages of closely reasoned Talmudic texts (including an entire tractate in the Talmud devoted to the topic entitled "Ketubot," Hebrew plural of *ketubah*), describes marriage as a contract that is freely entered into by both parties, and dissolvable by divorce — with little sacred to it. Further refinements to marriage in the immediate post-Talmudic period were in keeping with the spirit of this contract or partnership model of marriage.

These two divergent perspectives on marriage in the Jewish tradition are not merely variant strands of Jewish law and lore, nor are they parallel courses that never crossed paths. In the second millennium c.e., European Jewish law worked to minimize the contractual view of marriage found in the earlier Talmudic *ketubah* literature. This backlash against the long-running Talmudic tradition moved Jewish marriage closer to a covenantal scheme and also established the normal mode of marriage as one husband and one wife for life. But in the past fifty years, Jewish law has perforce reemphasized and restored some elements of the contractual view of marriage.

This shifting between marriage as covenant and contract, coupled with the absence of authority of rabbinical courts in America to enforce even an equitable divorce settlement, has created a situation in which Jewish law in America is unable to regulate (or even determine) its own marriage constructs. This, in turn, has led to an absolutely unique situation — the regulation of Jewish marriage by the state of New York since 1983, and the creation of the first covenant marriage statute in the United States, to solve the problems created by Jewish marriage doctrines.

In this chapter, I shall describe the covenant-contract conflict and interplay in three parts. The first section will lead the reader though the Talmudic history of family law, emphasizing its contractual roots.[5] The second section will ex-

---

5. A full survey of the sources of godliness, sanctity, and especially the use of the specific term "covenant" with regard to Jewish marriage is beyond the scope of this chapter. Indeed, the collation and analysis of these sources would be a significant contribution to the field, which, to my knowledge, has yet to be undertaken. This would be particularly helpful to distinguish between variant understandings of covenant in Judaism and Christianity. For example, while a number of Christian Bible commentators take the use of the term in Proverbs 2:16-17, which extols the virtue of wisdom "To deliver thee from the strange woman. . . . That forsaketh the lord of her youth, and forgetteth the covenant of her God," as an explicit reference to the marriage covenant, three of the four classic medieval Jewish commentaries printed in the standard *mikraot gedolot* editions (Rashi, Ralbag, and Metzudot) understand the phrase as referring to the covenant of commandments between God and Israel, not a covenant of marriage. Only Ibn Ezra connects the repeated imagery of straying and adultery to the particular use of covenant: "For women enter with men into a covenant of God not to forsake them, and so too men with women, and she forsook him by straying." (Ibn Ezra also offers a second explanation indicating that God is a partner to the marriage, lending his name to the Hebrew words "man" and "wife"

plain the post-Talmudic developments in family law, and the rise of the marriage as covenant. The third section will examine the dialectic tension of Jewish covenant and contract marriage in the laws of New York state and explain how New York had, in effect, the nation's first covenant marriage act, and why it was a Jewish covenant marriage act.

## Jewish Marriage Laws: Marriage As Contract in Talmudic Times

Marriage and divorce in Jewish law differ from many other mainstream legal and religious systems in that entry into marriage and exit from marriage through divorce are private contractual rights rather than public rights. In the Jewish view, one does not need a governmental "license" to marry or divorce. Private marriages are fundamentally proper; a political and even a religious official's regulation of marriage or divorce is the exception rather than the rule.[6]

As a brief aside, the mechanics of contracts in the Jewish tradition are different as well. While Jewish law requires the clear consent of both parties to a contract, the contract itself is executed by only one party.[7] Thus one who is transferring property drafts a contract, has it signed by witnesses, and finally hands it to the acquirer, thereby effecting the sale. Furthermore, Jewish law contracts encompass more than financial transactions — they may effect changes of personal or ritual statuses.[8] Marriage and divorce, it should be noted, fall into the latter category.[9]

While the Bible has a number of stories and incidents concerning marriage,[10]

---

— though this seems to imply that the marriage itself is not a covenant to God, but a human bond which God joins.)

6. This view stands in sharp contrast to the historical Anglo-American common law view, which treats private contracts to marry or divorce as the classic examples of an illegal and void contract; the Catholic view, which treats marriage and annulment (divorce) as sacraments requiring ecclesiastical cooperation or blessing; or the European view, which has treated marriage and divorce as an area of public law. This should not be misunderstood as denying the sacramental parts of Jewish marriage (of which there are many); the contractual view, however, predominates in the beginning-of-marriage and end-of-marriage rites. This is ably demonstrated by David Bleich, "Jewish Divorce: Judicial Misconceptions and Possible Means of Civil Enforcement," *Connecticut Law Review* 16 (1984): 201-89.

7. See Moshe Meiselman, *Jewish Woman in Jewish Law* (New York: Ktav, 1978), pp. 97-98.

8. Meiselman, *Jewish Woman*, pp. 96-97.

9. For more on this topic, see Menachem Elon, *Principles of Jewish Law* (Jerusalem: Keter, 1973), s.v. contracts.

10. See, e.g., Genesis 4:19-23, 25:1-6, 35:22, and Exodus 21:10-11, among many other instances.

in terms of divorce law little is known other than the Talmudic description of biblical law and the brief verses that incidentally mention divorce in the course of describing the remarriage of one's divorcee. Deuteronomy states,

> When a man marries a woman and lives with her, and she does not find favor in his eyes, as he finds a sexual blemish on her part, and he gives her a bill of divorce, puts it in her hand, and sends her from the house, she leaves his house and goes to the house of another. However, if the second husband hates her and writes her a bill of divorce, gives it to her and sends her from the house, or the second husband dies, the first husband, who sent her out, cannot remarry her. (24:1-4)[11]

According to the Talmudic understanding of biblical law, the husband has a unilateral right to divorce; the wife has no right to divorce except in cases of hard fault.[12] Because there was a clear biblical concept of divorce, no stigma was associated with its use.[13] In addition, marriages could be polygamous, although polyandry was never permitted in the Jewish tradition. Thus, according to biblical law, exit from marriage differed fundamentally from entry into marriage in that it did not require the consent of both parties. The marriage could end when the husband alone wished to end it. This was accomplished by the husband executing a writ of divorce (in Hebrew called a *get*, or plural *gittin*).

As soon as Jewish law was redacted, the notion of the dower *(ketubah)* was developed for all brides. The dower was payable upon divorce or death of the husband, and this became, by rabbinic decree, a precondition to every marriage. Thus, while the right to divorce remained unilateral with the husband, it was now restricted by a clear contractual financial obligation imposed on the

11. See also incidental mentions of divorce in Genesis 21:10, Leviticus 21:7, and Leviticus 22:13.

12. The Talmud records a three-sided dispute as to when divorce was proper. The school of Shammai recounted that divorce was only proper in cases of fault. The school of Hillel asserted that divorce was proper for any displeasing conduct. Rabbi Akiva maintained that a man could divorce his wife simply because he wished to marry another and could not support both wives. See BT *Gittin* 90a-b. As is always the rule in Jewish law, the school of Shammai is rejected as incorrect.

13. The exception is the case that proves the rule. There are a small number of cases where marriage is not discretionary but ethically mandatory. See, e.g., Deuteronomy 22:19. These cases involve either fault or detrimental reliance by the other. In the case of seduction, the Bible mandates that the seducer is under a religious duty to marry the seduced, should she wish to marry him. That marriage does not require the same type of free-will consent to marry, in that the religious and ethical component to the Jewish tradition directs the man to marry this woman; indeed, in certain circumstances he can be punished if he does not marry her. No divorce is permitted in such cases.

husband to compensate his wife if he exercised his right to engage in unilateral divorce absent judicially declared fault on her part.

The wife, as a precondition to entry into the marriage, could insist on a dower higher than the minimum promulgated by the rabbis.[14] Furthermore, the wife or husband could use the *ketubah* as a forum for addressing other matters between them that ought to be regulated by contract, such as whether polygamy would be permitted or what would be the response to childlessness or other potential issues in the marriage. These *ketubah* documents followed the standard formulation of contracts and openly contemplated divorce.[15] They said little about marriage as sacred or covenantal.

The *ketubah* also stipulated the wife's right to sue for divorce where her husband was at fault. These included not only hard faults such as adultery, but also softer faults such as repugnancy, impotence, cruelty, and a host of other such grounds. In such cases, the husband had to divorce his wife (and in most instances pay his wife her dower, too). The wife's access to fault-based divorce was expanded into a clear and concrete legal right in the Talmud. She also had a right to have children, and her husband's refusal to have children was grounds for divorce by her.[16] Though she could not sue for divorce as a general rule, she could restrict his rights through a *ketubah* provision.[17] Soon after the close of the Talmudic period, the rabbis of that time (called *Geonim*) changed or reinterpreted[18] Jewish law to increase vastly the right of a woman to sue for divorce. That change, however, had little impact on the basic nature of marriage as essentially contractual.[19]

In sum, the contractual model of marriage was basic to Talmudic Jewish law that prevailed until around 1000 C.E. While the Talmud imposed some limi-

14. See Michael Broyde and Jonathan Reiss, "The Ketubah in America: Its Value in Dollars, Its Significance in *Halacha,* and Its Enforceability in American Law," *Journal of Halacha and Contemporary Society* 47 (2004): 101-24. Nonetheless, in the case of divorce for provable fault by the wife, the obligation to pay the dower was removed.

15. For an excellent survey of the *ketubot* from Talmudic and the immediate post-Talmudic time, see Mordechai Akiva Friedman, *Jewish Marriage in Palestine,* 2 vols. (Tel Aviv: Tel Aviv University, 1983). Volume 2 contains dozens of actual *ketubot* from before the year 1000 C.E.

16. See BT *Yevamot* 64a, *Shulhan Arukh, Even HaEzer* 154:6-7, and *Arukh HaShulhan, Even HaEzer* 154:52-53.

17. BT *Yevamot* 65a; but see view of Rav Ammi.

18. Through a mechanism called *takanta demitivta,* or decree of the academy, whose exact mechanism is unclear. See Irving A. Breitowitz, *Between Civil and Religious Law: The Plight of the Agunah in American Society* (Westport, Conn.: Greenwood, 1993), pp. 50-53.

19. A more detailed explanation of this historical event and its mechanism is recounted in Michael J. Broyde, *Marriage, Divorce and the Abandoned Wife in Jewish Law: A Conceptual Approach to the Agunah Problems in America* (New York: Ktav, 2001).

tations on the private right to marry (such as castigating one who marries through a sexual act alone, without any public ceremony[20]), and the later Shulhan Arukh imposed other requirements (such as insisting that there be an engagement period[21]), Talmudic Jewish law treated marriage formation as a private contract requiring the consent of both parties,[22] and divorce as the other side of that marriage contract, albeit with certain limitations.

There was little notion in this Talmudic period of marriage as an inabrogable covenant. Three basic points highlight this. First, marriage was never centrally constructed as monogamous, and monogamy was never constructed in its hard form of one husband with one wife for life. Second, divorce was always recognized as normative and permissible; it was free of governmental or religious restrictions. Finally, couples constructed the social, fiscal, and logistical basis of their own marriage as they wished through contract.

## Jewish Marriage Laws: The Rise of Covenant in Jewish Marriage

Among European Jews, this contractual model of marriage did not continue much beyond the end of the first millennium of the common era. Through the efforts of the luminous leader of tenth-century European Jewry, Rabbenu Gershom, a decree[23] was enacted that moved Jewish law toward a covenantal model of marriage. Rabbenu Gershom's view was that it was necessary to restrict the rights of the husband and prohibit unilateral no-fault divorce by either husband or wife. Divorce was limited to cases of provable fault or mutual consent. In addition, fault was redefined to exclude cases of soft fault such as repugnancy. In only a few cases could the husband be actually forced to divorce his wife or the reverse.[24] Equally significant, these decrees prohibited polygamy, thus placing

20. Even though such an activity validly marries the couple; see BT *Yevamot* 52a; *Shulhan Arukh, Even HaEzer* 26:4.

21. *Shulhan Arukh, Even HaEzer* 26:4.

22. Marriages entered into without consent, with consent predicated on fraud or duress, or grounded in other classical defects that modern law might find more applicable to commercial agreements are under certain circumstances void in the Jewish tradition. See Broyde, *Marriage, Divorce and the Abandoned Wife*, Appendix B.

23. The decree of Rabbenu Gershom was enacted under penalty of the ban of excommunication *(herem)*. The collective decrees of Rabbenu Gershom are thus known as *Herem deRabbenu Gershom*. See *Herem deRabbenu Gershom, Encyclopedia Talmudit* (Yad Harav Herzog, 1996), 17:378.

24. This insight is generally ascribed to the eleventh-century Tosafist Rabbenu Tam in his view of the repugnancy claim (Heb.: *mais alay*). In fact it flows logically from the view of Rabbenu Gershom, who had to prohibit not only polygamy in order to end coerced divorce, but even divorce for soft fault.

considerable pressure on the man and woman in a troubled marriage to stay married. Since, absent fault, he could not divorce her without her consent, and she could not seek divorce without his consent, unless divorce was in the best interest of both of them (an unlikely scenario), neither would be able to divorce.[25] Divorce thus became exceedingly rare and possible only in cases of dire fault.

Once the refinements of Rabbenu Gershom were implemented, the basis for Jewish marriage changed. In Talmudic times, the parties negotiated the amount the husband would have to pay the wife if he divorced her against her will or if he died. She could not prevent the husband from divorcing her, except by setting the payment level high enough that the husband was deterred from divorce by dint of its cost. All this changed in light of the decrees of Rabbenu Gershom, which simply prohibited what the Talmudic sages had only discouraged. Together, the decrees severely restricted the likelihood of divorce and essentially vacated the economic provisions of the *ketubah.* As a result, though the original mechanism stayed in place, marriage in effect became a covenant between the parties, and not a contract.

Rabbenu Gershom's ban against divorcing a woman without her consent or without a showing of hard fault[26] called into question the value of the marriage contract itself. The Talmudic rabbis had instituted the *ketubah* payments to deter the husband from rashly divorcing his wife. But now, since the husband could not divorce his wife without her consent, there seemed to be no further need for the *ketubah.*[27] As the leading codifier of European Jewry, Rabbi Moses Isserles (Rama), put it:

> See Shulhan Arukh Even Haezer 177:3 [the case of rape discussed in note 27] where it states that in a situation where one only may divorce with the con-

25. Absent the prohibition on polygamy, the decree restricting the right to divorce would not work, as the husband who could not divorce would simply remarry and abandon his first wife. This decree prevented that conduct.

26. In which case, the value of the *ketubah* need not be paid as a penalty for misconduct imposed on the woman. What exactly is hard fault remains a matter of dispute, but it generally includes adultery, spouse beating, insanity, and frigidity; see *Shulhan Arukh, Even HaEzer* 154.

27. Thus, for example, *Shulhan Arukh (Even HaEzer* 177:3) states that "a man who rapes a woman . . . is obligated to marry her, so long as she . . . wish[es] to marry him, even if she is crippled or blind, and he is not permitted to divorce her forever, except with her consent, and thus he does not have to write her a *ketubah.*" The logic seems clear. Since he cannot divorce her under any circumstances without her consent, the presence or absence of a *ketubah* seems to make no difference to her economic status or marital security. When both want to get divorced, they will agree on financial terms independent of the *ketubah,* and until then, the *ketubah* sets no payment schedule. Should she insist that she will consent to be divorced only if he gives her $1,000,000 in buffalo nickels, they either reach an agreement or stay married.

sent of the woman, one does not need a *ketubah*. Thus, nowadays, in our countries, where we do not divorce against the will of the wife because of the ban of Rabbenu Gershom . . . it is possible to be lenient and not write a *ketubah* at all. . . .[28]

The *ketubah* did remain a fixture of Jewish weddings after the tenth century,[29] but it was transformed from a marriage contract to a ritual document whose transfer initiated the covenantal ceremony of marriage. The *ketubah* held no economic or other value as a contract. Indeed, the contractual model of marriage ended for those Jews — all European Jews — who accepted the refinements of Rabbenu Gershom. Consider the observation of Rabbi Moses Feinstein, the leading American Jewish law authority of the last century, on this matter:

> The value of the ketubah is not known to rabbis and decisors of Jewish law, or rabbinical court judges; indeed we have not examined this matter intensely as for nearly all matters of divorce it has no practical ramifications — since it is impossible for the man to divorce against the will of the woman, [the economics of] divorce are dependent on who desires to be divorced. . . .[30]

Elsewhere Rabbi Feinstein writes,

> One should know that in divorce there is no place for evaluating the ketubah, since the ban of Rabbenu Gershom prohibited a man from divorcing his wife without her consent. Thus, divorce is dependent on who wants to give or receive the *get*. . . . Only infrequently, in farfetched cases, is it relevant to divorce.[31]

The contrast between those Jewish communities that accepted the enactments of Rabbenu Gershom and those that did not can be clearly seen in the juxtaposed comments of the European and Oriental authorities which comprise the classic law code of the *Shulhan Arukh* in the area of family law. Rabbi Moses Isserles (of Poland) accepts these refinements and values the essence of marriage as a covenant. Rabbi Joseph Karo (of Palestine), who does not incorporate them, portrays a less lofty ideal of marriage. Consider the opening discussion of marriage which states:

> Karo: Every man must marry a woman in order to reproduce. Anyone who is not having children is, as if, they are killers, reducers of the place of people on

---

28. *Shulhan Arukh, Even HaEzer* 66:3.
29. See Broyde and Reiss, "The Ketubah in America."
30. Moses Feinstein, *Iggrot Moshe, Even HaEzer* 4:91. (This *responsum* was written in 1980.)
31. Moses Feinstein, *Iggrot Moshe, Even HaEzer* 4:92. (This *responsum* was written in 1982.)

this earth, and causing God to leave the Jewish people. *Isserles: Anyone who is without a wife lives without blessing and without Torah and is not called a person. Once one marries a woman, all of one's sins are forgiven, as it states, "One who finds a wife finds goodness, and obtains the favor of God;" Proverbs 18:22.*[32]

Rabbi Karo subscribes to a view that marriage, though mandatory, is but a necessary precondition to the fulfillment of the Jewish law obligation to have children. The marriage is a means to an end and governed by mutually agreeable contractual provisions. Rabbi Isserles, by contrast, sees the value of taking a wife in and of itself. One who marries moves beyond a state of incompleteness to the goodness inherent to finding one's life mate. It is the union of marriage itself that "obtains the favor of God." This is a marriage of covenantal nature.

The covenantal model of marriage set out by Rabbi Isserles, however, suffers from a grave defect. It eliminates the clear rules that are the foundation of Jewish divorce law. In the Talmudic period and beyond, Jewish divorce law was contractual: Women and men protected themselves from the consequences of divorce by contractually agreeing to the process and the costs of divorce. Although that approach had failings, it functioned and at least led to predictable results that the parties had negotiated in their *ketubah*. After Rabbenu Gershom's decree, Jewish divorce law lacked the basic element of a rules-based legal system, namely, clear rules to follow. Except in cases of fault (where a Jewish law court could order a divorce) all Jewish divorces became negotiated exercises between a husband and a wife. Jewish decisors could not force a divorce and could not direct its financial arrangements. At best, Jewish law courts could enact a settlement based on the principles of equitable authority, conferred or vested in them by the principalities and, later, nation-states. But these resolutions were not at all based on any provisions of the *ketubah*, but on the product of the later negotiation between the estranged parties.

This covenant understanding of marriage and divorce has proved difficult to maintain. It was workable only in pre-modern Europe because divorce was not common and was limited, given the social and economic reality of that time and place, to cases of hard fault.[33] Moreover, in these communities, Jewish law courts had the authority to provide equitable relief in cases where the parties appearing before the court desired to divorce but could not agree on the terms.

---

32. *Shulhan Arukh, Even HaEzer* 1:1.

33. For a detailed discussion of the problems posed in pre-emancipation Russia by this construct of Jewish law, see CheaRan Y. Freeze, "Making and Unmaking the Jewish Family: Marriage and Divorce in Imperial Russia, 1850-1914" (Ph.D. Diss., Brandeis University, 1997), who notes that Jewish divorce was more common than Orthodox Christian divorce but still relatively uncommon.

## Jewish Marriage Contracts and American Law

This use of the secular legal system to produce Jewish law solutions is unique and represents a noteworthy break from the Jewish tradition, which had a deep resistance to allowing a secular legal authority into the details of Jewish law. By contrast, Jews in the United States faced a central challenge in implementing this covenantal vision of marriage. Until the massive Jewish migration to the United States, there was no substantive Jewish family law that could be examined to compel the rabbinical courts to grant divorces except in cases of hard fault and where there was clear equitable authority in rabbinical courts to resolve matters of divorce fairly. The laws of nearly all European states recognized the authority of Jewish law courts in many matters to be binding and enforceable. The American states did not. American rabbinical courts thus ceased to be a significant source of authority in the American Jewish community unless and until the individuals in a particular marriage not only empowered the rabbinical court to resolve their dispute, but also refused to challenge the outcome in a secular court. In America, the Jewish marriage covenant was — in essence — unenforceable.

Three different solutions have been advanced to preserve the legal status of Jewish marriage. Each has involved the secular law of the United States in some form. None has worked very well.[34]

### *The Enforceability of the* Ketubah *in American Law*

The earliest effort sought to have the provisions of the *ketubah* enforced as a matter of American contract law.[35] This was litigated in a number of cases. For example, in 1974 a widow tried to collect the amount of her husband's *ketubah* and claimed that the *ketubah* superseded her prior waiver of any future claims pursuant to a prenuptial agreement between herself and her husband. (The *ketubah* had been signed after the prenuptial agreement, and thus, if it were a valid contract, would have superseded it.) The New York Supreme Court denied the claim, concluding that, even for the observant Orthodox Jew, the *ketubah* had become more a matter of form and ceremony than a legal obligation.[36] The basic claim of the litigant seemed reasonable from a Jewish law

---

34. For more on this, see Michael Broyde, "Informing on Others for Violating American Law: A Jewish Law View," *Journal of Halacha and Contemporary Society* 41 (2002): 5-49.

35. See, e.g., *Hurwitz v. Hurwitz*, 215 N.Y.S. 184 (N.Y. App. Div. Second, 1926), where the court refers to the *ketubah* by the term "koshuba" and has no context to examine it.

36. *In Re Estate of White*, 356 N.Y.S.2d 208, at 210 (N.Y. Sup. Ct., 1974).

view. She had entered a marriage, which was bound by Jewish law, and the courts ought to enforce it. The New York courts did not agree.

There is not a single case that I know of where a secular court has enforced the *ketubah* provision mandating payments.[37] The financial obligations described in the *ketubah* — in *zuzim* and *zekukim*, which require determinations of Jewish law to ascertain the proper value — are not considered specific enough to be enforceable.[38] Moreover, since the *ketubah* texts are not in English and are not signed by the husband and wife, they are regarded as void contracts at American law.

### Rabbinic Arbitration Agreements to Construct Jewish Marriages

The second method to provide American law support for Jewish marriage has been use of private arbitration law. The earliest use of arbitration agreements to govern Jewish marriages was in 1954 under the direction of Rabbi Dr. Saul Lieberman. These arbitration agreements were included in an additional clause to the *ketubah:*

> [W]e the bride and the bridegroom . . . hereby agree to recognize the Beth Din of the Rabbinical Assembly and the Jewish Theological Seminary of America or its duly appointed representatives, as having the authority to counsel us in the light of Jewish tradition which requires husband and wife to give each other complete love and devotion and to summon either party at the request of the other in order to enable the party so requesting to live in accordance with the standards of the Jewish law of marriage throughout his or her lifetime. We authorize the Beth Din to impose such terms of compensation as it may see fit for failure to respond to its summons or to carry out its decision.[39]

This exact formulation was upheld as a valid arbitration agreement by the New York Court of Appeals in the now famous case of *Avitzur*.[40] It is generally understood as a matter of secular law that all binding arbitration agreements

---

37. While it is true that in dicta, an Arizona court suggested that financial obligations described in a *ketubah* could perhaps be enforceable if described with sufficient specificity, *Victor v. Victor*, 866 P.2d at 902 (Arizona, 1993), the practice has never been to seek to conform the text of the *ketubah* to the contract requirements of American law.

38. Whether or not the language of a *ketubah* forms a basis for compelling a *get* according to secular law doctrine is a question beyond the scope of this essay.

39. *Proceedings of the Rabbinical Assembly of America XVIII* (1954), 67.

40. *Avitzur v. Avitzur*, 459 N.Y.S.2d 572 (1983).

undertaken to enforce religious values in a marriage are thus binding on the parties so long as they follow the procedure and forms mandated by New York (or whatever local jurisdiction governs procedure).[41]

While the particular form used in the Lieberman clause (as it became known) has been subject to intense criticism,[42] and ultimately not accepted by the vast majority of the Jewish law community, the idea of using binding arbitration agreements to enforce the promises and expectations of Jewish marriage has taken firm hold. Over the last fifty years, many different Jewish law–based arbitration agreements have been composed in an attempt to create a legal construct in which Jewish law has a significant stake in the outcome of a divorce and cannot simply be ignored when one of the parties wishes to ignore it. Indeed, there is an organization with a section of its Internet site devoted to sharing such agreements (and I myself have been involved in such).[43] The most recent version of the binding arbitration agreement widely used in the Orthodox Jewish community incorporates a binding arbitration agreement into a prenuptial agreement, such that one who signs this form of an agreement integrates Jewish law into the divorce process in a legally binding manner according to American law.[44]

Although Jewish law–based binding arbitration agreements designed to mandate adherence to Jewish law are quite common in the community that observes Jewish law, such agreements suffer from a number of defects. First, they require forethought. They must be composed, executed, and filed in anticipation of difficulty in the pending marriage. Second, they require — prior to the commencement of the marriage — a clear comprehension of the process of divorce and the various options available to the couple in terms of divorce. Such foresight is rare in newlyweds. Finally, they are subject to litigation that can hinder their effectiveness. Thus, while such agreements are clearly a part of the process of returning the legal covenant of Jewish marriage to its place among couples who seek a genuinely Jewish marriage, they are not the global solution they were thought to be when first developed.[45]

41. See, e.g., Linda Kahan, "Jewish Divorce and Secular Court: The Promise of *Avitzur*," *Georgetown Law Journal* 73 (1984): 193-224; Lawrence M. Warmflash, "The New York Approach to Enforcing Religious Marriage Contracts," *Brooklyn Law Review* 50 (1984): 229-54.

42. See Norman Lamm, "Recent Additions to the Ketubah," *Tradition* 2 (1959): 93-119; A. Leo Levin and Meyer Kramer, *New Provisions in the Ketubah: A Legal Opinion* (New York: Yeshiva University Press, 1955).

43. See www.orthodoxcaucus.org.

44. This document and its attendant instructions are available as a PDF file at www.orthodoxcaucus.org/prenup/PNA_2003.pdf.

45. For more on this issue and the many practical problems with these arbitration agreements, see Breitowitz, *Between Civil and Religious Law*.

## The New York State Jewish Divorce Laws

A third way of using secular law to uphold Jewish marriage came with the passage of the New York Jewish Divorce Law in 1983, which was revised in 1984 and modified again in 1992.

Jewish law recognizes that marriage and divorce in their essential form require private conduct rather than court supervision. Both private marriages and private divorces are valid in the Jewish tradition, so long as the requisite number of witnesses (two) is present. Indeed, the Jewish tradition does not mandate the participation of a rabbi in any manner in either the marriage or divorce rite (although the custom has been to do so).[46] In the past thirty years, however, Jewish women have appealed to the state of New York to address the pressing problem of recalcitrant husbands who refused to participate in Jewish divorces or who were using the requirements of Jewish divorce to seek advantages in the division of finances in the secular divorce proceedings.

The 1983 Jewish Divorce Law responded to their plight.[47] The purpose of the 1983 statute was not to compel a secular vision of marriage and divorce onto the Jewish community. It was rather to tailor the model of divorce employed by the state of New York to the needs of those Jews who have an alternative model of marriage and divorce grounded in Jewish law. The New York statute recognized that it was fundamentally wrong to allow a husband who had been married in a Jewish ceremony to be civilly divorced, but not to allow his wife to divorce until a Jewish divorce had first been executed.

How did the 1983 law fix this problem? It prevented the civil authorities from exercising their authority to divorce a Jewish couple civilly if they had not yet received a religious divorce. The law prevented a splitting of the civil and religious statuses by precluding the civil authorities from acting in Jewish divorces absent prior action by religious authorities.[48] This law harmonized civil law with Jewish law: Jewish law maintains that the couple is married until a *get*, a Jewish divorce, is issued. New York committed itself to not issuing a civil divorce in such cases until a *get* had been issued. The law contained no incentive for a person to issue a Jewish divorce unless that person genuinely desires to be divorced. To put this in a different way, the divorce process employed by the state of New York was different for those married in the Jewish faith than for anyone else. In that, the 1983 New York Jewish Law was very

---

46. Indeed, as is demonstrated in Bleich, "Jewish Divorce," the term "rite" is a misnomer; "contract" would be more accurate.

47. N.Y. Dom. Rel. Law §213 (McKinney 1992).

48. N.Y. Dom. Rel. Law §236(b) (McKinney 1992).

much like the current covenant marriage schemes of Louisiana, Arkansas, and Arizona.[49] It enabled Jewish parties to opt out of the prevailing contract marriage governed by state law.

Although the 1983 New York Jewish divorce law addressed certain cases, it had one obvious limitation. It was written to be applicable only in cases where the plaintiff was seeking the secular divorce and not providing a religious divorce. Only the plaintiff was obligated to remove barriers to remarriage, and a defending spouse, who did not desire to comply with Jewish law, need not. To remedy this, the 1992 New York Jewish divorce law took a completely different approach. It allowed the secular divorce law to impose penalties on the recalcitrant spouse in order to encourage participation in the religious divorce. It did so by changing the division of the marital assets in cases in which a Jewish divorce has been withheld.[50] The 1992 law sought to prevent the splitting of the religious and civil marital statuses by encouraging the issuance of the religious divorce when a civil divorce was to be granted. This law, still in effect, functions in the opposite manner of the 1983 law. It harmonizes Jewish law with New York law by committing state authorities to a policy of encouraging Jewish divorce. This, too, is a form of covenant marriage, albeit one with a totally different focus on the relationship between Jewish and secular law.

The technicalities of both these laws are beyond the scope of this chapter. They have generated a considerable amount of scholarly debate, both within the Jewish tradition[51] and within the secular law community,[52] precisely be-

49. See discussion and citations in the chapters by Katherine Spaht and Peter Hay in this volume.

50. Domestic Relations Law §236 was modified to add: "In any decision made pursuant to this subdivision the court shall, where appropriate, consider the effect of a barrier to remarriage, as defined in subdivision six of section two hundred fifty-three of this article, on the factors enumerated in paragraph (d) of this subdivision," thus allowing a judge to change the equitable distribution in a situation where the husband or wife will not give or receive a Jewish divorce. Section 253(6) limits "barriers to remarriage" to situations where a *get* is withheld.

51. For an examination of the issues raised in the Jewish tradition, see Michael Broyde, "The New York State *Get* [Jewish Divorce] Law," *Tradition: A Journal of Jewish Thought* 29, no. 4 (1995): 3-14; this article was followed by Michael Broyde and Chaim Malinowitz, "The 1992 New York *Get* Law: An Exchange," *Tradition: A Journal of Jewish Thought* 31, no. 3 (1997): 23-41; Michael Broyde and Chaim Malinowitz, "The 1992 New York *Get* Law: An Exchange III," *Tradition: A Journal of Jewish Thought* 32, no. 2 (1999): 99-100, and 33, no. 1 (1999): 101-9.

52. See, e.g., Michelle Greenberg-Kobrin, "Civil Enforceability of Religious Prenuptial Agreements," *Columbia Journal of Law and Social Problems* 32 (summer 1999): 359-400; Kent Greenawalt, "Religious Law and Civil Law: Using Secular Law to Assure Observance of Practices with Religious Significance," *Southern California Law Review* 71 (1998): 781-844; Patti A. Scott, "New York Divorce Law and the Religion Clauses: An Unconstitutional Exorcism of the Jewish Get Laws," *Seton Hall Constitutional Law Journal* 6 (summer 1996): 1117-81; Lisa Zornberg, "Be-

cause they were an attempt to impose a vision of religious marriage on a subset of the population through the vehicle of secular law. The 1983 New York state *get* law did so by restricting access to secular divorce when the rules of religious divorce were not followed. The 1992 statute did so by compelling religious divorce. Both approaches, however, are grounded in the centrality of Jewish marriage to its adherents.

One could claim therefore that New York state not only had the first covenant marriage law, but the first two such laws — the 1983 Jewish divorce law and the 1992 Jewish divorce law, each with a different approach to Jewish marriage. Granted, New York does not offer a covenant marriage option to all, since, practically speaking, Jewish clergy will not allow non-Jews to opt into Jewish marriage. But in terms of reframing or superimposing secular and religious definitions of marriage and divorce and offering a state-sanctioned model of religious union and dissolution, these statutes pave the way.[53]

Indeed, not only does New York pave *the* way, but it actually paves *two* ways: The view of Jewish law in the 1983 New York law is a model of religious law superceding secular law and supplanting its values. The vision in the 1992 New York law is a model of secular law seeking to coerce the Jewish tradition into a particular model of Jewish marriage. Not only do both these models exist in New York, but they are both part of Jewish law also. In fact, there is a vast theological dispute within the Jewish tradition about the nature of Jewish marriage, which becomes particularly apparent when Jewish law discusses the natural law of marriage and divorce (that is to say, the universal laws which Judaism believes to be binding on all and which Jewish legal theory posits were revealed at creation and supplemented after the great flood). The basic theological dispute is simple: What was the Divine image of the marital bond and divorce? Should divorce be a simple ending of the contract, with no difficulties and complexities, or should marriage be viewed as a covenant that can end only in cases of dramatic breach?

This dispute between marriage as contract and marriage as covenant goes to core theology in the Jewish tradition. The natural law formulation of marriage is found in Genesis 2:24: "Thus a man shall leave his father and mother and cleave

---

yond the Constitution: Is the New York Get Legislation Good Law?" *Pace Law Review* 15 (spring 1995): 703-84; Edward S. Nadel, "A Bad Marriage: Jewish Divorce and the First Amendment," *Cardozo Women's Law Journal* 2 (1995): 131-72; Paul Finkelman, "New York's *Get* Laws: A Constitutional Analysis," *Columbia Journal of Law and Social Problems* 27 (1993): 55-100.

53. The question of the applicability of this statute to Islamic marriages (a result never contemplated by the New York state legislature) is a fascinating one and requires further analysis; See Ghada G. Quaisi, "Religious Marriage Contracts: Judicial Enforcement of Mahar Agreements in American Courts," *Journal of Law and Religion* 15 (2000-2001): 67-82.

to his wife, and they shall be one flesh." In what instances and for what reasons is divorce proper? The biblical narrative here is quite silent on this point.

One answer is provided by the modern scholar of Jewish law, Rabbi Moses Feinstein.[54] He adopts the view that prior to the giving of Jewish law, *there was no institution of marriage and no institution of divorce*. Jewish law invented marriage, and divorce, he claims; prior to the giving of the Torah there was mere coupling, and when the coupling was over, the relationship was over. What then is the covenant that Jewish law added in terms of the marital relationship? This approach answers that Jewish law created marriage itself as part of the Divine covenant with the Giver of Jewish law, and restricted uncoupling to a written bill of divorce, issued by the husband to the wife.[55] It should be limited to cases where the covenant itself has been breached. Jewish law added divorce only as a rare escape valve for marriages gone very bad.

A diametrically opposite view is taken by Rabbi David ben Levi of Narbonne, a medieval scholar who adopts the view that under natural law, there is no divorce at all, for marriage was a permanent arrangement.[56] This model (similar to the ultimate conclusion reached in canon law) is that prior to the revelation of Jewish law, the marriage verses in Genesis dictate that marriage shall be permanent. Marriage — perhaps even monogamous marriage[57] without any possibility of divorce — was the legal norm prior to the Sinai revelation that created the Jewish people and Jewish law. The covenant of marriage granted to the Jewish people changed that, and permitted divorce. Marriage

---

54. Moses Feinstein, *Iggrot Moshe, Even HaEzer* 4:9(1).

55. A related answer is presented as derived from Maimonides, even as it is not explicitly stated; see commentary of Rabbeinu Nissim on *Sanhedrin* 58b in the name of Maimonides. Maimonides' ruling that following the Sinaitic revelation, Jewish marriage required a formal transaction parallels a similar development in divorce law, this theory claims. Prior to the revelation, marriage and divorce were purely functional relationships, and divorce (i.e., dissolution) was allowed through the simple activity of abandonment. When a husband or wife wished to end the marriage, either one of them could leave. Until such a time, they were married — but divorce was simple, informal, and grounded in natural law. It could be verbal or even simply an action (such as leaving the marital home). The Jewish law of divorce, by contrast, was procedural in nature, in that it derived from the need to create formal statuses, reflected in documentation. For more on this see Broyde, *Marriage, Divorce and the Abandoned Wife in Jewish Law*.

56. Quoted in *Novellae of the RaN* (Rabbenu Nissim), *Sanhedrin* 58b.

57. A small number of medieval commentators derive the monogamous ideal from the verse in Genesis 2:24; see *Baal haTurim* and *Hizkuni* ad. loc., and the notes in Menachem Mendel Kasher, *Torah Shelaimah*, Genesis 2:24. There are, however, no Talmudic homilies on the joys of monogamy, but one; see *Avot DeRabbi Natan* (Proverbs of Rabbi Nathan), version 2, chapter 2:1 (page 5a in the standard pagination), which states: "Rabbi Judah ben Betera states: Job would observe to himself that . . . if it had been proper for the first Adam to be given ten wives, it would have been done. But it was proper to give him only one wife, and I too need but one wife."

was not a part of the Divine covenant with the Jewish people — divorce was! Jewish law permitted divorce. Jewish law has, in this view, a weaker marital bond than its natural law predecessor, and marriages should end in the Jewish tradition when the parties want them to — and not only upon covenant-breaching events.

The ongoing relevance of this dispute is clear. On one view, the essential Jewish contribution to marriage doctrine is marriage, and in the other, it is divorce! The first model is theological and covenantal; the second is contractual and formal. These two views have parallels in the two models of Jewish marriage advocated by the 1983 and 1992 New York laws.

## Conclusions

Jewish marriage is not a single institution that has been unchanged during its three-thousand-year history. The contests between conceptions of marriage as covenant and marriage as contract run deep in the Jewish tradition. Although these disputes are rarely manifested in the details of marriage law, they appear in full bloom in Jewish divorce law. There is no consensus regarding the earlier natural law rules of divorce which later Jewish law changed. There is no agreement about the path Jewish law has taken since it was revealed at Sinai or about the nature of and need for rules and procedures governing marriage formation and dissolution. There is not even agreement whether divorce is a salutary innovation of Jewish law or a concession to natural law. Furthermore, the recent interaction of Jewish law with American family law has been fraught with conceptual difficulty and even some missteps. The New York state experiment with Jewish divorce law is the best example of the problems that can be created when two different legal systems — one religious, one secular — are forced to mesh.

That said, it must also be said that the covenantal basis of marriage and divorce law in the Jewish tradition strongly affirms two basic values. The first is that sanctity is a basic component of the marriage relationship that spouses have with each other and with their Creator. The second is that divorce is a natural possibility in the covenantal process, which was created in the same Divine moment that Jewish marriage was created.

# 3 Marriage As Covenant in the Catholic Tradition

*Michael G. Lawler*

The focus of this chapter is on marriage as covenant in the Catholic tradition. It addresses four related questions and, therefore, develops in four cumulative parts. First, since both Judaism and Christianity root all talk of covenant in the Hebrew Bible, it confronts the hermeneutical question, what is the meaning of covenant in the Bible? Second, it considers an exegetical question: is the notion of marriage as covenant supported in the Bible? Third, there is a historical question: how have Catholic theologians dealt with marriage in theological history? Fourth, that history raises a theological question: what is the meaning of the Second Vatican Council's description of marriage as "an intimate partnership of life and love . . . rooted in the conjugal covenant of irrevocable personal consent,"[1] and how is that meaning situated within the broad scope of the Catholic theological tradition?

## Covenant in the Bible

In both Judaism and Christianity, all talk of covenant has its roots in the Hebrew Bible. It is there that every analysis of covenant must begin. The paradigmatic covenant *(berit)*, "the classical example of covenanting as a theo-political act,"[2] is between the God Yahweh and the People Israel at Sinai, the climax of the Exodus liberation story. *Gaudium et Spes* likens the covenant of marriage to the covenant of love and fidelity through which "God of old made himself pres-

---

1. Pastoral Constitution on the Church in the Modern World, 48. Hereinafter this document will be referred to by its Latin title, *Gaudium et Spes*.

2. Daniel J. Elazar, *Covenant and Polity in Biblical Israel: Biblical Foundations and Jewish Expressions* (New Brunswick, N.J.: Transaction, 1995), vol. 1, p. 163.

ent to his people," and promotes it as a reflection and participation in "the loving covenant uniting Christ with the Church."[3] It is in the biblical covenants, therefore, that we begin. An initial, linguistic issue is relevant.

Walter Eichrodt showed that the Hebrew *berit* is found 286 times in the Old Testament.[4] Scholars agree that the term is either derived from, or closely related to, the Akkadian *biritu,* which means to bind together. *Berit,* or covenant, at root, means to bind together, but it connotes more. The parties bound together are originally free and unbound, and they agree to be bound in a relationship that both limits and guarantees their freedom in accord with the terms of the covenant. It matters not whether the covenant is between equals *(bnai berit)* or between a superior and a subordinate *(ba'alei berit);* both parties are equally bound by the terms of the covenant. The standard term for making a covenant, *likhrot berit,* literally to cut a covenant, derives from an ancient ritual of covenant-making in which an animal was cut in half, the covenanting parties walked between the two halves, and the halves were then bound together. The unitive symbolism of this rite is further underscored by the sacred, sacrificial meal which commonly accompanied the covenant and invoked God as its witness (cf. Exod. 24:1-12).

Daniel Elazar comments that "it is significant that cutting [dividing] and binding are the principal elements in the terminology and early practice of covenant-making since a covenant both divides and binds, that is to say, it clarifies and institutionalizes both the distinction between or separate identities of the partners and their linkage."[5] Covenants constitute two or more distinct parties in a relationship of mutual dialogue and justice, to which they are *morally* as well as *legally* bound. The covenant partners are to be faithful to the covenant; they are to be *lumen fidelitatis gentium,* a light of faithfulness to the nations. As the notion of covenant was adapted in cultural settings beyond the ancient Near East, *berit* successively gave way to the Greek *diatheke,* the Latin *foedus,* more technical than *testamentum,* the old English *troth,* and the modern English sacred promise, oath, and even contract, though this latter results in the loss of the essential moral overtones of covenant.

Careful study of ancient covenantal forms leads Delbert Hillers to list the standard elements in a covenant: first, an opening prologue that names the parties making the covenant; second, an identification of the purposes of the covenant relationship; third, specification of the duration of the covenant;

---

3. *Gaudium et Spes,* 48.

4. Walter Eichrodt, *Theology of the Old Testament,* trans. J. A. Baker, 2 vols. (Philadelphia: Westminster, 1961, 1967).

5. Elazar, *Covenant and Polity,* vol. 1, p. 65.

fourth, enumeration of the blessings and woes embedded in the covenant agreement; fifth, the swearing of a public oath; and, finally, the publication of a permanent record of the covenant ceremony.[6] Elazar's definition suggests the essential elements:

> A covenant is a morally informed agreement or pact based upon voluntary consent, established by mutual oaths or promises, involving or witnessed by some transcendent authority, between peoples or parties having indepen- dent status, equal in connection with the purposes of the pact, that provides for joint action or obligation to achieve defined ends (limited or comprehen- sive) under conditions of mutual respect, which protect the individual integrities of all the parties to it.[7]

Every covenant involves a mutual solemn promise or oath, with God as witness, to achieve specified ends in a context of mutual respect and justice. It also de- mands fidelity to the terms of the covenant as exemplified by Yahweh's steadfast love and faithfulness. These elements will be important to the claim later in this chapter that marriage is a solemn covenant.

## Marriage As Covenant

The idea of a covenant between the God Yahweh and the people of Israel, and the maintenance of that covenant in Israelite history, is the central idea that binds the Old Testament writings together. Whether it is the covenant with Noah, Abraham, or the Israelites led by Moses, Joshua, Ezra, and Nehemiah, Jews and Christians trace their roots back to covenants between Yahweh and Is- rael. That is clear, but it is not a central issue of this chapter. Not so clear in the Bible is the central issue, namely, marriage as a covenant between a man and a woman, like the covenant between Yahweh and Israel.

Since the prophet Hosea is frequently advanced as the origin of the idea of marriage as covenant, I begin with him. An immediate problem must be con- fronted, for "from centuries of critical debate only one consensus on the book of Hosea emerges: this is a disturbing, fragmented, outrageous, and notoriously problematic text."[8] From Jerome in the fifth century ("If we have need of the help of the Holy Spirit in the interpretation of all the prophets . . . how much

---

6. Delbert R. Hillers, *Covenant: The History of a Biblical Idea* (Baltimore: Johns Hopkins Press, 1969), pp. 25-39.

7. Elazar, *Covenant and Polity*, pp. 22-23.

8. Yvonne Sherwood, *The Prostitute and the Prophet: Hosea's Marriage in Literary- Theoretical Perspective* (Sheffield: Sheffield Academic Press, 1996), p. 11.

more when we come to the interpretation of the prophet Hosea"[9]) to Anderson and Freedman in the twentieth century ("[Hosea] competes with Job for the distinction of containing more unintelligible passages than any other book of the Bible"[10]), interpreting Hosea has always been a frustrating task. To cut through the frustration, I state from the outset my own reading. The covenantal view of marriage is not explicit in Hosea; at most, Hosea is arguing for the marriage between a man and a woman as an analogy of the covenant between Yahweh and Israel. Any claim of covenantal marriage in Hosea is not a reading of the text but an interpretive inference.

There is widespread agreement that Hosea divides in two sections, chapters 1-3 and 4-14, though Hans Wolff's subdivision of the second part into chapters 4-11 and 12-14,[11] yielding a tripartite structure, has won many followers.[12] It is the first part, Hosea 1-3, that is of interest to us here, because it speaks of marriage: in chapters 1 and 3 the marriage of Hosea and Gomer, a "wife of harlotry" (1:2) and an "adulteress" (3:1), in chapter 2 of Yahweh and Israel, a wife of "harlotry" and "adultery" (2:2). My judgment is that the final redactor created 3:1-5 as an interpretive commentary on the connection between the marriages of Hosea and Gomer and Yahweh and Israel,[13] both of which converge in the covenantal love of Yahweh for Israel. Yahweh will forgive his unfaithful wife when she repents and returns to her husband; as an ongoing prophetic symbol of this covenantal promise of forgiveness and reconciliation, so, too, will Hosea forgive his unfaithful wife.

In significant contrast to Hosea 1:2, where he is instructed only to "*take* a wife of harlotry," in 3:1 Hosea is instructed to "go again and *love* a woman who is beloved of a paramour." This love, which is to mirror prophetically Yahweh's love for unfaithful Israel, is a love that is the opposite of hatred (9:15), a helping love (11:1), a healing love (14:5), a love that wins back an unfaithful wife (3:4-5), a covenantal love that is "loyalty, service, and obedience."[14] Weiser and Elliger

9. Jerome, *Comment In Osee*, J. P. Migne, ed., *Patrologiae Cursus Completus, Series Latina* (Paris: Vrayet de Surcy, 1845), p. 815.

10. F. I. Andersen and David Noel Freedman, *Hosea: A New Translation with Introduction and Commentary* (New York: Doubleday, 1980), p. 166.

11. Hans W. Wolff, *Hosea: A Commentary on the Book of the Prophet Hosea* (Philadelphia: Fortress, 1974), pp. xxix-xxxii. The first German edition was in 1961.

12. For example, E. Jacob, *Osee* (Neuchâtel: Delachaux et Niestlé, 1965); Martin J. Buss, *The Prophetic Words of Hosea: A Morphological Study* (Berlin: Töpelmann, 1969); Gale A. Yee, *Composition and Tradition in the Book of Hosea: A Redaction Critical Investigation* (Atlanta: Scholars Press, 1987).

13. See Yee, *Composition and Tradition*, pp. 90-95.

14. William Moran, "The Ancient Near Eastern Background of the Love of God in Deuteronomy," *Catholic Biblical Quarterly* 25 (1963): 82.

claim that "something of the incomprehensible and indestructible love of God becomes apparent to Hosea in his own love for his adulterous wife," but it is the other way round.[15] As Hosea discovered the steadfast, forgiving, and reconciling love of God, he discovered also how he must act as a faithful husband toward an unfaithful wife. There is modeling here, from the heavenly marriage of Yahweh and Israel to the earthly marriage of Hosea and Gomer; there is analogy, from the marriage of Hosea and Gomer to the marriage between Yahweh and Israel; there is covenant, between Yahweh and Israel but not between Hosea and Gomer, at least not directly.

An interpreter can infer from the fact that the marriage between a man and a woman is a prophetic analogy of the covenant between Yahweh and Israel to the fact that human marriage is itself a solemn covenant. But neither Hosea himself nor his later redactor made that inference. All Hosea did, and it was religiously important then and continues to be religiously important now, was to represent in his own marriage to a faithless spouse the marriage of Yahweh to a faithless but still loved and, therefore, forgiven Israel. Hosea constructed a theology, not of marriage but of the covenant of grace between God and Israel, which he represented in the common human experience of marriage. That he represented the divine covenant in human marriage established subjective and objective connections between that covenant and marriage, and led later theologians to conclude that marriage itself was a covenant like the great covenant between God and Israel.

Malachi is the first theologian to articulate that conclusion. "The Lord," Malachi proclaims, "was witness to the covenant between you and the wife of your youth, to whom you have been faithless, though she is your companion and your wife by covenant" (2:14). Two things in this verse suggest that marriage is a covenant, first the statement that God was a witness to the covenant, second the phrase, "your wife by covenant." There is, however, widespread disagreement, centering on the precise meaning of "your wife by covenant." An equal number of reputable scholars are arrayed on each side of the divide, one side arguing that the phrase refers to marriage as covenant, the other that it does not. Gordon Hugenberger's densely detailed study collects all the opinions, examines them minutely, and arrives at the thesis "that Malachi, along with several other biblical authors, identified marriage as a covenant and that the implications of such a theory of marriage are not contradicted by other biblical texts."[16] I agree with

---

15. Artur Weiser and K. Elliger, *Das Buch der zwölf Kleinen Propheten* (Göttingen: Vandenhoeck & Ruprecht, 1967), cited in Wolff, *Hosea*, p. 60.

16. Gordon P. Hugenberger, *Marriage As a Covenant: A Study of Biblical Law and Ethics Governing Marriage Developed from the Perspective of Malachi* (Leiden: Brill, 1994), p. 12.

Hugenberger's judgment that "the burden of proof must rest with any interpreters who deny an identification of marriage as covenant in Malachi 2:14."[17] And, since I do not find that proof forthcoming, I further agree with him that Malachi portrays marriage as a solemn covenant. I cannot agree with him, however, in his further claims that the marriage oath is attested in the *verba solemnia* of the papyri,[18] which lie outside the biblical corpus and attest to legal contracts rather than to covenants, and that Hosea 2:16-20 and Proverbs 2:17, where the phrase "covenant of her God" occurs, refer to the marital covenant.

In summary, then, we can say that the approach to understanding marriage in the Bible under the rubric of covenant is questionable. Marriage as covenant is attested in Malachi 2:14, but explicitly nowhere else. Hosea, by common scholarly agreement, was the first to portray Israel's covenant infidelity as adultery (Hos. 2:2-23) and, because of his chronological priority, probably also the source of the same analogy in Isaiah (1:21-22; 54:5-8; 57:3-10; 61:10-11; 62:4-5), Jeremiah (2:2-3; 3:1-5, 6-25; 13:27; 23:10; 31:32), and Ezekiel (16:1-63; 23:1-49). But marriage as an *analogy* of the covenant does not translate to marriage itself *as covenant*, except by inferential interpretation. Neither Hosea, Isaiah, Jeremiah, nor Ezekiel goes beyond marriage as analogy of the covenant between Yahweh and Israel to claim that marriage itself is covenant. The claim that marriage is presented in the Hebrew Bible as a covenant is sparsely supported by a single text in Malachi, and even that text is not without significant naysayers.

Despite the claims made in Paul Palmer's quasi-classic essay on marriage as contract or covenant for the presence of the idea of marriage as covenant in the New Testament and in the Roman Empire,[19] my research convinces me such claims are unnuanced and unreliably inferential; moreover, there is also sparse support for marriage as covenant among Christian theologians of the first millennium. There are, however, several ritual allusions. The fourth-century convert Arnobius, lampooning the pagan gods, uses the Latin word for covenant, *foedus:* "Do the gods have wives, and do they enter conjugal covenants [*coniugalia foedera*] on agreed conditions? Do they swear to each other the oaths [*sacramenta*] of the marriage couch by use, by cake, or by purchase?"[20] The ninth-century pope Nicholas I, responding to a series of questions posed to him by Bulgarians evangelized by Greeks, uses *foedus* not only of marriage but also of betrothal. "After betrothal [*sponsalia*], which is a covenant promise [*promissa foedera*] of future marriage, made by those who are contracting and

17. Hugenberger, *Marriage As a Covenant*, p. 30.

18. Hugenberger, *Marriage As a Covenant*, pp. 216-79.

19. Paul F. Palmer, "Christian Marriage: Contract or Covenant," *Theological Studies* 33 (1972): 617-65.

20. Arnobius, *Adversus Gentes*, 4, 20, *Patrologia Latina* 5, p. 1040.

those under whose authority they live . . . [the couple] is led to the nuptial covenant *[nuptilia foedera]*.[21] There are also allusions to marriage as covenant in both the Gelasian and Gregorian Sacramentaries, though it is to be noted that they are greatly outnumbered by allusions in other rites to marriage as *copula carnalis*.[22]

## Marriage As Sacrament and Covenant

The difficulty in viewing marriage as covenant created by the sparse biblical evidence was compounded further by Tertullian's translation of *mysterion* (Eph. 5:32) as *sacramentum*, a translation replicated in Jerome's Vulgate.[23] From Tertullian through Augustine, Aquinas, Luther, and onward into the twentieth century, *sacramentum* would be the major Catholic theological category at the expense of *foedus*. Theologians began to concentrate on *sacrament* after Augustine, though his definition of sacrament, a sign of a sacred thing, was universally judged to be too broad. The search for a more precise definition took six hundred years and was made acute by Berengar of Tours who, in 1047, proposed a teaching opposed to the Roman realist approach to the sacrament of the Eucharist.

The uproar provoked by Berengar was the turning point in the Catholic history of sacrament in general and of its definition in particular. Several early Scholastic definitions followed, but the one that prevailed was Hugh of St. Victor's in the first half of the twelfth century. A sacrament is a sign of a sacred thing which not only signifies but also efficaciously confers what it signifies.[24] Hugh's notion of *efficacy* enabled Western theologians to distinguish sacrament from every other sign and led to Peter Lombard's definitive definition from around 1150: "a sacrament is a sign of the grace of God and the form of invisible grace in such a way that it is its image and its cause."[25] That definition controlled every approach to sacrament from the twelfth to the sixteenth century, when the Reformers rejected it.[26]

---

21. Nicolas I, *Responsa ad Consulta Bulgarorum*, III, *Patrologia Latina* 119, pp. 979-80.

22. See Korbinian Ritzer, *Formen, Riten und Religiöses Brauchtum der Eheschliessung in den Christlichen Kirchen des Ersten Jahrtausends* (Münster: Aschendorffsche, 1962), pp. 339-79, esp. 344, 346. See also Jean-Baptiste Molin and Protais Mutembe, *Le rituel du mariage en France du XIIe au XVIe siècle* (Paris: Beauchesne, 1974), pp. 319-27.

23. See Emile de Backer, "Tertullian," in *Pour l'histoire du mot sacramentum*, ed. J. de Ghellinck (Louvain: Spicilegium Sacrum Lovaniensis, 1924), pp. 143-46.

24. *Dialogus de Sacramentis Legis Naturalis et Scriptae*, 33D-34A, 34D-35A.

25. *Liber Sententiarum* 4, d. 1, c. 4.

26. For the history of the search for a definition of sacrament, see Michael G. Lawler, *Sym-*

The notion of sacramental efficacy excluded marriage from the list of sacraments. Theologians, who never doubted that marriage was a *sign* of grace, under the influence of Augustine's sexual theories seriously doubted that it was a *cause* of grace. Peter Lombard, for instance, carefully excluded marriage from the list of sacraments of the new law, explaining that "some offer a remedy for sin and confer helping grace, as baptism, others offer a remedy only, as marriage."[27] Marriage is a sign, "a sacred sign of a sacred reality, namely, the union of Christ and Church,"[28] but it is not a sacrament in the strict, efficacious sense. Albert the Great and his famous pupil, Thomas Aquinas, forever changed this opinion and firmly established marriage among the sacraments of the Catholic church.

In his obligatory commentary on Lombard's *Sentences,* Albert characterized as "very probable" the opinion that marriage "confers grace for doing good, not just any good but specifically the good that a married person should do."[29] In his commentary on the *Sentences,* Aquinas advanced to "most probable" the opinion that "marriage, insofar as it is contracted in faith in Christ, confers grace to do those things which are required in marriage."[30] He is even more positive in his *Summa Contra Gentiles,* stating bluntly that "it is to be believed that through this sacrament [marriage] grace is given to the married."[31] By the time he reached his *Summa Theologiae,* he listed marriage among seven sacraments with no demur about its efficacy to confer grace. The combined authority of these two theological giants ensured for marriage a place among the sacraments of the Catholic church and, on the eve of the Reformation, their opinion was universally held by theologians and solemnly taught by the church.[32] That pacific agreement was shattered by the Lutheran doctrine of the two kingdoms.

Though the doctrine of the two kingdoms and, especially, its interpretation have been matter for intense debate in recent decades,[33] there is widespread

---

bol and Sacrament: A Contemporary Sacramental Theology* (Omaha: Creighton University Press, 1995), pp. 29-34; D. Van den Eynde, *Les définitions des sacrements pendant la première période de la théologie scholastique* (Rome: Antonianum, 1950), pp. 40-52.

27. *Sententiae* 4, d. 2, c. 1.

28. *Sententiae,* 4, d. 26, c. 6.

29. *In IV Sent.* d. 26, a. 14, q. 2 ad 1.

30. *In IV Sent.* d. 26, q. 2, a. 3; repeated in *Supplement* 42, 3 corp.

31. Aquinas, *Summa Contra Gentiles* 4, 78.

32. At the Council of Lyons (1274) and the Council of Florence (1439); see Henricus Denzinger and Adolphus Schönmetzer, *Enchiridion Symbolorum Definitionum et Declarationum de Rebus Fidei et Morum* (Freiburg: Herder, 1965), pp. 860 and 1310.

33. John Witte Jr., *Law and Protestantism: The Legal Teachings of the Lutheran Reformation* (Cambridge: Cambridge University Press), pp. 89-119.

agreement that the doctrine is "the key to Luther's mature social, political, and legal thought."[34] God has ordained two kingdoms in which Christians are destined to live, the earthly or political kingdom and the heavenly or spiritual kingdom. The earthly kingdom, the realm of creation and civic life, is ruled by law; the heavenly kingdom, the realm of redemption and spiritual life, is ruled by gospel and grace. Marriage belongs to the earthly kingdom. It is "a rather secular and outward thing, having to do with wife and children, house and home, and with other matters that belong to the realm of the government,"[35] "an external, worldly matter, like clothing and food, house and property, subject to temporal authority."[36]

By placing marriage in the earthly kingdom, Luther supplanted the Catholic sacramental model of marriage with a social model. Marriage is not a sacrament which contains the promise of grace.[37] On occasion, Luther does teach that marriage is a sacrament, but it is a sacrament only in the Augustinian and early Scholastic sense. It is not an efficacious cause of grace but only "an outward and spiritual sign of the greatest, holiest, worthiest, and noblest thing that has ever existed or ever will exist: the union of the divine and human natures in Christ."[38] A four-hundred-year theological agreement was exploded, although, despite Luther's bitter invectives against the Catholic canon law, symbolized in his burning of the *Corpus Iuris Canonici* in 1520, Protestant jurists and rulers appropriated much of that law as it related to marriage and family.

Calvin also grounded his rejection of the Roman theology of marriage on the doctrine of the two kingdoms.

> There is a twofold government in man: one aspect is spiritual, whereby the conscience is instructed in piety and in reverencing God; the second is political, whereby man is educated for the duties of humanity and citizenship. . . . These are usually called the "spiritual" and the "temporal" jurisdiction[39] . . .

34. W. D. J. Cargill Thompson, *The Political Thought of Martin Luther* (New York: Barnes and Noble, 1984), p. 11.

35. Martin Luther, "The Sermon on the Mount," *Luther's Works*, vol. 21, ed. Jaroslav Pelikan (St. Louis: Concordia, 1956), p. 93.

36. Martin Luther, "On Marriage Matters," *Luther's Works,* vol. 46, ed. Robert C. Shultz (Philadelphia: Fortress, 1967), p. 265.

37. Philip Melanchthon, *Apology of the Augsburg Confession*, Article XIII, 14, in *The Book of Concord*, ed. Theodore G. Tappert (Philadelphia: Fortress, 1959), p. 213.

38. Martin Luther, "A Sermon on the Estate of Marriage," *Luther's Works*, vol. 44, ed. James Atkinson (Philadelphia: Fortress, 1966), p. 10.

39. Thirteenth-century popes claimed fullness of power in both spiritual and temporal matters. Calvin may have had this claim in mind.

by which is meant the former sort of government pertains to the life of the soul, while the latter has to do with the concerns of the present life.[40]

Marriage belongs to the earthly kingdom. It is "a good and holy ordinance of God" as are "farming, building, cobbling, and barbering."[41] It is of such worth and dignity that "Christ wills it to be an image of his sacred union with the Church."[42] It is not, however, a sacrament, any more than farming, building, cobbling, or barbering. Calvin concedes, as does Luther, that marriage may be a *sign* of the "spiritual joining of Christ with the Church,"[43] but it is only a sign, not a cause, of grace. It confirms no divine promise and grants no grace, as do true sacraments, and anyone who would classify it with the sacraments "ought to be sent to a mental hospital."[44]

If Calvin's earliest theology of marriage was grounded in the doctrine of the two kingdoms, his mature theology was grounded in the idea of covenant.[45] Marriage undoubtedly belongs to the earthly kingdom, but it has also a spiritual dimension. It is a "covenant which God has consecrated,"[46] a "sacred bond," the "principal and most sacred of all offices pertaining to human society."[47] It cannot be otherwise since God is its founder.[48]

> When a marriage takes place between a man and a woman, God presides and requires a mutual pledge from both. Therefore, Solomon in Proverbs 2:17 calls marriage the covenant of God. . . . So also Malachi declares that God is as it were the stipulator [of marriage] who by his authority joins the man to the woman and sanctions the marriage.[49]

God participates in the formation of the covenant of marriage through designated agents in the earthly kingdom, parents who give their consent to the union,[50] ministers who bless the union and admonish both couple and com-

---

40. John Calvin, *Institutes of the Christian Religion*, ed. John T. McNeill (Philadelphia: Westminster, 1960), III.19.15.

41. Calvin, *Institutes*, IV.19.34.

42. Calvin, *Institutes*, IV.12.24.

43. Calvin, *Institutes*, IV.19.34.

44. Calvin, *Institutes*, IV.19.34.

45. For a detailed treatment of Calvin's doctrine, see John Witte Jr., *From Sacrament to Contract: Marriage, Religion, and Law in the Western Tradition* (Louisville: Westminster John Knox, 1997), pp. 74-129.

46. *Comm in Mal* 2:14.

47. *Comm in Gen* 2:21, 24; *Contra la Secte des Libertines*, CO, 7:212.

48. Cf. *Serm in Eph* 5:22-26; *Serm in Deut* 5:18.

49. *Comm in Mal* 2:14.

50. *Comm in Lev* 19:29; *Serm in Deut* 5:16; *Comm in Eph* 6:1-3; *Comm in 1 Cor* 7:36, 38.

munity about their respective rights and duties,[51] two witnesses who testify to the couple's faith and sincerity,[52] and the magistrate, the representative of God's power in the earthly kingdom, who "registers the parties, ensures the legality of their union, and protects them in their conjoined persons and properties."[53] Parents, peers, ministers, and magistrates represent different dimensions of God's involvement in the marriage covenant, and their participation is indispensable. Should any one of them be missing from the covenant ceremony, God is missing.

Luther and Melanchthon taught that marriage was of the earthly kingdom alone. Calvin agreed that it belonged to the earthly kingdom, but not to the earthly kingdom alone. His doctrine of marriage as covenant established marriage as also a sacred reality. It is not a sacrament in the Roman sense, for it does not confirm any promise of grace, but it is a sign in the earthly kingdom of Christ's relationship with the church and God's relationship with God's chosen people. The image of Christ's relationship with the church was a favorite theme to which Calvin returned often, one which he held up constantly as a model to which spouses should aspire.[54] The basis on which he proved that marriage was a covenant can be disputed, particularly his reliance on doubtful biblical texts we have already considered, but it cannot be disputed that Calvin clearly taught that marriage is presented in the Bible as a covenant. He is the first post-biblical Western theologian to do so.

The Catholic response to the teaching of the reformers, the Council of Trent, was charged to consider two things: dogma and reform. The Council was faithful to this charge when it considered both sacraments in general and the sacrament of marriage in particular. Its work on sacraments was prefaced by the creation of a list of thirty-five errors drawn from the writings of Luther, Melanchthon, and Bucer, with no mention of Calvin, probably because he was newer on the list of reformers. This list was given to the consulting theologians to distinguish the propositions that were heretical and to be condemned from those which were merely erroneous and to be corrected and those which might be explained in an orthodox manner. The judgment of the theologians was then passed on to the council delegates for discussion and decision.[55]

Given the four-hundred-year doctrinal agreement that preceded the outbreak of reform, the task of both theologians and delegates, who had been in-

51. *Serm in Eph* 5:31-33.
52. *Comm in 1 Thess* 4:3.
53. CO, 45:529.
54. *Serm in Eph* 5:28-30; *Comm in Eph* 5:30-32.
55. See Hubert Jedin, *A History of the Council of Trent*, trans. Ernest Graf (St. Louis: Herder, 1958), vol. 2, pp. 370-95.

structed to focus on Catholic teaching and eschew the disputations of the schools, was an easy one. And so the Council of Trent solemnly taught again that there are no more and no less than seven sacraments, all of them instituted by Christ[56] to contain and confer grace on all who place no obstacle,[57] among them the sacrament of matrimony,[58] which is permanent and indissoluble when the marriage is consummated.[59] The Tridentine doctrine controlled every discussion of sacrament in general and of the sacrament of marriage in particular for the next four hundred years. There was no mention of Calvin in the discussion on marriage, no mention of marriage as covenant, and, therefore, no mention of marriage as covenant in the post-Tridentine Catholic church. The pre-Tridentine doctrinal agreement on matters sacramental continued to be the post-Tridentine norm. The Catholic theological focus in marriage continued to be on *sacrament* and marital realities connected to sacrament, with *covenant* clearly designated as a Calvinist approach. That situation was ended, rather abruptly, by another ecumenical council, the Second Vatican Council, in the second half of the twentieth century.

## The Second Vatican Council and Marriage

For the purposes of this chapter, two facts about the Second Vatican Council are relevant. First, among the schemas prepared for discussion at the Council was one related to marriage, entitled *De Castitate, Virginitate, Matrimonio, Familia,* drawn up by the Theological Commission under the chairmanship of Cardinal Ottaviani. Second, there was no schema examining the situation of the Catholic church in the modern world, which was surprising given Pope John XXIII's sermon at the opening of the Council, in which he emphasized that he wanted the Council to be about the church not only in itself *(ad intra)* but also in its relations with the world outside itself *(ad extra).* These two facts are closely related. Ottaviani's *De Castitate* was discussed by the Central Preparatory Commission in May, 1962, and overwhelmingly rejected. A sampling from the schema and the explanatory note accompanying illustrates two things: first, "the negative and rigoristic casuistry" which characterized the document; second, the doctrine that was rejected, both in the Preparatory Commission and in the Council itself, as a contemporary Catholic theological approach to

56. Denzinger and Schönmetzer, *Enchiridion Symbolorum Definitionum,* p. 1601.
57. Denzinger and Schönmetzer, *Enchiridion Symbolorum Definitionum,* p. 1606.
58. Denzinger and Schönmetzer, *Enchiridion Symbolorum Definitionum,* p. 1801.
59. Denzinger and Schönmetzer, *Enchiridion Symbolorum Definitionum,* p. 1806.

marriage. The Council's teaching on marriage in *Gaudium et Spes* grew out of that rejection, after many meanderings and spiteful contradictions.

Among those intimately connected with the development of *Gaudium et Spes,* and specifically with its chapter on marriage, was Bernard Häring.[60] He comments that the schema of *De Castitate* "was intended to perpetuate the negative and rigoristic casuistry of the standard textbooks. The events of the First Session of the Council made it perfectly clear that this schema could expect no better fate than the almost equally bad schema on the Sources of Revelation."[61] It is safe to assume that Häring's judgment on the inadequacies of these two schemas is based not only on an *a priori* personal preference but especially on the *a posteriori* basis of their actual fate. Some background on that fate will serve to introduce a contemporary Catholic approach to marriage.

Along with his schema, Ottaviani sent the Preparatory Commission a note of explanation. "Before all else the Theological Commission has set out the objective order, that is, that which God himself willed in instituting marriage and Christ the Lord willed in raising it to the dignity of sacrament. Only in this way can the modern errors that have spread everywhere be vanquished."[62] Among those errors were "those theories which subvert the right order of values and make the primary end of marriage inferior to the biological and personal values of the spouses, and proclaim that conjugal love itself is in the objective order the primary end."[63] The schema offers the hierarchy of ends theologically traditional since Aquinas. "The one and only primary end is the procreation and nurture of children. . . . The other objective ends of marriage, rooted in the character itself of marriage but still secondary — such as the spouses' mutual help and the remedying of concupiscence — constitute genuine, even if subordinate, rights in marriage when they are rightly intended."[64] The relative values of these two ends, procreation and conjugal love, became the focus of the debate, both in the Preparatory Commission and in the Council itself. The tortuous, and sometimes far from edifying, history of that debate need not be rehearsed again here, but only its outcome in part two, chapter one of *Gaudium et Spes.*

From the first paragraph of the chapter on marriage, it is described as a

60. See Philippe Delhaye, "Dignité du mariage et de la famille," in *L'Église dans le Monde de ce temps,* ed. Yves Congar and Michael Peuchmaurd, vol. 2 (Paris: Du Cerf, 1967), pp. 387-453.

61. Bernhard Häring, *Commentary on the Documents of Vatican II,* vol. 5 (New York: Herder and Herder, 1969), p. 225.

62. *Acta et Documenta Concilio Oecumenico Vaticano Apparando,* series 2 (Praeparatoria), vol. 2, part 3 (Roma: Typis Polyglottis Vaticanis, 1968), p. 937.

63. *Acta et Documenta,* series 2, vol. 2, part 3, pp. 910, 917 n. 50.

64. *Acta et Documenta,* series 2, vol. 2, part 3, p. 909.

*community* or *partnership,* even a *community of love.* "The well-being of the individual person and of both human and Christian society is closely bound up with the healthy state of that *community* produced by marriage and family. Hence Christians and all men who hold this *community* in high esteem sincerely rejoice in the various ways by which men today find help in fostering this *community of love.*"[65] The intent of *community* was to suggest a total, psychological and physical, communion between two persons, a two-in-one-oneness[66] which transforms the individual "I" and "Thou" into a communal "We." It is in their very *being,* and not just in their *having* or *doing* together, that a husband and wife are one.[67]

In the debate on marriage at the last session of the Council, Bishop De Roo specified what marital two-in-oneness means. "Marital love cannot be considered only as a physical and pleasurable attraction. Marital love is a very deep spiritual experience. It throws light into [the spouses'] very depths, showing them what they might mean for one another, and highlighting their mutual communion in an irrevocable union."[68] The Bishops of Asia sought to offer a moderating Catholic perspective, pointing out that the proposed schema was exclusively Western in tone and took no account of the way in which marriage was perceived in the cultures of Asia. Westerners marry because they love one another, Asians love one another because they are united in marriage. Marital love, for them, is often born after marriage.

Marriage, then, the Council taught, is "a community of love,"[69] "an intimate partnership of life and love."[70] In the face of strident demands to downplay conjugal love as too subjective a norm,[71] the Council, agreeing with Cardinal Alfrink's intervention that "conjugal love is an essential element of marriage rather than its consequence,"[72] declared love to be of the essence of marriage. Marriage is something more than a mere juridical contract about material

65. *Gaudium et Spes,* n. 47, emphases added.

66. See Herbert Doms, *The Meaning of Marriage,* trans. George Sayer (London: Sheed and Ward, 1939), pp. 94-95.

67. L'Action Populaire, *Constitution Pastorale Gaudium et Spes* (Paris: Spes, 1966), nn. 86, 190.

68. Cited in G. Caprile, ed., *Concilio Vaticano II* (Roma: Edizioni La Civilta Cattolica, 1969), pp. 5, 137.

69. *Gaudium et Spes,* 47.

70. *Gaudium et Spes,* 48.

71. See Giovanni Turbanti, *Un Concilio per il Mundo Moderno: La Redazione della Costituzione Pastorale 'Gaudium et Spes' del Vaticano secundo* (Bologna: Il Mulino, 2000), pp. 435-40, 581-83; also the interventions in *Acta Synodalia Sacrosancti Concilii Oecumenici Vaticani II,* vol. 4, Periodus Quarta, part 3 (Roma: Typis Polyglottis Vaticanis, 1977), pp. 13-51.

72. *Acta et Documenta,* series 2, vol. 2, part 3, p. 961.

things; it is something human, something personal, something religio-biblical. This approach was bolstered theologically by the insertion into the text of the biblical notion of *covenant,* an insertion which was explained in the commentary given to the Council Fathers along with the revised text in September, 1965. "There is no mention of 'matrimonial contract' but, in clearer words, of 'irrevocable personal consent.' The biblical term 'covenant' *(foedus)* is added at the intuition of the Eastern Churches for whom 'contract' raises some difficulties."[73] The understanding of *covenant* as used by the Council is dependent upon the intuition of the Eastern churches, and to that intuition, therefore, we must briefly turn.

The Orthodox intuition of marriage as covenant is located within the *oikonomia* of the biblical covenants of God with Israel and the church. Covenantal election involves, as we have seen, both God and people in a steadfast commitment, and in the church the fullest expression of that commitment takes place in the sacrament of marriage. "The covenantal bond within which God works out our salvation is in essence a nuptial bond. And, conversely, the nuptial relationship achieves its true purpose and attains its true fullness only insofar as it is based upon an eternal covenantal commitment."[74] The purpose of marriage between a man and woman is to create between them "a bond of covenant responsibility and faithfulness that represents and reactualizes the eternal bond established by God with his chosen people,"[75] and so it is that marriage is "a great mystery" which refers to Christ and the church (Eph. 5:32). In such an expansive vision of marriage, it is little wonder that the narrow juridical vision of "contract" would create "some difficulties." The use of *covenant* rather than *contract* deliberately takes marriage out of its narrow, traditional, juridical sphere and situates it in the sphere of interpersonal, religious, steadfast commitment and responsibility. Its identification as a "biblical term" insinuates its connection to the sempiternal covenants between God and Israel and Christ and church.

The Council took traditional Catholic canonical and contractual language and rendered it in covenantal terms, teaching that marriage, the intimate partnership of life and love, is rooted in a "conjugal covenant of irrevocable personal consent."[76] There were minority demands to retain the juridical word

---

73. *Acta Synodalia,* vol. 4, Periodus Quarta, part 1, p. 536.

74. John Breck, *The Sacred Gift of Life: Orthodox Christianity and Bioethics* (New York: St. Vladimir's Seminary Press, 2000), p. 63.

75. Breck, *Sacred Gift of Life,* p. 62. While preferring *mysterion* or *sacrament* and eschewing *covenant,* John Meyendorff, *Marriage: An Orthodox Prespective* (New York: St. Vladimir's Seminary Press, 1984), articulates the meanings Breck associates with covenant. See, especially, pp. 18-20, 33-42.

76. *Gaudium et Spes,* 48.

*contract,*[77] but the Council demurred and intentionally selected the more biblical, religious, and personal word *covenant*. Contractual language about marriage had been traditional among Western theologians and canonists since Gratian and Lombard, but had been canonized in official church documents only since the 1917 Code of Canon Law.[78] *Covenant* was intentionally chosen over *contract* to insinuate that the intimate partnership of life and love that is marriage is more than a legally witnessed contract regulating mutual rights over bodies for the purpose of procreation.[79] It is an interpersonal vow witnessed by God in and through which the spouses "mutually give and accept each other in order to establish marriage."[80] *Covenant* encompasses all that is legally and institutionally encompassed by *contract*, but it also insinuates more. It insinuates that the free, loving, mutual gifting and accepting that creates the community of marriage is not temporary and revocable, as it could be under contract, but permanent, irrevocable, and "no longer [dependent] on human actions alone."[81]

This interpersonal approach to marriage and the highlighting of conjugal love as a prime end of marriage necessitated a reshaping of the traditional hierarchical ordering of the ends. The Council emphasized that both marriage and the marital love of the spouses "are ordained for the procreation and education of children, and find in them their ultimate crown,"[82] but, again deaf to minority voices to the contrary, refused to employ the traditional primary end/secondary end language. The Theological Commission was careful to explain that the text just cited "does not suggest this [a hierarchy of ends] in any way."[83] *Gaudium et Spes* finally taught that "marriage and conjugal love are by their nature ordained to the generation of children," but that this "does not make the other purposes of marriage of less account," and that marriage "is not instituted solely for procreation."[84] The outcome of the core debate about marriage was, for the first time in Catholic history, both a clear statement that conjugal love and procreation are co-essential prime ends of marriage[85] and a refusal to

77. See, for instance, the speech of Bishop Louis Alonso Munoyerro, *Acta Synodalia*, vol. 4, Periodus Quarta, part 3, pp. 37-38.

78. See Michael G. Lawler, "Faith, Contract, and Sacrament in Christian Marriage: A Theological Approach," *Theological Studies* 52 (1991): 725-29.

79. See Code of Canon Law (1917), Can 1081, 2.

80. Code of Canon Law (1983), Can 1057, 2; *Gaudium et Spes*, 48.

81. *Gaudium et Spes*, 48.

82. *Gaudium et Spes*, 48.

83. *Commentary on the Documents of Vatican II*, vol. 5, p. 234.

84. *Gaudium et Spes*, 50.

85. In his speech before the Council, Cardinal Colombo of Milan observed that "it is very pleasing that, rooted in a doctrine that is fully human and personalistic, as well as supernatural,

order these two ends hierarchically. Mutual, including sexual, love between spouses is "eminently human," "good," "noble and worthy,"[86] irrespective of procreative intent or outcome.

This approach was confirmed as a Catholic approach by "the last conciliar document,"[87] the revised Code of Canon Law. Though the revised Code is schizophrenic in its appropriation of the marital teaching of Vatican II, it does generally embrace that teaching and make significant changes to the 1917 Code. The first canon on marriage sets the tone. "The marriage *covenant*, by which a man and a woman establish between themselves a partnership of their whole life, and which of its very nature is ordered to the well-being of the spouses and to the procreation and upbringing of children, has, between the baptized, been raised by Christ the Lord to the dignity of a sacrament."[88] Marriage is "brought into being by the lawfully manifested consent of persons who are legally capable," and that consent "is an act of the will by which a man and a woman by irrevocable *covenant* mutually give and accept one another for the purpose of establishing a marriage."[89] Contemporary Catholic theology and law of marriage stress, in a personalistic and dynamic perspective, the spouses and the willed communion created in their marriage. Their marital love, their intimate partnership of life and love, their solemn covenant which creates their irrevocable community, are now all part of Roman Catholic theology and law.

One thing remains for this marriage as sacrament and covenant chapter: to ask what the teaching about marriage as covenant and sacrament means in its Catholic incarnation. To covenant is to commit oneself radically forever and to call upon God to witness one's commitment. When a man and a woman covenant in the sacrament of marriage, they commit themselves mutually to a life of equal and intimate partnership in loyal and steadfast love. They commit themselves mutually to create and sustain a climate of personal openness, availability, and trust. They commit themselves mutually to behavior that will respect, nurture, and sustain covenant, two-in-one-bodiness, and steadfast love. They commit themselves mutually to explore together the religious depth of human

---

the schema sets forth the ends and goods of marriage in such a way that conjugal love is declared an intrinsic end of marriage, co-essential with the procreative end." *Acta Synodalia*, vol. 4, part 3, p. 33.

86. *Gaudium et Spes*, 49.

87. Raymond L. Burke, "Vatican Council II and Matrimonial Law," in *Vatican II: Assessment and Perspectives*, ed. René Latourelle, 3 vols. (New York: Paulist, 1988-89), p. 217.

88. Canon 1055, 1. Emphasis added. See my critique of the theological naivete of this canon in Michael G. Lawler, *Marriage and the Catholic Church: Disputed Questions* (Collegeville: Liturgical Press, 2002), pp. 43-65.

89. Canon 1057. Emphasis added.

life in general, and of their marriage in particular, and to respond to that depth in the light of their shared Christian faith. They commit themselves, finally, to abide in love, in covenant, in marriage, and in sacrament for the whole of life.[90]

It is sometimes said that covenant and contract are in reality much the same. That is true if only legal consequences are considered; it is far from true if their specific witnesses and moral consequences are considered. Contracts have people as witnesses and states as guarantors; covenants have people as witnesses too, but their primary witness and guarantor is God. Akkadian covenants of the eighth century B.C.E. stipulate that the gods are "Lords of the oaths" and that the gods reward those who live up to the covenant and "pursue relentlessly" those who do not.[91] In the Sinai covenant, God stipulates, "if you will obey my voice and keep my covenant, you shall be my own possession among all the peoples" (Exod. 19:5). The inverse, which is implied in Exodus, is spelled out in Joshua: "if you forsake the Lord and serve foreign gods, then he will turn and do you harm, and consume you after having done you good" (24:20). This involvement of the eternal God is what makes covenants steadfast, permanent, and irrevocable.

Contracts can be made for a stipulated period of time and, even in that time, can be voided, albeit with material loss to one or both parties to the contract. Covenants are forever and are irrevocable. They can be violated, but they cannot be voided. When they are violated, the result is personal, not just material, loss for one or both of the covenanters. That is why *Gaudium et Spes* teaches that, when a couple enter into the conjugal covenant, "a relationship arises which by divine will and in the eyes of society too is a lasting one . . . the existence of this sacred bond no longer depends on human decisions alone."[92] Though the covenant of marriage is brought into being by the human act of free consent on the part of the couple, God is intimately involved in it as its author, its primary witness, and its guarantor. Covenants, therefore, are essentially religious and moral affairs, in distinction from contracts, which are secular, legal affairs. The parties bound by covenant are obligated to deal with one another in mutual respect and justice beyond the letter of the law. When a covenant is violated, the aggrieved party can always legitimately complain, "but you solemnly promised." The involvement of God in a covenant marriage makes the marriage not just a legal institution but also a *mystery* or a *sacrament*.

In a covenantal-sacramental marriage, spouses consent and commit them-

90. The thoughts that follow are inspired by Wilson Yates, "The Protestant View of Marriage," *Journal of Ecumenical Studies* 22 (1985): 41-54.

91. Klaus Baltzer, *The Covenant Formulary in Old Testament, Jewish, and Early Christian Writings* (Philadelphia: Fortress, 1971), pp. 14-15.

92. *Gaudium et Spes*, 48.

selves to create a life of equal and intimate partnership in loyal and steadfast love. When God created the heavens and the earth, when no plant had yet sprung up from the earth because God had not yet brought rain, a mist rose up and watered the earth. The mist turned the dry earth to mud, in Hebrew 'adamah, and from that 'adamah God formed 'adam and breathed into her and his nostrils the breath of life. And 'adam became a living being (Gen. 2:4-7). "When the Lord Yahweh created 'adam, he made 'adam in the likeness of Yahweh. Male and female he created them, and he blessed them and he named them 'adam" (Gen. 5:1-2).

This myth, for it is indeed a myth, responds to the perennial human question: where did we come from? We — in Hebrew 'adam, in English humankind — came from God. Male and female as we are, we are from God, and together we make up humankind. This fact alone, that God names woman and man together 'adam, establishes the equality of men and women as human beings. The further myth that speaks of the creation of woman from man's rib intends in the Hebrew metaphor to emphasize that equality, not their separate creation. The Catholic bishops of the United States underscore this reading in their pastoral response to the concerns of women in the church. Since "in the divine image . . . male and female [God] created them" (Gen. 1:27), woman and man are equal in everything that is human; they are "bone of bone and flesh of flesh" (Gen. 2:23). It is only because they are so equal, says the myth, that they may marry and "become one body" (Gen. 2:24). When they marry in a covenant marriage, their equality is further underscored and solidified by the extent to which they are both equally bound by the terms of their covenant.

Christian marital covenant demands not only the creation of a life of equal partnership but also the maintenance of that life. As the God revealed in Jesus is not a God who creates and then abandons creation to its own laws, as Jesus is not a Christ who gives himself up for the church (Eph. 5:25) and then abandons her, so no Christian believer creates a covenant, a marriage, a sacrament, and leaves the spouse to survive by himself or herself. When a Christian man and a woman marry, they commit themselves mutually to create rules of behavior that will nurture and sustain their marriage, their sacrament, their covenant. As Christian believers, they will find those rules articulated in their Christian tradition.

Scholars today, across all Christian traditions, are moving away from what may be called a "biblical rules" approach to morality. Realizing the difficulty of rigidly transposing rules from biblical times to our own, interpreters look for larger themes and ideals that can inform moral reflection without determining specific practices in advance. Christian spouses will find the ideals to inform their covenant marriage succinctly summarized in the biblical letter to the Ephesians. The author critiques the list of traditional household duties in first-century Palestine, together with the inequality embedded in it, and challenges all Christians to "give way to one another because you stand in awe of Christ" (Eph. 5:21). The critique both challenges the absolute authority of any Christian individual over another, including that of a husband over a wife, and establishes the basic attitude required of all Christians.

Since all Christians are to give way to one another, it is not surprising that wives are challenged to give way to their husbands (Eph. 5:22). What is surprising, at least to those husbands who see themselves as lords and masters of their wives and who seek to found this unchristian attitude in Ephesians, is the challenge to husbands. The challenge is that "the husband is the head of the wife *as* [that is, in the same way as] Christ is head of the church" (5:23). In immediate response to the obvious question, "how is Christ head of the church?" the writer explains, "he gave himself up for her" (5:25), a clear echo of Mark's description of the Son of Man who "came not to be served but to serve" (Mark 10:45). There is loud echo also of the teaching Jesus constantly sought to inculcate in his power-hungry disciples, namely, that in the kingdom of God the leader is the servant of all (Luke 22:26). The Christian way to exercise authority is to serve. Christ-like authority is not domination of another human being; it is not making unilateral decisions and transmitting them to another to carry out; it is not reducing another to the status of a slave. To be head as Christ is head is to serve. The Christian husband, as Markus Barth puts it so beautifully, is called to be "the first servant of his wife,"[93] and she is equally called to be his first servant. One rule of behavior by which Christian spouses may nurture both their marriage and their sacrament is the Christian rule of service — to God, to one another, and to the needs around them.

Another Christian rule for behavior, in and out of marriage, is the great commandment: "You shall love your neighbor as yourself" (Lev. 19:18; Mark 12:31). Husbands, the author of Ephesians instructs, are to "love their wives as their own bodies," for the husband "who loves his wife loves himself" (5:28). We can rightfully assume that the same instruction is intended also for wives. The great Torah and Gospel commandment to love one's neighbor as oneself applies in marriage to one's spouse who, in that most beautiful and sexual of Jewish love songs, the *Song of Songs*, is addressed nine times as *plesion*, literally neighbor (1:9, 15; 2:2, 10, 13; 4:1, 7; 5:2; 6:4), suggesting that *neighbor* is a term of endearment for the beloved. A paraphrase of Paul clinches the rule of love for Christian spouses: those who love their spouses have fulfilled all the rules of behavior for nurturing and sustaining a covenant marriage (Rom. 13:8).

---

93. Markus Barth, *Ephesians: Translation and Commentary on Chapters Four to Six*, The Anchor Bible (New York: Doubleday, 1974), p. 618.

A sacramental marriage is not just a wedding to be celebrated; it is more critically an equal and loving partnership to be lived for the whole of life. When spouses covenant to one another in the sacrament of marriage, they commit themselves to explore together the religious depth of their married life and to respond to that depth in the light of their mutual covenant to Christ and to the church in which he abides. A central invitation of Christian faith is the invitation to discipleship enshrined in Jesus' "Follow me" (Mark 1:17). "Disciple" is a gospel word, implying both a call from Jesus and an intentional response from a believer. Disciples learn from a Master, and the disciples of Jesus learn from him the triune mystery. They learn the mystery of God as Father who calls them to live as God's daughters and sons, of God as Son who calls them to be his brothers and sisters, of God as Spirit who calls them to neighbor-love and mutual service. They ponder the mystery of Christ, in whom this God is embodied and revealed, and the mystery of the church which is the Body of Christ (Eph. 1:22-23; Col. 1:18, 24) and which calls them to communion and to service. Christian spouses, members of the church, disciples of the Christ, and believers in the God he reveals, consent in covenant to ponder together these mysteries, to discern their implications for marital life, and to structure their marital life accordingly. It is their marital life, lived in faith, friendship, and mutual love and service, that is ultimately the Catholic sacrament of the presence of God and God's Christ in the world.

In our age, when marriage and family are in such disarray,[94] followers of Christ have to discern and decide what sign their marriage will offer to a world that is sinful, broken, and divided by racism, sexism, and classism. Since they are believing Christians, that sign will depend, at least in part, on Jesus' assertion, already considered, that he came "not to be served but to serve" (Mark 10:45). Nobody claiming to be Christian, no individual, no couple, no church, can be anything less than for others. No Christian family can be anything less than a "domestic church"[95] for others, reaching out to heal the brokenness in the communities in which it exists.[96] Service to the society in which they live is the responsibility of all Christians, married or unmarried. Sacramental, covenant marriage adds only the specification that the spouses exercise their service as part of their marital life.

This section concludes with another characterization of marriage, only now a more fully elaborated characterization of *Christian* marriage. Christian mar-

---

94. See Michael G. Lawler, *Family: American and Christian* (Chicago: Loyola, 1998).

95. *Lumen Gentium*, 11.

96. See William P. Roberts, "The Family As Domestic Church: Contemporary Implications," in *Christian Marriage and Family: Contemporary Theological and Pastoral Perspectives,* ed. Michael G. Lawler and William P. Roberts (Collegeville: Liturgical Press, 1996), pp. 79-92.

riage is an intimate and equal partnership of life and love. Its origin is, ultimately, in God's act of creating *'adam,* male and female, proximately, in the covenant of the spouses' free, willed, and irrevocable consent. Its goal is the continuation of Christ's mission to establish the reign of God in the lives of the spouses, their family, and in the world in which they live. The wedding ceremony by which they enter into marriage is a covenant ceremony, according to the covenant requirements listed by Hillers in the opening section of this chapter. There is, first, a prologue that identifies the parties making the covenant ("I, Michael, take you, Susan"); second, the identification of the purpose of the covenant ("as my lawful wedded wife . . . wedded husband"); third, a specification of the irrevocable duration of the covenant ("until death do us part"); fourth, an enumeration of covenantal blessings and woes ("to have and to hold . . . for better or for worse, in sickness and in health"); fifth, a publicly sworn oath (the marital consent); and, finally, a public and permanent record of the covenant ceremony (the marriage certificate). During the ceremony, the spouses are instructed about the requirements of a Christian, covenantal marriage. "Father, keep them always true to your commandments. Let them be living examples of Christian life. Give them the strength which comes from the gospels so that they may be witnesses of Christ to others."[97] If ritual prayers are always the best indicators of ritual meaning, and they are, there can be no doubt about the Catholic meaning of sacramental, covenantal marriage.

97. *The Rites of the Catholic Church* (New York: Pueblo, 1976), p. 544.

## 4 Covenant Marriage: Reflections from an Eastern Orthodox Perspective

*Stanley Samuel Harakas*

Is there a concept of "covenant" in the Orthodox approach to marriage? The first part of this chapter will seek to address this question, with not too encouraging results. The second part will try to reinterpret the covenant dimension of holy matrimony into Orthodox theological categories, and in particular the place of the marital relations, especially sexual union, in the sacramental relationship of the Christian spouses. The third part will be an equally brief sketch of what I shall call two complementary ecclesial trajectories regarding the intimacy of marriage. It will highlight some of the manuscript evidence regarding the development of marital rituals, in early Eastern and Western Christianity. These will serve as the context for the thesis of this chapter that the present betrothal and marriage texts of the Orthodox Church can be understood as a theological tract, presenting a positive view of marriage in general, and sex in marriage specifically, against those who would denigrate marriage and its relationships in favor of a "higher view" of the celibate monastic life. The chapter concludes with an effort to relate the above thesis theologically with the concept of covenant.

The first draft of this chapter was a paper prepared for a scholarly meeting organized by the Ecumenical Patriarchate of Constantinople on the general topic, "The Creation of the World and the Creation of Humanity: Challenges and Problematics of 2000," as part of an ongoing program of observances of the Jubilee for the beginning of the third millennium of the Christian era. The original title, indicating a different focus, was "Human Life and the Demographic Problem: The Two Genders." It has not been published as of this writing.

## Covenant in Eastern Orthodox Theological Reflection

Is there a concept of "covenant" in the Orthodox approach to marriage? Since one of the hallmarks of Orthodoxy is its fidelity to the patristic tradition, this question translates easily into the question of whether one can find in the tradition of the church fathers, particularly the Eastern fathers, an application of the idea of "covenant" to the marital relationship.

Generally in the Eastern patristic tradition the focus of the term *covenant* is on the divinely initiated gracious act of God for humanity. Speaking of the covenant of God, the *Epistle of Barnabas* (c. 85 C.E.) declared that "Moses received it as a servant, but the Lord himself gave it to us, that we might become the people of the inheritance."[1] This may be an apt early Christian summary of the mainline understanding of *covenant*. A bit later, Irenaeus of Lyons (130-200 C.E.) sometimes discerned that there were more than two covenants, but all had the same dynamic: God initiates the relationship, and we humans are called to either accept or reject it. Irenaeus said,

> [F]our principal covenants were given to the human race: the first was under Adam, prior to the deluge. The second was the one after the deluge, under Noah. The third was the giving of the law under Moses. The fourth is that which renovates man, and sums up all things in itself, by means of the Gospel.[2]

The church more commonly spoke of two covenants in the divine economy for the world's salvation: the "Old" and the "New," referring to the covenant with the Israelites, and the covenant in Jesus Christ. Irenaeus himself used this approach, declaring that "in both Testaments [covenants] there is the same righteousness of God."[3]

It would be too great a task, if not impossible, for a chapter such as this to survey the whole Eastern patristic corpus in search of all uses of the term *covenant*. A wiser and more realistic course is to examine the major writings of a church father who excels in his appreciation of the institution of marriage and to seek to discern how and where the idea of "covenant" appears in his writings.

I shall use St. John Chrysostom as a case study to answer the question, "Is there a concept of *covenant* in the Orthodox approach to marriage?" I was able

---

1. Michael W. Holmes, ed., *The Apostolic Fathers: Greek Texts and English Translations* (Grand Rapids: Baker Books, 1999), vol. 4, p. 313.

2. *Against Heresies*, bk. 3.11.8, in *The Ante-Nicene Fathers*, ed. Alexander Roberts and James Donaldson, 10 vols. (Buffalo: Christian Literature Publishing, 1885-1896), vol. 1, p. 429.

3. *Against Heresies*, bk. 4.28.1.

to find over one hundred and sixty references to *covenant* in the writings of St. John Chrysostom.[4] The vast majority of these references use the term *covenant* to refer to the dual "old" and "new" covenants of God with humanity — the first with the Hebrew people, the second with the whole created world, and, in particular, in the dispensation of Christ with his Church. Almost always, Chrysostom uses the Greek scriptural word *diatheke* when speaking of this phenomenon. An example of this widespread, biblically based understanding of *covenant* is found in the following passages from Chrysostom's *Gospel according to Matthew*. In the first homily he writes,

> [L]et us give strict heed unto the things that are written; and let us learn how the Old Law was given on the one hand, how on the other the New Covenant.
>
> How then was that law given in time past, and when, and where? After the destruction of the Egyptians, in the wilderness, on Mount Sinai, when smoke and fire were rising up out of the mountain, a trumpet sounding, thunders and lightnings, and Moses entering into the very depth of the cloud. But in the new covenant not so — neither in a wilderness, nor in a mountain, nor with smoke and darkness and cloud and tempest; but at the beginning of the day, in a house, while all were sitting together, with great quietness, all took place.[5]

And in the second homily he continues,

> [It is] as though any one were to place himself in the space between any two persons that were standing apart, and stretching forth both his hands were to lay hold on either side, and tie them together; even so hath He done, joining the old covenant with the new, God's nature with man's, the things that are His with ours.[6]

Another example is a passage where Chrysostom discusses the commandments of God, comparing those of the old covenant with those of the new and affirming their essential unity:

> [W]e say, that there is but one and the same Legislator of either covenant, who dispensed all meetly, and adapted to the difference of the times the difference between the two systems of law. Therefore neither are the first com-

4. As presented in *A Select Library of the Nicene and Post-Nicene Fathers*, first series, ed. Philip Schaff, 14 vols. (New York: Scribners, 1886-1889), vols. 9-12.

5. *Gospel According to Matthew*, Homily 1:2-3, in *Nicene and Post-Nicene Fathers*, vol. 10, pp. 1-2.

6. *Gospel According to Matthew*, Homily 2:3, in *Nicene and Post-Nicene Fathers*, vol. 10, p. 3.

mandments cruel, nor the second hard and grievous, but all of one and the same providential care.[7]

These examples of the use of the term *covenant* by Chrysostom refer to the core biblical understanding of the gracious action of God toward humanity and the creation, initiated by God and received by those who are made thus, God's people. This understanding of covenant predominates in Chrysostom.

From this perspective, the Protestant "covenant marriage" approach is problematic for the Orthodox. On the one hand, it is probably correct that translating the biblical idea of covenant into the kind of mutual agreement and commitment between husband and wife implied in the term *covenant* has a great deal to do with extra-ecclesial movements such as the legal emphasis of the West, the Enlightenment project, the rise of individualism, and the *syntheke* (contractual) mindset of capitalism. Yet, the Protestant effort to reconceptualize Christian marriage after the model of the biblical covenant(s) was an effort to elevate marriage and grant it a special nobility within the Christian framework of relationships. What I do not see is how contemporary Orthodox Christianity can adopt this position with integrity if it is to continue to claim rootedness in the patristic mindset *(phronema)*.

This observation should either signal the end of this contribution to the present volume or provoke an effort to do another kind of "translation" in a contemporary context. I propose to do that in terms of the biblically based tension regarding marriage and the monastic celibate life, including the assessment of marital sexual relations. The mutuality inherent in the idea of covenant marriage is reflected in the Orthodox tradition's understanding of the purposes and goals of marriage.

In the patristic and contemporary Orthodox Christian tradition, there are sharply differing views about marriage and the place of sex in marriage. On one side in the scriptural and patristic traditions, there are those who hold that marriage's only purpose is procreation. On the other, there are those who hold to a view that is much more compatible to the covenant idea of marriage: they hold that marriage is a multifaceted interrelationship of husband and wife in the unity of their persons, in which marital conjugal relations are not only for procreation but also for expressing the loving unity of the couple. In the history of the development of marriage in Eastern Christianity, a struggle between these two orientations or trajectories has and continues to take place. The touchstone for delineating these two orientations to marriage is the place of sex

---

7. *Gospel According to Matthew*, Homily 16:1, in *Nicene and Post-Nicene Fathers*, vol. 10, p. 109, sec. 8.

in marriage as part of the larger whole of the mutual relationships of spouses in their mutual love.

## Marriage as Sacramental, Interpersonal, and Incarnational

Chrysostom sometimes used the idea of covenant in ways that allow an understanding of marriage that goes beyond procreation to a more sacramental, interpersonal, and incarnational conceptionalization. In a letter to some Antiochian Presbyters, Chrysostom spoke of a "covenant of love," which he contrasts with business-type covenants. In business covenants, upon payment, one is poorer, the other richer. "But this is not what commonly happens in the covenant of love," Chrysostom wrote, referring to his brotherly relationship with the Presbyters. "[T]he payment of love makes him who pays richer than before."[8] Here, Chrysostom focused on the mutuality of relationships, a concept that emphasizes the quality of human affiliation that creates bonds of empathy and support. This kind of relationship may draw upon the covenant relationship between God and God's people, but it is not identical with it. In marriage, it would be proper to speak of a "covenant of love" between the spouses under and with God. The marriage is then seen as a sacrament in which the material dimensions of the couple's relationships on every level are vehicles for their exercise of mutual love.

Chrysostom also translated the concept of the covenant between God and his people to the personal relationship of catechumens and believers with Christ. In a letter to a lapsed believer Chrysostom expressed deep sorrow "because you have blotted out your name from the list of the brethren . . . knowing that the rejection of this covenant will bring great condemnation."[9] Such an approach affirms the voluntary dimension of commitment, which is needed to maintain deeply held relationships, even though in this case the commitment to God is interpreted as taking place among "the brethren." That commitment in a well-developing marriage is necessary and made possible for the Christian spouses by the sense that their marriage is a holy relationship in all of its expressions from the most mundane to the most lofty and spiritual. Marriage potentially incarnates the grace-filled presence of God only if it is consciously willed and chosen by the spouses.

In another place, speaking of the dying process, Chrysostom spoke of the

---

8. *To Castus, Valerius, Diophantus, Cyriacus, Presbyters of Antioch*, in *Nicene and Post-Nicene Fathers*, vol. 9, p. 304.

9. *Letter II*, in *Nicene and Post-Nicene Fathers*, vol. 9, p. 111.

soul making "that blessed covenant with the common master of us all."[10] Yet, the term used here is not *diatheke* but *suntheke,* a term used usually in human treaties and agreements.[11] The focus here seems to be not on externals but on the shared experience of the many, pointing, in the case of marriage, to a corporate, shared, communal dimension of the marital relationship. Husband and wife are more than two negotiating agents; partners in a common enterprise, in a shared life, they work out their salvation together.

Elsewhere, speaking to catechumens, who are about to confess their faith and be baptized, Chrysostom says of their commitment, "this word is a covenant with the Master."[12] Again, the term for covenant is not *diatheke* but *syntheke,* implying that here we are dealing with another kind of relationship of agreement, not the biblical understanding of covenant.[13] It is the shared sense that their agreement is not only between the two of them, like some legal contract, but that it includes Christ in the *syntheke.* Each Christian marriage is a partnership in life of spouses and Christ.

Nevertheless, nowhere does Chrysostom use the biblical understanding of the term *covenant (diatheke)* to discuss marriage and the relationships of spouses. In short, Chrysostom reserves the term *covenant* exclusively for the God-initiated saving economy, to which humanity is called to respond, accept, and remain faithful.

This case, I believe, is a model for the Eastern fathers in general. Authors such as John Witte Jr. and Max Stackhouse are thus correct in pointing to the Protestant source of the idea of "covenant marriage."[14] Covenant marriage is not a teaching of the patristic or the Eastern Orthodox tradition. Yet, there are some coincidences of content between the two views. Those who approach marriage as a "covenant," I believe, will find much to appreciate in the "sacramental" approach as expressed in the Eastern patristic and Orthodox Church traditions, and I would think the converse is also true.

For the Orthodox, however, there is an internal issue that places strains on its holistic "sacramental" approach, which expresses itself in deeply held positions about sexuality in marriage. These views have created a tension

10. *Instructions to Catechumens,* First Instruction, 1, in *Nicene and Post-Nicene Fathers,* vol. 9, p. 160; Migne, *Patrologia Graeca* (hereafter MPG), vol. 49, p. 225.

11. *Di' on ten makarian syntheken pros ton koinon emon apanton katathesetai Despoten.*

12. *Instructions to Catechumens,* Second Instruction, 5, in *Nicene and Post-Nicene Fathers,* vol. 9, p. 170.

13. *Aute gar he fone; syntheke pros ton Despoten estin,* in MPG, vol. 49, p. 239.

14. Max L. Stackhouse, *Covenant and Commitments: Faith, Family, and Economic Life* (Louisville: Westminster John Knox, 1997); John Witte Jr., *From Sacrament to Contract: Marriage, Religion, and Law in the Western Tradition* (Louisville: Westminster John Knox, 1997).

*within* Orthodox Christianity, which I describe in the categories of two "trajectories."

## Two Ecclesial Trajectories Regarding Marriage

Two views regarding marriage, and in particular sex in marriage, have been held in greater or lesser intensity almost continually in the history of the Orthodox Church. Sometimes, they are cast in mutually exclusive categories; sometimes they have reached an uneasy *modus vivendi;* sometimes they are treated as mutually complementary. Their coexistence in the life of the Church can be described in the category of "trajectories."[15]

David G. Hunter describes the New Testament as presenting what he calls an "ambivalent" view of marriage.[16] Within the apocalyptic milieu of the earliest strata of the Christian movement, marriage was a hindrance and procreation unessential, given the expected impending end of the inhabited world. The radical tone of this perspective is a powerful appeal that can be fulfilled only in an exclusive renunciation of the world, including the relationships of marriage and family. Christ says, "Whoever comes to me and does not hate father and mother, wife and children, yes, and even life itself, cannot be my disciple" (Luke 14:26; cf. Matt. 10:37). Note also the sharp and demanding approach of St. Paul: "It is well for a man not to touch a woman" (1 Cor. 7:1).

Nevertheless, the Gospels present another side to the picture. Jesus, in the context of speaking about celibacy, affirms that "not all men can receive this saying," and that "only he who is able to receive this, let him receive it" (Matt. 19:9-12). The words imply that there are those who have a calling *(klesis)* for abstinence from marriage and its sexual dimensions, and those who do not. Similarly, St. Paul recognized that not all are able to follow the celibate path as he does, approving of marriage not for procreation primarily but for the fulfillment of sexual needs. "Because of the temptation to immorality, each man should have his own wife and each woman, her own husband" (1 Cor. 7:2).

---

15. The term *trajectory* is applied primarily "to the curve that a body (as a planet or comet in its orbit or a rocket) describes in space." It is also applied metaphorically to describe "a path, progression, or line of development resembling a physical trajectory." *Merriam-Webster's Collegiate Dictionary,* tenth ed. (Springfield, Mass.: Merriam-Webster, 2000), p. 1248. In this chapter, the narrow understanding of sex in marriage as permissible only for the one purpose of procreation is called "the first trajectory"; and the view that holds that there are more purposes to relationships in marriage than procreation, is called "the second trajectory."

16. David G. Hunter, trans. and ed., *Marriage in the Early Church* (Minneapolis: Fortress, 1992), p. 4.

Ephesians 5 served to elevate the importance of marriage in the Christian value system by comparing the relationship of the spouses with that of Christ and the church. Love and respect are introduced into the marital relationship as a reflection of the intimate bond of Christ with the ecclesial body.

These juxtaposed biblical teachings have led the Eastern Christian tradition to what Father John Meyendorff has called "internal tensions." "In its interpretation of human sexuality, the family, and marriage itself, the Christian tradition, which was accepted as a norm in Byzantine society, is marked by internal tensions."[17] A few Gnostic Christians may have interpreted Christian freedom as a call to sexual excess.[18] More, by far, tended to the opposite extreme, condemning marriage and the sexual relations in it as a form of dualism. Movements such as Manichaeism, the Encratites, and Messalianism pushed strongly against the propriety of marriage. Thus, in the East, Meyendorff notes, "The two great Syrian writers of the fourth century, Aphrahat and St. Ephrem, considered sexual abstinence as normative after baptism, even for married couples."[19] Though a series of canons restricted such extreme ascetic teachings, anathematizing those who condemned marriage,[20] the first trajectory of suspicion toward sex, even in marriage, remained alive and strong throughout the first Christian millennium. Marriage in this trajectory was barely tolerated, but accepted primarily because of its reproductive function.[21]

Nevertheless, there are also positive evaluations of marriage in the patristic tradition. This we call "the second trajectory." For example, Clement of Alexandria followed St. Paul (1 Cor. 7:5) in counseling that couples who avoided marital sexual relations by agreement and for a time should then resume marital sexual relations, "for if he abstains from intercourse with his own wife, he may conceive a desire for another woman."[22] Clement held to the view that sexual

17. John Meyendorff, "Christian Marriage in Byzantium: The Canonical and Liturgical Tradition," Dumbarton Oaks Papers, number 44 (Washington, D.C.: Dumbarton Oaks Research Library and Collection, 1990), p. 99.

18. See Romans 6: "What shall we say then? Are we to continue in sin that grace may abound? By no means! How can we who died to sin still live in it?" (vv. 1-2) and "What then? Are we to sin because we are not under law but under grace? By no means!" (v. 15).

19. Meyendorff, "Christian Marriage in Byzantium"; Meyendorff cites A. A. Vöörbus, *Celibacy, A Requirement for Admission to Baptism in the Syrian Church* (Stockholm: Estonian Theological Society, 1951).

20. Council of Gangra (340 A.D.), canons 1, 9, 10, 14; and reaffirmed by the Sixth Ecumenical Council in Trullo (692).

21. Alexander Khazdan, "Byzantine Hagiography and Sex in the Fifth through Twelfth Centuries," Dumbarton Oaks Papers, number 44 (Washington, D.C.: Dumbarton Oaks Research Library and Collection, 1990), pp. 141-43.

22. Miscellenies 3, 12.79, translated in *Marriage in the Early Church*, ed. Hunter, p. 55.

intercourse in marriage is for procreation only, but he also agreed that it meets normal sexual needs. Though the rationale he provided for the procreation-only approach has been questioned as inadequate,[23] his *Miscellanies* (bk. 3, 12, 84) includes a beautiful and touching praise of other spiritual and interpersonal dimensions of Christian marriage.

Chrysostom pointed to the unitive and agapaic aspects of the marital relationship in writing, "The apostle wants each man to have as much love for his wife as he has for himself. It is not because we share one nature; no, the responsibility toward a wife is greater than that. It is because they are no longer two bodies, but one."[24] Thus, Chrysostom taught that marriage, according to Christ, is "a spiritual marriage,"[25] in which the Christian life is lived out in the partnership and yoke of lifelong commitment. In his *Commentary on Genesis,* Chrysostom came tantalizingly close to stating (at least the implications of) the Protestant idea of "covenant marriage" in emphasizing the mutuality of Christian spouses in their shared, but different, roles. Though the passage reflects some fourth-century social realities, it stands as a witness to a high and rich understanding of Christian marriage:

> The two spouses try to eradicate every cause for sorrow, to reinforce the harmony of the family and make it grow.
>
> The wife should abandon herself to her husband; and the husband, when he is free from the anxieties and troubles of public life, should find in the heart of his wife a safe haven where he can enjoy help and comfort.
>
> The wife in fact is the one who can help her husband. She has been given to him precisely for this purpose to be his consolation and strength.
>
> Her virtue and her sweetness are the joy of her husband; she is not only his companion but his helper in all sorts of circumstances. She makes everything easy and trouble-free for him; she does not weary him further by telling him the innumerable little complications that arise every day in the home. Like a capable pilot she succeeds in steering her husband's storm-tossed mind towards perfect serenity. Her steadiness is a source of great relaxation for him.
>
> Two souls united thus have nothing to fear either from present circumstances or future events. When there is harmony, peace and mutual love, the

23. See my article, "Christian Faith Concerning Creation and Biology," in *La Theologie dans L'Eglise et dans le Monde: Les Études theologiques de Chambesy - 4* (Chambesy, Switzerland: Publications of the Orthodox Center of the Ecumenical Patriarchate, 1984), pp. 226-47.

24. Homily 20 on Ephesians, 4, translated in *Marriage in the Early Church,* ed. Hunter, p. 83.

25. Homily 20 on Ephesians, p. 85.

man and his wife already possess everything good. No preoccupation vexes them and they can live serene behind the impregnable fortifications, which protect them, namely harmony in conformity with God.

For that reason they are harder than diamonds and tougher than steel. They walk with a firm step on the road to eternal life, enjoying the continual increase of divine grace. I urge you; let us place harmony above all good things, and undertake with all our strength to maintain peace and tranquility in our homes.[26]

The focus on multiple aspects of marriage in this passage, in which there is not even a single mention of procreation, provides an alternative approach to marriage, with multiple interrelated goals, values, goods, and purposes of the Christian marital relationship, and is a good example of the second trajectory.

## The Development of Marital Rituals

We turn now to sketch the development of the blessing of the marital relationship in and by the church in Byzantium and contemporary Orthodox Christianity.[27]

In its earliest forms, the marital blessings seem to have been brief, informal, and occasional. There are no marital rituals extant from the first strata of church history. The earliest indication we have of some sort of blessing comes from St. Ignatius of Antioch (35-107) when he wrote, "It is right for men and women who marry to contract their union with the advice of their bishop, so that their marriage is made in the Lord, and not for the sake of passion."[28] Tertullian (160-225) also indicated that some blessing of marriage, connected

26. John Chrysostom, *On Genesis*, 38, 7 (MPG, vol. 53, p. 359), translated in *Drinking from the Hidden Fountain: A Patristic Breviary*, Cistercian Studies Series no. 148 (Kalamazoo, Mich.: Cistercian Publications, 1993), pp. 194-95.

27. For material regarding the liturgical development of marital rites, East and West, see E. O. James, *Christian Myth and Ritual: A Historical Study* (Gloucester, Mass.: Peter Smith, 1973); John Meyendorff, "Christian Marriage in Byzantium," pp. 99-108; Demetrios Moraites, "Leitourgike - Ethike," in the general article "Gamos," in *Threskeutike kai Hthike Egkuklopaideia*, ed. A. Martinos (Athens: Martinos Publications, 1964), pp. 210-17; Kenneth Stevenson, *Nuptial Blessing: A Study of Christian Marriage Rites* (New York: Oxford University Press, 1983); Mark Searle and Kenneth W. Stevenson, *Documents of the Marriage Liturgy* (Collegeville, Minn.: Liturgical Press, 1992); Panagiotes N. Trembelas, *Mikron Euchologion. Tomos A'. Ai Akolouthvai kai Taxeis Mnestron kai Gamou, Euchelaiou, Cheirotonion kai Baptismatos Kata tous en Athenais Kodikas* (Athens: 1950); translations of this text are my own.

28. *Letter to Polycarp* 5.2.

with the Eucharist, took place at least in some places of the Christian church. He spoke of "that marriage which is made by the Church, confirmed by the oblation, sealed with the benediction which the angels proclaim, and which is ratified by our Father in heaven."[29] Contemporary scholars are reluctant to assign too much significance to these and similar statements. At most, Christians continued to be married in accordance with the requirements of Roman law, but it seems far-fetched to assume that a Christian bishop would simply give permission to a couple to marry without offering to them some sort of blessing as well. It seems hard to understand, also, how Tertullian's reference to the "oblation" could take place without some sort of blessing, which might easily become formalized with the passing of time.

According to Mark Searle and Kenneth Stevenson, "The presence of the clergy at Christian betrothals and marriages is attested as early as the third century in the East, but it was as honored guests that they attended and their role was restricted to giving a blessing at some point in the proceedings." "By the seventh century, however, the practice was becoming universal and mandatory, and the scene of both rites shifted from house to church."[30] Panagiotes Trembelas, in his liturgical textual studies, notes that the services of engagement and marriage are "presented according to the oldest and most authentic manuscripts as exceptionally brief and short."[31] Indications from the writings of Paulinus of Nola in the fifth century, the *Veronese Sacramentary* in the sixth century, and the Gelasian liturgical tradition dating from the mid 700s are characterized by brief prayers of blessings, not rites in and of themselves.

A distinct set of services for betrothal and marriage in the East appears in eighth-century manuscripts — in particular the *Barberini 336*. Even so, they are simple, direct, and relatively plain. Trembelas notes, for example, that only two prayers appear in the Barberini manuscript for the betrothal. The marriage service is also very brief, consisting of a few petitions, the prayer at the joining of the hands, and the crowning of the couple. By the tenth century, the Eastern marital services began to develop in complexity, even as the older, simpler forms remained dominant in the manuscript tradition. New prayers fill out the services in twelfth- and thirteenth-century manuscripts. But these extended texts are not uniform among themselves, varying in the texts used and in the order in which they appear. Trembelas notes that while the shorter and simpler form remained stable in the manuscript tradition, the longer and richer forms were "unstable and wavering" *(astatheis kai kumainomena).* One contribution

---

29. *To His Wife* II.9.
30. Searle and Stevenson, *Documents of the Marriage Liturgy,* p. 55.
31. Trembelas, *Mikron Euchologion,* p. 9.

to this development may well have been the development of imperial wedding rituals.

Both Trembelas and Phaedon Koukoules in his *Byzantinon Bios kai Politismos* see one source of this development in the spread of Byzantine imperial marriage practices to the rest of society. Trembelas adds that the first printed Orthodox service books were issued in Venice in the sixteenth century, with the longer version of the engagement and marriage ceremonies drawn primarily from manuscripts from southern Italy. These two observations will contribute to the conclusions to be drawn at the end of this chapter.

## The Positive View of Marriage in Contemporary Marital Rituals

To this point, I have argued that there are two trajectories in the Eastern Christian tradition regarding the goals, goods, ends, and purposes of marriage. Both have roots in the Bible and in the patristic tradition. One trajectory sees procreation as the only goal of marriage. It generally holds that the sexual relations that lead to procreation are essentially a submission of marriage to an otherwise unchristian and undesirable involvement with pleasure *(hedone)*. The second trajectory has a much broader conception of the goals, goods, ends, and purposes of marriage, a view that consequently allows for greater sexual expression within marriage, as a good. The development of increasingly complex and rich liturgical rites for the sanctification of marriage in the engagement service and the sacrament of holy matrimony is an embodiment of the second broader trajectory.

There is no doubt that the values incorporated in the texts of the engagement service and the sacrament of holy matrimony affirm the idea that the Orthodox Christian approach to marriage, while including procreation as a major purpose of marriage, includes other goals, goods, ends, and purposes, and that the liturgical rites themselves are a powerful statement of support and advocacy for marriage as a part and expression of the Christian life. Further, a close examination of the texts of these two services, now conducted exclusively as a single liturgical act, will show that there is a deliberate mixing of these goals so that none of them, including procreation, is given priority.

### Theological Groundings

The rites of marriage highlight numerous theological teachings that promote and enhance marriage in the Orthodox Christian framework of life. Among these are (1) the doctrine of creation and marriage as part of it; (2) the connection of the married with the people of God, in particular with the married couples of sacred history; and (3) their relationship to the kingdom of God and the church, the Scriptures, and salvation. To these are added the affirmation that those who are being engaged or married are servants of God, that the marriage is conducted in the name of the Holy Trinity, and most important, that the one who blesses the marriage is the Lord himself.

First, one of the most important affirmations regarding the existence of marriage is that it is the result of God's divine creative action. There are several repeated affirmations in this regard. Thus, for example, in the engagement service the priest affirms, "You, O Lord, from the beginning have created male and female, and by You is a woman joined to a man for assistance and for the continuation of the human race."[32] The first prayer in the sacrament of holy matrimony, following the litany, repeats God's declaration in Genesis — "It is not good for man to be alone upon the earth; let us make a helpmate for him" — as well as the subsequent events, affirming that "'whom God has joined together, let no man put asunder.'" Immediately following is the invocation: "And now, O Master, Lord our God, send down Your heavenly Grace upon these Your servants, *(Name)* and *(Name)*."[33] The reminder that God is the author of marriage and that God joins the spouses together is not only a theological position, it is an affirmation of the holiness of the married state.

Second, the inclusion of the couple about to be married as being part of the people of God is another affirmation of the sanctity of the marital union. Thus, the rite declares: "Therefore, O Lord God, Who has sent forth Your truth to Your inheritance and Your promise to Your servants, our fathers, who were Your elect, do You give regard unto this Your servant *(Name)* and Your servant *(Name)*."[34] Perhaps one of the most striking illustrations of this affirmation

32. Fr. John von Holzhausen and Fr. Michael Gelsinger, trans., Fr. N. M. Vaporis, ed., *An Orthodox Prayer Book* (Brookline, Mass.: Holy Cross Orthodox Press, 1977), Service of Betrothal (Final Prayer), p. 78. All subsequent references to the liturgical marital texts in this section are from this translation and edition.

33. The relevant portion of the prayer says ". . . do You Yourself now, O Master, Who in the beginning created man, and appointed him as the king of creation, and said, 'It is not good for man to be alone upon the earth; let us make a helpmate for him;' then, taking one of his ribs, made woman, whom when Adam saw, he said, 'This is now bone of my bones, and flesh of my flesh, for she was taken out of her man. For this cause shall a man forsake his father and his mother, and cleave unto his wife, and two shall be one flesh;' and 'whom God has joined together, let no man put asunder.' And now, O Master, Lord our God, send down Your heavenly Grace upon these Your servants, *(Name)* and *(Name)*." Sacrament of Holy Matrimony (First Prayer), p. 83.

34. Service of Betrothal (Prayer of Engagement), p. 78.

that the married are among the people of God is the liturgical procession around the table in front of the iconostasis, known as the Dance of Isaiah. Different interpretations of this ritual act have been offered through the centuries. What is clear is that the circumlocution, led by the priest sometimes holding the Gospel book, calls for hymns that connect the names of Isaiah, the Virgin Mother, her Son, "Emmanuel, Who came as both God and man," the holy martyrs, and the apostles to the marriage and to the married couple. They are surrounded by divine and holy persons, affirming the sanctity of their new relationship.[35]

One of the striking theological emphases in the Byzantine marriage rituals is the long and sustained connection of the couple about to be married with the married persons of the Old and New Testaments. The new couple is thus seen as joining the ranks of a whole line of holy married figures in sacred history. One might even suggest that these prayers envisage a parade of married persons beginning with Adam and Eve and including both Old and New Testament couples, at the end of which the church places those whose marriage is now taking place. Thus, in the second prayer following the litany in the sacrament of holy matrimony, God is called upon to bless the couple, just as he blessed Abraham and Sara, Isaac and Rebecca, Jacob and all the prophets, Joseph and Asenath, Moses and Zipporah from the Old Testament; and Joakim and Anna, Zacharias and Elizabeth from the New Testament. The couple is also made part of the history of salvation, when prayers are offered that God preserve them as he protected "Noah in the ark, Jonah in the whale, and the Three holy Youths from the fiery furnace." The prayer also connects them with the discovery of the True Cross by St. Helena, and the Forty Holy Martyrs who received crowns from heaven.[36] It is clear that this prayer functions to associate not only mar-

---

35. The full text is as follows:

> *Then he takes the Bridal Pair, while the Groomsman holds the Crowns behind and above them, and leads them in a circle around the Analogion thrice. The people sing:*
>
> O Isaiah, dance your joy, for the Virgin was indeed with child; and brought to birth — a Son, that Emmanuel, Who came as both God and man; Day-at-the-Dawn is the Name He bears, and by extolling Him, We hail the Virgin as blessed.
>
> Hear us, you martyred Saints, who fought the good fight, gaining crowns: entreat the Lord to shed His tender mercy on our souls.
>
> Glory to You, O Christ our God, Your Apostles' proudest boast and treasure of Your Martyrs' joy, Who to all proclaimed the Consubstantial Trinity.
>
> Sacrament of Holy Matrimony (Dance of Isaiah), p. 94.

36. The text reads as follows: "(+) Bless them, O Lord our God, as you blessed Abraham and Sara. (+) Bless them, O Lord our God, as You blessed Isaac and Rebecca. (+) Bless them, O Lord our God, as you blessed Jacob and all the Prophets. (+) Bless them, O Lord our God, as You

riage, but the specific married couple, with the married couples of the history of salvation, thus assuring the acceptance, blessedness, legitimacy, uprightness, and sanctity of the marital state.[37]

Third, the ancient connection of the sacrament of holy matrimony with the Eucharist has left its traces in the present service that begins with the blessing of the "Kingdom of the Father, and of the Son and of the Holy Spirit."[38] This should be contrasted with the beginning words of the Engagement or Betrothal Service, "Blessed is our God always, both now and ever, and to the ages of ages."[39] The late Father Alexander Schmemann highlighted this aspect of marriage, describing marriage as the induction of an ordinary pan-human social institution into the life of the kingdom of God.

Considered sacramentally, the sanctification of the married state as incorporated in the kingdom of God is sharply emphasized in the selection of the Epistle reading for the sacrament of holy matrimony — Ephesians 5:20-33. This passage describes the relationship of Christ to the church as the church's loving head and Lord and compares this relationship to the relationship of the spouses:

> Husbands, love your wives, as Christ loved the church and gave himself up for her, that he might sanctify her, having cleansed her by the washing of water with the word, that he might present the church to himself in splendor, without spot or wrinkle or any such thing, that she might be holy and without blemish. Even so husbands should love their wives as their own bodies.

---

blessed Joseph and Asenath. (+) Bless them, O Lord our God, as You blessed Moses and Zipporah. (+) Bless them, O Lord our God, as You blessed Joakim and Anna. (+) Bless them, O Lord our God, as You blessed Zacharias and Elizabeth. Preserve them, O Lord our God, as You preserved Noah in the Ark. Preserve them, O Lord our God, as You preserved Jonah in the jaw of the seabeast. Preserve them, O Lord our God, as You preserved the holy Three Children from the fire, when You sent down upon them the dew of the Heavens. And may that joy come upon them which the blessed Helen had when she found the Precious Cross. Remember them, O Lord our God, as You remembered Enoch, Shem, and Elias. Remember them, O Lord our God, as You remembered Your holy Forty Martyrs, sending down upon them the crowns from the Heavens." Sacrament of Holy Matrimony (Second part of second prayer after the Litany), pp. 85-86.

37. Note also this same connection in the *Apolysis* or dismissal benediction of the Sacrament of Holy Matrimony: "He, Who by His presence in Cana of Galilee declared marriage to be honorable, Christ our true God, through the intercessions of His all-pure Mother, of the holy, glorious, and all-praiseworthy Apostles, of the holy, God-crowned and Equal-to-the-Apostles Constantine and Helen, of the Holy, great Martyr Procopios, and of all the holy Saints, have mercy on us and save us, as our good and loving Lord." Sacrament of Holy Matrimony (Benediction/Apolysis), p. 96.

38. Sacrament of Holy Matrimony *(Enarxis)*, p. 81.

39. Service of Betrothal *(Enarxis)*, p. 75.

The headship of Christ is a concept that reflects the kingdom of God. In the Ephesians text an analogy between the kingdom of God and marriage is clearly drawn.[40]

Of special interest here and below (where the liturgical texts focus on the relationship of the spouses-to-be) is the comparison between the Byzantine Orthodox selection of biblical readings for the marriage rite and those in the Western Latin tradition. As E. O. James puts it, referring to ninth-century texts, "[T]he Mass of the Holy Trinity was said with 1 Corinthians vi, 15-20 as the Epistle — in which the physical union constituting the obligation of the marriage bond is taught — and St. Matthew xiv, 3-6 as the Gospel, setting forth the indissolubility of the alliance."[41] The tone of these contrasting selections for the marital blessing is significant. The emphasis on "the obligation of the marriage bond" together with the emphasis on the "indissolubility of the alliance" are legal concepts. The choice of Ephesians 5 with its emphasis on the kingdom, churchly, and love elements of marriage provides a contrast, placing the marital relationship in an ecclesial and interpersonal context. Ephesians 5 concludes with the verse, "This is a great mystery, and I take it to mean Christ and the church; however, let each one of you love his wife as himself, and let the wife see that she respects her husband."[42]

The Gospel passage for the Western marital mass (Matt. 19:3-9) warns the couple of the indissolubility of their marriage. The Gospel passage in the Byzantine liturgy of marriage (John 2:1-11) presents the joyous occasion of the marriage in Cana of Galilee and Christ's miracle of changing water to wine. The last line of the pericope connects the joy of the wedding and the first of Jesus' public miracles with the manifestation of divine glory: "This, the first of his signs, Jesus did at Cana in Galilee, and manifested his glory; and his disciples believed in him." Surely, the progression of marriage, messianic sign, manifestation of glory, and apostolic belief occasioned by the presence of Christ at the marriage observance serves to send a message of affirmation and acceptance.[43]

Marriage is thus presented very positively and as an integral element of living the life of the kingdom of God. The ecclesial dimension, when related to marriage and its functions, affirms the inclusion of marriage in the work of redemption and the sanctifying presence of the Holy Spirit. Thus, at the blessing of the rings in the Service of the Engagement, the priest prays: "O Lord our God, Who espoused the Church as a pure virgin called from out of the Gentiles,

---

40. Sacrament of Holy Matrimony (Epistle), pp. 88-89.
41. James, *Christian Myth and Ritual*, p. 167.
42. Sacrament of Holy Matrimony (Epistle), pp. 88-89.
43. Sacrament of Holy Matrimony (Gospel), p. 90.

bless this Betrothal (+), uniting these Your servants, keeping them in peace and oneness of mind."[44] The relationship of the forthcoming marriage of the couple and the purity of the church is thus accented and affirmed.

## Scriptures

This discussion leads directly to positive and affirmative connections between biblical stories and events and marriage. The old Roman practice of using a ring or rings as symbols of the pledge given between spouses is transformed by being subsumed to biblical imagery. Note also that in the prayer regarding the blessing of the rings, God is incorporated into the action: "For You, O Lord, have declared that a pledge is to be given and held inviolate in all things." The exchange of rings is related to the authority of Joseph in Egypt, the Babylonian exaltation of Daniel, and the compassionate father's acceptance of the prodigal son.[45] We have already seen other examples of the marital rite's effort to repeatedly connect the couple being married with other biblical personages and events.

Perhaps the most dominant scriptural theme in the service, in addition to the creation passages that apply to marriage, is the parallelism between the marital sacrament and the presence of Christ and his mother at the marriage of Cana. There, Christ's public ministry was inaugurated with the miracle of transforming water to wine, as one of the petitions puts it, calling the congregation to pray, "That this marriage may be blessed as was that of Cana of Galilee."[46] Thus, biblical material is included, exegeted, interpreted, and presented in the services of betrothal and marriage in the Byzantine rites so as to affirm the propriety of marriage. This heavy biblical emphasis affirms the second trajectory of the church's attitude toward marriage.

## Salvation

A striking theologically oriented inclusion in the rites for marriage is the repeated connection of marriage with the reality of salvation. Salvation is fre-

44. Service of Betrothal (Prayer at Blessing of Rings), p. 77.

45. The text affirms that "By a ring Joseph was given might in Egypt; by a ring Daniel was exalted in Babylon; by a ring the truth of Thamar was made manifest; by a ring our heavenly Father showed compassion upon His prodigal son, for He said, 'Put a ring upon his right hand, kill the fatted calf, and let us eat and rejoice.' Your own right hand, O Lord, armed Moses in the Red Sea." Service of Betrothal (Prayer of Engagement), pp. 78-79.

46. Sacrament of Holy Matrimony (Inserted Matrimonial Litanies, Petition 3), p. 82.

quently associated with the rites of matrimony. If one were seeking to shore up marriage in the face of negative assessments of it, certainly one of the most powerful concepts to highlight is that salvation is associated with it. Thus, salvation is the first thing that is mentioned in the betrothal service: "For the servant of God *(Name)* and the servant of God *(Name)* who now pledge themselves to one another, and for their salvation; let us pray to the Lord."[47] Later, a petition asks, "That there may be granted unto them and unto us all prayers that tend unto salvation."[48] At the sharing of the common cup, the chant from the Psalms is intoned: "I will drink from the cup of salvation; I will call upon the name of the Lord."[49] Though initially this most certainly was included to refer to participation in the Eucharist by the marital couple, its retention with the exclusive use of the common and shared cup of ordinary wine continues the affirmation in principle that marriage and salvation are mutually inclusive.

Furthermore, the couple is frequently identified as "servants of God," a powerfully positive term applied to the prophets of the Old Testament and to the saints of the New Testament.[50] Thus, in the litany of the sacrament, the priest or deacon intones, "For the servants of God, *(Name)* and *(Name)*, who are now being joined to one another in the community of Marriage, and for their salvation; let us pray to the Lord."[51] Theologically, a "servant of God" is one who is a faithful and committed part of the ecclesial household and living in the context of church life, and in the framework of the growth toward God-likeness *(theosis)* and spiritual illumination *(photismos)*.

Another element in the theological framework of the marital rites is that repeatedly the prayers and liturgical actions are connected intimately with the sacred name of the Holy Trinity. The crowning rite provides us with just one example:

*After the Amen, the Priest, taking up the Crowns, crowns first the Bridegroom, saying:* The servant of God *(Name)* is crowned for the servant of God *(Name)*, in the Name of the Father, and of the Son, and of the Holy Spirit. Amen. *(Thrice) And he crowns the Bride, saying:* The servant of God *(Name)*

47. Service of Betrothal (Inserted Engagement Litanies, Petition 1), p. 75.

48. Sacrament of Holy Matrimony (Inserted Matrimonial Litanies, Petition 5), p. 82.

49. Psalm 116:13. Sacrament of Holy Matrimony (Common Cup), p. 94. The Septuagint version in 115:4 is "poterion soteriou lepsomai kai to onoma Kyriou epikalesomai."

50. See: 2 Corinthians 6:4, "but as servants of God we commend ourselves in every way"; Titus 1:1, "Paul, a servant of God and an apostle of Jesus Christ"; James 1:1, "James, a servant of God and of the Lord Jesus Christ"; 1 Peter 2:16, "Live as free men, yet without using your freedom as a pretext for evil, but live as servants of God."

51. Sacrament of Holy Matrimony (Inserted Matrimonial Litanies, Petition 5), p. 82.

is crowned for the servant of God *(Name)*, in the Name of the Father, and of the Son, and of the Holy Spirit. Amen. *(Thrice)*[52]

Finally, unlike the Roman Catholic theological understanding, based on old Roman law, that the couple marries themselves with the church as a witness, and the usual Protestant practice in which the presiding minister pronounces the couple man and wife after vows are exchanged, the texts of the Orthodox services of betrothal and marriage clearly express the view that it is God who officiates, and blesses the union. In this is a close resemblance to the epiclesis in the Eucharist, and the use of the passive voice in other sacramental actions (for example, "The servant of God is baptized. . ." rather than "I baptize you. . . ."). Thus, after the exchange of the rings in the engagement, the priest implores, "O Sovereign Lord, do You Yourself *[Autos oun kai nyn, Despota]* bless this putting on of rings with Your heavenly benediction *[eulogian ouranion];* and may Your Angel go before them all the days of their life."[53] So also the concluding prayer calls upon God to bless the betrothal: "[D]o You Yourself bless *[Autos eulogeson]* the betrothal of these Your servants *(Name)* and *(Name)* and confirm the word that has been spoken by them."[54] This is clearly more emphatic than simply having the clergyman bless the marriage with prayers and invocations. These petitions affirm that it is God himself who officiates at the wedding.

In the second of the three prayers prior to the crowning of the couple, the role of God is made explicit when the priest prays, "Blessed are You, O Lord our God, Holy Celebrant of mystical and pure marriage *[ho tou mystikou kai acharantou Hierourgos].* . . ."[55] And, at the joining of the couple's hands, which might readily be considered the "epicletic moment" of the sacrament of holy matrimony, the priest prays, as he joins the hands of the couple,

Holy God, Who fashioned man from the dust, and from his rib fashioned woman, and joined her to him as a helpmate for him, for it was seemly unto Your Majesty for man not to be alone upon the earth, do You Yourself, O Sovereign Lord, stretch forth Your hand from Your holy dwelling place, and join together *(When this is said, the priest joins their right hands)* this Your servant *(Name)* and Your servant *(Name)*, *for by You is a wife joined to her husband.*[56]

---

52. Sacrament of Holy Matrimony (Exchange of Crowns), pp. 87-88.
53. Service of Betrothal (Final Prayer of Engagement), p. 79.
54. Service of Betrothal (Final Prayer of Engagement), p. 78.
55. Sacrament of Holy Matrimony (Second Prayer), p. 83.
56. Sacrament of Holy Matrimony (Prayer at the Joining of the Hands), p. 87; emphasis added.

Thus, when read from the perspective being emphasized in this chapter, we can discern a concerted effort to ground marriage and the relationship of the about-to-be-married couple in a fully theological matrix. A series of theologically based arguments — which can be perceived as an argument supporting marriage in the face of those who would ecclesially and spiritually denigrate it — are inserted in the services of marriage and in reference to married persons, which connect them to core elements of the Christian faith and life.

## Relationships

In addition to these theologically focused elements, the marriage rites also emphasize numerous elements of Christian virtue, with particular emphasis on interpersonal relationships that are intimately embodied in the Christian ethos and life in God. In the face of the first trajectory's denigration of married life and its assumptions that sexual intimacy cannot be a vehicle for authentic Christian living, except in the most limited ways, the marriage rites exemplify the view that Christian marriage can be a vehicle for Christian virtue.

An excellent example can be found in the litany at the beginning of the service of betrothal. The first petition having to do with marriage emphasizes the relationship created by the mutual pledge given by the couple, expressing trustworthiness in the context of living out their salvation in Christ. Implied is a parallel between the monastic commitment for life *(monachike koura),* which is permanent and lifelong, and the marital commitment for life, which is also permanent and lifelong: "For the servant of God *(Name)* and the servant of God *(Name)* who now pledge themselves to one another, and for their salvation; let us pray to the Lord."[57] In the course of that litany, God is asked to grant the couple a long series of virtues including "perfect love," "peace," "divine protection," "oneness of mind," "steadfastness of Faith," "harmony," "perfect trust," a "blameless life," and, regarding their sexual life, "an honorable marriage and a bed undefiled."[58]

At the beginning of the service of holy matrimony, the first petition having to do with marriage in the litany uses a particularly striking phrase to describe the relationship of husband and wife, "who are now being joined to one another in the community of Marriage."[59] The Greek originals of these phrases are very powerful terms. "Being joined to one another" in Greek is *synaptomenon allelois,* composed of *syn,* together, and *apto,* which among its meanings includes touch,

---

57. Service of Betrothal (Inserted Engagement Litanies, Petition 1), p. 75.

58. Service of Betrothal (Inserted Engagement Litanies, Petitions 3-7), pp. 75-76.

59. Sacrament of Holy Matrimony (Inserted Matrimonial Litanies, Petition 1), p. 82.

embrace, and partake sacramentally.[60] The composite word *synapto* and its cognates carry meanings such as compounding, conjoining, uniting together, fastening, and attaching. St. Cyril of Alexandria notes that the term is used to emphasize the extreme fullness of union *(synapheian)*.[61] Not unexpectedly, the term *synapheian* also has theological implications,[62] relating to patristic teachings of the doctrines of both the Holy Trinity and the incarnation.

Similarly, the term *community of marriage (gamou koinonian)* has rich interpersonal and theological implications. Patristic uses of the term *koinonia* connote meanings such as communion, association, connection, sharing, community of life, sharing love and life, mutual imparting, and the like. This term is also frequently used theologically in reference to Trinitarian, christological, ecclesial, and sacramental patristic expositions, including union with Christ and Eucharistic participation, that it would be out of place to develop here.[63] The choice of these heavily laden terms to describe the physical, interpersonal relationships and the spiritual union of a married couple contributes to the elevation in estimation, value, and importance of Christian marriage.

The sexual relationship is also mentioned several times during these services. Phrases used, some of which have been noted above, include, "an honorable marriage" *(timion ton gamon)*, "a bed undefiled" *(he koite amiantos)*, and "fruit of the womb as may be most expedient for them." In the sacrament of holy matrimony, the petition is made, "Join them together in oneness of mind; crown them with wedlock into one flesh."[64] There is no embarrassment regarding the sexual aspect of marriage, no apology, no sense of its moral impropriety. It is, to be sure, not highlighted or focused upon, but nowhere in the marital rites is there any apology or reticence about it, either. Sexual relations are simply accepted as an essential aspect of marriage.

An extremely important relationship aspect of the marital rites is the striking presence of mutuality in the marital relationship. Clearly, the biblical formal headship of the husband is also found in the texts of the services, as seen, for example, in the fact that the blessing of the groom with the rings in the engagement service comes first, as is the case also with the crowns in the marriage sacrament proper. What is remarkable is how the common and shared aspects

60. G. W. H. Lampe, ed., *A Patristic Greek Lexicon* (Oxford: Clarendon, 1961), p. 222.
61. He says, *"tou synephthenai legein, to te kolleseos onoma, meizona pou pantos kai axiologoteran ten emphasin echei: eiper estin alethes eipein, os to tisi kollomenon, en epitasei polle ten sunapheian echei." Quod Unus Sit Christus,* 51.733, in Lampe, *A Patristic Greek Lexicon,* p. 1305a.
62. Lampe, *A Patristic Greek Lexicon,* pp. 1305b-1306a.
63. Lampe, *A Patristic Greek Lexicon,* pp. 762-64.
64. Sacrament of Holy Matrimony (Third Prayer, Joining of Hands), p. 87.

of the marital relationship is, nevertheless, repeatedly emphasized. Again, there is a contrast to early Western practices, when the engagement would take place with only one ring, given by the groom-to-be to the bride-to-be.[65] E. O. James describes one aspect of a tenth-century English marriage ceremony, the giving of the dowry by the husband to the wife. He writes: "The bride prostrated herself at the feet of her husband if he gave her land, where the *Sarum Manual* required her to kiss his right foot."[66]

By contrast, the present Byzantine texts show a remarkable and striking emphasis on the mutuality of the relationship between husband and wife. The exact same words are used for both the man and the woman in the exchange of the rings and of the crowns, and both share equally in drinking from the common cup. Further, the mutuality of these symbolic acts is highlighted with their threefold repetition. While the man's name is placed first in the first exchange and repeated three times, in the second threefold exchange, the woman's name is placed first and the husband's second. The pledge is mutual, the exchange of rings is mutual, the exchange of the crowns is mutual, since they are pledged and crowned "for each other."[67] The mutuality theme is further emphasized by the older practice of the couple receiving Holy Communion side by side and by the later practice of the couple drinking from the common cup, a symbol, also, of their pledge to share "the cup of life" together.

A final aspect of the mutuality emphasized in these rites is the differentiation of roles in the marital relationship at the removal of the crowns at the end of the service. The priest lifts first the crown of the husband, exalting him by comparing him with Abraham, Isaac, and Jacob, and calling for him to be magnified, blessed, and increased. He is enjoined to leave the rite as a married man, "in peace, performing in righteousness the commandments of God."[68] Then

65. James, *Christian Myth and Ritual*, p. 159.
66. James, *Christian Myth and Ritual*, p. 160.
67. The text is as follows:

> "*After the Amen, the Priest, taking up the Crowns, crowns first the Bridegroom, saying:*
> "The servant of God *(Name)* is crowned for the servant of God *(Name)*, in the Name of the Father, and of the Son, and of the Holy Spirit. Amen. *(Thrice)*
> "*And he crowns the Bride, saying:*
> "The servant of God *(Name)* is crowned for the servant of God *(Name)*, in the Name of the Father, and of the Son, and of the Holy Spirit. Amen. *(Thrice)*
> "*The Priest takes the Crown of the Groom in his right hand, and the Crown of the Bride in his left, and places them on their heads while he intones:* O Lord, our God, crown them with glory and honor."
> Sacrament of Holy Matrimony (Crowning), pp. 87-88.

68. The text is as follows: "*Then the Priest removes the Crowns, taking first that of the Groom*

the wife's crown is raised above her head as she is exalted by being compared with Sarah, Rebecca, and Rachel. The prayer for her is that she be magnified, rejoiced and increased. She is to be "glad in [her] husband, keeping the paths of the law, for so God is well pleased."[69] In their distinct roles, they are mutually blessed, and they are mutually expected to perform righteousness, follow the commandments of God and his law, and in doing so, they will please God.

The virtues of relationship emphasized in the marriage rites are those that are appropriate and most fitting to Christians in marriage. They are not essentially different from those of the monastic and celibate callings, but they are expressed in different ways and contexts. The married are also called to spiritual exercise and struggle *(askesis kai agona)*, but in a quite different way. Their calling does not have the single-mindedness of the monastic, since it focuses more on relationships with others, including spouse, children, family, and social life. That is why the Orthodox tradition consistently places it in second place to the celibate ascetic life. Nevertheless, in marriage, the same virtues of the monastic life (sexual purity, poverty, and obedience) are lived in different ways, in what Russian Orthodox theologian Paul Evdokimov called "Interiorized Monasticism."[70]

I have summarized elsewhere the meaning of this concept of "interiorized monasticism" — that nonmonastic Christians are called upon to transform the vows of monastics in a way that gives deeper and richer meaning to their own Christian lives. Thus, those who are married are not to deny the sexual aspect of their married life, but they are to keep the whole of their marriage relationships wholesome, pure, and undefiled. They are to "interiorize" the proper use of their material resources by using them in the service of love for the needs of the poor, downtrodden, and suffering. And they are to take their own role as followers of Christ seriously, in the home, at work, in recreation, in friendship, as citizens, and as Christians in the world.[71] Thus, all relationships in marriage are essential aspects of living the Christian life. From the perspective of this chap-

---

*and saying:* Be magnified, O Bridegroom, as Abraham, and blessed as Isaac, and increased as was Jacob. Go your way in peace, performing in righteousness the commandments of God." Sacrament of Holy Matrimony (Prayer at the Removal of the Crowns), pp. 94-95.

69. The text reads: "*He takes the Crown of the Bride and says:* And you, O Bride, be magnified as was Sarah and rejoiced as was Rebecca, and increased as was Rachel, being glad in your husband, keeping the paths of the Law, for so God is well pleased." Sacrament of Holy Matrimony (Prayer at the Removal of Crowns), pp. 94-95.

70. P. Evdokimov, *Sacrement de l'amour: Le Mystere conjugal a la lumiere de la tradition orthodoxe* (Paris: Editions de l'Epi, 1962), subsequently published in Greek, 1967, as *To Mysterion tes Agapes* (The Mystery of Love), and in English as *The Sacrament of Love: The Nuptial Mystery in the Light of the Orthodox Tradition* (Crestwood, N.Y.: St. Vladimir's Seminary Press, 1985).

71. Stanley S. Harakas, "Religious Question Box," *Hellenic Chronicle* (November 13, 1986), p. 4.

ter, interpersonal relationships in marriage also serve to highlight the Christian legitimacy and spiritual content of marriage as the church sees it. As a statement of values, it affirms the importance and significance of marriage as an aspect of the Christian life.

## Multiplicity of Goals

The first trajectory limits the purpose of marriage to the procreation of children, as we have seen. Any other sexual expression is considered to be an improper submission of marital sexual union to pleasure-seeking. It is important to note, as we have above, that the second trajectory understands the goals, goods, ends, and purposes of marriage in a much larger context, though certainly not excluding the goal of procreation. When we examine the marital texts we can affirm that they are an excellent expression of a wider and more comprehensive understanding of the goals and purposes of marriage, and that there does not seem to be any ranking of these goals in any kind of hierarchy.

There is no question at all that the rites of engagement and the sacrament of holy matrimony affirm the importance and desirability of the procreation of children. Early in the engagement text, the congregation is instructed to pray "that there may be promised unto them children for the continuation of their race, granting unto them all their prayers unto salvation."[72] In the sacrament proper, the initial processional psalm proclaims: "Your wife shall be as a fruitful vine on the sides of your house. . . . Your children like young olive plants around your table. . . . Yea! You shall see your children's children."[73] The importance of procreation as one of the purposes of marriage is highlighted from the beginning of the text of the sacrament of holy matrimony in the initial litany.

72. Service of Betrothal (Inserted Engagement Litanies, Petition 2), p. 75.
73. The abbreviated text, with its refrain, as usually sung, is:

> Your wife shall be as a fruitful vine on the sides of your house.
> Glory to You, O our God, Glory to You.
> Your children like young olive plants around your table.
> Glory to You, O our God, Glory to You.
> Behold! The man shall be blessed that fears the Lord.
> Glory to You, O our God, Glory to You.
> The Lord shall bless you out of Zion, and you shall see the good things of
> Jerusalem all the days of your life.
> Glory to You, O our God, Glory to You.
> Yea! You shall see your children's children, and peace be upon Israel.
> Glory to You, O our God, Glory to You.
>                    Sacrament of Holy Matrimony (Processional Psalm), pp. 80-81.

In these petitions the congregation is exhorted to pray for the couple that they may be given "fruit of the womb as may be most expedient for them," that they "rejoice in the beholding of sons and daughters," and "[t]hat there may be granted unto them the happiness of abundant fertility."[74]

But the rites also emphasize other goals of marriage beyond procreation. We have already seen in the petitions of the service of holy matrimony the concept of "soberness of life," indicating that the sexual aspects of life are properly exercised in marriage only, thus calling for marital fidelity and proscribing adultery. The appeal that the couple be blessed with "fruit of the womb as may be most expedient for them" at least allows for the idea that procreation may have limitations attached to it, allowing other values and goals to influence the number and spacing of children. Their life as a married couple is not blameworthy nor something for which they are to sense any shame. The petition asks "That there may be granted unto them . . . a course of life blameless and unashamed."[75]

The goal of companionship and mutual assistance is also noted in the rites, including the biblical passage: "'It is not good for man to be alone upon the earth; let us make a helpmate for him'; then, taking one of his ribs, [God] made woman." This goal takes precedence even over the goal of procreation. This same passage is paraphrased in the third prayer of the sacrament: "Holy God, Who fashioned man from the dust, and from his rib fashioned woman, and joined her to him as a helpmate for him, for it was seemly unto Your Majesty for man not to be alone upon the earth."

The unity of the couple is another value and goal included in the rites. Thus, the first prayer of the sacrament refers to their union, with sexual implications. It speaks of their "conjoining," which "declared them both to be one member." Similarly, in the same prayer, marital sexual intercourse is "a lawful union," and Christ's presence at the marriage in Cana "blessed the marriage there" and was to show that marriage "is according to [God's] Will."[76]

---

74. The full text reads:

> That there may be given unto them soberness of life, and fruit of the womb as may be most expedient for them; let us pray to the Lord.
> That they may rejoice in the beholding of sons and daughters; let us pray to the Lord.
> That there may be granted unto them the happiness of abundant fertility, and a course of life blameless and unashamed; let us pray to the Lord.
>
> Sacrament of Holy Matrimony<br>(Inserted Litanies, Petitions 3, 4, and 5), p. 82.

75. Sacrament of Holy Matrimony (Inserted Litanies, Petition 4).

76. "Who through Your unspeakable Grace and plentiful goodness were present in Cana of

It is illuminating to compare the order of some of the lists that identify the ends, goals, and purposes of marriage in the marriage rites. There does not seem to be any pattern or ranking among them. In particular, in spite of the importance of procreation, it is not listed with regularity in the first place. For example, the first prayer of the sacrament calls for the following: "a peaceful life, length of days, chastity, love for one another in a bond of peace, offspring long-lived, fair fame by reason of their children, and a crown of glory that does not fade away." It continues the listing by saying,

> Account them worthy to see their children's children. Keep their wedlock safe against every hostile scheme; give them of the dew from the Heavens above, and of the fatness of the earth. Fill their houses with bountiful food, and with every good thing, that they may have to give to them that are in need, bestowing also on them that are here assembled with us all their supplications that are unto salvation.[77]

We see that material and spiritual goals — such as peaceful cohabitation, long life, marital chastity (that is, marital fidelity), and love — are intermixed. These precede procreation (it is fifth in the list). Prayers for material prosperity, the goal of marital philanthropy, and the salvation of the couple follow references to procreation.

A shorter list of marital goods in the prayer at the joining of the couple's hands orders the goods of marriage differently: "Join them together in oneness of mind, crown them with wedlock into one flesh, grant to them the fruit of the womb and the gain of well-favored children." Interpersonal compatibility is followed by sexual union, ending with procreation, in the last place.[78]

Still another order is seen in the blessings prayed for in the second prayer of the marriage sacrament:

> Give to them fruit of the womb, fair children, concord of soul and body. Exalt them as the cedars of Lebanon, and as well-cultured vine; bestow on them a rich store of sustenance, so that having a sufficiency of all things for themselves, they may abound in every good work that is good and acceptable before You. Let them behold their children's children as newly planted olive

---

Galilee, and blessed the marriage there, that You might show a lawful union, and a generation therefrom, is according to Your Will [*ina phaneroses oti son thelema estin he ennomos syzygia kai he ex autes paidopoiia*]; do You Yourself, O Most Holy Master, accept the prayer of us, Your servants; and as You were present there, be present also here with Your invisible protection."

77. Sacrament of Holy Matrimony (First Prayer), pp. 83-84.

78. Sacrament of Holy Matrimony (Prayer at the Joining of the Hands), p. 87.

trees round about their table; and, being accepted before You, let them shine as stars in the Heavens, in You, our Lord. . . .[79]

Here, procreation is first in the list, psychosomatic partnership is second, dignity and good repute is third, material abundance is fourth, marital philanthropy is fifth, longevity of life together is sixth, and acceptability before God and the consequent glorification is seventh. This is hardly an ordered hierarchy of values. But if it is, it would seem that procreation is at the bottom of the list, for certainly, "being accepted before God" is the highest of goals.

In the blessing before the benediction, concluding the sacrament of holy matrimony, the list changes: The Holy Trinity is invoked to bless the couple and to "grant to [them] long life, well-favored children, progress in life and in Faith; replenish [them] with all the good things of the earth, and count [them] worthy of the promised blessings."[80] Here the order is shared longevity, procreation, material and spiritual growth and development (*prokopen biou kai pisteos*), material necessities in abundance, and participation in eternal life.

Finally, in the prayer after the Gospel, the priest addresses Christ as declaring "marriage honorable" by his presence, and then asks that he

> preserve in peace and oneness of mind these Your servants (*Name*) and (*Name*), whom You are well pleased should be joined to one another. Declare their marriage honorable. Preserve their bed undefiled. Grant that their life together be without spot of sin. And assure that they may be worthy to attain unto a ripe old age, keeping Your commandments in a pure heart.[81]

In this list, peace and mutual harmony head the list; living together as husband and wife in honor comes next; sexual fidelity follows; living sinlessly is next; followed by marital longevity; ending with conformity to the divine commandments with inner goodness and righteousness. This prayer is particularly notable because procreation is not mentioned at all in this list of the goals of marriage.

## The Marital Rites As Theological Tract

The preceding sections have been examined in the light of a suspicion that the present texts of the Orthodox marriage rites can be read in the historical con-

79. Sacrament of Holy Matrimony (Second Prayer, second part), p. 86.
80. Sacrament of Holy Matrimony (Prayer before Benediction), pp. 95-96.
81. Sacrament of Holy Matrimony (Prayer after Gospel), p. 91.

text of the Church's continuing effort to balance the first trajectory, honoring and respecting monastic celibacy, with the implications of the second trajectory. While respecting the monastic calling, the contemporary service seeks to affirm the spiritual and ecclesial dignity and honor of the "other way," the way of honorable and virtuous married life.

A way of summarizing what we have seen so far in the marshalling of theological contexts, interpersonal virtues in marriage, and the rite's way of listing the goals, goods, ends, and purposes of marriage, is to simply count the frequency of the use of a number of key terms in the texts of the services of betrothal and marriage. Thus, the word "bless," when applied to the couple only, appears twenty times in the texts. The Holy Trinity is referred to seventeen times. Children are mentioned ten times, excluding the redundancy of the phrase "children's children," while to these must be added three references to "the fruit of the womb," making a total of thirteen references to children. This is followed by twelve references to love, eleven inclusions of the word "salvation," ten variant forms of "creation," ten references to "servants" or "servants of God," eight citations of the words "one another," seven mentions of peace in marriage, seven references to the faith of the couple, four uses of the phrase an "honorable marriage," and three mentions of the phrase "community of marriage."

In my book *Health and Medicine in the Eastern Orthodox Tradition*,[82] there is a discussion of the church's involvement in the East with physical and spiritual healing.[83] Part of that discussion deals with the history of the Eastern Christian establishment and supervision of hospitals from the fifth to the eleventh centuries. Parallel to this deep involvement in medical healing, one of the liturgical expressions of spiritual healing was the sacrament of holy unction, or anointing *(Euchelaion)*. It, too, like the blessings of engagement and marriage, consisted of just a few prayers, usually connected with the divine liturgy. The prayers date from the time of the fourth-century *Sacramentary of Serapion,* in which we find one prayer to consecrate the oil and one prayer for the anointing of the sick. It was only when the church lost control of the hospitals, which it had established, to the medical guilds, and was excluded from that aspect of its healing ministry in the eleventh and twelfth centuries, that the sacrament of holy unction was enriched and expanded. Thus, it should not surprise us that the church sought some way of responding to this exclusion from the healing process in the society of that day. In the subsequent century tendencies to en-

---

82. Stanley Samuel Harakas, *Health and Medicine in the Eastern Orthodox Tradition: Faith, Liturgy, and Wholeness* (New York: Crossroad, 1990), repr. ed. (Minneapolis: Light and Life, 1996).

83. Harakas, *Health and Medicine,* pp. 100-106.

hance the liturgical form of the sacrament of healing led to its separation from the context of the divine liturgy and to the formation of a service complete in itself. It is possible to trace the development of this service through the thirteenth, fourteenth, and fifteenth centuries and to show how the present-day pattern of seven Epistle and seven Gospel readings and seven prayers emerged. With the introduction of printed service books the text of the service became more or less fixed.[84]

I propose that something similar happened with the services of betrothal and holy matrimony. Events in both East and West may well have served to promote the enhancement and development of these marital rites, so as to encourage greater appreciation for marriage. Several contributing factors may have provoked this reaction.

In the East, Phaedon Koukoules, in his *Life and Culture of the Byzantines,* treats the liturgical aspects of marriage in two sections, popular marriage *(laikos gamos)* and imperial marriage *(basilikos gamos).*[85] As would be expected, the imperial marriage customs and liturgical practices were much more impressive and complex than those for ordinary people. The widespread development of monasticism in Byzantium, especially as Hesychasm spread during the last centuries of the Byzantine Empire, with its basic commitment to what we have called the first trajectory, had a strong impact on how people thought about marriage.

It would not be unreasonable to assume that this would provoke a need on the part of those who wished to defend the dignity and importance of marriage to react in some way. Similar to the case of holy unction, expanding and enriching the marital rites was a way to affirm and articulate the second trajectory. One of the ways it did this was to incorporate elements from the imperial marriage tradition into the services used for the common people. It was a natural solution. Trembelas points to the connection of this development with royal practices. We see something like this at work in the Slavic practice of using elaborate crowns made of metal and jewels as an example of this enhancement of the service.[86] Thus, it seems likely that in the East, the enhancement of the marital rites was motivated by an effort to counter an extreme emphasis on monastic asceticism that served to denigrate the value and importance of marriage.

In the West, the manuscript tradition with the expanded version of the marital rites points to another, though related, reason for this enhancement.

---

84. Harakas, *Health and Medicine*, p. 102.

85. Phaidon Koukoules, *Byzantinon Bios kai Politismos* (Athens: French Institute of Athens, 1951), vol. 4, pp. 95-143.

86. Trembelas, *Mikron Euchologion*, pp. 22-24.

Trembelas describes how many of the manuscripts of the expanded marital rites have their source in "Orthodox southern Italy." He observes, "It should not be forgotten that the first printed Prayer Books *[entypa euchologia]* were published in Venice. As such it was natural that they should have had before them in the publication the best manuscripts belonging to the Orthodox southern-Italian tradition *[ton Notio-Italikon Orthodoxon typon]*."[87] These manuscripts were especially plentiful from the eleventh century onward, as Trembelas notes in the catalog of manuscripts he uses for his study of the texts.[88] What was happening in the West at this time? The gradual imposition of clergy celibacy. This took place from the eighth century onward, but with special emphasis under Pope Gregory VII, also known as Hildebrand, who reigned from 1073 to 1085. Clerical celibacy was finally made mandatory by the Third Lateran Council in 1123. The obvious message of required clerical celibacy is that marriage is somehow tainted and incompatible with the sacred calling and the holiness required of the clergy.

What I suggest is that there may be a causal connection between the imposition of clergy celibacy in the West and the appearance of the expanded Orthodox marital rites in the locale where their confrontation was most evident. Clerical celibacy clearly embodies the values and emphases of the first trajectory. The enhancement of the marital rites in southern Italy could well have been provoked by the imposition of clerical celibacy by the Western tradition, since that practice would be a present and direct challenge to the Eastern Orthodox tradition of married clergy.

This suggestion, at least in part, is not my own. In 1979 G. Baldanza published an important article on the marriage rites in the *"Euchologio Barberini."*[89] Baldanza advanced the case that this first authenticated expansion and development of earlier simple blessing prayers "was written by Greek monks in Italy in order to defend marriage against Marcionist or Tatianist tendencies," which according to our terminology belong to the first trajectory. Stevenson expresses doubt about this, especially the reaction to Marcion and Tatian, who are much earlier figures.[90] But Baldanza's view coincides in many ways with the thesis of this chapter. The development of Orthodox betrothal and marital rites is a reaction against the tendencies minimizing the significance of marriage. It is also a response to a more current development, the al-

---

87. Trembelas, *Mikron Euchologion*, p. 15.

88. Trembelas, *Mikron Euchologion*, pp. 6-8.

89. G. Baldanza, "Il rito de Matrimonio nel 'Euchologio Barberini 336,'" *Ephemerides Liturgicae* 93 (1979): 316-51.

90. Stevenson, *Nuptial Blessing*, p. 99.

most exclusive identification of the Christian life with monasticism in the East and the imposition of clerical celibacy in the West.

Thus, it is possible to see the expansion of the liturgical texts of the betrothal and marriage services as something more that the simple accretion of liturgical material over the years. The present-day Orthodox rites of marriage are also a statement defending and promoting the importance, theological validity, spiritual authenticity, and moral value of Christian marriage, in the face of forces that denigrated and minimized marriage. As such, it is not only a liturgical text. It is a powerful and articulate theological tract in support of the second trajectory.

## Conclusion: The "Second Trajectory" and the Idea of "Covenant Marriage"

This chapter has made the case that there are two discernable trajectories in the Eastern Christian tradition regarding marriage. The first trajectory identifies only one goal and purpose to marriage, procreation. Sex in marriage is permissible only for the purpose of procreation. No focus exists for the ideas of the interpersonal relationships of spouses, or for marital sexual relations as an incarnational expression of the couple's love for each other in the sanctity of holy matrimony, or for the living of the Christian life in its fullness in the context of marital relationships. The second trajectory has a much broader understanding of the goals, purposes, values, and intentions of marriage. My thesis is that the current marriage rites are an expression of this broader trajectory and allow a fuller, richer, and sacramental understanding of the goodness, holiness, and graciousness of the spiritual, emotional, relational, and physical aspects of the wholeness and mutuality of marriage. I have presented evidence to support the view that the existing marital rites of the Orthodox Church for betrothal and the sacrament of marriage support this view. Sex in marriage is celebrated there along with many other goals, purposes, and values interrelated in Orthodox Christian marriage.

This rich understanding of marriage in the Orthodox tradition also has resonance with some aspects of approaches to the marital union in the "covenant marriage" tradition. There, too, interpersonal, loving, committed, and mutually supportive relationships of spouses are affirmed. Though the term *covenant marriage* is foreign to the patristic and Eastern Orthodox Christian tradition, the second trajectory of marriage in Orthodox Christianity resonates in many ways with the covenant marriage tradition of the West.

Perhaps the view of someone who stands outside the Eastern Orthodox tradition could serve to support this conclusion and provide a fitting ending to this chapter. In his book *Nuptial Blessing: A Study of Christian Marriage Rites,* after discussing the structure and values of the Orthodox marital services, Kenneth Stevenson writes the following:

> [M]ore important than this basic community of ideas is the strongly positive view of marriage, and the enjoyment of the things of the flesh when blessed by God; all this the Byzantine marriage liturgy reinforces. You could never find a Troparion invoking the joy of the saints and martyrs at a wedding in any medieval Western rite! Moreover marriage is about *both* partners, an insight given symbolic expression in that the couple are crowned, instead of the bride alone being veiled. It is not for nothing . . . that two rings first appear in the East [which] shows that the Byzantine understanding of the marriage relationship was not only highly developed but given liturgical expression. Perhaps the choice of lections clinches the matter, if we are looking for a distinctively Byzantine view of marriage compared with Western ones. . . . The gospel-reading appears always to be John 2:1-11 — Christ at the wedding in Cana — a tradition that may probably go right back to the fourth century . . . and the epistle is usually Eph. 5:20-33 — the Christ-Church analogy. . . . Byzantine-rite Christians got married with a liturgy that did not encourage them to go home to bed feeling slightly guilty.[91]

91. Stevenson, *Nuptial Blessing,* p. 104.

# 5  Marriage As Covenant in Early Protestant Thought: Its Development and Implications

*James Turner Johnson*

The covenant model of marriage was a distinctive element in the Protestant re-casting of marriage that took place during the sixteenth-century Reformation era. Though the covenant model of marriage was the particular work of the Puritan movement in England, it was shaped by the theology of Martin Luther and other sixteenth-century Reformers as they dealt with issues such as the nature and purpose of sexual difference, the nature and purpose of marriage, and the place of the society created by marriage within the larger frame of the social order. Perhaps because of this incorporation of earlier ideas from the core of Reformation theology, the influence of the covenant understanding of marriage continues to be felt long after the end of Puritanism as a distinct religious movement.

In this chapter, I first examine the origins, development, and lines of influence of the idea of marriage as covenant, beginning with the sixteenth-century Reformers and their rejection of the inherited Catholic doctrine and its implications, and the main lines of their reconstruction of how to think about these matters. I turn next to the covenant idea itself as developed within the Puritan movement in both England and America. Finally, I look at the continuing influence and relevance of the idea of covenant for understanding sexuality, marriage, and society in the context of the United States.

## The Inherited Tradition and the Reformers' Reaction

Let me begin by painting in very broad strokes the main features of the Catholic tradition against which the sixteenth-century Reformers reacted and the nature of their reaction. The Catholic understanding of sexuality and marriage at the dawn of the Reformation was an amalgam of ideas and attitudes drawn variously from both Augustinian and scholastic theology, from the tradition of sacramental theology, and from canon law. From Augustine came an underlying suspicion of human sexual activity. This was formally rejected but not entirely discarded by Thomas Aquinas's natural-law recasting of the nature of human sexuality after the fall. The suspicion of human sexuality was most notably present in the preference of celibacy over marriage and the canonical requirement of priestly celibacy.

From Augustine also came the basic framework for conceiving marriage in terms of three goods or ends: *proles, fides,* and *sacramentum. Proles,* for Augustine, referred not only to the organic connection between sexual relations and procreation. Since, in his conception, sexual arousal also reflected the sin of concupiscence, the good of *proles* for Augustine referred more fundamentally to the right intention necessary in sexual activity if its inherent sinfulness was to be forgiven by God. *Fides,* for Augustine, was a broad category denoting "keeping faith" with one's partner in a variety of ways and for various purposes. It included reserving oneself sexually for one's spouse, giving oneself sexually to one's spouse for the purpose of restraining and remedying the impulse to sin, assisting the spouse in his or her own moral growth, and creating a bond of mutual love between the spouses — initially, even for Christians, a bond based in cupidity but, for Christians, growing increasingly to be an expression of charity *(caritas). Sacramentum,* for Augustine, was the only good specific to Christian marriage; for him it denoted the oath of indissolubility Christians took when marrying, an oath not taken in non-Christian unions.[1]

Between Augustine in the fifth century and Aquinas in the thirteenth, the development of sacramental theology transformed the meaning of the good of *sacramentum.* By the time of Aquinas, *sacramentum* had taken on the technical meaning of "sacrament," that is, a visible sign of an invisible grace. Thus, in Aquinas's treatment of the ends of marriage, *sacramentum* became something quite different in meaning from what it was for Augustine. For Aquinas, it functioned as a kind of "super-end" of marriage, denoting the transforming effect of grace *ex opere operato* throughout all elements of every Christian marriage. This reconception of the good of *sacramentum* meant effectively that there are only two ends of marriage in the sense of what might be achieved by the parties, both by their own efforts and by the help of grace:

1. Augustine treated marriage directly in two treatises, *The Good of Marriage* and *Marriage and Concupiscence,* and indirectly in others on different subjects. For a theological exploration of Augustine on human sexuality and marriage see Paul Ramsey, "Human Sexuality in the History of Redemption," in *The Ethics of St. Augustine,* ed. William S. Babcock (Atlanta: Scholars, 1991), pp. 115-45.

*proles* and *fides*. *Proles*, for Aquinas, denoted what is particular to sexuality in the natural law, namely, its orientation toward procreation. *Proles* was thus the distinctive end of marriage, understood as the one human relationship in which sexual activity is proper according to natural law, where the procreation of children and their care and education for life distinguishes this relationship from all others. Because Aquinas understood the natural-law purpose of human sexuality to be unharmed by the fall into sin, his conception of marriage did not regard sexual activity as inherently sinful. Indeed, when properly undertaken and oriented toward procreation, sexual activity has a positive end. But still, such activity belongs only to the natural order, in Aquinas's view; in the higher supernatural order of grace, it has no place. So the relative devaluation of marriage relative to celibacy remained in place in Aquinas's thought, though placed on a different footing from that in Augustine's thought.

The end of *fides*, for Aquinas, suffered somewhat because of the overall structure of the conception of morality in which it was placed. So far as it was natural, *fides* was associated with natural human love *(amor)*, which for Aquinas was a drive that found its perfection in the virtue of temperance, the lowest of the four natural virtues. So far as it was supernatural, *fides* was associated with the virtue of charity *(caritas)*, the highest of the supernatural virtues. Thus on the natural level, *fides* implied restraint in the exercise of what was distinctive to marriage, while, on the supernatural level, it implied a love directed toward God as rooted in but transcending human loves.

Aquinas also reshaped the breadth and variety of meanings associated with the idea of *fides* in Augustine's thought and in the subsequent Augustinian tradition. Not in Aquinas proper, but in medieval treatments of the ends of marriage after him, the idea of *fides* was gradually separated into two distinct but related ends: restraint and remedy of sin and mutual love. While this was not important for Luther and sixteenth-century Reformed theologians, it surfaced as an important issue in the Puritan rethinking of the inherited Catholic tradition, and I will return to it in that context.

As for the matter of the indissolubility of marriage, Aquinas understood it to follow from the natural purposes of this union, namely, to procreate and raise offspring and to exercise mutuality to that end. That is to say, the conception of marriage as sacrament in the technical medieval sense was not itself the source of the indissolubility of marriage; its effect was only to strengthen Christians in their achievement of actual indissolubility in their marriages by the work of the grace conferred through the sacrament. This was, though, for practical purposes a distinction without a difference since, except for the relatively small presence of Jews, Europe in the late Middle Ages and the Reformation era was a society of Christians, and all formal marriages were in fact conducted by the church and were thus sacramental.[2]

The thrust of Martin Luther's reaction to the system that resulted from all this, as he knew it in the early sixteenth century, was essentially negative. He rejected major elements in it: priestly and monastic celibacy as leading to immoral sexual relationships and practices; the conception of marriage as sacrament as not grounded in Scripture; the doctrine of marital indissolubility as wrongly yoking together people not genuinely married in the sight of God; the conception of the consent of the two parties, followed by sexual intercourse, as the sole efficient cause of a marriage as weakening parental authority and the bonds necessary to society, a problem manifest in the practice of clandestine marriage.

Luther provided alternatives in each of these cases, alternatives that became centrally characteristic of the Protestant approach to sexuality and marriage as they were taken up and developed by later Protestant thought and practice. The rejection of priestly celibacy was replaced by the assumption that marriage is the normal state for all, the clergy included. The idea of marriage as sacramental was replaced by a conception of marriage reflecting Luther's doctrine of the two kingdoms. In its ideal state, as originally created by God and possible to Christian spouses through grace — that is, in marriage conceived as a relationship in the Kingdom on the Right Hand — it is indissoluble because of the perfection of love between the spouses. Yet in the world as it is, the Kingdom on the Left Hand, people marry who do not enjoy perfect mutual love; serious incompatibilities may arise, and one or both spouses may take actions which destroy the marital bond. In this kingdom, indissolubility is not an inherent characteristic of the marital state but an ordering imposed by the temporal authorities for the common good. Luther did not extend this reasoning, as John Milton did a century later, to justify allowing divorce in the public law, for he feared that for an individual sovereign to allow divorce would endanger the public order. Yet Luther did entertain a possible, if extreme, remedy in cases such as infidelity, where it is clear that there is really no marriage in the proper sense: that the wronged partner may remove to another sovereignty and there be free to marry again. In place of the idea that the consent of the two parties, followed by sexual intercourse, makes a marriage, Luther took a position requiring parental permission, wit-

---

2. Thomas Aquinas treats the subjects of sexuality and marriage in various places in the *Summa Theologica* and the *Summa Contra Gentiles*. For a theological exploration of some of the themes found there see Lisa Sowle Cahill, *Between the Sexes: Foundations for a Christian Ethics of Sexuality* (Philadelphia: Fortress, 1985), pp. 105-22.

nesses, and public profession of the marriage vows. Luther thus redefined marriage in terms that tied it closely to the social and even political structure of the society in which it existed, while at the same time setting a high ideal for performance not only for the husband-wife relationship but also for familial relationships considered more broadly. We see here several main features of the covenant idea of marriage developed in the next century by the English Puritans.[3]

Closer to Luther's time, though, these same ideas were also taken up and elaborated by the theologians of the Reformed movement. In contrast to the emphasis placed on procreation in the inherited Catholic tradition, the Reformed theologians stressed elements of what Augustine had termed *fides:* mutual love and the restraint and remedy of sin. They did this by giving new attention to Genesis 2, in contrast to Genesis 1, where "Be fruitful and multiply" had been taken to underscore the fundamental procreative purpose of human sexuality. Martin Bucer thus commented as follows on Genesis 2:23:

> In this verse God shows what marriage is and why He instituted it. The communion of man and woman is such that in all things they are one flesh, i.e., one being, and that each of them has a willingness to remain with the other more than with anyone else on earth.[4]

This led him, in another place, to define marriage in the following terms:

> True marriage, as instituted by God, . . . is a society and conjunction of man and woman, in which they are obliged to mutually communicate all things, divine and human, throughout their whole life and to live together in giving their bodies to one another whenever required or because of warm affection and genuine friendship.[5]

John Calvin, in discussing the purpose of marriage in the *Institutes,* likewise gave primacy to the Genesis 2 account, though his focus was on Genesis 2:18, "And the LORD God said, It is not good that the man should be alone; I will make him an help meet for him" (KJV). Calvin wrote:

> As the law under which man was created was not to lead a life of solitude, but enjoy a help-meet for him — and ever since he fell under the curse the neces-

3. For further discussion of Luther's views and references to his diverse discussions of sexuality and marriage, see Cahill, *Between the Sexes,* pp. 123-37; Eric Fuchs, *Sexual Desire and Love* (Cambridge: J. Clarke, 1983), pp. 136-38.

4. Martin Bucer, *Von der Ehe,* quoted in Fuchs, *Sexual Desire and Love,* p. 140, n. 22.

5. Bucer, *De Regno Christi,* quoted in Fuchs, *Sexual Desire and Love,* p. 140, n. 23.

sity for this mode of life is increased — the Lord made the requisite provision for us in this respect by the institution of marriage. . . .[6]

This new way of thinking about the marital relationship in terms of the society it creates rather than its procreative end gave broader meaning to the emphasis already found in Luther on the need for parental consent for children to marry. Luther linked marriage strongly to the public sphere by insisting on not only parental consent but also witnesses and public celebration. For Bucer, parental consent was an implication of the commandment, "Honor thy father and mother," but enforcing it was a matter for public law.[7] Calvin's *Ecclesiastical Ordinances* of 1561 interwove the levels of responsibility in contracting marriage — that of the would-be husband and wife, their parents, and the public authorities — by insisting on parental approval for minor children to marry, but by giving the consistory authority over both.[8] The significance of this was to place marriage in the framework of God's plan for government of the world, to link the sociality which should be the core of marriage to the sociality that is part of the larger society.

To sum up: In the early decades of the Reformation era the Continental Reformers undertook to reshape the conception of marriage as an integral and important part of their reshaping the understanding of and restructuring church and society. In doing this, they rejected the conception of marriage as sacramental, the state of marriage as ordained distinctively for procreation, the creation of a state of marriage by the consent only of the two parties to live together and have sexual relations for the purpose of procreation, and the whole idea of marriage as subordinate in value to celibacy and virginity. In place of these ideas they offered a new conception of marriage based on mutual love, founded on affection, friendship, and mutual assistance in all of life; a relationship blessed by God but not sacramental; one to be viewed not solely through the couple but rather through the family as a whole and the place of the marriage in the larger society; and thus a relationship to be understood as part of God's redemptive plan for the government of the fallen world, to be regulated not by the church but by the civil authorities. This was a radically different understanding of the purpose of sexual difference, of marriage, and of the place of marriage within society from the inherited Catholic doctrine.

The English Puritans came in contact with these ideas from the Continental Reformers in various ways through the last part of the sixteenth century. By

---

6. John Calvin, *Institutes of the Christian Religion*, 2 vols., trans. Henry Beveridge (Grand Rapids: Eerdmans, 1957), 1:348.

7. Bucer, *Von der Ehe*, quoted in Fuchs, *Sexual Desire and Love*, p. 143, n. 35.

8. Fuchs, *Sexual Desire and Love*, p. 143, n. 36.

the beginning of the seventeenth century these ideas of marriage were well known and had been incorporated in the thinking of leading Puritan intellectuals like Robert Cleaver and William Perkins. But in recasting these ideas in covenantal terms the Puritans gave them new focus, emphasis, and structure.

## The Covenant Model of Marriage
## As Defined by the Puritan Movement

Puritan theology developed the model of marriage as covenant as part of a broader emphasis on the biblical idea of covenant as defining the divine-human relationship and the divine plan for government and redemption of the world through the working of grace in those to whom it had been given. Calvin had introduced the idea of the third use of the law, "the principal use," in his judgment, by which Christians through grace are brought "to learn with greater truth and certainty what that will of the Lord is which they aspire to follow" and, through meditation on this knowledge, to be "excited to obedience, and confirmed in it, and so drawn away from the slippery paths of sin."[9] Through the work of grace in them Christians were no longer slaves to sin, but could actually do good; they could cooperate with God in their own redemption and in the transformation of society according to the divine will.

Within Puritanism the implications of this conception of the third use of the law were worked out by use of the Old Testament model of the covenant between God and Israel. The terms of the covenant came to be understood as the divine law, and each side had its responsibilities: God was not to forsake Israel, and Israel was to obey the law, that is, to fulfill the terms of the covenant. This latter responsibility was both individual and social; it bound each individual Israelite as well as the people of Israel as a whole. Similarly, in Puritan covenant theology, the gift of grace to the individual Christian established a covenant between him or her and God, by which God let the Christian know of God's good will (that is, the election to salvation) and gave the Christian the ability to know and do God's will; in response, the Christian, having been given the ability and the motivation to do this will, could be held to account for failure. Collectively, in turn, Christians were given knowledge of what a godly society should be, were charged with creating it, and were granted the motivation and ability to achieve it. This conception applied to all the relationships which collectively make up society. Thus marriage understood and described as covenant was not a conception which stood alone; rather, it was

9. Calvin, *Institutes*, 1:309.

one part of a larger way of conceiving the ideal nature of all the relationships to be found in society.

Working within this covenant framework led Puritan thinkers on marriage to compare it with other major forms of social relationships, themselves conceived as covenants: the relationship of government, that of friendship, that of the business partnership, and that of the church. These analogies overlapped and interlocked in Puritan writings on marriage; some of the authors emphasized certain comparisons, while other authors placed their emphases differently. Nonetheless, taken together these various descriptions of the covenant character of marriage make a whole, and the analogies are fundamental to the Puritans' covenantal understanding of marriage.

One of the central issues in the Puritan use of these analogies was to work out the balance between distinctive authority and mutuality. The Puritan conception of the divine-human covenant was that it was "a true contract of mutual obligation,"[10] and so, by extension, are all human covenants, including that by which government is established and maintained. The obligations are mutual but not equal; God and the Christian have different, but nonetheless obligatory, responsibilities, and so are the responsibilities of governor and governed, as well as all the rest of relationships in society. This way of thinking meant that Puritan theorists had no difficulty in dealing with hierarchical relationships within covenants. Just as God's choice of Israel was an act of *ahabhah,* a free, unconditioned act of love that implied taking responsibility for Israel and caring for it, so all authority within government was understood to imply active measures of responsibility and care for the members of society. The same was true of authority within the household as well as relationships of friendship, of business partnerships, and of fellow Christians within the church. These were all inherently relationships of unequals, but still genuinely mutual.

It is also important to note that marriage understood as a covenant, like that of God with Israel, is a sphere of obligation, of duty. Husband and wife have certain duties in common, other duties that are different but owed mutually to one another, others that are owed toward the children and servants within the household, and still others that are owed back from these toward the husband-father-master and the wife-mother-mistress, singly or together. In early Puritan writing on marriage these duties were not developed in detail. By the 1620s, however, spelling out these duties and their implications became a major feature — sometimes the *only* feature — of Puritan sermons and treatises on marriage. These duties were developed as a spiritually motivated disci-

10. Perry Miller, *The New England Mind: The Seventeenth Century* (Boston: Beacon, 1961), p. 377.

pline — a discipline rooted in the divine grace first given in election and particularly given in the choice of husband and wife for each other, so that each particular marriage was understood as a work of grace. The duties of marriage, in their turn, were the specific expressions of the requirements of the divine will able to be known and fulfilled by those who have received grace. The Puritan understanding of marriage as covenant, then, was deeply theological in its nature: the relationship of marriage is a form taken by God's work of redemption.

The distinctive understanding of marriage that resulted from this perspective and from the use of analogies from different kinds of covenantally conceived relationships first began to appear at the very end of the sixteenth century. A good example was Robert Cleaver's *A Godlie Forme of Household Government*, published in London in 1598, in which the analogy between marriage and government was tempered by a conception of the husband-wife relationship as a form of friendship.[11] Cleaver began with the analogy to government: "A household is as it were a little common wealth, by the good government whereof, Gods glorie may be advaunced, the common wealth which standeth of severall familes, benefited, and al that live in that familie may receive much comfort and commoditie."[12] With these words Cleaver concisely linked the relationship and responsibilities of marriage to those of the national society. Both are forms of government; they both aim at the common good; and they are interlocked in their aim of achieving that common good. What differentiates them is not their respective size or level of responsibility, but whether they are Christian or not. If the householder or ruler seeks only to provide for the necessities of life, "then Papists, Atheists, yea, Turkes, and Infidels, do yeelde this dutie as well as [the Christian]."[13] The Christian householder is first to seek to ensure "christian holiness," and then "secondlie the things of this life."[14] The first aim of ensuring Christian holiness rendered the householder's responsibility toward the household like that of the minister to his congregation: the householder should get everyone to worship services together and on time; "[s]econdly, hee must set an order in his house for the service of God"; "[t]he

11. Robert Cleaver, *A Godlie Forme of Householde Government* (London, 1598). This and the works of other English Puritan writers from the sixteenth and seventeenth centuries cited in this chapter are catalogued in A. W. Pollard and G. R. Redgrave, *A Short-Title Catalogue of Books Printed in England, Scotland, and Ireland, and of English Books Printed Abroad 1475-1640* (London: Bibliographical Society, 1926), abbreviated *STC*. For Cleaver's work and the other works cited in this chapter I provide the catalogue number, which for Cleaver is *STC* 5382.

12. Cleaver, *A Godlie Forme*, p. 5.

13. Cleaver, *A Godlie Forme*, p. A3.

14. Cleaver, *A Godlie Forme*, p. 17.

third dutie . . . is private instruction . . . in matters of religion."[15] The same applies, by extension, to the government of society.

But who specifically, in the household, is to exercise this responsibility? Cleaver's answer was one that became typical throughout the development of the Puritan understanding of marriage. Though in the passages I have just quoted he was speaking of the obligations of the husband as the head of household, elsewhere he made clear that the government of the household is shared. "The governours of families . . upon whom the charge of government lyeth, though unequally, are first the Cheefe governour, which is the Husband, secondly a fellow helper, which is the Wife."[16]

Now, all the Protestant Reformers would have accepted this statement of the superiority of the husband over the wife; for that matter, so would Catholic marriage theory. But, by contrast with Catholic theory, this is presented here as a matter not of natural law but of the order of redemption, and the husband's preeminence and the wife's submission are tempered in various ways. First, the order is one that is defined by office, not by personal qualities; the wife is not inherently inferior to the husband, or woman to man. Second, the order of precedence is defined by the order of responsibility. "Heavy is the head that wears the crown" might apply to husbands as well as to kings, and the responsibilities of precedence do not, therefore, give husbands any right to tyrannize their wives and families. Third, the wife's strong second place is secured in detail: she has the authority of the husband within the household when he is absent, and near equal authority when he is present; indeed, in some respects within the household her authority is superior to his. She is to be obeyed and revered by the children and the servants in the household just as he is.[17] The husband and wife are, after all, Cleaver noted, co-founders of the household, though the first initiative toward that end was properly the husband's.

In developing this conception of precedence with mutuality, Cleaver drove toward the following definition of marriage:

> Wedlocke or Matrimonie, is a lawful knot, and unto God an acceptable yoking and joyning together of one man, and one woman, with the good consent of them both: to the end that they may dwell together in friendship and honestie, one helping and comforting the other, eschewing whoredome, and all uncleannesse, bringing up their children in the feare of God. . . .[18]

15. Cleaver, *A Godlie Forme*, pp. 34, 43, 49.
16. Cleaver, *A Godlie Forme*, p. 19.
17. Cleaver, *A Godlie Forme*, pp. 60-61.
18. Cleaver, *A Godlie Forme*, p. 98.

Here the precedence of the husband is forgotten. The images are those of mutuality: "one helping and comforting the other." Note also the image of friendship, another of the relationships the Puritans conceived on the model of covenant and to which they regularly compared marriage. Note, too, the reference to the "good consent of them both," but without saying that it is this which makes the marriage. Rather, Cleaver assumed the Reformed idea of marriage as resulting from broader social approval to which the parties add their consent.

Cleaver also showed here that he assumed what was already implied, though not always explicitly stated, in the Protestant rethinking of marriage, and would become increasingly explicit in Puritan thought on marriage, namely, the reversal of priorities among the ends or goods of marriage. The first end of marriage is the end of mutuality, expressed through commonality, friendship, and reciprocal help and comfort. Then, as a result of mutuality, follow the ends of restraint and remedy of sin and the procreation and upbringing of offspring. Cleaver thus reversed the traditional order of the ends of marriage: mutual society, not procreation, is most fundamental, and procreation is presented not as the defining purpose of marriage but as one of the results of a good marriage.

This reconception and reordering of the ends of marriage was broadly characteristic of the Reformation idea of marriage. In the context of the Puritan covenant model of marriage, it took on special importance, for it symbolized centrally the importance of the married partners' relationship of mutual care and responsibility as a reflection of the right ordering of the world through the work of grace. Acting out this right ordering, with the help of grace, is what restrains and remedies sin. In turn, the physical expression of love is what leads to the procreation of children, whose care and education can be rightly carried through only from the perspective of such a rightly ordered relationship. Put simply: love makes the marriage, leading to restraint and remedy of sin and to the procreation of offspring. What is definitively unique in the covenant model of marriage is not the purpose of procreation, as the natural law model taught, but the right ordering of the man-woman relationship according to God's redemptive plan. This reconception of the priorities of the ends of marriage became one of the most important long-term influences of the covenant idea of marriage, as we shall see further below.

The same explicit use of covenant imagery, the analogy of marriage to national life and to the church, an emphasis on mutuality, and a conception of married life as a kind of spiritually created discipline mark Robert Pricke's *The Doctrine of Superioritie, and of Subjection*,[19] a work that appeared about a de-

---

19. Robert Pricke, *The Doctrine of Superioritie, and of Subjection* (London, 1609), *STC* 20337.

cade after Cleaver's *A Godlie Forme of Household Government*. Working from the fifth commandment, "Honor thy father and thy mother," Pricke argued that this implies broad duties. Honoring one's father also implies honoring "Kings, Princes, and Magistrates, Ministers of the word of God, Householders, Schoolemaisters, and Teachers." These relationships, for Pricke, are all grounded in the relationship of marriage, which is the fundamental form of society. But marriage itself, for Christians, is understood as a work of grace. The husband-wife relationship is like that between God and the elect: God "hath joyned to himselfe, and as it were married in a speciall covenant of mercie and compassion, all the faithfull and elect ones; so that he is head and husband of his people."[20] The relation between God and the church is like that of the husband and wife in marriage; both forms of relationship are covenants like that brought into being by God with Israel: created by divine action, covenantal in structure.

Cambridge theologian William Perkins, whose *Christian Oeconomie*[21] was published a year after Pricke's treatise, depicted marriage in terms of government, economic life, and friendship.[21] Marriage, he wrote, is "the Seminarie of all other Societies," distinguished by being brought about for a particular purpose, having its specific obligations, and ruled by its own particular government.[22] Marriage "was ordained by God in Paradise" after God said, "It is not good that [the man] should be himselfe alone, I will make him an helpe meete for him" (Gen. 2:18). In Paradise, God joined the first couple together "immediately," that is, directly, effectively, and without intermediary. Procreation came as a blessing added to this relationship, in the words of Genesis 1:28, "Increase and multiply, and fill the earth." And finally, argued Perkins, "marriage was made & appointed by God himselfe, to be the fountaine and seminarie of al other sorts and kinds of life, in the Common-wealth and in the Church."[23]

Perkins amplified this conception through examination of the idea of mutual companionship, his way of using the analogy of friendship, through the duties implied by it. In so doing he laid down a pathway for the subsequent development of the Puritan understanding of marriage: the covenant model as one of "dutiful companionship" in marriage. This model implied not simply love as affection but love as act, act in accord with the obligations of the covenant relationship. On the basis of their conception of the working of grace, Perkins and subsequent Puritan writers held that husband and wife should be

20. Pricke, *Doctrine of Superioritie*, p. B6.
21. William Perkins, *Christian Oeconomie*, vol. 3 of William Perkins, *Workes*, 3 vols. (Cambridge, 1609), STC 19649.
22. Perkins, *Christian Oeconomie*, 3:10.
23. Perkins, *Christian Oeconomie*, 3:670-71.

bound together in caring for each other. Yet, at the same time, by marrying, the husband and wife undertook to act in defined, specific ways so as to manifest this care. Love in marriage is a discipline, ideally one which originates from inside, but one which may be imposed from outside if necessary.

This was essentially a statement of the two sides of Calvin's third use of the law for the specific context of the marriage relationship. Marriage was needed because a man and a woman needed each other. In response to that neediness, God, through grace, brings couples together to provide "meet help." The nature of such help is defined in various specific ways because of the social character of marriage. The parties in a true marriage are able to provide the necessary companionship because of the grace which has been manifested in them. Thus they should hold themselves to the requirements of such companionship, and an external discipline serves as an aid to doing so. That is, just as the people of Israel experienced the law as a manifestation both of God's favor and of God's requirements for their lives, so Christians in marriage should look on their union as effected by God through grace and as a relationship defined by specific duties in accord with God's will.

Perkins described the duties of marriage as "principally two: Cohabitation and Communion." The duty of cohabitation has to do with married persons living together in the same household, sharing the government of that household for the common good. The duty here is for each partner to the marriage to join in this mutual society. The duty of communion adds to this: it requires mutual communication of "both their persons, and their goods each to other, for their helpe, necessitie and comfort" and the satisfaction of the marriage debt. The marriage or conjugal debt, however, is described here not simply in terms of restraint and remedy of sin but also as "cherishing one another," that is, "the performing of any duties, that tend to the preserving of the lives one of another."[24] Two things stand out here: the emphasis on the communal interaction of husband and wife in all things, including their specifically sexual interaction, for each other's and the mutual good, and the conception of this interaction in terms of duty. For Perkins, this duty is deeply personally felt; it comes from the presence of grace in the individual heart. Nonetheless, he does not hesitate to describe what this must mean in terms of "cohabitation" and "communion." The duties of companionship in marriage may be felt subjectively, but they are also able to be known and described objectively. While Perkins held together these two sides of the idea of dutiful companionship, later Puritan writers on marriage tended to split them, either emphasizing the duties of marriage in terms of an objectively knowable discipline or stressing the need

24. Perkins, *Christian Oeconomie*, 3:686-90.

for grace to motivate marriage partners to act in accord with the end of providing mutual meet help.

By the early 1620s the distinctively Puritan conception of marriage was being laid out in more direct and popular form, as in the titles of the marriage sermons published by clergyman Thomas Gataker: *A Good Wife Gods Gift, A Wife Indeed,* and *Marriage Duties.*[25] These were sermons that might have been preached originally as part of a celebration of marriage in Gataker's parish. They laid out the divine institution of marriage and the particular work of God that Christians should see in each individual marriage, the meaning of the wife as "helpmeet" to the husband, a concept involving a certain authority of its own alongside that of the husband, and, more generally, a summary of the duties of marriage as implications and expressions of mutual love and companionship.

In *Marriage Duties,* the first and most comprehensive of these three sermons, Gataker began with the idea of love as given to Christian spouses equally through grace. This love serves as the motive force behind the performance of companionable duties in marriage. Gataker blended equality and difference, nature and grace into a particular unity in explaining this. Christian husbands and wives equally receive grace to perform the different and unequal duties required of them by their positions according to nature. As we saw earlier, Robert Pricke used the fifth commandment to enjoin wives to honor their husbands; Gataker, in his turn, cited 1 Peter 3:7 to enjoin the husband to honor "the wife, as unto the weaker vessel."[26] The relation of husband and wife is mutual and reciprocal, but not equal, because husbands and wives are of different natures as man and woman as well as of different offices in marriage. But such difference does not diminish their fundamental equality in grace; nor does it in any way impair their ability to function as true partners in their common enterprise. Gataker wrote:

> [I]f Christian men are to observe one another, that they may whet on each other to godlinesse and good workes: then much more should Christian man and wife so doe: that having lived togither for a time as copartners in grace here, they might reigne togither as co-heires in glory hereafter.[27]

For Gataker, each individual Christian marriage, properly understood, is a society ordained and brought into being by God. Its prime end is companion-

---

25. Thomas Gataker, *Marriage Duties* (London, 1620), *STC* 11667; Thomas Gataker, *A Good Wife Gods Gift;* and Thomas Gataker, *A Wife Indeed: Two Marriage Sermons* (London, 1623), *STC* 11659.

26. Gataker, *Marriage Duties,* p. 48.

27. Gataker, *Marriage Duties,* p. 48.

ship, with the chief ways of proving a companion being the performance of duties based in love. Gataker described these duties only in the most general terms, focusing instead on the mutual love that is inspired by grace. That is, his work represented one side of the argument made by Perkins, as noted above: that side which stressed loving companionship in marriage as a result of the work of divine grace in the spouses. Other Puritan writers of the same period, though, took up the opposite side of Perkins's thought, stressing the definition of duties to be performed in Christian marriages.

This latter "duty-based" approach is epitomized by another work of the same period, William Gouge's *Of Domesticall Duties Eight Treatises.*[28] This was a massive and compendious work, laying out the duties to be performed by all the parties involved in the covenant of marriage: the duties of the husband to wife and those of wife to husband; the duties of father to the male children and the female children, respectively, and those of the mother to the female and male children, in her turn; the duties of the male and female children to father and mother, respectively; the duties of the master to the male and female servants and their duties to him; the duties of the mistress to the female and male servants, and theirs to her; the duties of each member of the household toward the world outside the household. For Gouge, living a disciplined life, performing these individually defined duties, is what covenantal marriage requires. Still, the theological argument at work in Gouge's writing is the same as that found in Gataker: Love is the source of duty in Christian marriage, and the source of love is divine grace. When God's providence puts two people together in wedlock, they are given the grace to be what is necessary for each other.

In all this, Gouge and Gataker agree, and both echo Perkins. But Gouge, far more than Gataker and Perkins, was confident that it is possible to lay out the particulars of all the duties in objective detail. In doing so, he shifted the terms of the covenant of marriage from emphasis on the inward assent to grace of two Christian spouses toward the idea that adherence to an objective discipline might itself be a sign of the presence of grace. This same kind of shift occurred elsewhere in the Reformed tradition as it matured, making religion less a matter of the inclination of the will and more a matter of behavior according to objective moral standards. Further, Gouge's detailed description of the duties of married life provided a blueprint for the external regulation of marriage, whether by the church, by the community, or, especially in the deliberately covenant-based Puritan society of New England, by law.

The examples of Gataker and Gouge thus show the covenant idea of marriage in two distinctively different lights. In Perkins, on whom both these later

28. William Gouge, *Of Domesticall Duties Eight Treatises* (London, 1622), *STC* 12119.

thinkers depend, the concept of marriage as covenant is explicitly connected to the performance of certain duties by the spouses, duties which themselves follow from God's will that they be "helpmeets" for each other. Both the duties themselves and the ability and will to perform them arise from God's gift of grace. Marriage understood as covenant is a model for Christian marriage, or more precisely, marriage between persons who have both received divine grace in their respective individual covenants with God. But the covenant theology as a whole understood all the Christian community as having common and mutual responsibilities one toward another, and as the authority given to the head of household implied care for imposing discipline where it was not being observed, so ministers had that responsibility for the people in their congregations, and the national government had that responsibility for the nation as a whole. So the idea of duty in covenant relationships had two faces from the start, an internal one and an external one. In Perkins's thought they coexist together, a balance his successors found hard to maintain. Gataker represents those in the Puritan tradition who emphasized the internal working of love, while Gouge exemplifies the trend toward defining the Christian life as adherence to objectively defined duty. Marriage as covenant means different things from each perspective.

We can see this particularly in the argument for divorce put forward by John Milton. Already in Gataker's thought we see how the covenant conception of marriage could be developed to emphasize the work of grace and Christian freedom in love. These ideas were taken up and developed with great sophistication and detail by Milton in his *Tetrachordon* and *Doctrine and Discipline of Divorce* — works arguing for divorce on the grounds of mutual incompatibility.[29] The gist of Milton's argument was that when one or both partners in a marriage find it impossible to perform their proper duties to each other, this shows that their relationship is not a product of the love that only grace can produce, for such grace would have made for the performance of these duties. Such incompatible unions, Milton thus reasoned, are not marriages created by God; they are in fact not marriages at all, and the partners should be allowed to go their separate ways.

Gataker himself did not make this argument, though other Puritan writers of the same period did — as in William Whatley's reasoning that nonperformance of the marriage duties could "stretch" the bond of marriage.[30] Gataker

---

29. John Milton, *The Complete Prose Works of John Milton,* general ed. Don M. Wolfe, vol. 2, ed. Ernest Sirluck (New Haven/London, 1959); Milton, *The Doctrine and Discipline of Divorce,* in *Complete Prose Works of John Milton,* pp. 217-356; Milton, *Tetrachordon,* in *Complete Prose Works of John Milton,* pp. 571-718.

30. William Whatley, *A Bride-Bush; or, A Wedding Sermon* (London: Imprinted by Felix Kyngston for Thomas Man, 1617), pp. 6-7, STC 25296.

took the opposite road, arguing that the husband has taken the wife as his "perpetuall companion," that he is to continue loving her despite all difficulties, and that the wife in her turn is so to love her husband as to "draw love from him."[31] This illustrates the tension within the Puritan conception of marriage. Within a covenant relationship in which the parties are obligated to perform certain duties, failure to perform those duties is, on the face of it, a violation of the covenant and grounds for its dissolution. Yet as its partners have been brought together by grace, and as the duties are in their turn defined and made possible of fulfillment by grace, the partners ultimately cannot fail in the performance of these duties, and they may be held to them by an external discipline imposed by the church and by the laws of the state. This was the line of argument, based on Calvin's conception of the third use of the law, implied by Gouge's description of marriage in terms of specific duties.

Normative Puritanism took this latter position on the subject of divorce. Milton's answer to it was that given the assumptions of the conception of marriage as covenant initiated by God, where there was severe incompatibility in a union, it was clearly not a union God had any hand in creating. The implication of this was either that one or both parties had sinned through willful disobedience, or else that one or both were in fact not among those elected to grace. In either case, responding to Milton's challenge required the imposition of an external discipline, even if all it could achieve was to prevent the marriage from being formally dissolved, with right of remarriage. But given all that Puritan marriage doctrine says about the effects of grace in marriage, reducing its moral discipline to an external one calls into question whether the marriage is genuinely a work of God — which was exactly Milton's point. So the covenant model of marriage serves well to encourage those who understand themselves as motivated by grace and who are committed to a form of loving, companionable mutuality able to be described by a matrix of obligations. But it also implies that where there is no such understanding and no ability to live out such mutuality, there really is no true covenant and thus no real marriage.

## Application and Internalization of the Covenant Model of Marriage

As the dispute over divorce shows, the covenant model of marriage provided no panacea for the reality that some marriages may prove seriously incompatible. Its strength lay in its conception of marriage as loving companionship and its

31. Gataker, *Marriage Duties*, p. 31.

ability to draw out the meaning of this conception: on the one hand, as a manifestation of the loving grace of God, manifested as a sign of redemption, and, on the other hand, in terms of the ways married partners ought to act toward one another, toward their children, and toward other members of their household. But it takes little insight to recognize the difference between a marriage relationship founded on such internal affection and one where the companionship does not go beyond the performance of mutual duties, perhaps externally enforced, perhaps enforced on the wife and household by a husband imagining himself on the model of the ruler of the nation or even of God himself. Of course, there is a middle ground, where the motivation and discipline are held together, as in the thought of Perkins and, in their respective ways, also by Gataker and Gouge. But these two aspects of the covenant model of marriage also may be at war with one another, and in any case much is lost when they are separated. Let me illustrate this by a closer look at the New England experience, where the influence of the covenant model not only influenced the inner moral life but also shaped the laws.

Edmund S. Morgan, in his book *The Puritan Family,* shows that the analogy between marriage and civil government found in the covenant model was early reshaped in the Massachusetts colony into something else: a description of marriage as an element in the civil government of society as a whole. At first, as Morgan observes, the civil government left the family to its own particular sphere:

> Civil government, once established, did not supersede the family as a means of enforcing the laws of God. The state made no demand that the heads of families should "yield up their Family-Government over their Wives, Children, and Servants, respectively, to rule them in common with other Masters of Families." Rather, it gave additional support to their authority.[32]

This was in accord with the position we have found in Cleaver, Pricke, and Perkins, that the household is itself a form of government for its own members, analogous to but different from the government of the society as a whole. But in New England the analogy between these two forms of covenant was carried to the point of blending them.

Two examples from Morgan's study illustrate this blending. First, in 1629 the Massachusetts Bay Company ordered John Endicott, a deputy governor, to divide a group of male servants under his direction into artificial "families," setting up in each as its head a servant "grounded in religion." The end

---

32. Edmund S. Morgan, *The Puritan Family: Religion and Domestic Relations in Seventeenth-Century New England,* rev. ed. (New York: Harper and Row, 1966), pp. 142-43.

here was disciplinary, to keep order among these servants who had no regular connection with a household. Indeed, in these artificial families, created not by God's leading grace but by the authority of the civil government, there was little if anything left of the Puritans' ideal of marriage except the conception of the authority of the head of household and his duty to impose discipline on the subordinate members. The second example comes from the Connecticut and Plymouth colonies, both of which passed laws requiring any unmarried man with no servants to attach himself to an established household and submit to discipline by a family head.[33] A man with servants, of course, constituted a household in itself. Whatever one may say about the beauty of a conception of marriage so focused on the choice of one man and woman for each other by God directly, individually called to a life of loving companionship together, this has disappeared in these laws treating the family as a means of keeping a disciplined public order. Here the emphasis on the family as a vehicle for discipline has taken away the fundamental meaning of the relationship.

Looking at the matter from the opposite angle, the legal regulation of marriage, though it might attempt to follow the covenant model, could not in itself ensure that each marriage was brought into being according to the ideal at the root of that model. Without inner assurance of grace, effectively what remained was the discipline of companionship — at best the spur to a form of loving mutual care and perhaps a means of gaining confidence that grace was in fact present in the union, but at worst a hollow shell of a relationship.

But the covenantal ideal of marriage also had a happier history in the American experience. Consider this poem, "To My Dear and Loving Husband," from Anne Bradstreet, who came to Massachusetts in 1630 and lived there till she died in 1672:

> If ever two were one, then surely we.
> If ever man were loved by wife, then thee.
> If ever wife were happy in a man,
> Compare with me, ye women, if you can.
> I prize thy love more than whole mines of gold,
> Or all the riches that the East can hold.
> My love is such that rivers cannot quench,
> Nor aught but love from thee give recompense.
> Thy love is such I can no way repay;
> The heavens reward thee manifold, I pray.

33. Morgan, *Puritan Family,* pp. 144-45.

Then, while we live, in love let's so persever,
That when we live no more we may live ever.[34]

Or consider this, from the beginning of another poem, "A Letter to Her Husband, Absent on Public Employment":

My head, my heart, mine eyes, my life — nay more,
My joy, my magazine of earthly store:
If two be one, as surely thou and I,
How stayest thou there, whilst I at Ipswich lie?[35]

Here, in literary form, is the ideal of the loving companionship assumed in Puritan theory to be the basis of the marital covenant. There is nothing here of obligation, of duty, considered externally; the husband's superiority lies only in his ability to give love and thus joy and meaning to life.

Alongside the incorporation of the covenant model into the legal regulation of marriage by church and state, this conception of marriage as mutual society, the closest form of human companionship, expressed in reciprocal love as well as common enterprise, remained also. A century later we find sentiments similar to Anne Bradstreet's in the correspondence between John and Abigail Adams — both, not incidentally, products of the Puritan sensibility relating to marriage and public life. The Adamses habitually addressed each other as "My dearest friend" in their letters. These letters were frequent, given the long separations caused by John Adams's absence on public service. During these times, Abigail functioned in his stead as head of their household, not only raising their children but choosing and directing servants and running their family farm. Thus their letters include much about the state of domestic and international politics, the war, and matters relating to the children and to the business. But they also regularly include language like this, which recalls that of Anne Bradstreet during her husband's absence on public affairs:

[S]hould I draw you the picture of my Heart, it would be what I hope you still call Love; though it contain nothing New; the early possession you obtained there, and the absolute power you have ever maintaind over it, leaves not the smallest space unoccupied. I look back to the early days of our acquaintance, and Friendship, as to the days of Love. . . . [N]or have the dreary

---

34. Anne Bradstreet, "To My Dear and Loving Husband," in *The American Puritans: Their Prose and Poetry,* ed. Perry Miller (Garden City, N.Y.: Doubleday, 1956), p. 271.

35. Anne Bradstreet, "A Letter to Her Husband, Absent on Public Employment," in *American Puritans.*

years of absence in the smallest degree effaced from my mind the Image of the dear . . . Man to whom I gave my heart.[36]

Among the most lasting influences of the covenant ideal of marriage, as the Adamses' letters suggest, is the emphasis on love not only as lasting dedication to the other and to the other's good, but also as the basis of a lifelong companionship in everything necessary to the life of the family. Though the covenantal model's emphasis on discipline easily elided into churchly and civil legal regulation of the state of marriage, there is nothing in either Anne Bradstreet's or the Adamses' writings about the need to maintain the discipline of married life; this, for them, came from within. And of course, this was the nature of the original conception of the relation of companionship and duty in the Puritans' covenantal model of matrimony. Love as the basis for lifelong companionship as friends, as fellow governors of their household, as business partners, and as heirs to grace, all expressed as the willing undertaking of common and mutual responsibilities — this was the essence of the covenantal model of marriage as defined by Cleaver, Perkins, and other Puritan thinkers of the early seventeenth century. The letters of John and Abigail Adams to each other, more than a century and a half later, contain all these elements. As far as these conceptions linger in later understandings of marriage, the covenant model also lingers.

## Institutionalization and Influence: The Covenant Idea of Marriage and Later Protestant Conceptions of Marriage

One can trace in various ways the influence of these ideas and the covenant model of marriage they collectively define. I shall focus on three examples: (1) the explicit reordering of the traditional ends of marriage;[37] (2) the emphasis on mutual companionship as the purpose of human sexuality and of marriage, as seen in the work of the twentieth-century Reformed theologian Eric Fuchs; and (3) the expression of covenantal thought present in several contemporary marriage liturgies.

*The Second Prayer Book of King Edward VI*, reflecting the inherited main

---

36. Abigail Adams to John Adams, December 23, 1782, in *The Book of Abigail and John: Selected Letters of the Adams Family*, ed. L. H. Butterfield, Marc Friedlaender, and Mary Jo Kline (Cambridge, Mass.: Harvard University Press, 1975), pp. 332-33.

37. This process of reordering the ends of marriage was already underway during the time of the sixteenth-century Reformers, but the seventeenth-century Puritan thinkers carried it to completion, and Richard Baxter later gave it liturgical expression in his marriage liturgy.

line of Christian tradition on marriage up to that point, listed the priorities among the ends of marriage as follows:

> One was for the procreation of children, to be brought up in the fear and nurture of the Lord, and praise of God. Secondly, [marriage] was ordained for a remedy against sin, and to avoid fornication. . . . Thirdly, for the mutual society, help, and comfort, that the one ought to have of the other, both in prosperity and in adversity.[38]

While Puritan writers of the early seventeenth century did not openly challenge this liturgical language, they made it clear that, in the context of the definition of marriage as a form of covenant relationship, the first end of marriage was "mutual society, help, and comfort" (in short, mutual love), with the procreative purpose of marriage reduced to a subordinate role. This ordering was done in theological works like William Perkins's *Christian Oeconomie*, in marriage sermons, many of which were subsequently published in amplified form, and in polemical works like the divorce tracts of John Milton.

This tension between the liturgical listing and the direction of covenantal marriage theology can be seen in the writings of Perkins. When listing the ends of marriage, he followed the prayer book format: procreation, restraint and remedy of sin, and mutual help. But in the same context, when describing the original institution of marriage, he used decisively different language:

> [F]irst, [marriage] was ordained by God in Paradise, above and before all other states of life, in Adams innocencie before the fall. Againe, it was instituted upon a most serious consultation among the three persons in the holy Trinitie. . . . Jehovah Elohim said, It is not good that the man should be himselfe alone, I will make him an helpe meete for him. Thirdly, the manner of the conjunction was excellent, for God joyned our first parents Adam and Eve together immediately. Fourthly, God gave a large blessing unto the estate of marriage, saying Increase and multiplie, and fill the earth. Lastly, marriage was made and appointed by God himselfe, to be the fountaine and seminarie of al other sorts and kinds of life, in the Common-wealth and in the Church.[39]

Perkins left the tension between these two ways of thinking about the nature of marriage unresolved. Yet his own preference was clear. He did not return

38. Parker Society, eds., *The Two Liturgies* (Cambridge: Printed at the University Press, 1844), p. 303.
39. Perkins, *Christian Oeconomie*, 3:671.

to the matter of the priority of procreation among the ends of marriage but rather developed his theology of marriage as covenant around the "helpmeet" passage of Genesis 2:18, where the remedy for human loneliness is paramount and that remedy is mutual love, with procreation an added blessing that follows such love.

This theme received great new emphasis a generation later, when publication of Puritan marriage sermons was at its height. Thomas Gataker, author of three works on marriage, provides an example of this unequivocal Puritan reordering of the essential ends of marriage. A good wife, he wrote, "was one of the first reall and royall gifts that God with his owne hand bestowed upon Adam. And it must needs be no small matter that God giveth with his owne hand."[40] Gataker went on to amplify and clarify his meaning:

> Is a good wife such a speciall gift of God? Then is Marriage questionles a blessing, and no small one, of it selfe: one of the greatest outward blessings that in this world man enjoyeth. In the first place commeth the Wife, as the first and principall blessing, and the Children in the next. . . . If Children bee a Blessing, then the root whence they spring ought much more to bee so esteemed. . . . Children are the gift of God; but the Wife is a more special gift of God: shee commeth in the first place, they in the second.[41]

Gataker here made direct use of the Calvinist categories of general and special providence. The gift of a good wife — that which instituted the relationship of marriage in Paradise and continues to institute true marriages since — is an act of God's special providence. Correspondingly, "if a good Wife bee such a speciall gift of God, then a good Husband is no lesse. For the Husband is needful for the Wife, as the Wife is for the Husband."[42] The gift of children, by contrast, comes from God's general providential governance of the world. So special is the gift of a good mate and the creation of a marriage based on that gift that, for Gataker, it compares in this life to the gift of salvation in the next.[43]

Such is the overwhelming thrust of all Gataker's published marriage sermons. While he nowhere challenged the official marriage liturgy, in the one place where he explicitly listed the ends of marriage, they fit his theological conception of the priority of the husband-wife relationship and not the ordering found in the liturgy. Marriage, said Gataker, is first for "societie"; second, for "assistance"; third, for "Comfort and Solace"; fourth, "for Issue"; and fifth,

40. Gataker, *A Good Wife*, p. 9.
41. Gataker, *A Good Wife*, p. 12.
42. Gataker, *A Good Wife*, p. 24.
43. Gataker, *A Good Wife*, p. 15.

for "Remedie against Incontinencie."[44] His emphasis was so strong on the importance of the husband-wife relationship that here it has become three of the five ends listed. The fifth end, Gataker points out, was added only as a result of the fall. Thus of those ends originally purposed by God in Paradise, procreation — the procreation of "Issue" — is the last of the four.

Another two decades later, this same prioritization of the relationship of husband and wife over the procreative purpose of marriage became a major theme of John Milton's theology of marriage. Milton, who like many other Puritan thinkers of the first half of the seventeenth century had studied with Perkins while at Cambridge, found what is definitive on "what is marriage, and what is no marriage" to be the words of Genesis 2:18: "It is not good that man should be alone; I will make him a help meet for him." He continued:

> Frome these words so plain lesse cannot be concluded, . . . than that in Gods intention a meet and happy conversation is the chiefest and noblest end of marriage; for we find here no expression so necessarily implying carnall knowledg, as the prevention of loneliness to the mind and spirit of man.[45]

The marriage of Adam and Eve is archetypal; the gift of Eve to Adam responds to a loneliness that man has in his nature even before the fall into sin. Thus marriage is not first of all for the procreation of children or the remedy of lust; the latter comes only after the fall, and the former, while it is a blessing given in Paradise, comes only after the gift of a suitable companion.

Elsewhere Milton was even more explicit about the ordering of the ends of marriage. Commenting on Genesis 1:27-28 (which includes the "be fruitful and multiply" passage) and 2:18-24 (which contains the "helpmeet" passage), he asserted: God has "treatably and distinctly . . . heer taught us what the prime ends of marriage are, mutual solace and help."[46] By his exegesis, the preferred order of the ends of marriage is to be found already in Genesis 1:27: "So God created man in his own image, in the image of God created he him; male and female created he them." This passage, Milton argued, refers to the end of mutual meet help: man's imaging God describes the proper (meet) relationship of mutuality as humanity was originally created and as it remains after the fall. This is the conception made even more explicit in Genesis 2:18. Marriage is instituted for the prevention and remedy of loneliness in the mind and soul of man; the other goods or ends of marriage follow from the husband's and wife's providing meet help to each other.

44. Gataker, *A Wife Indeed*, p. 24.
45. Milton, *Complete Prose Works*, 2:246.
46. Milton, *Complete Prose Works*, 2:601.

As the examples of Perkins, Gataker, and Milton all show, the normative center of the Puritan covenantal conception of marriage was an understanding of the ends or purposes of marriage which placed the mutual, loving relationship of husband and wife first, and treated procreation as having a subordinate and dependent role relative to that relationship. It was no great step at all to a marriage liturgy incorporating that revised prioritization of the ends of marriage, but it was only finally with the work of Richard Baxter, some thirty years after Milton, that this was carried through. In the order "Of the Service of Matrimony" in his *Reformed Liturgy*,[47] Baxter incorporated the reprioritization of the marriage ends that was at the core of the covenant theology of marriage. His order of marriage as a whole is quite short. Following a brief charge to the couple, the minister offers a prayer. Then follow the vows, the pronouncement by the minister that the marriage is made, a statement of the duties of married persons (this is, in Baxter's liturgy, to be read from Scripture; the category, however, reflects the subject of the Puritan marriage sermons of the 1620s), and a final prayer and benediction. The first and most explicit statement of the reprioritized ends of marriage comes in the initial prayer: "Most merciful Father, who has ordained marriage for mutual help, and for the increase of mankind with a legitimate issue, and of the church with a holy seed, and for the prevention of uncleanness. . . ."[48] In two other places this same prayer restates this hierarchy of ends: God's blessing is asked that the pair about to be married "may there entirely devote themselves to thee, and be faithful in all conjugal affections and duties to each other; and if thou blest them with children, let them be devoted unto thee" (language which underscores the essential character of the conjugal relationship and the contingent character of procreation); and later, a supplication to God, "Make them meet helps to each other in thy fear."[49]

Baxter's theology and his *Reformed Liturgy* continued to be read and republished in England and the United States up into the Victorian era. He was also read on the Continent, sometimes in translation. As church historian Williston Walker has noted, Baxter was read in Dutch by at least one major figure in the Continental Pietist movement.[50] The influence of his thought, one of the last major expressions of the theology of the Puritan movement, thus lasted well beyond that movement proper.

The Puritan conception of marriage, as I have argued above, drew directly

---

47. Richard Baxter, *The Reformed Liturgy: "Of the Service of Matrimony,"* in his *The Practical Works*, 4 vols. (London: G. Virtue, 1838), 1:937-38.

48. Baxter, *Reformed Liturgy*, 1:637.

49. Baxter, *Reformed Liturgy*, 1:637.

50. Williston Walker, *A History of the Christian Church*, rev. ed. (New York: Scribner, 1959), p. 445.

on major themes of the thought of the sixteenth-century Reformers and shared with them the belief that the Bible itself provided the normative understanding of the purpose of human sexual difference, the relationship of marriage, and the place of the marital relationship within the larger sphere of human social existence as intended by God. These same themes have recently been taken up and developed by a contemporary theologian of the Reformed tradition, Eric Fuchs, in his *Sexual Desire and Love*.[51] Working from the main line of the Continental Reformed tradition, without reference to the thought of the Puritans, and without dependence on the language of covenant, Fuchs (a European theologian) defines a conception of marriage focused on exactly those same conceptions of human nature — the fundamental purpose of marriage as being the male-female relationship, the centrality of love, the gift of that loving relationship as an act of God, and the role of procreation as a result of this primary purpose, not itself the first purpose of marriage — seen in Perkins, Gataker, Milton, and the other authors treated earlier.

"The couple," says Fuchs, "is the long-range objective of sexuality."[52] Like Milton, he roots this in the nature of the image of God in man, calling it "an openness and incompleteness, a sign that man can be fulfilled only through encounter with the [sexual] Other, through love of a particular other being."[53] The marriage partners, by marrying, enter into a project in which each of them assists the other to realize himself or herself more fully, to experience a "freedom which is discovered through a liberating trust in each other."[54] For Fuchs, the help and assistance given the other in the context of marriage is the meaning of marital fidelity.[55] But the marriage relationship is not simply that of two individuals; it has a necessary social dimension as well. Like the Reformers, Fuchs insists that the mutual consent of the two parties is not in itself enough to constitute a marriage; the social dimension must also be present. Their consent must be declared publicly, and the social group to which they belong must recognize them as a married couple.[56] The result is to knit the marriage relationship together with other forms of sociality in an integrated whole. "It is the sexual love relationship which gives meaning to all the other relationships by permitting a unique and total experience of what relationship to another really is."[57] Shifting focus to the society, Fuchs argues that in acknowledging and ac-

51. Fuchs, *Sexual Desire and Love* (Cambridge: J. Clarke, 1983).
52. Fuchs, *Sexual Desire and Love*, p. 176.
53. Fuchs, *Sexual Desire and Love*, p. 176.
54. Fuchs, *Sexual Desire and Love*, p. 182.
55. Fuchs, *Sexual Desire and Love*, pp. 179-80.
56. Fuchs, *Sexual Desire and Love*, p. 184.
57. Fuchs, *Sexual Desire and Love*, p. 185.

cepting the marriage relationship society recognizes that it itself is not the center of human meaning. "The State, the nation, the community, do not constitute the goal of individual life; what is structural and primary is the couple."[58] Fuchs's argument here, which recalls vividly the analogies made by Puritan writers between the marriage relationship and other forms of social life, like them draws on the core of the Reformed tradition on marriage as central to the constitution and good working of human society.

Fuchs's central affirmation, that "[t]he couple is the goal, the objective of sexuality," has to be understood in this broader context. Reaching this goal requires of the married partners as individuals, fidelity, mutual help toward each other's growth and fulfillment, and constant, caring love. It also requires that their relationship be engaged with society as a whole, to knit together the bonds of sociality and to assist toward their fulfillment the other relationships that make up society. Fuchs does not use the language of covenant here, but the conception he describes is of a piece with the Puritans' description of the marriage covenant's dependence on the spouses' mutual love and assistance of each other toward perfection and with their conception of marriage as the ground of all human social relationships.

Fuchs's position on the relative priority of the ends of marriage clearly puts mutual love first. When he comes to discuss procreation and the role of the child in marriage, his language is of the dependence of this end on the first. Procreation, he notes, may be no more than the result of "a loveless sexual reaction." The ideal toward which Christian marriage aims is much more: "[T]he child is the sign par excellence of love's creativity." "It is thus clear," he concludes, "that the child should not be the primary goal of the relationship between a man and a woman, and even less should he be its only justification. . . . [The child should] symbolize the covenant exchanged between his parents."[59]

I have introduced the thought of Fuchs to illustrate the essential continuity between the English Puritans' conception of marriage as covenant, within their own larger conceptual frame of the covenant theology, and the main line of the Reformed tradition on human sexuality and marriage. If it is objected that the thought of the Puritans is too particular, too circumscribed by their own time and abilities, the similarity of Fuchs's position serves as a reminder that their conception of marriage as covenant had, and has, a larger reference to fundamental Reformation ideas about human sexuality and human nature as a whole, about the relationship of marriage as ordained toward human fulfillment, and about the essential connection between the marriage relationship

58. Fuchs, *Sexual Desire and Love,* p. 187.
59. Fuchs, *Sexual Desire and Love,* p. 191.

and other forms of human sociality. That Fuchs in his closing paragraph finds himself turning to the word *covenant* to describe this complex reality is indicative of the importance of this conception.

Finally, let us return to the American context and the example provided by some contemporary marriage liturgies. A convenient point of reference is the compilation by Perry H. Biddle Jr., in *A Marriage Manual*,[60] which provides marriage liturgies from several contemporary American denominations. Of these the only one which, rather conspicuously, lacks any reference to the idea of marriage as a covenant relationship grounded in the mutual love of the spouses is the Lutheran one, which comes out of a theological tradition that developed differently from the Reformed tradition on which the others, in various ways, depend or in which they participate. In the other liturgies provided — Episcopal, Presbyterian, and United Methodist — the language used reflects the tradition of marriage as a covenantal relationship of mutual love. "Christian marriage is a solemn and public covenant," reads the Episcopal marriage liturgy.[61] "God gave us marriage for the full expression of the love between a man and a woman," reads the Presbyterian order of marriage.[62] And in the United Methodist service the language employs both these themes: "The covenant of marriage was established by God, . . . grounded in the love of husband and wife."[63] These marriage liturgies all honor the conception of marriage as a covenant whose origin is with God and whose effective form is the relation of mutual love between the husband and the wife.

Thus far, the covenant idea of marriage lives on. Yet as the Puritan example shows, and as the contemporary work of Fuchs demonstrates in another way, language like this reaches its fullest resonance and meaningfulness only in the presence of a thick and robust theological context and of a Christian community whose members, singly and together, aid and encourage spouses in their seeking to serve as mutual meet helps to each other — for the covenant conception of marriage is more than a civil contract between the two consenting parties, and it is more than the formal linking of two people who believe themselves to be in love with each other. The purposiveness and meaning of marriage understood as covenant go well beyond either of these to encompass the conviction that God's blessing is needed already to bring the two parties together, and then is needed to help them to be all they need to be in the service of the other. Such marriage is not simply a relationship of two individuals but a relationship that forms part of

---

60. Perry H. Biddle Jr., *A Marriage Manual*, rev. ed. (Grand Rapids: Eerdmans, 1994).

61. Biddle, *Marriage Manual*, p. 119.

62. Biddle, *Marriage Manual*, pp. 136-37.

63. Biddle, *Marriage Manual*, pp. 150-51.

the bonds which create and sustain community. The place of children in such a marriage is one that is subordinate to the spouses' mutual meet help, to be sure, but it is an organic result of their ongoing commitment to participate in human life in its fullest dimensions. Perhaps no marriage liturgy can do more than hint at these broader dimensions. But without the broader dimensions even the hint may go unheeded or perhaps not be understood at all. This is the problem of the covenant conception of marriage today, four centuries after thinkers like Cleaver and Perkins first described it.

# 6 Covenantal Marriage: Protestant Views and Contemporary Life

*Max L. Stackhouse*

A decade ago, a series of volumes on "Family, Religion, and Culture" was launched to renew discussion of the theological and ethical understanding of marriage in interaction with the newer perspectives and findings of historical and social scientific scholarship.[1] One key motif in parts of that series was the idea of the "covenant," a dominant concept in the biblical tradition that was taken up in the Reformation by a number of the Protestant leaders and applied not only to the decisive divine-human relationship but to a variety of social relationships, including marriage and the family, in ways that have had implications for contemporary life.[2] The Christian tradition had already developed a sacramental system, codified in canon law, but the system was generally held by the Protestant Reformers to have departed from the biblical tradition and to be ineffective in guiding and nurturing love.

The sacrament of marriage had been developed to dignify, sanctify, and give moral order to the rather crude, often chaotic, and sometimes brutal relationships that existed between men and women and parents and children in Europe after the decline of the legal constraints of the Roman Empire, and to actualize the implications of the gospel by the use of creed, cult, and code. That sacrament thus brought a new sense of holiness to the estate of marriage and reduced the double standard between men and women with regard to expected sexual behavior. The sacramental practices seemed, for several centuries, to have dignified and given moral order to eros — especially during the feudal pe-

---

1. A summary volume was written by Don Browning, general editor of the series, with Bonnie Miller-McLemore, Pamela Couture, Brynolf Lyon, and Robert Franklin, *From Culture Wars to Common Ground: Religion and the American Family Debate* (Louisville: Westminster John Knox, 1997).

2. See, e.g., my *Covenant and Commitments: Faith, Family, and Economic Life* (Louisville: Westminster John Knox, 1995).

riod when the dominant power in society was the land-owning aristocracy, who kept their power by enforced hereditary ownership — but it did not fully sanctify it. Since land was the primary mode of production, both economic and political-military authority was concentrated in the hands of elite families who also had considerable control over the peasants who worked the land and who inherited their positions as well. The church in this period could easily have been swallowed into the system of feudal estates, and, indeed, hereditary bishops (with the offspring of bishops succeeding to the position) were not unknown. But the church also developed the monastic system as the center and ideal of the church, with its vows of poverty, chastity, and obedience (to the abbot, and thus not to the holders of economic, familial, or political authority). The preservation of the church as an institution, in principle independent of these powers, decisively shaped the contours of civil society in the West, and from this independent position the church not only formed a new kind of structurally differentiated pluralistic society but was able to influence other spheres of life, including the family, from this sovereign spiritual position.

The significance of this can be seen in comparative perspective. One cannot understand the dynamics of tribal societies without charting the sacred genealogical traditions behind them: the caste-structured social fabric of India without reference to the Hindu *Laws of Manu;* the familistic loyalties of Chinese society without reference to the Confucian traditions; or the patterns of authority in household or regime in the Islamic world without awareness of the *Shar'ia* — not because the people in these societies always follow what is prescribed in these sacred sources, but because these provide the normative models around which varieties and exceptions swirl, guilt is experienced, respect is accorded, and law and morality are debated.[3] It is also doubtful that the West can be understood without recognition of the ideals of celibacy, on the one hand, the sacramental marriage, on the other, plus the efforts to reform this system in subsequent traditions by the Protestant Reformation, and efforts to overthrow all of these by later secular movements.

The efforts to reform that heritage were profound. These efforts changed ideals and behaviors in large proportions of the population, and they deeply in-

3. I am indebted to the writings of scholars John Mbiti regarding tribal traditions, Sze-kar Wan regarding Confucian ones, Thomas Thangaraj regarding Hindu ones, Kosuki Koyama regarding Buddhist ones, and Lamin Sanneh regarding Islamic ones. They are all Christian scholars who come from, and have studied, these great religions and civilizations and have recognized that while they are all being influenced by globalization, they each maintain distinctive social and cultural patterns. Each scholar contributed a major essay to *Christ and the Dominions of Civilization* (volume 3 of the series *God and Globalization*), which I edited with comparative religionist Diane Obenchain (Harrisburg, Pa.: Trinity Press International, 2002).

fluenced the normative models by which sexuality and marriage, child rearing and social roles were defined in Western culture. The change was brought about both by the propagation of a revised view of biblical motifs and by offering new accounts of the changing experiences of people's lives in altered social contexts. As the free cities of northern Europe, the harbingers of modernity, began to develop, and as the clergy who served in the parishes were newly required to be celibate like the monks — as evidence of a graced state of existence that allowed them to handle the elements of the Communion — it was at first believed then later doubted that the two-leveled system of celibate clergy and married laity made sense. For one thing, unmarried laity were expected to avoid "fornication," but in fact "common-law" marriages, cohabitation, extra-marital affairs, and casual sex were frequent among the poorer segments of the population and not uncommon among the elites. For another, the official codes were ill-observed by the clergy, and the sale of indulgences later made a mockery of efforts to discipline "deviant" behavior. The system seemed to many to have become incapable of offering compelling guidance to old village or new city, or even to function in monastery, manse, or manor house.[4]

The Protestant Reformers, centered in these cities, sought to purify the faith and the church first of all, but they soon saw that the changes they sought entailed also the reform of the economic, political, cultural, and familial spheres of life as well. Thus they gradually turned to a more expansive view of covenantal relationships as the model for organizing the common life. This is the idea that God calls people into a divine-human relationship that is ordered not only to right belief and worship in this world and salvation in the next, but also to rightly ordered human relations in church and society. That order could be formed by committed people living their lives according to the laws of God, serving the purposes of God, and forming those institutions that served the well-being of the community as well as contributing to the happiness and fidelity of the partners. The Reformers did not, of course, transform everything, nor did they work out these ideas unambiguously or immediately. But they were well aware that sex is such a compelling urge for such a high percentage of the population so much of the time that a rightly ordered family life could provide a structured context in which it could fulfill its divinely intended purposes and reduce temptations to behaviors disruptive to the community and the soul. The covenantal model seemed, to many of the Reformers, to provide a faithful and practical framework for sex and family that fit the economic and political systems that Protestantism also fomented.

---

4. See Muriel Porter, *Sex, Marriage, and the Church: Patterns of Change* (North Blackburn, Australia: Dove, 1996), chap. 1.

Covenantal relationships involved a structured companionship that fostered love and gave stable shape to one of the key institutions of civil society that recognized that life was often beset by difficulty in this fallen world. Indeed, one of the most commonly used phrases in marriage rituals recognized this: the promise of fidelity was made "for better, for worse; for richer, for poorer; in sickness and in health, until death do us part." Those words suggest that the parties to a marriage pledge themselves to a life in which material conditions, messy and unreliable as they are, are nevertheless the loci of incarnate moral and spiritual possibilities that can be made reliable and trustworthy by the "owning" of the covenantal patterns of life that are a gift of God. Further, these moral and spiritual possibilities are more important than the social, material, and physical realities themselves. They make concrete the covenantal principles of fidelity, fecundity, and family formation that allow love to be temporally embodied, and without which love might well dissipate.

The fact that wedding vows are highly ritualized in every society, especially among the higher classes but usually by others who imitate them, is very significant. In rites, rituals, and liturgies, the core moral and spiritual convictions of faith are congealed into a cultural form that is intended to articulate the guiding values for the relationship, and to draw attention in an outward and publicly legitimated way to stabilize and guide a set of inward urges and commitments.[5] What is enacted ritually entails the public declaration of a binding agreement with established norms that also involves the formation of a social unit with established roles. For Protestants, the question was how to recognize that a divinely initiated gift of grace calls persons into a set of holy relationships that accord with God's laws and purposes as made manifest already in the initial divine creation of complementary sexes. "It is not good that one should be alone," says Genesis 2:18; and when a man and a woman recognize that they are made for each other, each is to "cleave" to the other in the presence of God and in accord with God's creational intent. Moreover, according to the mythic poetry that was held to articulate the primal architecture of human social existence, a human pair is so designed that they may become co-creators with God as the "two become one flesh." Even those who marry when they are beyond the child-bearing age, according to later accounts, replicate the structure of this divine design for the purposes of companionship, mutuality of regard, and relief from wanton temptations.

The covenant tradition holds that a covenant is not only a relationship be-

---

5. See Catherine Bell, "Ritual Behavior" (Ph.D. diss., Berkeley, 1989); Catherine Bell, *Ritual, Theory, Ritual Practice: Perspectives and Dimensions,* rev. ed. (New York: Oxford University Press, 1995).

tween two people; there is always a third party present. The formation of such a social unit involves a pledge of fidelity to the other partner in the presence of God, a promise to share the mutual delights of both the marriage bed and a sustained friendship that anticipates the joys of heaven, and a commitment to the future of human existence. Thus, wherever this belief is accepted, it also means accepting personal responsibility for the general shape of society, so that the children of the community, and their children after them, can know a morally and spiritually formed, as well as an economically and politically sound, world. This ideal now appears to be recognized in at least more recent Roman Catholic teachings, current legal codes, and social-psychological research.[6]

Today, it is arguable that, with rapid globalization and massive urbanization, and with dynamic changes in the common culture, the world is undergoing a transformation at least as dramatic as the shift from the early to the medieval world and from medieval feudalism to more urban modernity. Further, it is a widespread perception that the church traditions that derive from the classic Roman and Reformation heritages are not being sustained in their older forms. An important question for these traditions is whether a renewal of the theology and ethic of covenant in the midst of changing social conditions is possible and, if so, whether it can again help the society deepen and broaden its views of sexuality and marriage. If so, it could help nurture a renewed vision of family life that is faithful to the deepest strands of faith, compelling to those forming families, and able to shape the public ethos such that, along with appropriate changes in the economic, political, and legal systems, we can reconstruct a viable, just, and life-sustaining family system. This question is important not only for the happiness and well-being of believers and their children; it is arguable that no civilization can survive over time without an ordered and operative normative pattern for relating of male and female and of parents and children. Familial patterns of life and senses of obligation derived from theological or ethical sources have to be lived out in a context of political, economic, cultural, and legal institutions in a way that is both adaptable to changing conditions and supportive of perennial first principles, the common life, and the uniqueness of each person in the relationship; but it is arguably the case that over time religious thought and practice are decisive influences in all these areas of life. Thus, a closer look at these religious influences is warranted. For this reason, we take up the issues from the past with one eye always glancing toward the issues families are facing today and are likely to face tomorrow.

6. See the chapters herein by Michael G. Lawler, Katherine Shaw Spaht, and Margaret Brinig and Steven Nock.

## A Brief Review of Reformation Views[7]

The meaning of *covenant* in regard to marriage, however, was not univocal during or since the Reformation. John Witte Jr., as well as James T. Johnson, has shown that the Reformers did not speak with one voice on the matter of marriage and that not all of them used the idea of covenant in the same way, although they agreed in rejecting earlier views of sacrament and code.[8] Above all, they did not believe that celibacy was in any way superior to marriage. That view, they held, misunderstood the basic relationship of materiality and spirituality. The latter may be more important than the former, but the increase of one does not entail the decrease of the other. Spiritual realities, indeed, are usually manifest in the material areas of life. Thus a sharp distinction between the "natural laws" and "supernatural graces" falsely divides the character of life. This attitude was not only immediately pertinent to issues of marriage; it also shaped Protestant attitudes toward economic and technological life and toward active engagement by the people in social and political life — in contrast to the older ideal of a celibate, contemplative life. At least a century of debate about the hypothesis of Max Weber that the "Protestant ethic" was instrumental in making the modern socio-economic world what it is, has largely established that it did play a significant role in ways that continue to make a difference.[9]

Behind the Reformers' critique of the previous theological assumption that good but imperfect nature needed ministrations of supernatural grace to be complete, was a doubt that the church had the power and authority to confer grace on nature by a sacramental action, especially if it were claimed that the action altered the very being of the recipient of that grace. In contrast, the Reformers held that grace was already present in the gift of creation, in what some called "common grace" or "general revelation." When, however, humans exercised the freedom given by God to distort God's creational intent, sin, corruption, and death entered human existence and the world of nature in ways that required redemption — which could not be mediated or dispensed by any church or priestly action, but only by God's grace known in Christ through faith. The Reformers, thus, did not believe that the priestly performance of a

7. See chapter by James T. Johnson herein for a fuller history of early Reformation and Puritan teachings, which I shall set in the context of other social developments.

8. See John Witte Jr., *From Sacrament to Contract: Marriage, Religion, and Law in the Western Tradition* (Louisville: Westminster John Knox, 1997), esp. chaps. 2 on Lutheranism, 3 on Calvinism, and 4 on Anglicanism.

9. See Max Weber, *The Protestant Ethic and the Spirit of Capitalism*, second Roxbury ed., trans. Talcott Parsons (Los Angeles: Roxbury, 1998); David Landes, *The Wealth and Poverty of Nations* (New York: W. W. Norton, 1998).

sacrament in the taking of sacred vows of marriage or celibacy mediated divine grace, conferred an ontological change of status, or infused a potential to perfect what was already good or contribute to the soul's salvation. John Witte has put the matter this way:

> [The Reformers] rejected the subordination of marriage to celibacy and the celebration of marriage as a sacrament. . . . [Rather, it was] a covenantal association of the entire community. A variety of parties played a part in the formation of the marriage covenant. The marital couple themselves swore their betrothals and espousals before each other and God — rendering all marriages triparty agreements with God as party, witness, and judge. The couple's parents, as God's bishops for children, gave their consent to the union. Two witnesses, as God's priests to their peers, served as witnesses to the marriage. The minister, holding the spiritual power of the Word, blessed the couple and admonished them in their spiritual duties. [And] the magistrate, holding the temporal power of the sword, registered the parties and their properties and ensured the legality of their union.[10]

This covenantal theory put the issues more widely into the hands of the community of the laity — a "priesthood of believers." This theory was at once more "liberal" than previous ontocratic views, and more "conservative" in that it sought to use the wider biblical sources and networks of community life. The friends and family of the pledged couple were more widely empowered, even if monitored by clerical and civil authority, to take responsibility for the family as a part of the temporal civil society. This entailed a major reformation of the previous system, this time with reduced hierarchical emphasis and with stronger proto-democratic elements that eventually also inclined the West toward a transformation of economic and political life.

The basic background beliefs for interpreting and guiding sexuality and marriage did not congeal immediately, however. Martin Luther emphasized the idea that marriage is one of the "orders of creation" — built into the way God created the world and a practical remedy for the temptations to lustful behaviors for sinful humanity. John Calvin and others in the Reformed tradition, especially Heinrich Bullinger and Martin Bucer, followed Luther at first, but gradually elaborated a theory of overlapping covenants — between God and the persons who formed the couple, between the parents of the marriage partners and the couple, and between the larger society and the particular couple, with God present in all these relationships. This, then, is what was celebrated

---

10. John Witte, Jr., *An Apt and Cheerful Conversation on Marriage* (Atlanta: Emory University, 2001), p. 6.

and made known to all in public worship services where various rites were devised to acknowledge these creational and covenanted relationships.[11] Together these invite what Joseph Allen calls "a network of mutual entrustment."[12]

The biblical tradition recognizes that the people of God do not always keep the covenants to which God calls them, and that these covenants sometimes break down so that new ones have to be formed or old ones renewed under the overarching covenant that God has made with humanity, Israel, and the church. If breakdown happens in marriages, efforts at reconciliation and re-covenanting are advised; but divorce and remarriage become a possibility — one not given in the earlier sacramental tradition, as James T. Johnson has convincingly argued.[13] In practice, breakdown happened in the sacramental system also, but it was conceptually very awkward, for the ontological status thought to be conferred by the sacrament made marital change theoretically impossible. A church court had to determine that no marriage had taken place; thus the "relationship" was "annulled."

A key moment in the development of Protestant understandings of marriage came precisely when this issue of annulment was a highly visible international issue. Henry VIII, King of England, required a male heir to succeed him, at a time when primogeniture was the least violent means of political succession acknowledged. Although the story is lengthy and complex, and the motivations mixed, the main plot is simple: Henry needed a divorce to marry a wife who might give him a son, and Rome would not grant one because of the classic doctrines and laws regarding the sacrament of marriage.[14] So, as the breezes of humanism wafted through Amsterdam and Oxford, the gustier winds of Reformation blew through Wittenberg, Geneva, and Zurich in the 1530s, and the storms of nationalism gathered in Paris, Edinburgh, and London, Henry felt he had to break with Rome. The obvious result is the Anglican church,

11. These several paragraphs are indebted to Witte, *From Sacrament to Contract*. But I interpret the Reformed tradition somewhat differently in that I see a closer connection between Calvin, Bullinger, Bucer, and the Anglo-American Puritans, whereas he focuses on Calvin in one chapter and treats Bullinger, Bucer, and so on in the context of the Anglican tradition. As we will see, I agree that the Anglican tradition was influenced by them, but agree with James T. Johnson's chapter herein that the Puritan tradition was particularly important in shaping much modern practice, and served as the target of many criticisms of "Christian" teachings on family and sexuality. In this connection, see, e.g., Tracy Fessenden, N. Radel, and M. J. Zaborowska, *The Puritan Origins of American Sex* (New York: Routledge, 2001).

12. Joseph L. Allen, *Love and Conflict: A Covenantal Model of Christian Ethics* (Nashville: Abingdon, 1984).

13. See James T. Johnson, *A Society Ordained by God: English Puritan Marriage Doctrine in the First Half of the Seventeenth Century* (Nashville: Abingdon, 1970), and his chapter herein.

14. See Witte, *From Sacrament to Contract*, pp. 143-56.

whose bishops allowed him to divorce while basically keeping the Catholic theory of sacraments, but with a modified view of marriage!

A new prayer book was developed, drawing on Lutheran-evangelical and Calvinist-Reformed theories of marriage to render an integrated distillation of normative teaching about marriage. It echoed scriptural passages that pointed to the "orders of creation" and to "covenantal bonding," without mentioning these characteristic Protestant doctrines by name. The new liturgy shows, nevertheless, a new understanding of the relationship of materiality and spirituality, nature and grace. Marriage, it says, instructing both couple and witnessing congregation,

> is an honorable estate, instituted of God in paradise in the time of man's innocency, signifying unto us the mystical union that is betwixt Christ and his Church: which holy estate Christ adorned and beautified with his presence and first miracle that he wrought in Cana of Galilee, and is commended of St. Paul to be honorable among all men, and therefore is not to be enterprised nor taken in hand unadvisedly, lightly, or wantonly, to satisfy men's carnal lusts and appetites, like brute beasts that have no understanding, but reverently, discreetly, advisedly, soberly and in the fear of God, duly considering the causes of which matrimony was ordained. One was, the procreation of children to be brought up in the fear of the Lord, and praise of God. Secondly, it was ordained for a remedy against sin, and to avoid fornication, that such persons as have not the gift of continency might marry, and keep themselves undefiled members of Christ's body. Thirdly for the mutual society, help, and comfort, that the one ought to have of the other, both in prosperity and adversity. . . .[15]

The Lutheran traditions are generally suspicious of "covenant" language, for it seems so Reformed; but they use the words *bind* and *bond* with the echo of the fact that the Germanic word for covenant is *Bund*. Some Free-church Protestants use "mystery of marriage," an echo of the New Testament use of the Greek *mysterion* as one translation of *covenant*, without taking the next (Catholic) step to the Latin *sacramentum*. Versions of the themes in this instruction were adopted and adapted by the English-speaking world first through the influence of the Anglican church in Great Britain and America, later around the world as the British Empire rose to dominance, and then through the missionary activity of, particularly, the Methodists and the London Missionary Society,

---

15. John Booty, ed., *The Book of Common Prayer 1559* (Charlottesville: Published for the Folger Shakespeare Library by the University Press of Virginia, 1976), pp. 290-91, quoted by Witte, *From Sacrament to Contract*, p. 155.

and later the Reformed, Presbyterian, and Congregational missions of the nineteenth and twentieth centuries, who already had a parallel tradition.[16] The particular formulas have been modified over time — primarily in the direction of the more and more explicit use of covenant theology as a guide to social life became predominant through the influence of the Puritan theologies of England and New England, but the themes are remarkably constant. The revised *Book of Common Prayer,* used by the Protestant Episcopal Church in the United States, for instance, begins the service with these words:

> Beloved, We have come together in the presence of God to witness and bless the joining together of this man and this woman in Holy Matrimony. The bond and covenant of marriage was established by God in creation, and our Lord Jesus adorned this manner of life by his presence and first miracle at the wedding in Cana of Galilee.

This is echoed by the United Methodist service:

> Friends, we are gathered together in the sight of God to witness and bless the joining of this man and this woman in Christian Marriage. The Covenant of marriage was established by God, who created us male and female for each other.

The Presbyterians do not put the term *covenant* in the general statement to the couple or in the explanation of what marriage is about to the congregation at the opening of service, but instead in the direct questions put to the couple. Thus they accent the voluntary human activity in this area of human covenanting under God, even if, in other areas of doctrine, the emphasis on predestination suggests that humans have little choice about the fact that God elects and calls them to various duties and relationships in life:

> "John" (or "Jane"), understanding that God has created, ordered, and blessed the covenant of marriage, do you affirm your desire and intention to enter this covenant?[17]

16. The Methodist adaptation was influenced by the subsequent impact on Anglicanism of the Puritan and Presbyterian traditions, such as John Knox's *Book of Common Order.* In these the term *covenant* appears more directly, especially in the inquiry made to the pair. See the formulation in the Methodist Discipline based in the "abridgement" of the *Book of Common Prayer* that John Wesley sent in 1792 to the Methodists in the United States, *The Sunday Service of the Methodists in North America, with Other Occasional Services* (Nashville: Methodist Publishing House, 1792). Direct parallels, with local adaptations, can be found in, among other locations, India, Burma, South Africa, Kenya, Singapore, Hong Kong, Canada, Australia.

17. I draw these four samples from the convenient collection of wedding ceremonies edited

In all cases, the covenantal form is understood to be a free, voluntary agreement that accords with a pre-given order and a divine set of purposes that correspond not only to the basic patterns of creation but to rightly ordered human desires. The couple, in the context of a caring community and the presence of God, is asked to declare publicly that they wish to "enter" this form of life and make it their own.

## Between the Reformation and the Twentieth Century

Considerable continuity can be traced between the Continental and the British Reformations and the dominant understandings of the nature, character, and purposes of marriage as represented in most liturgies of the twentieth century, especially in Protestant-influenced countries. Of course, the Roman Catholic sacramental traditions continued, as did the Eastern Orthodox, Jewish, and other distinctive traditions. But the practices of the Protestant churches formed the core of the pluralistic civil society in much of the West; they allowed these several traditions their own place in the fabric of the common life, while still generating an ethos that reinforced covenantal social, political, and economic presumptions about roles, responsibilities, and the nature and character of a loving home, presumptions that were often formulated into legal codes. The majority of governmental policies fomented these patterns through laws concerning marriage licensing, divorce, child custody, inheritance, and property provisions. Indeed, the rites used by justices of the peace and sea captains, who also had the legal authority to perform weddings, basically followed the pattern of these rituals, often without using the word "God," and usually omitting reference to "Christ."[18]

This is not to say that there were not tensions within the Protestant tradition. On the whole, although there are variations in specific times and places, the Lutherans were more willing to make marriage more a matter of civil law, with a church blessing to follow, while the Reformed and Puritan traditions saw the church-centered wedding as prior, to be then registered by civil authority.[19] We must also remember that in Europe until the 1830s and the United States until the 1860s, slavery was legal and seen by many as consistent with both nat-

---

by Andy Langford, *Christian Weddings: Resources to Make Your Ceremony Unique* (Nashville: Abingdon, 1995).

18. Nancy F. Cott, *Public Vows: A History of Marriage and Nation* (Cambridge: Harvard University Press, 2000).

19. Roman Catholic and Anglican parish records were themselves often the legal registration, since these churches were directly established by the states.

ural law and the Scriptures. This had considerable impact on family life in that the control over the sexual lives of the slaves varied widely — from direct exploitation, to programmed breeding by assigned pairing (a practice that was neither sacramental nor covenantal nor contractual), to the breaking up of families by sale. This scandalous chapter in American history has had enduring effects, even if some slave owners made attempts to replicate "Christian" marriage among the slaves and the slaves themselves mixed these traditions with remembered African ones.

Further, since the Reformation put the Bible in the hands of the laity, the laity as well as the clergy learned to turn to it as the authority in all matters. Protestantism is not constitutionally fundamentalist, but it has a biblio-centric dimension, a tendency that gave rise to contrary accents and interpretations about the issue of the authority of the father and husband in relation to that of the mother and wife. On the one hand, there are the famous passages from Genesis which tell us that humanity was made in the image of God and given the mandate to "have dominion" and thus become stewards of creation together (Gen. 1:26). When humanity became conscious of the fact that they were formed as complementary partners, they recognized the other as "bone of my bones and flesh of my flesh" (Gen. 2:23).[20] Further, much later, during the early formation of the church, it was held that "in Christ . . . there is neither male nor female" (Gal. 3:28). These passages, some related to creation, others to the prospect of redemption, press toward a sense of the equal dignity and authority of male and female, with each having some distinct capabilities. Time and again in the history of Protestantism, these were used to point toward a nonsubservient partnership, even if one can find strong evidence of patriarchy in the ancient Hebraic, Greek, Latin, and Reformation traditions that are present in the Scriptures, and some direct commands that seem to re-enforce it normatively. In Ephesians 5:22, for example, we read: "Wives, be subject to your husbands. . . ." Of course, the previous verse says, "Be subject to one another. . . ." And three verses later, one can find, "Husbands, love your wives, as Christ loves the church and gave himself up for her" — a verse that suggests a kind of voluntary sacrificial subjection of the husband to the welfare of the wife that turns patriarchy upside down. But it was less these verses than the direct instruction to the wives that was most quoted. Indeed, in many wedding liturgies written prior to the mid twentieth century, the wife is asked in the "pledges" to "love, honor, and

20. The continuing importance of this is clearly stated in Mary Stewart Van Leeuwen, "Faith, Feminism, and the Family in an Age of Globalization," in *Religion and the Powers of the Common Life,* ed. Max L. Stackhouse and Peter Paris, vol. 1 of the God and Globalization series (Harrisburg, Pa.: Trinity Press International, 2000), pp. 184-230.

obey" her new husband, while the husband is asked to "love, honor, and cherish" his new wife — phrases now usually made parallel by the use of alternative wording.

Catherine Hall has studied a representative case of how this patriarchy came to be normative in Protestant thought, despite much scriptural evidence to the contrary. She sees the roots in the evangelical movement that followed on the heels of earlier Puritanism, became widespread after the rise of Methodism, and carried into the Victorian period, and she turns to the writings of Hannah More as exemplary of these developments. More, at first, was entranced by the French Revolution and was a friend of William Wilberforce, the key advocate for the abolition of slavery. But she became converted to the new evangelicalism before the end of the 1700s. She wrote a series of tracts that became standard fare for the newly urbanizing working populations as industrialism increased, and she later wrote a novel for the growing middle classes. Hall summarizes More's writings as an

> Evangelically inspired attempt to win the hearts and minds of the people through propagandizing traditional paternalism combined with Christian revivalism. . . . More preached obedience to those in authority and emphasized the joys to come in the heavenly home. A modest, humble, and hardworking life would find pleasure in God's eyes. . . . [She was] . . . one of the most widely read authors of her period. More's fundamental quest was for religious salvation. She saw the family as crucial for that salvation and familial duties were preeminent in the attempt to lead a Christian life. All men and women possessed individual souls and, therefore, the possibility of life eternal; but the duties of men and women were markedly different. [Her hero was] a model of Christian manliness, exemplifying all those virtues that the Evangelicals were defining as necessary to a new form of masculinity that would challenge the older patterns of rude vigor and sportsmanship and celebrate instead gentleness and tenderness combined with manly authority. . . . He is immensely serious about family duties . . . as a husband or a father. . . . The new Christian man must allow his religious calling to be the center of his being, whether that calling is to be a gentleman farmer, a merchant, a clergyman, or a worker. Whatever his employment, he must perform it in a religious spirit. . . . [In contrast,] Evangelical ideas about femininity began with the assumption that woman's godliness was linked to her maternal and wifely duties. Eve had fallen because of her unabashed sensuality. But Mary, the Mother of Christ, had given new hope to womanhood by bearing Jesus. Saint Paul . . . had instructed women that their duty was to manage the house. . . . The home was the proper sphere of

her influence and her action. The wider theaters of public life were not for her. . . .[21]

These ideas became almost as widespread as the covenantal wedding liturgies, but other key developments in society and culture, prompted by certain developments of modern technology and economics, were also deeply stamped by ideas of vocation. These fed a new spiritual dedication to profession that altered perceptions as to how these normative principles and purposes were to be applied. The family historically was the primary center of production, distribution, nurture, and consumption, as well as reproduction, the unit where husband and wife often shared tasks in the field or the shop with older children for the good of the whole family unit. The household was the place where one learned to share the relatively more or less that was available to all members. Ideally, it was also where one's character was most directly formed and where one learned to love and pray. All these functions of life were understood to be holy gifts and sacred duties, ratified by a legal act, celebrated in a public sacramental or covenantal bonding. In many cases the economic order, the family structure, the dominant religious practices, and their relationship were more or less integrated and enforced by political and legal authority.

But even during the period in which More was writing, the changing relationships of the different spheres in society became more rapid and more extensive and soon began to challenge that pattern of distinction between the public male and the domestic female. Of course, the influential lay theologian and political theorist John Locke had already written his critical analysis of traditional patriarchy in both familial and political authority in his famous *First Treatise on Government*. He developed an influential theory of economic life that was to take place in a much more democratic family in his *Second Treatise*.[22] He may well have articulated what others were to experience in the next century: the family was being fundamentally reshaped by social developments. Ironically, these developments were largely the unintended by-product of Protestant influences in the English-speaking world. Modern pluralistic, representative democracy can trace many of its roots to the Puritan Revolution in England of the 1640s to 1680s, and to the American and French Revolutions a century later — the first sympathetic to Protestant Christianity and covenantal theory, the second especially hostile to Catholic Christianity and in favor of

21. Catherine Hall, "The Sweet Delights of Home," in *A History of Private Life*, gen. ed. Michelle Perrot, Philippe Ariés, and Georges Duby (Cambridge, Mass.: Belknap Press of Harvard University Press, 1990), 4:29-30, 55-57.

22. *John Locke's Two Treatises of Government*, ed. Peter Laslett (Cambridge: Cambridge University Press, 1960). The original drafts were completed about 1689 and published the next year.

adopting a militantly secular social contract theory.[23] These revolutions included the celebration of the ideas of human equality and human rights — for the former, first of all, in communities of faith with implications for society; for the latter, first of all, in the political order, which was expected to create a national social solidarity on nonreligious grounds.

The implications of these revolutionary trends for the family are quite remarkable, but the ways in which the different revolutionary traditions worked them out were divergent. The idea of a society based in contract was intended to recognize the freedom of the individuals to contract with each other as each party wants. When this model is projected on a larger social scene, however, it begins to force a new kind of conformity. Lynn Hunt, in her research on the impact of the French Revolution on family life during this period, found that

> In no domain was the invasion of public authority more evident than in family life. Marriage was secularized and the ceremony, to be considered binding, had to be performed before a municipal official [rather than before a priest]. By the far-reaching decree of 20 September 1792, . . . the state determined the [conditions for] marriage; [granted the rights of children] . . . ; instituted divorce; and limited parental powers. . . . [A]s Danton said, [the children] "belong to the Republic before they belong to their parents." Bonaparte himself insisted that "the law takes the child at birth, provides for his education, prepares him for a profession, regulates how and under what conditions he can marry, travel and choose a profession." . . . In general, the state often limited family or church control only in order to increase its own. . . .[24]

The French Revolutionary developments extended the centralized state of earlier French royalty, now republican in form, in unanticipated ways. It developed a system that focused on the individual as a citizen of the collective state, with many of the intermediate institutions (church, school, the arts, and medicine, for example) subjected to the life of the state. It anticipated the political structure that reappeared in the other great revolutionary state — the twentieth-century Soviet Union. The family became a contracted unit between

23. See Michael Walzer, *The Revolution of the Saints: A Study in the Origins of Radical Politics* (Cambridge: Harvard University Press, 1965). See also A. S. P. Woodhouse, ed., *Puritanism and Liberty,* second ed. (Chicago: University of Chicago Press, 1950); James Hastings Nichols, *Democracy and the Churches* (Philadelphia: Westminster, 1951). In this period the distinction between a "covenant" and a "contract" began to be more refined, with the one thought to be initiated by God and in accord with a universal moral law, and the second by human will according to the perceived needs or wants of the human parties.

24. L. Hunt, "The Unstable Boundaries of the French Revolution," in *A History of Private Life,* 4:27-28.

two individuals, essentially permitted, guided, and controlled by governmental regulation.

The covenantal tradition, by contrast, saw the role of the state as a limited, even a dependent, one. The decisive social relations were between God and humans, and, in that context, between persons of commitment in communities of worship, in families, or in cooperative ventures that morally served the common good. People in these public bodies could associate to form, dissolve, or reform a political order accordingly as it served and protected these social communities of commitment that were prior to the state. This implied the priority of civil societal relationships, including church and family, to the state, whose role it was to protect these pre-political associations.

These pre-political organizations were economic as well as familial and ecclesial. Without explicitly intending capitalism in its modern forms, Lutheran, Reformed, Methodist, and many sectarian Protestant groups held an overlapping doctrine of "vocation" that encouraged those ascetic habits of devotionally driven work, constrained consumption, and rationally organized labor known previously only in the monastery. The Protestants applied these habits to business life that was regulated, but not managed, by political authority — in part because it took the idea of the medieval corporation that had been developed for monastic orders, independent towns, and charitable institutions and applied it to the business corporation.[25] In that context, they applied the findings of science to new technologies, and through new bookkeeping methods applied the rational calculation of costs and gains to every stage of production and distribution; in addition, they developed new technological innovations that changed the structure of the economy. The "Weberian thesis" regarding this development, that religion is a formative factor in social history, has, as was mentioned above, been extensively studied, widely doubted, but essentially confirmed in modified forms by subsequent scholarship in the key respects that concern us here.[26] It helps explain why successful economic development appears among some parts of the population in an area, and why some cultures seem to develop in one direction while others develop quite differently, when other factors are essentially similar. Economic development may not be entirely a matter of economic natural laws. Weber had argued that the Reformation had, in basic ways, shaped the industrializing economy of modernity.

25. See my "The Moral Roots of the Corporation," *Theology and Public Policy* 5, no. 1 (1993): 29-39.

26. See, e.g., I. Bernard Cohen, ed., *Puritanism and the Rise of Modern Science* (New Brunswick, N.J.: Rutgers University Press, 1990); E. Digby Balzell, *Puritan Boston and Quaker Philadelphia* (New York: Free Press, 1979); Francis Fukuyama, *Trust: The Social Virtues and the Creation of Prosperity* (New York: Free Press, 1995).

But he also held that modern humanity was likely to leave the consciously religious motivations behind; yet the frameworks developed by that now-lost consciousness would shape the social habits of the culture. Today, a number of scholars are arguing that, in order to grasp what is driving the "cultural DNA" of modern society — and determine whether to embrace it, repudiate it, or modulate it — it is necessary to exhume the deep religiocultural factors that shaped what is going on.[27]

## Other Indirect Influences

However the details of these historical arguments are assessed over the next several decades, the formation of a technological, corporate, and global market economy in a democratic political order that seeks to guarantee human rights to everyone has generated not only a polity today thought to be based on a "social contract," but a set of economic and social contractual relationships that influence how, where, and with whom people interact, earn their livings, meet and relate to each other outside the home, and, increasingly, view the relationships they have made to family, church, and society. These social, political, and economic transformations have deeply affected the contemporary family, and the kinds of expectations people have of marriage.

Whereas in most of human history, the family was the center of production, nurture, distribution, and consumption as well as reproduction, the centering of the economy and work in the corporation and the market — the factory, the office, or the store — has brought with it the separation of production and much of distribution from the family unit. Not only does the family less and less often work together in the same location, the economic skills demanded for the changing world of work make obsolete the parental knowledge of how to do things. At the same time, the common, volatile relationships of economic life, focused on temporary cooperative teamwork with changing work-mates, has given rise to a new form of contractual interactions. Further, the development of a series of markets — labor, financial, goods and services, all increasingly open to women as well as men, to the young as well as the old, to unmarried as well as married — has also taken much distribution out of the collective hands of familial dynamics and made consumer offerings of the market available to anyone with resources. The family has become (or is becoming

---

27. See Peter Berger, *The Capitalist Revolution* (New York: Basic Books, 1986). Cf. L. E. Harrison and S. P. Huntington, *Culture Matters: How Values Shape Human Progress* (New York: Basic, 2000).

in those parts of the world that are changing most rapidly) essentially a center for certain kinds of consumption and recreation, in the double sense of the term — one spends time with the family when one is off-duty because, and if, one enjoys it; and it is re-creational in that it allows the recharging of the physical and emotional batteries so that one may reenter the work world refreshed. Of course, many couples genuinely love each other, spend as much time with each other and the children as possible, and stick together through thick and thin, but it appears to be the case that if the prospects of consumption and recreation are not fulfilled in their relationship, other couples are inclined to shop around.

There are doubtless many other factors influencing relational behaviors and human commitments. The high-tech culture produced out of these deeper historical influences not only produced labor-saving devices that made sex-role stereotypes less pertinent, it brought new birth-control methods, cars with mobility and privacy, safer methods of abortion, and mass media with a popular culture celebrating "post-conventional" behavior. Until the advent of AIDS, the human costs of casual, serial relationships were reduced, and the themes of "sex, drugs, and rock-and-roll" that became prominent during the 1960s by new recording methods and the mass media seemed to legitimate non-celibate and pre-marital sexual experimentation.

Colin Campbell, in a highly suggestive study, has argued that such developments derive from the development of a parallel culture to that formed by "the Protestant ethic," the earlier ascetic "Catholic ethic," and the "rational control of the world" of Enlightenment scientism, including the disciplined life and chaste marriages that were, in rather different ways, advocated by these traditions. A "Romantic ethic," in which nothing was thought to be worse than to deny the felt impulses of the heart, even if it meant breaking all "bourgeois," "Victorian," "old-fashioned religious," "out-of-date moralistic," or "cold rationalist" values, began to dominate the libidinous, consumption side of the also furiously productive side of modern economic culture.[28]

The effects of these changes were partially visible in the Gay Nineties at the turn of the twentieth century, and in the Roaring Twenties a couple of decades later. They were temporarily obscured by the Depression and preoccupations with defeating the Fascists and containing the Communists at mid century; even then, they were well preserved in the Romantic movies of those years. And, after the Depression and World War II was over, higher and higher percentages of the population began to go to college and more and more women

28. Colin Campbell, *The Romantic Ethic and the Spirit of Modern Consumerism* (Oxford: B. Blackwell, 1987).

joined the campuses. The extended education, away from home, not only implied a longer adolescence exactly during the years when hormones are most active; it removed the youth from parental, community, and church influence and supervision. "Dating, rating, and mating" became a primary function of higher education, reinforcing both more highly autonomous decisions about relationships and the idealization of the romantic wedding.[29]

The churches grew in the 1950s, and during this time mainline Protestant pastors increasingly turned to existentialist and psychological understandings of the faith and morality, and became more focused on persons in their particular context than on forming stable institutions in society. This shift involved a situational ethic rather than one that sought to provide normative guidance about the conduct of life. A new optimism developed as a kind of "confidence in love." This was supplemented over the next two decades as liberation theology became the dominant influence among the leadership of the mainline churches. That theology supported the de-colonial movements that were taking place in the developing world, and it joined those efforts to overcome cultural imperialism. The domestic counterpart to these movements not only supported the "freedom movement" as it was led by Martin Luther King Jr., it gave new conceptual resources to the developing women's movements.

In all cases, these newer movements tended to raise the values of liberty and equality above all others, a tendency that had remarkable implications when joined to the confidence in love. Whereas once people thought that God is loving as well as righteous and just, increasingly Love became god, equality the norm of all justice, and righteousness appeared only in the term *self-righteous*. Knowing something about the perils, according to newer psychoanalytical theories, of any repressed feelings, many mainline church leaders were reluctant to be judgmental, or to impose their values on anyone else. Some simply declared the old standards obsolete. In this context, both the Catholic sacramental views and the Protestant covenantal views of marriage began to decline in the operating convictions of the new generation of church leaders who might have been expected to advocate these classical views.

The domestic cultural revolution of the 1960s and 1970s, for all the gains it made in terms of racial justice and increased opportunities for women, also radicalized a tolerant and permissive ethos and generated (as the slogans of the period reveal) both the "make love, not war" hippies and the militant "New Left" cadres, both of which repudiated the ideals of the bourgeois family, sought alternative lifestyles, and legitimized the idea that one may have to leave one's spouse, partner, and/or children to find oneself or to fight every hege-

29. See Porter, *Sex, Marriage, and the Church.*

mony. Many of the youth left the churches and turned East, often with highly imaginary models of Asian religions and their understandings of sexuality and marriage, while others turned Left, taking Latin American revolutionary figures as their heroes. During this same time, in part reacting against these developments, neo-conservative, evangelical, and pentecostal movements grew, holding staunchly to the older standards and generating ideological debates over the changing patterns of family life.[30]

Governmental programs that more nearly approximated the French and Marxist theories of democracy than Puritan-influenced Anglo-American ones reduced some of the aristocratic privileges in society. But they also fomented a shift away from classical, normative understandings of marriage and the family toward a more secular, contractual understanding that was not without consequences. Specifically, it fostered a "two agent" theory of social life: The individual and the state were increasingly acknowledged as the only substantive social agents, family basically defined as a living unit of some kind, and the intermediary institutions of civil society, including religious ones, were programmatically reduced in importance, although many held that these are the decisive carriers of the ethical fabric of the common life, the primary source of social capital.[31] Welfare policies implemented by the war on poverty aided many in difficult circumstances; they also made it much more possible to have and raise children alone. The rates of divorce, of cohabitation, and of the percentage of children born out of wedlock increased exponentially, although all the reasons for this continue to be debated.[32]

Today the classical traditions are largely eclipsed in the popular mind by an entirely secular theory of contract, in which many see a great peril. Indeed, in a remarkable Millennium Lecture, Jonathan Sacks, the Chief Rabbi of Great Britain, states the issues quite directly. He argues that since the idea of natural hierarchies is discredited, there are only two great remaining ways of thinking of human association. They are "contract," essentially an idea from political economics in which interests and mutual suspicion are the determinants; and "covenant," essentially a social concept in which trust, moral commitments, and mutual accountability are the determinants that modulate power, interests, and suspicion. The idea of covenant, he writes, "creates the institutions of civil society: families, communities, voluntary associations, and moral tradi-

30. See, e.g., Brigitte Berger and Peter L. Berger, *The War over the Family* (Garden City, N.Y.: Anchor Press/Doubleday, 1983).

31. See Corwin Smidt, ed., *Religion As Social Capital: Producing the Common Good* (Waco, Tex.: Baylor University Press, 2003).

32. I have traced and evaluated a number of these debates in Stackhouse, *Covenant and Commitments.*

tions. . . . [T]he reinvigoration of these civil institutions is the single greatest challenge facing . . . liberal democracies. . . ."[33]

The scholar of American religion Bradford Wilcox, with a nod to sociologist Alan Wolfe, also recently summarized the effects that all this secularizing, contractual theory of the common life has had on the ethos of America:

> [C]urrent interpretations of the Constitution require that there be a secular purpose for governmental action and that that action must not have the primary effect of advancing religion (with which concern for the family is widely thought to be connected). . . . [Further, many] politicians and activists . . . came to realize that language invoking distinctly Christian conceptions of biblical truth was counter-productive if the objective is to win elections and pass legislation. . . . [Moreover,] the recent cultural turn toward "moral freedom" has left many Americans, including politicians, unwilling to make strong arguments in public settings — both political and civic — about moral obligations where there is substantial cultural disagreement. Many Americans are now under the misapprehension that the virtue of tolerance requires them to make no public claims about the good life, especially if such claims would impinge upon the behavior of others.[34]

In addition, as theologian and ethicist Don Browning has argued in a new study, the general patterns that are held to be a part of modernization and globalization and that have altered lifestyles and social thought in a number of other ways at home are also being exported around the world, causing hostility to the West in many places. This globalization effect is not only appearing in the new formation of middle classes, it is also bringing new levels of divorce in the rapidly developing cultures of Asia where it was previously rare. Moreover, fathers are more likely than before to leave their families, and the devastation of AIDS seems to signal more casual patterns of sexual intimacy and the breakdown of older constraints. These factors increase the poverty of those left behind and limit their chances of taking advantage of the promise of the globalizing economies.[35]

33. Reprinted as "Social Contract or Social Covenant," in *Policy Review* (July/August, 1996): 54-57.

34. W. Bradford Wilcox, *Sacred Vows, Public Purposes* (Washington, D.C.: The Pew Forum on Religion and Public Life, 2002), pp. 15-16. He cites Alan Wolfe, *Moral Freedom: The Search for Virtue in a World of Choice* (New York: W. W. Norton, 2001).

35. Don S. Browning, *Marriage and Modernization: How Globalization Threatens Marriage and What to Do about It* (Grand Rapids: Eerdmans, 2003). A supplementary view of the globalizing trends can be found in my *Capitalism, Civil Society, Religion and the Poor* (Wilmington, 2002), written with Larry Stratton.

Wilcox and Browning utilize political, economic, and sociological views, and illumine some aspects of human behavior. But they know that such methods are methodologically reductionistic and seldom are capable of conveying the deeper meanings that people associate with falling in love and planning to get married for life. Such methods also fail to fully explain how increasingly complex civil societies that erode traditional authoritarian structures of family life also may open the way to patterns of family life that can best flourish in the midst of rapid social change, that reward the formation of specific kinds of relationship, and that enhance the prospects of humanizing the globalizing tendencies that seem presently so powerful and so pervasive. They fail to offer an understanding of the nature of sexuality in the context of love, of the power of love in personal lives, or of the distinctive forms of marriage and the family that various cultures have produced because of the theological, metaphysical, moral, and religious meanings implicit in these matters. Rarely do they convey a compelling interpretation of the religious or spiritual elements that shape the nature of the society of which the families are always a part, and thereby offer a normative view of family life or the place of the family in the larger culture.[36] Fortunately, a series of other authors have also begun to grapple with these issues of the nature and character of love in fresh and creative ways.[37]

## The Most Heated Debates

All of these efforts, however, may be obscured if the church and the society do not find a way to deal with the current debates about homosexuality. Every denomination is presently in the midst of debates about this matter that threaten to divide the communities of faith. Every politician must sooner or later declare a position and risk losing half of his or her constituency. Especially worrisome to some religious leaders is the way in which an increasingly secular view of

36. The new yearbook of the American Society for Political and Legal Philosophy evidently found it entirely unnecessary to include any treatment of religious perspectives in their *Nomos* series, volume 44, Stephen Macedo and Iris Marion Young, eds., *Child, Family, and State* (New York: New York University Press, 2003).

37. See, e.g., Diogenes Allen, *Love: Christian Romance, Marriage, and Friendship* (Cambridge, Mass.: Cowley, 1987); Gilbert Meilander, *The Limits of Love: Some Theological Explorations* (University Park, Pa.: Pennsylvania State University Press, 1987); Mary Stewart Van Leeuwen et al., *After Eden: Facing the Challenge of Gender Reconciliation* (Grand Rapids: Eerdmans, 1993); Lisa Sowle Cahill, *Sex, Gender and Christian Ethics* (Cambridge/New York: Cambridge University Press, 1996); Stephen Post, *Spheres of Love: Toward a New Ethics of the Family* (Dallas: Southern Methodist University Press, 1994).

marriage as a private, temporary, contract, entered into for the advantage of the parties, is eroding classic sacramental and covenantal views of marriage. Already the Netherlands and Belgium have made the marriage of same-sex couples legal, several states in North America have approved civil unions, and the Massachusetts courts have declared that marriage laws must be applied equally to opposite-sex and same-sex pairs.

While, in regard to economic and political life, mainline Protestants have criticized individualistic autonomy and arbitrary contracts as a morally insufficient way of organizing these areas of the common life, this is the view of family life that has begun to triumph in the popular mind. No longer is sex viewed as a dimorphic gift of God designed for procreation and the cultivation of love within a sacred, bonded, and publicly approved institution; it is seen as a natural happening, a secular choice, and a private matter according to one's inclinations. Some wonder what religion and law have to do with it, for what really counts is a subjective consciousness, preference, or orientation and a right of privacy. Indeed, in the 2003 case of *Lawrence v. Texas,* the Supreme Court seemed to confirm the legal side of the question when it ruled that sexual behavior between two persons of the same sex, in private, is legal. But many who are self-designating lesbian or gay, and many who support them, are also believers and want to have the fuller moral and spiritual legitimation of their union recognized by the churches.

Although many mainline Protestants have faced these changes with a great deal of anxiety, sensibilities inherited from the civil rights movement have shaped attitudes toward this issue. Since the churches came to oppose the segregation of minority ethnic groups and the exclusion of women from leadership in church and society as decisive moral issues, why is it not the case for homosexual persons? Concerns for the rights of gays have led some mainline church leaders to mute their support for traditional heterosexual marriage.[38] Indeed, debates about the ordination of homosexual persons and the possible recognition of same-sex marriages by the churches have been a rancorous and divisive issue in the mainline Protestant churches for a quarter of a century. These disputes became most visible in 2003 when the Episcopalians ordained an openly gay bishop. That decision almost overshadowed the fact that they also both rejected a proposal to authorize the writing of an official liturgy for

38. For example, Dr. Robert Edgar, General Secretary, National Council of Churches, withdrew his name three days after he signed "A Christian Declaration of Marriage," also signed by the Chairman of the National Conference of Catholic Bishops, the President of the Southern Baptist Convention, and the President of the National Association of Evangelicals. He explained that he was concerned that the statement would become "an oblique statement on same-sex unions" (http://www.ncccusa.org/news/2000GA/marriage.html).

same-sex unions and allowed, as an informal local option, the pastoral blessing of same-sex couples — as minorities in other churches have been doing for some years. At stake are not only questions of church polity (that is, how the various denominational groups believe that God wants humanity to order its common life when it is faithful), but also the discernment of what is genuine and what is false prophecy, the fundamental question of the authority of the Bible and classic doctrines on matters of "personal" morality today, and the relationship of personal to public morality and law.[39]

All but two of the major denominations in America have sought to preserve the classical traditions in official teachings — the United Church of Christ and the Episcopal Church. All the others — the Baptists, Lutherans, Perbyterians, Methodists, etc. — however, have strong minority voices who are persistent advocates of the full acceptance of gay and lesbian persons and behaviors as co-equal in moral standing to heterosexual ones.[40] Catholics, Orthodox, and evangelical groups have much smaller minorities but sometimes vociferous voices as well. Moreover, mainline Protestants on the whole have yet to make a concerted, institutionalized effort to make the case for a normative shape to Christian marriage that entails the joining of a man and a woman in holy matrimony that is compelling to the public. Some advocate the view that recognizing same-sex marriage or unions will strengthen the patterns of marital life by extending its boundaries. Many denominational leaders have viewed evangelically oriented organizations attempting to address family values, such as Promise Keepers, with deep suspicion. They oppose both evangelical and Roman Catholic attempts to limit abortion, to prevent the ordination of gay candidates for ministry, to stop legislative approval of same-sex civil unions or marriage, to limit programs of sex education in the public schools that treat all sexual orientations and family forms as equal in value, or to gain support for private or parochial schools that could teach traditional values. And, it must be said, some are rather gleefully eager to point out the failures and hypocrisy of rigid standards when popular television evangelists are exposed as having had affairs, or Catholic priests are proven to have been molesters of youth.

In this context, two highly pertinent developments are taking place. One is what is happening to the wedding ceremonies among the population. A search of the web using the keyword *marriage* reveals more than 3.5 million sites, more than one hundred thousand listings of "wedding providers," almost one hun-

39. The most complete, if controversial, treatment of these last two issues is found in Robert A. J. Gagnon, *The Bible and Homosexual Practice* (Nashville: Abingdon, 2001).

40. These patterns are paralleled in the Jewish traditions. The Reformed wing has approved the blessing of same-sexed relationships, whereas the Conservative and Orthodox wings oppose it.

dred thousand sites dealing with "wedding rituals," and thirteen thousand options for "marriage liturgies." Although no systematic analysis of all these sites has been done, to my knowledge, a number of hours reading what is posted on these sites suggests the following.

- First, people want "religious" weddings, but they want them on their own terms, and they want help in planning them — from invitations to suggested reception toasts.
- Second, many church-related sites indicate the kind of service they provide, a description of the beauty of the facilities, and the variety of liturgies that are available.
- Third, there is seldom a distinction between the religious meanings and customary practices (shower for the bride; bachelor party for the groom) that imply a correct way of carrying out these rituals.
- Fourth, while most of the major branches of Christianity and the great world religions are represented, more striking is the willingness of so many to use religious poetry, prayers, songs, or chants from any religious tradition or cultural tradition, including medieval, Native American, Elvis, gothic, rock, rap, and so on.
- Fifth, much of the variety is determined by ethnicity, with distinctive food and music — most obvious in Indian and Chinese ads, but present also in Irish, Italian, and Latin ones.
- Sixth, thousands of "wedding planners," "marriage advisors," or "providers," many indicating that they are ordained, clearly indicate that they are open to mix and match liturgies, with the bride and groom writing parts or all of the services, and are available to perform ceremonies with or without references to God for any sex couple.

Of course, it is still the case that more than 85 percent of Americans (and some 60 percent of Europeans) are married in church services that are, on the whole, quite traditional. Whether the parties to the wedding are otherwise actively religious or not, I suspect that it is not wrong to say that the cultural impact of the sacramental and, even more, the covenantal traditions remains so deeply embedded in the ethos of the common life that some view the provision of wedding services by the churches as nearly a public utility. This would account for the fact that the increased toleration of homosexuals, according to several recent polls, has not substantively altered the view that the term *marriage* should be reserved for heterosexual couples with the deepest intention of long-term, "sacred" obligations, a view recently stated publicly by the U.S. President and most candidates running for political positions. Marriage is, to overwhelm-

ing numbers, a "holy estate" with divine overtones that entail a relationship between a male and a female — even if people are vague, undecided, or skeptical
about God or God's law and purposes, and want to be tolerant and forgiving.[41]

It is possible that the Internet represents one indicator of the consciousness
of the future, a primary source of opinion and possibility that the younger generations consult. If so, marriages of the future will be, as many pastors already
know, designer events, with no two being any more alike than pastoral counseling follows one format. Pastors will have to be prepared with a discerning and
careful mix of what the great, deep traditions of the past have to offer that is of
perennial value, and what the sensibilities of the couple and their communities
already believe can validly be celebrated. In a way that is much more profound
than items of clothing, the service will have to involve "something old and
something new." It will also likely involve "something borrowed" from the culture or some ethnic tradition, and possibly "something blue," an insight derived
from heaven knows where.

It is, of course, quite possible for the churches to withdraw from such debates into their enclaves of piety and insist on their own dogmas and practices
without revision. This is likely to be quite important for those who are already
deeply committed to a specific church subculture and are alienated from or
hostile to the culture at large. It is also possible, at the opposite extreme, for
some churches to accept the current cultural drift toward the acceptance and
approval of all lifestyles, and to see these as prophetic of a new tolerance.[42] But
neither an intentionally sectarian church nor the identification of the faith with
secular trends is likely to generate vision able to shape the common life of the
future.

This leads to a central issue: Is it the task of communities of faith and, indeed, of every believer as an active agent and advocate of the life of faith, to
form and model the most loving, just, and functional relationships possible in a
flawed world in every area of social, political, economic, professional, and familial life? If it is, then the formation of a family in an extremely complex civilization where great pressures are on those who have fallen in love is one of the
most intense and highly personal opportunities, potentially available to almost
all the population, to manifest a gracious, creative community marked by a just

41. See the excellent report on new surveys and opinions by Elisabeth Bumiller, "Why
America Has Gay Marriage Jitters," *New York Times Week in Review* (Aug. 10, 2003): section 4,
pp. 1, 4.

42. Rabbi Gerald Zelizer posed this question for all clergy in a recent column: "Should
Clergy Endorse 'Living in Sin'?" *USA Today* (July 24, 2003): 13A. He points out that while cohabitation and toleration for it is on the increase, extra-marital relationships are viewed as clearly
morally wrong. People tend to honor exclusivity and fidelity.

and enduring love in a morally ambiguous world. Every cleric who holds sessions in premarital counseling and writes a liturgy of marriage with the couple will have an opportunity to draw on the rich traditions of sacrament and covenant, and to craft a tailored ceremony that can be a sermon for a lifetime. Every religion and denomination will have the responsibility of charting out the acceptable models according to their deepest convictions. Preparing people for this will require a new and deeper understanding of the theological and contextual aspects of family life today, and this can be done only by patient preaching, careful teaching, compassionate persuasion, and exemplary pastoral care.

One can see some of the issues that are likely to be on the horizon in the United Church of Christ, the only member of ecumenical Christian bodies that has become, at the national level, an active advocate of the ordination of homosexuals and officially approving of same-sex marriage. It nevertheless has still a rather classical statement about marriage in its official *Book of Worship*. The liturgy for weddings is quite flexible and open to inclusion of non-official materials, yet the opening statement in the wedding ceremony affirms the tradition with these words:

> We come to share in their joy and to ask God to bless [them]. . . . Marriage is a gift of God, sealed by a sacred covenant. God gives human love. Through that love, husband and wife come to know each other with mutual care and companionship.
>
> God gives Joy. Through that joy, wife and husband may share their new life with others as Jesus shared new wine at the wedding in Cana.[43]

This church is the direct descendant of those British Puritans who came to New England as Congregationalists, and who have now joined with immigrants from the evangelical and Reformed Churches of Germany and branches of African-American denominations that split off from Southern Methodist or Baptist churches over slavery. Their central message on this matter for more than a decade has been that Christians should be "open and affirming" toward others. In fact, in this highly democratic church, the people in the churches *are* for the most part "open" and accepting of homosexual persons. But it is doubtful that the majority of the believers can soon be persuaded to be "affirming" of gay marriage, for there is little evidence in Scripture or any parts of the classic tradition — or, for that matter, in scholarly, scientific studies (which this denomination holds in high esteem) — that homosexual behavior should be affirmed, and that the issues are directly parallel to issues posed by the exclusion

43. United Church of Christ, *Book of Worship* (New York: United Church of Christ Office for Church Life and Leadership, 1986).

of ethnic groups or women from society. Also, the resentment about being pressured by church leaders to make affirmations against conscience is reducing loyalty to the national church organization and strengthening the sense of historic congregational sovereignty. Ironically, similar developments are taking place in Episcopal and Presbyterian bodies, contrary to their more centralized traditions. The harvest of Protestant "covenantalism" is that the people must decide in their own hearts, minds, and communities of faith what is truly godly, loving, and just.

The actual practice of the churches will likely include, as did the sacramental and covenantal traditions of the past, the element of legal contract; but it is also likely that the contractual element will come to dominance in legal theory for the foreseeable future and that political pressures will be brought against the use of historic theological arguments in defending heterosexual marriage as the only socially legitimated marriage. Yet, the battles are already at hand on this point as well. At one level, common law marriages are already legally recognized in many places: heterosexual couples who live together and take some responsibility for each other, the common expenses, and any children over any serious period of time are, for purposes of the law (or, increasingly, aspects of social services policy), viewed as a family. At another level, a number of states are following Vermont in passing one or another statute granting recognition to "civil unions" — an act that allows homosexual partners to have a civil ceremony that guarantees legal rights to health and tax benefits, and so on, that are comparable to those of heterosexual couples. Arguments for this are based on the equal standing of all citizens before the law, freedom of contract, and the rights of privacy.

At still a third level stand the marriage laws, which, while they differ somewhat from state to state, basically presume that marriage is a relationship between a man and a woman, as the earlier liturgies and codes said, except in Massachusetts, as mentioned above. This is so even if there are increasing numbers of prenuptial contracts specifying how to dispose of common property and care for any issue should a couple divorce. But the inner logic and theological presumptions behind the legal heritage have sufficiently eroded that marriage in the eyes of the law seems more and more like the registration of a common law marriage or contractual civil union, and the belief has grown that this is all that the state should be responsible for. In this context, however, movements to establish the legal category of "covenant marriage" are gaining ground, as Katherine Shaw Spaht and Margaret Brinig, among others, have documented.[44] The attempt to specify *covenant* as more than a legal contract in

44. See note 6 above.

marriage, and to get states to recognize this as an optional possibility, suggests that there is something basic and valid in what the religious traditions have recognized, something shared by many psychiatrists and social scientists as a quality of relationship different from a totally voluntary or negotiated agreement by autonomous human beings. On the whole, this has to do with the insight of the biblical tradition that the just God is also the God of love, and that love to be validly acknowledged, structured, and lived out requires an awareness of a transcendent moral order that humans did not construct and cannot reconstruct. If Protestantism is to make a difference in this area of life in the future, this is the context in which it must make its case anew, within the churches, among the people, before the academic critics, and in the halls of justice.

## 7 The Nature of the Islamic Marriage: Sacramental, Covenantal, or Contractual?

*Azizah Y. al-Hibri*

The nature of the Islamic marriage contract *(kitab)* has been largely misunderstood by Muslims and non-Muslims alike. On the Muslim side, the problem has been one of over-secularization of the law of contract, a trend that led to a trivialization of the marriage contract, and hence of the commitment of some marriage partners to it. On the non-Muslim side, the problem has been one of trying to explain the Islamic marriage contract from world perspectives that are at times incongruent with it. This has led to unintended distortions in characterizing its nature.

For example, Muslims and non-Muslims often assert the purely contractual nature of the Muslim marriage contract in order to draw a distinction between it and the nature of marriage in other traditions. Unlike Catholic marriages, for example, it is pointed out that a Muslim man can dissolve the marriage bond at will and pay his wife a set amount (called the *mahr* or *sadaq*) agreed upon in advance in the marriage contract. The marriage ceremony may take place at home, and thus, it is argued, is not "before God" as in a church, but rather "temporal."

I was one of those propagating this point of view until I started researching Islamic law, especially in the areas of marriage and divorce, more seriously. As it turns out, Islamic law is a seamless web, and it is quite difficult to understand

The author thanks Prof. Robert Shepherd, University of Richmond, for his valuable comments on the American law aspects of this chapter. The author also thanks Ms. Raja El Habti, Senior Scholar and Director of Research at KARAMAH: MUSLIM WOMEN LAWYERS FOR HUMAN RIGHTS, for her valuable comments on matters of Islamic law and her assistance in footnoting the chapter. Finally, the author thanks Ms. Cheryl Call, her student assistant, Ms. Safia al-Kharsa, KARAMAH intern, for their help in the footnoting process.

one part of it without having some knowledge of the other parts. I can safely assert now that almost every claim in the preceding paragraph is false.[1]

In this chapter, I shall remove some of the confusion and misunderstanding about the Islamic marriage contract by taking the reader with me on a brief tour of the fundamentals of Islamic law as they pertain to our subject. I shall start with an introductory discussion of the Islamic worldview in general, and the Islamic view of gender relations in particular. It will be followed by a discussion of the nature of contract in Islam. I shall then turn to the Islamic marriage contract and its special status in Islamic law and religion, and, finally, examine the nature of marriage among Muslims in the United States.

## The Islamic Worldview

The Islamic worldview is based on the fundamental concept of *tawhid* (the unicity of God).[2] There is only one Creator and one Supreme Will. Any view which associates partners with this Supreme Will, whether directly or indirectly, results in *shirk* (the opposite of *tawhid*), which is a sin that God tells us in the Qur'an he will not forgive (4:48). Iblis (Satan) missed this important point and disobeyed God when God ordered him to bow to Adam (15:31). By refusing to obey a divine command, Iblis made his own will supersede that of God. For that unforgivable sin he was cursed (15:35). But the critical question in this Qur'anic story is this: What prompted Iblis to disobey God? The answer is his vanity. The Qur'an tells us that in justifying his disobedience, Iblis told God, "I am better than he [Adam] is" (7:12). This Iblisi worldview, which is based on vanity intertwined with hierarchy, is directly opposed to divine logic, which celebrates diversity and the fundamental equality of all human beings as signs of God's miracles on earth.

The Qur'an tells us,

---

1. The full extent of this error will be made clear in my forthcoming book on marriage contracts.

2. This is most clearly stated in Chapter 112 of the Qur'an itself. It states in its entirety, "Say: He is God the One and Only. God the Eternal, Absolute; He begetteth not, Nor is He begotten; And there is none Like unto Him."

In this chapter, I use *The Meaning of the Holy Qur'an,* trans. A. Yusuf Ali, 11th ed. (Maryland: Amana Corp., 2004). However, where critical for our discussion, I have revised some of the translations that are inaccurate linguistically or legally, or are unjustifiably patriarchal. I have also consistently replaced the word "Allah" with "God" since that is the proper translation of the word into English. Leaving it in its Arabic form will cause confusion as to the identity of the God in which Muslims believe. He is the same God of the other Abrahamic religions. All the translations of the Arabic sources, other than the Qur'an, are mine.

> O people! We created you from a single [pair] of a male and a female, and
> made you into nations and tribes, that ye may know each other. . . . Verily, the
> most honored of you in the sight of [God] is [the one who is] most righteous
> [atqakum] of you. . . . (49:13)

It also states, "And among His Signs [miracles] is the creation of the heavens
and the earth, and the variations in your languages and your colors; verily in
that are Signs for those who know" (30:22). The Prophet also asserted the same
worldview in *Khutbat al-Wadaa'* (Farewell Address) when he reminded his au-
dience, "O kin of Quraysh, God has removed from you the arrogance of
*Jahiliyyah* and its patriarchal dynastic pride *[ta'ath.thumaha bi al-abaa']*. People are of Adam and Adam is of dust."[3]

Jurists saw in such Qur'anic verses and Hadiths (statements of the
Prophet) a conclusive proof of the equality of all humans before God. They also
saw in the stories of the fall of Iblis, and of Adam and Eve, the pitfalls of vanity
and the pursuit of power.[4] These realizations prompted jurists to be modest in
asserting their views and in disputing the views of others. It also led them to eschew hierarchies and opt for an egalitarian system of relationships.

In the case of gender relations within and outside the family, both the
Qur'an and the Prophet were quite clear. Men and women were created of the
same *nafs* (soul) (Qur'an 4:1; 7:189), and as a previous verse indicates, they are
measured not by their gender but by their individual righteousness (49:13).
Further, the Qur'an assures both genders that as to this world, "Never will I suffer to be lost the work of any of you, be [it] male or female; ye are from one another" (3:195). The last part of the passage refers to the fact that not only are the
two genders interdependent in reproductive life, they are also constituted of the
same basic elements, a sign of true equality. In matters of faith, "Whoever
works righteousness, man or woman, and has faith, verily to him will We give a
new life, a life that is good and pure, and we will bestow on such their reward
according to the best of their actions" (16:97). As for family relations, the
Qur'an tells us, "And among His signs is this: that He created for you mates
from among yourselves, that ye may dwell in tranquility with them, and He has
put love and mercy between your [hearts]: Verily in that are signs for those who
reflect" (30:21). Finally, the guiding principle in family relations was articulated
by the Qur'an with striking simplicity: "[It is either holding together] on equitable terms, or [separating] with kindness" (2:229).

3. Zayd Ibn Ali al-Wazir, *Al-Fardiyah: Bahth fi Azmat al-Fiqh al-Fardi al-Siyasi 'inda al-
Muslimin* (Virginia: Yemen Heritage and Research Center, 2000), p. 62.

4. See, e.g., Muhammad Ibn Ali al-Shawkani, *Fath al-Qadir* (Beirut: Dar al-Khayr, 1992),
vol. 3, pp. 438-39.

Clearly, all these verses articulate an egalitarian view of relationships between the sexes. Yet, many traditional jurists living in highly patriarchal societies managed to provide a patriarchal jurisprudence for spousal relationships. They seized on a couple of verses in the Qur'an and interpreted them so as to introduce a full-fledged hierarchy between husband and wife. Extreme statements about this hierarchy were then made that relegated the wife to a subservient status.[5] Yet the Qur'an clearly states that male and female believers are each other's *walis* (protectors, guardians, advisors). Since Muslims believe that the Qur'an is internally consistent, the hierarchical interpretations of the spousal relationship must be reexamined to uncover the underlying patriarchal cultural influences.[6]

The deeply rooted egalitarian view of gender relations in the Qur'an and the life-affirming view of family relations discussed above are critical to understanding the fact that the Islamic marriage contract is a contract based on the consent of two equal parties. But before we turn to this discussion, we need also to understand the theory of contract in Islam.

## The Islamic Contract

The Islamic marriage contract is a variant of Islamic contracts. Therefore, it is important to understand the underlying Islamic theory of contracts before embarking on the more specialized discussion of the jurisprudence of the Islamic marriage contract. Unfortunately, little attention has been given to the study of Islamic contract theory, which arose originally in the commercial context. Further, when this body of law is studied, it is usually examined within the commercial contexts of the modern Western capital markets. While this is an important endeavor, it is unhelpful for understanding the basics of Islamic contract law and the logic behind its various rules. Indeed, it has led many writers to misunderstand and mischaracterize the nature of the Islamic marriage contract. Yet this fact is not fully comprehended even by some Muslims today who unwittingly tend to think of Islamic contract theory as essentially secular, as is exemplified by the popular belief that the Islamic marriage contract is simply a civil contract.

This distorted understanding of Islamic law is not surprising given that many Muslim countries abandoned that law decades ago as a result of modernization, the collapse of the Ottoman Empire, and the ensuing colonialism, to

5. See, e.g., Abu Ja'far al-Tabari, *Jami' al-Bayan fi Tafsir al-Qur'an*, 23 vols, repr. of ninth c. ed. (Beirut: Dar al-Ma'rifah, 1978) vol. 2, p. 275; vol. 5, pp. 37-39. See also Abu Bakr Muhammad Ibn al-'Arabi, *Ahkaam al-Qur'an* (Beirut: Dar al-Ma'rifah, 1987), vol. 1, pp. 188-89, 415-16.

6. See, e.g., Azizah al-Hibri, "Islam, Law and Custom: Redefining Muslim Women's Rights," *American Journal of International Law and Policy* 12 (1997): 1, 20.

list a few factors. They replaced it in most areas, but notably not in the area of family relations, with positive law modeled after Western secular law. The replacement severed the conceptual connection between contract law, which became secularized, and family law, which remained Islamic.[7] As a result, many modern Muslim jurists studied the second without reference to the first, in either its secular or religious manifestations. Important principles of Islamic contract law and its connections to family law were thus missed, leading to an important loss of insight in later generations. In the next few sections, we shall try to regain some of these insights in order to develop a deeper understanding of the Islamic marriage contract.

Traditional Islamic contract theory is based on reasonably well developed medieval jurisprudence. This jurisprudence, while quite suitable for the demands of its time, was not challenged by the complicated structures of our industrial and information-based societies. The jurisprudence of Islamic contract law is now in dire need of updating in order to be able to respond to these more recent developments. The task, however, is quite daunting. For the purposes of this chapter, we shall simply attempt to understand the basic principles of contract law as they relate to the issue at hand. We leave a more fundamental assessment and contribution to the field for another day, and we turn now to the basic principles of Islamic contract theory.

### What Is an ʿAqd?

The word ʿaqd, which has been translated into English as *contract*, means "to bind, tie, fasten or secure," as in the case of tying two ends of a rope.[8] It was later used figuratively to refer to firm commitments, whether in spiritual or legal contexts and whether unilateral or not. An ʿadq is also referred to also as an ʿahd (pl. ʿuhud), although an ʿahd, as we shall see later, may refer to commitment of a higher order, such as a treaty or a covenant.[9] An ʿaqd has a general meaning as well as a specialized meaning. The general meaning in the literature subsumes under ʿaqd any binding undertaking or commitment by a unilateral

---

7. Some countries like Saudi Arabia retained Islamic law in all its branches, including contract law.

8. Abd al-Hamid Mahmoud al-Baʾli, *Dhawabit al-ʿUqud* (Cairo: Maktabat Wihbah, 1989), pp. 39-40; Abd a-Razzaq al-Sanhuri, *Massadir al-Haqq fi al-Fiqh al-Islami* (Beirut: Dar Ihyaʾ al-Turath al-Islami, 1953-54), vol. 1, p. 75 (quoting al-Alousi in his Tafsir).

9. Muhammad Abu Zahrah, *Al-Milkiyah wa Nathariyat al-ʿAqd* (Cairo: Dar al-Fikr al-ʿArabi, 1996), pp. 173-75; Ali M. A. al-Qurra Daghi, *Mabdaʾ al-Ridha fi al-ʿUqud* (Beirut: Dar al-Bashaʾir al-Islamiyah, 1985), vol. 1, p. 106.

individual will, whether it was made in return for an undertaking by another or not.[10] Thus, there need not be two parties to an *'aqd*. Examples of a unilateral *'aqd* are oaths and vows.[11] Also, under this definition, every stipulation in a contract is an *'aqd* because of the undertaking to fulfill the condition it specifies.[12]

The specialized meaning of *'aqd*, however, is that which refers to the agreement of two wills resulting in a firm commitment. This has become the more prevalent meaning of *'aqd*. Many medieval jurists used the word *'aqd* in its specialized meaning.[13] Nevertheless, all Qur'anic interpreters agreed that the verse, "Fulfill all *'uqud*" (5:1), refers to the general meaning of *'aqd*, and, hence, covers both types of commitments, unilateral and otherwise.[14]

Given this broad Qur'anic interpretation, it follows that reneging on one's commitment, whether in exchange for another or not, is wrong.[15] This follows regardless of the presence or absence of formalities when the commitment was made, because the need to fulfill it does not derive from legal formalities but from divine orders and religious morality.[16] This point is made emphatically in *Taj al-Arus*, the classical Arabic lexicon, even in its discussion of mere promises (as opposed to contractual commitments). Under the entry *wa'd* (promise), it notes that "if a person promises [to do] something good and does not deliver it, they [the Arabs] would say: 'the person *akhlaf*' [breached his promise], and that is a grave vice *[al-'ayb al-fahish]*."[17] It also quotes the *'ulama*, who emphasized the importance of fulfilling promises and prohibited breaching them.[18] *Taj al-Arus* then continues,

and the Arabs found it [breaching a promise] an ugly vice and they said: "breaching a promise is of the morals of scoundrels"; and it is said that ful-

10. Malakah Yusuf Zirar, *Mawsu'at al-Zawaj wa Al-'Alāqah al-Zawjiyah* (Cairo: Dar al-Fath, 2000), vol. 1, pp. 134-35 (margins). Zirar admits only of the unilateral meaning of *'aqd*, however, while providing a different definition for the bilateral ones; see also p. 139.

11. Zirar, *Mawsu'at al-Zawaj*, vol. 1, p. 139.

12. Abu Zahrah, *Al-Milkiyah*, pp. 173-74.

13. Al-Qurrah Daghi, *Mabda' al-Ridha*, vol. 1, pp. 114-15 (quoting Ibn Nujaim, al-Babirti, ibn Hammam, al-Kasani, al-Dardir, al-Dusuqi, and many others).

14. Al-Qurrah Daghi, *Mabda' al-Ridha*, vol. 1, p. 115 (citing al-Tabari, Ibn 'Arabi, al-Jassas, Ibn Kathir, and others).

15. Muhammad Fakhr al-Din al-Razi, *Tafsir al-Fakhr al-Razi* (Beirut: Dar al-Fikr, 1985), vol. 5, pp. 47-48, vol. 11, pp. 125-26. See also al-Qurrah Daghi, *Mabda' al-Ridha*, vol. 1, p. 115.

16. Al-Qurrah Daghi, *Mabda' al-Ridha*, vol. 1, p. 116.

17. Muhammad Murtadha al-Zabidi, *Taj al-'Arus* (Beirut: Manshurat Dar Maktabat al-Hayat, eighteenth-century reprint, n.d), vol. 2, p. 537.

18. al-Zabidi, *Taj al-'Arus*, vol. 2, p. 537.

filling promises is a *Sunnah* [the example of the Prophet]. . . . Qadi [judge] Abu Bakr bin al-'Arabi said: ". . . breaching a promise is lying and hypocrisy, and if it is rare it [still] is disobedience to God."[19]

To understand better the interaction between the legal and spiritual world in Islam, I offer a brief overview of Islamic law. It is divided into two general categories: *'ibadat,* or matters of worship (between a person and God), and *mu'amalat,* or transactions (among people). The first category includes matters of faith, such as prayer, fasting, and tithing. The second category includes such matters as contract law, property law, and constitutional law. Both categories are proper subjects of Islamic jurisprudence and are governed by the Qur'an and Sunnah.[20] For example, as we shall see, the Qur'anic prohibition of usury *(riba)* resonates throughout the Islamic financial markets, affecting contract law, banking law, and even securities regulation.[21] This fact alone renders Islamic contract law essentially different from Western secular law. It is very important to keep these differences in mind, if we plan to understand Islamic law properly and not empty it, through facile translation or interpretation, from its very *raison d'être.*

## The Islamic Worldview and Its Impact on Contracts

The Qur'an enjoins Muslims to fulfill their contracts. It says, "O ye who believe, fulfill all *'uqud*" (5:1). This verse is the opening verse of a long passage which lists for Muslims those things permitted unto them, and those things forbidden. According to al-Tabari, whose exegesis of the Qur'an is among the most famous, the verse urges Muslims to fulfill *all* their *'uqud,* because there is no rational basis for differentiating among them.[22] So a Muslim should not breach a contract after affirming it. In fact, fulfilling one's *'ahd* is placed in the Qur'an alongside prayer, charity, chastity, and truthful testimony — qualities used to describe a pious and fair person (70:22-35).

The Prophet himself was no less emphatic about the importance of fulfilling one's contracts. He said, "Fulfill your *'uqud,* and the *'aqd* most worthy of

19. Al-Zabidi, *Taj al-'Arus,* vol. 2, p. 537.

20. The Sunnah is the Hadiths (sayings), deeds, and example of the Prophet. It is used by Muslim jurists as a source secondary only to the Qur'an for further clarification and guidance.

21. Abd a-Razzaq al-Sanhuri, *Massadir al-Haqq,* vol. 3, p. 14 (noting that *riba, gharar,* and the rule against multiple transactions in one contract have deep influence on various specific rulings and matters of Islamic jurisprudence).

22. Al-Tabari, *Jami' al-Bayan fi Tafsir al-Qur'an,* vol. 6, p. 33; al-Ba'li, *Dhawabit al-'Uqud,* pp. 34-36.

fulfillment is that of marriage."[23] This prophetic Hadith makes it very clear that, among all Islamic contracts, the marriage contract is the most worthy of fulfillment; yet by Qur'anic injunction even the least important contract in Islam must be fulfilled.

This fact also shows that an Islamic contract is not the same as a secular contract under American law. While the worldly repercussions for entering, fulfilling, or breaching an Islamic contract may overlap significantly with those under American contract law, these repercussions represent only *haqq al-'abd* (the right of the human being). But an Islamic contract also gives rise to *haqq Allah* (the right of God), which has been clearly distinguished and articulated in the Qur'an. That right arises when a Muslim violates the clear injunctions of the Qur'an to fulfill all her *'uqud.*

The Islamic view that all contracts are subject to Qur'anic injunctions is conceptually different from some Christian views. Christian theologians like John Calvin distinguished between two kingdoms — the temporal and the spiritual — with the former pertaining to the concerns of our daily life, and the latter pertaining to the life of the soul.[24] Calvin argued that marriage is an institution of the earthly kingdom, "just like farming, building, cobbling, and barbering."[25] It has no bearing on one's salvation or eternal standing, but it is a divine remedy for human lust. Muslims, on the other hand, believe that "farming, building, cobbling, and barbering" all have a bearing on our eternal standing, because, like marriage, they fall into the category of *mu'amalat,* which is an important part of the religion.

The overlap between the spiritual and the temporal realms in Islam explains why contracts that deal with everyday matters are also subject to God's law. Given this religious dimension of the Islamic contract, it is misleading to translate the Arabic word *'aqd* as *contract.* This distortion is most noticeable in the case of the Islamic marriage contract. To call the Islamic marriage contract "a civil contract," as many do, and analogize it to a modern secular contract, strips the marriage contract of its momentous religious status as the contract most worthy of fulfillment.

Recognizing the special importance and station of the marriage contract in Islam, jurists refused to apply to it *mutatis mutandis* the same rules as those that govern sales and other commercial contracts.[26] In each case the distinction was

23. Muhammad Ibn Isma'il al-Bukhari, *Sahih al-Bukhari* (Beirut: Dar al-Ma'rifah, n.d.), vol. 3, p. 252.

24. John Witte Jr., *From Sacrament to Contract: Marriage, Religion, and Law in the Western Tradition* (Louisville: Westminster John Knox, 1997), p. 79.

25. Witte, *From Sacrament to Contract,* p. 94.

26. For more on the distinction between the marriage contract and the commercial one,

based on the gravity of the marriage contract and the fact that, unlike a sale, it is not an exchange transaction (that is, one made for consideration).[27] While the marriage contract (like all other contracts) contains worldly terms negotiated by the parties, these terms address only the worldly aspect of the marriage. To assume that there is no more to the contract than these aspects is to commit a grievous error. Many Muslims primarily conduct marriage negotiations with a view to pleasing God. In fact, some women and their *walis* (guardians or advisors) pay so little attention to the worldly aspect of the marriage contract that they end up suffering worldly consequences.

## Exceptions to the Rule

The fact that even the least important contract in Islam must be fulfilled was not fully appreciated by some writers because they misconstrued a reported incident involving the Prophet.[28] The incident involves 'A'ishah, the wife of the Prophet, who agreed to purchase Barirah, a slave woman, upon the latter's request, in order to free her. Under Islamic law, the freeing of Barirah created between the two women a special relationship of *wala'* akin to that of a blood relationship.[29] Such relationships are very narrowly and carefully defined. They include the usual blood relationship, as well as others articulated by the Qur'an and Sunnah such as the milk relationship (based on nursing), the womb relationship *(silat al-rahm),* and the *wala'* relationship (based on freeing a slave). None of these relationships is transferable.[30]

---

see al-Ba'li, *Dhawabit al-'Uqud,* pp. 106-7. See also Zirar, *Mawsu'at al-Zawaj,* vol. 1, pp. 134-44, and al-Sanhuri, *Massadir al-Haqq,* vol. 3, p. 130.

27. See, e.g., Zirar, *Mawsu'at al-Zawaj,* vol. 1, pp. 134-44.

28. Frank E. Vogel, *Islamic Law and Finance: Religion, Risk, and Return* (The Hague, 1998), pp. 67-68. Based on this precedent and practice in Saudi Arabia, the author states that "[t]his *Hadith* is highly troubling for freedom of contract. It suggests that the very terms of contracts, not to mention contracts themselves, must be prescribed by God's writ" (pp. 67-68). But Vogel's statement is based on a narrow interpretation that has been rejected by various important jurists. This chapter adopts the better interpretation that contract terms (and contracts) may not violate God's law (i.e., Islamic public policy). This is the interpretation adopted by al-Sanhuri, *Massadir al-Haqq,* vol. 3, pp. 170-72, and al-Qurah Daghi, *Mabda' al-Ridha,* vol. 2, pp. 1193-96, among others.

29. Al-Bukhari, *Sahih al-Bukhari,* vol. 4, p. 169 (margin).

30. See, e.g., Taqi al-Din Ahmad Ibn Taymiyyah, *Nathariyat al-'Uqud* (Cairo: Markaz al-Kitab li al Nashr, n.d.), p. 23. This nontransferability requirement is quite important, as is obvious from the jurisprudence regarding adoption. A person may become the *kafeel* (guardian) of an orphaned child, but may not take away from the child the name of his or her own biological

The *wala'* relationship included, among other things, a commitment to mutual defense and protection.[31] This commitment was critical to the freed slave, who had no tribe of her own to defend or protect her. The owners of Barirah, however, stipulated that they would sell her only if the *wala'* relationship remained theirs.[32] Their aim in this case was not to defend Barirah's liberty or protect her. Rather, they wanted to inherit Barirah's property after her death, thus adding insult to injury by re-appropriating the property she had accumulated through her hard work.

When informed that the owners of Barirah were ready to sell her on the condition that her *wala'* remained theirs, 'A'ishah became reluctant to enter this untenable transaction.[33] In effect, the transaction would have required Barirah to dedicate her loyalty and *wala'* to her previous owners, even as she lived with 'A'ishah and was actually being protected by 'A'ishah's tribe. In other words, the stipulation created a classic case of divided loyalties in a tribal society where loyalty and *wala'* were critical for the well-being of its members.

'A'ishah's reluctance would have kept Barirah locked into slavery as a result of the unconscionable stipulation by her owners. The Prophet was understandably displeased with the attempt of Barirah's owners to overreach. He told 'A'ishah, "Free her, for the *wala'* relationship belongs to the one who frees."[34] Then he went to the mosque that evening and publicly chastised the owners, saying, "How is it that some people are demanding *shurut* [stipulations] not in God's book? Any *shart* [stipulation] not in God's book is null and void, even if it were a hundred *shurut*."[35] In another report, he said, "God's book is more worthy [of being followed] and God's *shart* is more binding."[36]

Some jurists were puzzled by this incident, which according to other ac-

---

father and mother. The Qur'an is clear on this point. Similarly, the child cannot inherit as a blood relative, but may inherit from the discretionary portion of the estate in accordance with a will by the *kafeel.* Thus inheritance in Islam, as well as naming, is one of the indicia of the closeness of a relationship. From this perspective, a *wala'* relationship is closer than that of a *kafeel.* This makes sense, given the fundamental importance of liberty to human beings, and the wish to encourage Muslims to liberate slaves.

31. Ibn Taymiyyah, *Nathariyat al-'Uqud,* p. 23.

32. Al-Bukhari, *Sahih al-Bukhari,* vol. 4, pp. 168-69; vol. 2, p. 116.

33. Al-Bukhari, *Sahih al-Bukhari,* vol. 4, pp. 168-69; vol. 2, p. 116.

34. Al-Bukhari, *Sahih al-Bukhari,* vol. 4, pp. 168-69; vol. 2, p. 116. The report is unclear as to whether 'A'ishah purchased Barirah under this condition or was contemplating purchasing her under the condition. The reports in the latter case state that the Prophet told 'A'ishah to go ahead and buy Barirah under the condition "because the *wala'* always belongs to the one who frees."

35. Al-Bukhari, *Sahih al-Bukhari,* vol. 4, pp. 168-69; vol. 2, p. 116.

36. Al-Bukhari, *Sahih al-Bukhari,* vol. 4, pp. 168-69; vol. 2, p. 116.

counts appeared to encourage 'A'ishah to agree to a contract that contained a stipulation she knew she would not keep.[37] Even if the latter accounts were true, the situation described is no different from one in which a person executes a contract containing a term that is inconsistent with public policy. Under our laws, such a term is null and void. It is also null and void under Islamic law.[38] Under Islamic law, once a slave is freed, all oppressive ties to the earlier status are severed. The freed slave acquires all the indicia of freedom others have. To drive this point home, the Prophet encouraged a woman from his own noble tribe of Quraish to marry a freed slave.[39]

Therefore, those who insist on including oppressive, overreaching, or unconscionable provisions in their contract have only themselves to blame. In the early days of Islam, this incident was an occasion for the Prophet to reiterate the fact that freedom of contract does not supersede Islamic public policy as articulated by the Qur'an and the Sunnah. His emphatic position regarding public policy does not detract from the fundamental Islamic position that even the most modest contract in an Islamic society must be fulfilled because of its religious nature. To argue otherwise would result in a *reductio ad absurdum,* since the opposite argument in favor of unlimited freedom of contract would oblige us to honor a contract even if it involved a criminal act.

This is in fact the view of the Andalusi scholar Ibn Hazm. In his notable work *al-Muhalla,* he states that a Muslim is not obligated to fulfill all his promises.[40] He argues that it is in fact a good thing for a Muslim to renege on a promise to commit adultery, drink alcohol, or commit other forbidden acts.[41] He was responding to other jurists who argued that a person who reneges on his promise must be forced to fulfill it, or that at least it would be preferred that he do so.[42] The arguments of those in favor of fulfilling a promise were also based on another Qur'anic verse that states, "O ye who believe! Why say ye that

37. See Taqi al-Din Ahmad Ibn Taymiyyah, *Majmou'at al-Fatawi* (al-Mansoura, Egypt: Dar al-Wafa', 1998), vol. 15, pp. 185-89 (stating among other things that the bond of *wala'* is like a familial bond).

38. Al-Sanhuri, *Massadir al-Haqq,* vol. 3, pp. 171-72; Wihbah al-Zuhayli, *Al-Fiqh al-Islami wa Adillatuhu* (Beirut: Dar al-Fikr al-Mu'asser, 1997), vol. 9, pp. 6540-47; Ibn Taymiyyah, *Nathariyat al-'Uqud,* p. 23; Abu Zahrah, *Al-Milkiyah,* pp. 235-37.

39. Ibn Hisham, *Al-Sirah al-Nabawiyah* (Beirut: al-Maktabah al-'Ilmiyah, n.d.), vol. 1, pp. 247-48; Omar Rida Kahalah, *A'lam al-Nisa' fi 'Alumay al-Arab wa al-Islam,* 5 vols. (Beirut: Mu'assasat al-Risalah, 1977), vol. 2, p. 59.

40. Abu Muhammad Ali Ibn Sa'ed Ibn Hazm, *Al-Muhalla bi al-Athar* (Beirut: Dar al-Kutub al-'Ilmiyah, 1988), vol. 6, pp. 278-79.

41. Ibn Hazm, *Al-Muhalla bi al-Athar,* vol. 6, pp. 278-79.

42. Ibn Hazm, *Al-Muhalla bi al-Athar,* vol. 6, p. 278 (discussing Ibn Shabramah and those who followed him).

which you do not do? Grievously odious it is in the sight of [God] that ye say that which ye do not do" (61:2-3).

Ibn Hazm is quite right, but he could have widened the scope of his examples; for, while a Muslim is enjoined to keep her promises, it cannot possibly be argued that a Muslim must keep that promise regardless of the nature of the promise or its circumstances. Under the well-known principles of "choosing the lesser of two evils" and "avoiding harm" *(la darar wa a dirar),* a person would be allowed to breach his promise if fulfilling it would result in harm or greater evil.[43] For example, a promise to give the baby milk is enforceable, unless it is discovered that the baby is allergic to milk. To insist on fulfilling the original promise in light of the changing circumstances would cause the child harm and hence is against Islamic public policy and moral principles.

For this reason, in discussing the importance of fulfilling promises, *Taj al-Arus* (the classical Arabic lexicon mentioned earlier) distinguished between two types of promises: *wa'd,* which involves doing something good, and *wa'eed,* which involves visiting harm upon someone or doing something bad. In the former case, the lexicon argues that a person who gives a *wa'd* must fulfill it; in the second case, it argues that it is better for a person who issues a *wa'eed* not to fulfill it. It adds that such failure to follow up on the threat would not constitute a breach. Rather, it would constitute an act of forgiveness and generosity. It then notes that it is the quality of God, the Almighty, that if he makes a *wa'd* he fulfills it, and if he issues a *wa'eed,* he forgives.[44]

The famous jurist Abu Hanifah disagrees with this analysis based on the clear and emphatic injunction in the Qur'an which states flatly, "Fulfill all [ *'uqud*]" (5:1). He argues that if a person vows to fast on the day of *'Eid* (the day after the end of fasting, which is prohibited), or to sacrifice (slaughter) his son, then he must fulfill his *'aqd.*[45] So, once the *'aqd* is made, it is such a grave and strict obligation that no considerations would permit its nonfulfillment. In my opinion, this view ignores the prophetic precedent that permitted a public policy exception in the case of Barirah. The Barirah precedent is critical for shed-

---

43. For further discussion of this principle, see Azizah al-Hibri, "Islamic Constitutionalism and the Concept of Democracy," *Case Western Reserve Journal of International Law* 24 (1992): 1, 8-9.

44. Al-Zabidi, *Taj al-'Arus,* vol. 2, p. 537.

45. Al-Razi, *Tafsir al-Fakhr al-Razi,* vol. 6, p. 126. Abu Hanifah argues that such a vow contains two parts. The first is the act of slaughtering and the second is the object of the act of slaughter, namely, one's own son. The first part of the vow — that is, the act of slaughtering itself — is binding. Only the second part of the vow, which involves the object of the act, is not binding. The person must therefore slaughter an animal to fulfill his vow and ask God for forgiveness for not fulfilling the rest of his vow.

ding light on the flat Qur'anic injunction to fulfill 'uqud. Another famous jurist, al-Shafi'i, understood this fact and disagreed vehemently with Abu Hanifah. He argued that a vow to fast on the day of *Eid* or to sacrifice one's son is null and void, because fulfilling such a vow would result in an act of disobedience toward God. He then quoted the Prophet: "There is no [valid] vow that disobeys God."[46]

Thus, to adopt the distinction introduced by *Taj al-Arus,* the Qur'an and Sunnah enjoined that a *wa'd* (but not a *wa'eed*) be fulfilled. Alternatively, if we drop this linguistic distinction, we could simply say that the Qur'an and Sunnah enjoin the fulfillment of 'uqud generally, but that the duty to fulfill such 'uqud is implicitly contingent (as the rest of the Qur'an and Sunnah indicate) on public policy, morality, and similar concerns. This is not an unusual feature for a body of law. As noted earlier, secular law has many such exceptions. Clearly, however, the question of damages (where appropriate) and other possible remedies can be raised in Islamic law as it can be raised in other legal systems.

In general, Muslim jurists agree that one who promises with intention to fulfill that promise but becomes unable to do so because of legitimate intervening circumstances is neither legally nor morally (religiously) liable.[47] They also agree on the moral culpability of a person who makes a promise he does not intend to keep, but they disagree on the legal enforceability of such a promise.[48] They all recognize such behavior as a sign of hypocrisy, a trait soundly condemned in the Qur'an and Sunnah. The Qur'an admonishes hypocrites who do not keep their promises. The Prophet does, too. In a famous Hadith, he says, "The sign of a hypocrite is three-pronged: if he speaks, he lies; if he promises, he breaches; and if he is trusted, he betrays."[49]

Clearly, people lie, breach, and betray. The majority of Muslim jurists reasoned that most of this behavior remains outside the reach of the courts but is within the realm of (religious) ethics.[50] Thus, while breaching a promise may not always be legally actionable, barring intervening circumstances, it is still ethically wrong. From an Islamic perspective, where the realms of ethics and law run into each other in a seamless web, this is not much of a break for a pious person who must live by the dictates of both. The Muslim will have to answer to a higher authority for an unjustified breach of promise, but the courts

46. Al-Razi, *Tafsir al-Fakhr al-Razi,* vol. 6, p. 126.

47. Al-Ba'li, *Dhawabit al-'Uqud,* p. 65.

48. Al-Ba'li, *Dhawabit al-'Uqud,* p. 65. See also al-Zuhayli, *Al-Fiqh al-Islami,* vol. 4, pp. 2928-29.

49. Al-Bukhari, *Sahih al-Bukhari, Kitab al-Iman,* vol. 1, p. 15.

50. See, e.g., al-Zuhayli, *Al-Fiqh al-Islami,* vol. 9, p. 6512.

cannot be responsible to enforce every single promise. This brings out clearly the difference between a promise and an *'aqd* under Islamic law from the majority perspective: the former is a personal undertaking that usually does not rise, like the second, to the level of a firm contractual commitment.

The minority view rejects the distinction between a simple promise *(wa'd)* and a firm undertaking *('aqd)*. It relies on Qur'anic verses, such as that which states, "Fulfill every *'ahd*, for every *'ahd* will be inquired into [on the Day of Reckoning]" (17:34). It also relies on prophetic Hadiths, such as the one which states, "There is no faith in one who is not trustworthy and no religion in one who does not keep his promise."[51] Based on these foundations, these jurists require that every promise be kept and be legally enforceable. They generally recognize, however, that certain intervening circumstances could operate as a legitimate excuse for breach.[52] Thus the difference between the majority view and the minority view is not really about ethical values and the importance of the fulfillment of promises. It is, rather, about the extent to which the state may use its judicial arm to enforce promises made among its citizens. The majority view upholds a less intrusive view of government, while the minority view advocates greater governmental intrusion. Our American system has undergone similar discussions. In the area of marriage promises, we have come out in favor of the majority view, namely, generally keeping government out of such matters.

## Engagement and Marriage

Before a marriage takes place in Islamic law, there usually is an engagement period during which the man and the woman determine their suitability to each other. The rules associated with this period reflect the importance of honoring one's commitments and preparing for a successful marriage. So we turn to the engagement process first.

### The Engagement Promise

An engagement involves a promise to marry. Hence it is a very significant promise. The engagement promise allows the man several privileges; foremost

---

51. Al-Ba'li, *Dhawabit al-'Uqud*, p. 68; there are also other Hadiths that have the same meaning, see Al-Bukhari, *Sahih al-Bukhari, Kitab al-Iman*, vol. 1, p. 15.

52. Al-Ba'li, *Dhawabit al-'Uqud*, pp. 66-71.

among them is the ability to have greater interaction with the woman he wishes to marry. Usually, all such interaction is chaperoned. Furthermore, a man who is seriously considering engagement to a veiled woman has the right to see her if his offer is likely to be taken seriously by her and her family. This is part of the Prophet's Sunnah. Jurists disagreed as to how much of the woman her prospective fiancé may legitimately see.[53] But, in any case, it is agreed that not only must he see her, but she must also see him to decide upon his suitability.[54] In other words, the feelings and preferences of the woman during engagement and marriage are equally important to those of the man. This state of affairs may be puzzling in a society like ours where everyone is seen by everybody else, but in a community of veiled women, extending to the man the right to see his prospective fiancée is quite significant. It makes clear that the engagement promise is a serious and important one which overcomes certain prohibitions. Consequently, it must be honored barring a legitimate intervening circumstance.

It is worth noting, however, that the reasoning behind permitting a man to see his prospective fiancée is not based on the importance of the "looks" of the woman or the man. The Prophet made that clear when he recommended to a man that he see his intended wife because seeing her could help them develop affection for each other.[55] On another occasion, the Prophet cautioned Muslim men against choosing a woman for her looks or riches. Instead, he recommended that they choose a woman for her piety.[56]

Nevertheless, despite the seriousness of the engagement promise, jurists have generally allowed parties to an engagement to change their minds about their proposed life-long commitment.[57] The major reason underlying this attitude is that the Islamic marriage contract requires *ridha* (psychological contentment), and not mere acceptance from the parties.[58] So, if the parties appear not to find such *ridha* with each other, then it would be better to break the engagement than embark on a life-long journey of misery. Furthermore, if the promise is treated as enforceable, then it would have the force of a contract,

53. See, e.g., Ibn Hajar al-'Asqalani, *Fath al-Bari Sharh Sahih al-Bukhari* (Beirut: Dar al-Kutub al-'Ilmiyah, 1989), vol. 9, pp. 225-27; Muwaffaq al-Din Ibn Qudamah, *Al-Mughni* (Beirut: Dar al-Kitab al-'Arabi, n.d), vol. 7, pp. 453-54. See also Muhammad Abu Zahrah, *Al-Ahwal al-Shakhsiyah* (Cairo: Dar al Fikr al'Arabi, 1957), pp. 28-30; al-Zuhayli, *Al-Fiqh al-Islami,* vol. 9, pp. 6501-6508.

54. Zirar, *Mawsu'at al-Zawaj,* vol. 1, pp. 150-51.

55. Zirar, *Mawsu'at al-Zawaj,* vol. 1, p. 147.

56. See, e.g., al-'Asqalani, *Fath al-Bari,* vol. 9, pp. 167-69.

57. See, e.g., Abu Zahrah, *Al-Ahwal al-Shakhsiyah,* pp. 36-37.

58. Al-Qurrah Daghi, *Mabda' al-Ridha,* vol. 2, p. 835. See also al-Ba'li, *Dhawabit al-'Uqud,* pp. 19-28.

which it is not;[59] it would also mean that the judiciary can force one person to marry another, which it cannot under Islamic law.[60]

On the other hand, if the "jilted" party sustains damages as a result of the break-up, such as those incurred by a woman who left her job upon the request of her fiancé, reparations must be made.[61] Note that under American common law, an action for breach of promise to marry existed for several centuries, entitling the plaintiff to recover for injury to his or her feelings, health, and reputation. Recently, however, most states abolished this cause of action through "anti–heart balm statutes."[62]

As mentioned above, the period of engagement is very important for helping the couple determine their compatibility. Therefore, this becomes an active period where families invite the couple to dinners and surround them with opportunities to be together. The man usually showers his intended with gifts (in addition to the required marital gift called *mahr*) in the spirit of the Qur'an that requires the man to give gifts to the woman upon marriage and recommends (some say requires) him to give additional gifts *(mut'at al-talaq)* in case of divorce.[63] While these gifts are not religiously required, they are viewed as signs of affection and commitment.

The reason the family surrounds the couple is that the two may not be left totally alone in private with each other. This is a significant requirement with legal ramifications, which I shall presently explain. In Islamic law, the interaction between male and female is circumscribed by the Qur'an to avoid sin. Thus only certain blood relatives of the prospective bride may have unfettered access to her.[64] The fiancé remains outside this circle until the marriage contract *(kitab)* is concluded. Thus, any intimate interaction between the two prior to the *kitab* is religiously unacceptable. For that reason, many families avoid having their children fall into sin by executing the *kitab* at the time of engagement, but not announcing it until the wedding.

The benefit of this approach is that the couple may now hold hands, even kiss, as they spend time together, without fear of breaking God's law regarding chastity. But there are also problems with this approach. First, if the engage-

59. Abu Zahrah, *Al-Ahwal al-Shakhsiyah*, p. 36.
60. Abu Zahrah, *Al-Ahwal al-Shakhsiyah*, p. 37.
61. Al-Zuhayli, *Al-Fiqh al-Islami*, vol. 9, p. 6511.
62. John De Witt Gregory et al., *Understanding Family Law* § 4.02 (New York: Matthew Bender, 1993).
63. Qur'an 2:241. See also al-Razi, *Tafsir al-Fakhr al-Razi*, vol. 6, p. 173; Abu al-Walid Muhammad Ibn Rushd, *Bidayat al-Mujtahid wa Nihayat al-Muqtasid* (Beirut: Dar Ibn Hazm, 1995), vol. 3, pp. 1108-1109; al-Zuhayli, *Al-Fiqh al-Islami*, vol. 9, pp. 6829-35.
64. Qur'an 24:31. See also Ibn Qudamah, *Al-Mughni*, vol. 7, pp. 454-57.

ment does not work out, a divorce will be needed to end it. Second, if the couple spends even a short period of time (a few minutes) alone in private, most jurists would presume the marriage consummated, whether a wedding had taken place or not. Thus, if the engagement is broken in such a situation, not only will it require a divorce, but the divorce will have to follow the rules pertaining to a consummated marriage (with full payment of *mahr* by the husband). This situation also affects the status of the woman, who will now be regarded as a divorcée. In some countries, this status could make her less marriageable.

In the United States, where males and females freely interact with one another, there is usually no need for an early *kitab*. Couples join their friends in public places and have a good time getting to know each other. As a result, the engagement period in the United States tends to achieve its intended purpose by allowing a couple to determine compatibility before it moves into the final stage of commitment, the *kitab*.

## The Islamic Marriage Contract

The Qur'an does not refer to the marriage contract as a contract based on offer and acceptance. Rather, it describes it as *mithaqan ghalithan* (a solemn covenant), which is carefully regulated by a body of laws. It admonishes men who are about to leave their wives, "But if ye decide to take one wife in place of another, even if ye have given the latter a whole treasure for dower, take not the least bit of it back; would ye take it by slander and a manifest wrong? And how could ye take it when ye have gone in unto each other, and they have taken from you a solemn covenant?" (4:20-21).[65]

The word *mithaq*, which means "covenant," appears in a number of places in the Qur'an. In each place it refers to a momentous context, such as the covenant between God and the children of Israel, or those with whom Muslims have concluded a treaty. Furthermore, Egyptian jurist Malakah Zirar notes that God has placed marriage within the category of *'ibadat*, which relate to God's worship, and not within *mu'amalat*, where contracts are usually placed.[66] This makes the marriage contract radically different from and superior to all other contracts.

---

65. These verses refer in particular to the *mahr*. The husband has no right to reclaim it if he initiates divorce, because it is the wife's pure right. Incidentally, despite this admonition, some Muslim men today do exactly what the Qur'an forbade upon divorce. They treat their wives miserably to force them to give up their financial rights in the marriage, or they make false allegations against them during divorce proceedings. I shall discuss these situations in my forthcoming book.

66. Zirar, *Mawsu'at al-Zawaj*, vol. 1, pp. 134-44 (also citing similar views by Shaykh Imam Shaltut, in *al-Islam 'Aqidah wa Shari'ah*).

The Sunnah of the Prophet is no less emphatic. The Prophet said that the marriage contract is the contract most worthy of fulfillment.[67] In other words, he viewed the marriage contract as superior to all other contracts. He is also reported as saying that "marriage is my *Sunnah*, so the one who turns away from my *Sunnah*, turns away from me."[68] After all, marriage concerns human happiness and progeny. Ideally, it brings into being a relationship of affection, tranquility, and mercy, [69] and usually results in offspring, who are not only very dear to the parents' hearts but also very critical to the future of the community.

Yet, despite the importance of marriage, jurists disagreed as to whether it was a duty for a Muslim to marry, or whether it was simply a desirable or just permissible act.[70] Some argued that marriage in Islam was not obligatory except to avoid sin.[71] Nevertheless, even jurists who viewed marriage as a duty prohibited a prospective husband from getting married in the presence of evidence that he was abusive.[72] The prohibition is based on the fact that abusive marriages do not fulfill the Qur'anic ideal of spousal relationships (see, for example, Qur'an 2:187 and 30:21).

In an Islamic marriage, the parties maintain their identity as well as independence. The woman, for example, keeps her (maiden) name, and financial independence.[73] The wife remains an independent entity under the law, capable of transacting her own business and other affairs.[74] Husbands and wives are expected to consult with each other in the upbringing of their children.[75] Further, the wife has no obligation to perform housework, and is entitled to main-

67. Al-Bukhari, *Sahih al-Bukhari,* vol. 2, p. 117; vol. 3, p. 252.

68. Abu Hamid al-Ghazali, *'Ihya' 'Ulum al-Deen,* eleventh century, repr. (Egypt: Mustafa Babi al-Halabi Press, 1939), vol. 2, p. 22.

69. See, e.g., Qur'an 30:21.

70. Zirar, *Mawsu'at al-Zawaj,* vol. 1, p. 156.

71. Zirar, *Mawsu'at al-Zawaj,* vol. 1, p. 159.

72. Al-Zuhayli, *Al-Fiqh al-Islami,* vol. 9, p. 6516; Muhammad Baltaji, *Fi Ahkam al-Usrah* (Cairo: Maktabat al-Shabab, 1987), pp. 147-48 (describing the Hanafi view); Abu Zahrah, *Al-Ahwal al-Shakhsiyah,* p. 24.

73. See, e.g., Muhammad Rashid Rida, *Huquq al-Nisa' Fi al-Islam,* repr. ed. (Beirut: al-Maktab al-Islami, 1975), pp. 19-20. See also Zaidan 'Abd al-Baqi, *Al-Mar'ah Bayna al-Din Wa al-Mujtama'* (Cairo: n.p., 1977), vol. 4, pp. 291-97; vol. 7, pp. 334-43.

74. See Abd al-Rahaman al-Jaziri, *Kitab al-Fiqh 'ala al-Madhahib al-Arba'ah* (Beirut: Dar Ihya' al-Turath al-Arabi, 1969), vol. 4, pp. 46-47. See also Muhammad Jawad Maghniyah, *Al-Fiqh 'ala al-Madhahib al-Khamsah,* sixth ed. (Beirut: Dar al-'Ilm li al-Malayin, 1969), p. 321; Ahmad Faraj, *Al-Zawaj wa Ahkamuhu fi Madhahib ahl al-Sunnah* (Mansourah, Egypt: Dar al-Wafa', 1989), pp. 126-34.

75. For a discussion of consultation within the family, see Abd al-Halim Abu Shuqqah, *Tahrir al-Mar'ah fi 'Asr al-Risalah,* 6 vols. (Kuwait: Dar al-Qalam, 1990), vol. 5, pp. 104-9.

tenance by her husband.[76] These facts are the result of the juristic position, based on the Qur'an, that the marriage contract is not a service contract. Rather, it is viewed as being about *nafsayn* (two souls), male and female, coming together in a relationship of tranquility, mercy, and affection, to enjoy each other, and procreate and raise children who are good Muslims and good members of their society. This relationship is so close that the Qur'an describes each spouse as being the "garment" of the other, that is, one who covers the other's shortcomings and protects his or her privacy (Qur'an 2:187).

Regarding the rights of women within marriage, the Qur'an says, "women shall have rights similar to the rights against them [that is, rights of men] . . ." (2:228). It is reported that a man called Bishr ibn al-Harth, who lived in the early period of Islam, refused to marry for fear of not being able to live up to this verse.[77] The Qur'an also sets the standard for dealing with marital discord. It describes proper marital relations as "[either holding together] on equitable terms, or [separating] with kindness . . ." (2:229).

These and other verses, as well as the Prophet's Sunnah and the description of marriage as a solemn covenant, have led some jurists (despite their patriarchal tendencies) to recommend gentle behavior in the treatment of women. Al-Ghazali, the preeminent medieval jurist, argued that to be well-mannered with one's wife does not simply mean that the husband should not harm his wife (verbally or physically); rather, it means that the husband must be prepared to endure the harm inflicted upon him by his wife, and be patient when she becomes angry. Al-Ghazali noted that God emphasized the importance of the rights of women when he described the marriage contract as a "solemn covenant"; and that the Prophet repeatedly counseled men to be kind to women, until his tongue became heavy and his voice inaudible.[78]

The Qur'an also cautions a man against taking the easy way out and leaving his wife (4:19).[79] It tells those who dislike their spouses, "If ye take a dislike to them, it may be that ye dislike a thing, and [God] brings about through it a great deal of good" (4:19). Thus, while Islam provided four ways to divorce, it did not encourage it; for, "ye have gone in unto each other, and they have taken

---

76. See, e.g., Ibn Qudamah, *Al-Mughni*, vol. 8, pp. 130-31. See also al-'Asqalani, *Fath al-Bari*, vol. 9, pp. 632-33, 640-41; Ibn Rushd, *Bidayat al-Mujtahid*, vol. 3, pp. 1028-29; al-Zuhayli, *Al-Fiqh al-Islami*, vol. 9, pp. 6591-92.

77. Al-Ghazali, *Ihya' 'Ulum al-Deen*, vol. 2, pp. 24, 34. Please note that the second part of this passage states, "But men have a degree of advantage over them." This has been interpreted by patriarchal men to refer to a superior status. In fact, it refers to a heightened duty, as discussed in al-Tabari, *Jami' al-Bayan fi Tafsir al-Qur'an*, vol. 2, p. 275.

78. Al-Ghazali, *'Ihya' 'Ulum al-Deen*, vol. 2, p. 44.

79. See also al-Ghazali, *'Ihya' 'Ulum al-Deen*, vol. 2, pp. 57-58.

from ye a solemn covenant . . ." (4:20-21). Al-Ghazali calls a man who abandons his family a run-away whose prayer and fasting will not be accepted by God until he returns.[80] After all, the Prophet told Muslims that "Each one of you is a shepherd, and each one of you is responsible for his flock."[81]

This discussion shows that, while divorce is permitted in Islam, it is seriously disliked. The Prophet calls it "the most disliked permissible act."[82] The Qur'an provided ways to reduce the divorce rate by instructing a troubled couple to seek arbiters, one from each side of the family (4:35). These arbiters are bound by the rules of justice in mediating disagreements. If mediation fails, then God will not force an unhappy couple to stay together.

The burden of divorce thus becomes a religious one, between God and the one who seeks it. So, if a spouse decides to divorce, a judge may not ask him or her about private matters, unless the divorce action is based on fault. Otherwise, it is left to the conscience of the spouse, and his or her relationship with God. So, in every divorce there is the right of the spouse *(haqq al-'abd)*, and the right of God *(haqq Allah)*. The courts deal with the former, God deals with the latter in the afterlife. Even where the courts conclude that a unilateral divorce by the husband is arbitrary and oppressive toward the wife, they are not entitled to prohibit it. Otherwise, courts would be intervening in the Muslims' freedom of contract. Instead, courts have allowed themselves the right to step in and protect the oppressed party by adjusting the final terms of the divorce settlement to reflect the equities of the situation.[83]

It is worth noting at this point that one of the forms of divorce permitted in Islam is that of *khul'*. This form, which gives the woman the right to initiate divorce, is often misunderstood. Recently, the Egyptian religious scholars of al-Azhar, the oldest Islamic school in the world, attempted to clarify (and correct) it. Historically, the Prophet granted this form of divorce to a woman who sought it because she was afraid that staying with her husband might cause her to violate God's laws (perhaps by looking to another relationship outside the marriage to console her). She informed the Prophet that there was no defect, moral or religious, in her husband, but that she simply could not stand him. The Prophet asked her if she would be willing to return the *mahr* (and only that) to her husband. When she agreed, he instructed the husband to divorce her.[84]

---

80. Al-Ghazali, *'Ihya' 'Ulum al-Deen*, vol. 2, pp. 34-35.

81. Al-Bukhari, *Sahih al-Bukhari*, bk. 62, *Kitab al-Nikah* (Marriage), vol. 3, p. 257.

82. Abu Dawud Sulayman Ibn al-Ash'ath al-Sijistani, *Sunan Abu Dawud* (Beirut: Dar al-Irshad, 1969), vol. 2, pp. 631-32; bk. *Kitab al-Talaq* (Divorce), nos. 2177, 2178.

83. See, e.g., Syrian family law, Decree No. 59 (1953) regarding Personal Status Law, *amended by* Law No. 34 (1975), Bk.1, Tit. 3, Ch. 5, Item 117.

84. Al-'Asqalani, *Fath al-Bari*, vol. 9, pp. 493-505, esp. pp. 500-501.

Despite the plain meaning of the story, patriarchal jurists interpreted this form of divorce to require the consent of the husband.[85] For centuries, Muslim women could not divorce at will. Recently, the situation became far more serious as less religious men began asking for large amounts of money in exchange for their consent, in clear contravention of the Prophetic tradition. The problem became so egregious that al-Azhar jurists decided to review the matter. As a result of this review, the consent requirement by the husband was eliminated.[86] In doing that, they reached the same conclusion that a Pakistani court reached decades earlier in a brilliant opinion that went largely unnoticed.[87]

The new Azhari interpretation rectifies the current jurisprudential situation by dropping the requirement of the husband's consent. This change prevents the husband from coercing his wife into staying with him ('adhl), or forcing her to pay a large amount of money for her divorce. The Qur'an expressly prohibits 'adhl, whether by a husband or by a father who tries to prevent his daughter from getting married (2:232). The Prophet's Sunnah specifies that the husband may not take from the wife more than the *mahr* he gave her upon marriage. Further, some jurists recommend that it would be better and more charitable if the husband forgives part of the *mahr*.[88] By doing so, the husband would soothe the wife's feelings as they part, in accordance with the Qur'anic injunction to part ways charitably.

As a result of the new jurisprudence, the Egyptian personal status law (family law) was amended.[89] Under the new law, a woman has the right to ask for *khul'* from her husband. She need not specify any grounds, except to state that she fears that the continuation of the marriage may cause her to violate God's law.[90] Once the wife utters these words, the judge is bound to grant her

85. See, e.g., Ahmed al-Khamlishi, *Al-Ta'liq 'Ala Qanun al-Ahwal al-Shakhsiyah*, 2 vols. (Rabat: Dar al-Ma'arif al-Jadidah, 1987), vol. 1, pp. 355-63, esp. pp. 361-63.

86. Egyptian Code, Act No. 20 (2000), Decree No. 1, regarding the regulation of certain situations and procedures of judiciary actions in matters of personal status (stating that the consent of the husband is no longer required in cases of *khul'* divorce).

87. See Keith Hodkinson, *Muslim Family Law: A Sourcebook* (London, 1984), pp. 285-87 (relating criticism by a Pakistani court of the consent requirement).

88. See al-'Asqalani, *Fath al-Bari*, esp. vol. 9, p. 503.

89. See Egyptian Code, note 86 above.

90. According to the Prophetic tradition, there was a woman who developed a great dislike for her husband, through no fault of his own. She went to the Prophet seeking a way out of the marriage. The Prophet instructed her to return to the man his *mahr* (in this case, a garden). She was so pleased by the prospect of ending the marriage that she offered to give the husband other things as well. The Prophet said, "As for the garden, yes. As for more, no." See Ibn Qudamah, *Al-Mughni*, vol. 8, pp. 173-75, 182-83; Muhammad Ibn Ali Muhammad al-Shawkani, *Nayl al-Awtar*, 9 vols. (Beirut: Dar al Jil, 1973), vol. 7, pp. 34-41.

divorce after an attempt to reconcile the parties. If the reconciliation fails, she is granted divorce but must return to the husband his *mahr*.[91] This is based on the rationale that the woman herself rejected her husband through no fault of his own, and hence must not profit by her action.

The fact that divorce is permissible in Islam is an integral part of the Islamic system of *'adalah*. *'Adalah* is another core concept in the Qur'an, and the backbone of *'adalah* is the *mizaan* (balance). Loosely translated, *'adalah* means "justice," but not just human retributive justice. Rather, it refers to a richer concept of justice which encompasses the whole universe as well as higher forms of justice, such as restorative justice and the concept of forgiveness.[92] It also provides the *mizaan* of the world.[93] God tells us in the Qur'an that God created the whole universe in due measure,[94] so that the sun would not overtake the moon, nor the night overtake the day;[95] that "the earth we have spread out [like a carpet] set thereon mountains firm and immovable and produced therein all kinds of things in due balance" (15:19). In other words, everything on earth was created according to Divine Balance. So was marriage. This is why the Islamic concept of marriage is based on tranquility and harmony. Discord upsets the balance, and oppressive divorces violate God's all-encompassing principle of *'adalah*. On the other hand, where the divorce is the result of a failed good-faith effort by both parties, then God will simply reward the parties for their attempts and open new doors to the divorcing spouses.

## Requirements of the Marriage Contract

The Islamic marriage contract is founded on the mutual consent of both parties.[96] This requirement again emphasizes the fact that the two parties to the

91. See, e.g., al-'Asqalani, *Fath al-Bari*, vol. 9, pp. 225-27. See also Abu Zahrah, *Al-Ahwal al-Shakhsiyah*, pp. 340-41.

92. For a discussion of Islamic criminal law and the concept of forgiveness, see Azizah al-Hibri, "The Muslim Perspective on the Clergy-Penitent Privilege," *Loyola Los Angeles Law Review* 29 (1996): 1723-32.

93. See, e.g., Qur'an 55:7-9: "And the Firmament has He raised high, and He has set up the Balance [of Justice], in order that ye may not transgress [due] balance. So establish weight with justice and fall not short in the balance."

94. Qur'an 25:2: "He to whom belongs the dominion of the heavens and the earth: no son has He begotten, nor has He a partner in His dominion: it is He who created all things, and ordered them in due proportions."

95. Qur'an 36:40: "It is not permitted to the Sun to catch up to the Moon, nor can the Night outstrip the Day: Each [just] swims along in [its own] orbit [according to Law]."

96. Al-Qurra Daghi, *Mabda' al-Ridha fi al-'Uqud*, vol. 2, p. 835. See also al-Ba'li, *Dhawabit al-'Uqud*, pp. 19-22.

marriage contract are equally important. The consent requirement is a *rukn* (formal element) of the marriage contract and without it no marriage contract will be properly established.[97] Where fraud or absence of true consent is discovered, the marriage contract can be annulled.[98] Further, the terms of the acceptance must coincide with those of the offer, and the language of the offer must be unconditional and clearly indicative of marriage.[99] According to Islamic tradition, either the woman or the man can make the offer, although in most cultures women have been assigned the more passive role.[100] Finally, the consenting parties must have the legal capacity to do so or the marriage contract will not be properly formed.[101]

To protect inexperienced, previously unmarried women from entering into unsuitable (and hence potentially unsuccessful) marriages, Islamic jurists have either required or recommended that a woman seek the approval of her *wali* (guardian or advisor) in marriage. So, we now turn briefly to the concept of *wali* and his role in the marriage contract.

## The Concept of Wali

This requirement affects the effectiveness of the marriage contract, as well as the possibility of annulling it. Most traditional Muslim jurisprudence requires a *wali* in marriage for a *bikr* (virgin) woman, even if she has reached maturity.[102] The requirement usually means that the young woman's marriage cannot be concluded without the presence (and acceptance) of her *wali*, who is usually her father or, in his absence, someone who truly cares about her interests.[103] So, what is a *wali* and what is the extent of his authority?

97. See, e.g., al-Zuhayli, *Al-Fiqh al-Islami*, vol. 9, pp. 6567-68; Abu Zahrah, *Al-Ahwal al-Shakhsiyah*, p. 41.

98. Abu Zahrah, *Al-Ahwal al-Shakhsiyah*, p. 60. But not for Abu Hanifah, who did not view marriage contracts as ones that can be annulled. See al-Zuhayli, *Al-Fiqh al-Islami*, vol. 9, pp. 6535, 6567-68, 6582-83; al-Khamlishi, *Al-Ta'liq*, vol. 1, pp. 82-83.

99. See, e.g., al-Zuhayli, *al-Fiqh al-Islami*, vol. 9, pp. 6522-32. See also Abu Zahrah, *Al-Ahwal al-Shakhsiyah*, pp. 41-47.

100. It is well known that Khadija, the first wife of the Prophet, took the initiative of proposing marriage to him; indeed, nothing prevents a woman from proposing to a man. See, e.g., al-ʿAsqalani, *Fath al-Bari*, vol. 9, pp. 217-18.

101. See, e.g., al-Zuhayli, *Al-Fiqh al-Islami*, vol. 9, p. 6534. See also Abu Zahrah, *Al-Ahwal al-Shakhsiyah*, p. 41.

102. See al-Jaziri, *Kitab al-Fiqh*, vol. 4, pp. 51-53. See also Muhammad Jawad Maghniyah, *Al-Fiqh ʿala al-Mathahib al-Khamsah*, p. 321; Faraj, *Al-Zawaj*, pp. 126-34.

103. Ahmad al-Ghandur, *Al-Ahwal al-Shakhsiyah fi al-Tashriʾ al-Islami* (Kuwait: Jamiʾat al-Kuwait Press, 1972), pp. 122, 135-36; Faraj, *Al-Zawaj*, p. 126; al-Jaziri, *Kitab al-Fiqh*, vol. 4, pp. 52-

Generally, a *wali* is a fiduciary who must guard the interests of his or her ward. For this reason, he or she must meet certain conditions to be eligible, such as full capacity (physical maturity, rationality, and liberty), and sameness of faith.[104] In the case of the marriage contract, most jurists required also that the *wali* be male, and he is usually the father of the bride.[105] This requirement was historically defended on several grounds. Most important, jurists instituted this requirement as a protective measure for women who may be swept by their emotions into the most important contract in their lives.[106] They feared that young, innocent women could be deceived by designing men.[107] To eliminate such a possibility, jurists required the consent of the father to the marriage, along with the consent of his daughter.[108] This requirement created a partnership relationship between the daughter and her father in the choice of a husband.[109]

The important scholar Abu Hanifah, however, rejected this paternalistic approach by arguing that women should be able to take charge of their own lives.[110] He noted that God has given Muslim women full financial independence.[111] Since life is more valuable than money, he concluded that it was even more important that women be entrusted with their lives.[112] Consequently, Hanafi jurisprudence permits a woman to execute her own marriage contract without the need for a *wali*. In other words, under Hanafi law, a marriage contract entered into by a Muslim woman without her *wali* is effective.

Another reason for the requirement of a *wali* was that it protected the fam-

---

53. See also Muhammad Abu Zahrah, *Muhadarat fi 'Aqd al-Zawaj wa Atharuh* (Cairo, 1958), pp. 135, 139; Ibn Qudamah, *Al-Mughni*, vol. 7, pp. 337, 346.

104. Ibn Qudamah, *Al-Mughni*, vol. 7, pp. 337, 346, 356-57; al-Zuhayli, *Al-Fiqh al-Islami*, vol. 9, pp. 6700-6703.

105. See, e.g., Ibn Qudamah, *Al-Mughni*, vol. 7, pp. 346-47. See also al-Ghandur, *Al-Ahwal al-Shakhsiyah*, pp. 121-22, 135-36; Faraj, *Al-Zawaj*, p. 126; Al-Jaziri, *Kitab al-Fiqh*, vol. 4, pp. 52-53; Abu Zahrah, *Al-Ahwal al-Shakhsiyah*, pp. 110-17, 118-19.

106. See, e.g., Abu Zahrah, *Al-Ahwal al-Shakhsiyah*, pp. 109, 126-30.

107. Abu Zahrah, *Al-Ahwal al-Shakhsiyah*, p. 128. See also Abu Zahrah, *Al-Milkiyah*, pp. 294-95.

108. Abu Zahrah, *Al-Ahwal al-Shakhsiyah*, p. 128. See also al-Zuhayli, *Al-Fiqh al-Islami*, vol. 9, p. 6574; Abu-Zahrah, *Al-Milkiyah*, p. 291.

109. Abu-Zahrah, *Al-Milkiyah*, p. 291.

110. Muhammad bin Ahmad al-Sarakhsi, *Kitab al-Mabsut*, 30 vols. (Beirut: Dar al-Ma'rifah, 1968), vol. 5, pp. 10-15. See also al-Ghandur, *Al-Ahwal al-Shakhsiyah*, p. 126; Abu-Zahrah, *Al-Milkiyah*, pp. 292-93.

111. See, e.g., al-Shafi'i, *Kitab al-Umm*, first ed. (Cairo: Maktabat al-Kuliyah al-Azhariyah, 1961), vol. 3, pp. 215-16, 219. See also Abu-Zahrah, *Al-Milkiyah*, pp. 291-97.

112. Abu-Zahrah, *Al-Milkiyah*, pp. 292-93; Al-Zuhayli, *Al-Fiqh al-Islami*, vol. 9, pp. 6698-99.

ily's honor and social standing, in cases where women may have elected to marry "ineligible" males.[113] This rationale was found so appealing that even Hanafis, who recognized the right of the adult woman to contract her own marriage without a *wali*, expressed their preference for the woman's delegation of that right to a *wali*.[114] Furthermore, even Abu Hanifah empowered the father to annul a marriage (where pregnancy had not yet occurred) if the husband was "ineligible."[115]

*Eligibility* in this context is a term of art, which has been endowed with a broad range of meanings. The Prophet defined eligibility in terms of faith and piety.[116] But the Hanafi School has departed from this basic definition. Hanafis define eligibility in accordance with hierarchical social customs, subsuming under this concept such factors as lineage, financial condition, and skill or profession.[117] Consequently, the Hanafi definition, which is currently used in Islamic courts, reflects traditional patriarchal concerns of the jurists' times. These concerns were so strong that they were viewed as sufficient for ignoring the woman's choice after the fact and voiding her marriage.

Note that the traditional patriarchal stereotype of women as irrational, emotional, and dependent plays an important role in justifying the Hanafi view that a *wali* may void an unsuitable marriage. Today, these assumptions are viewed by our society as unwarranted, and hence that part of the jurisprudence of marriage is ripe for review. Nevertheless, the Hanafi idea of an adviser to the woman who is preparing for marriage is an excellent one, although it is not necessary (or desirable) for the woman to delegate to him the power of executing her marriage contract.

In our American society, we have generally recognized the importance of legal advice for a less empowered spouse entering into a prenuptial agreement

---

113. See, e.g., Al-Jaziri, *Kitab al-Fiqh*, vol. 4, pp. 49-50; Ibn Rushd, *Bidayat al-Mujtahid*, vol. 3, pp. 953-54. See also Abu-Zahrah, *Al-Ahwal al-Shakhsiyah*, pp. 294-95; Abu Zahrah, *Muhadarat fi 'Aqd al-Zawaj wa Atharuh*, p. 135; Mohammad al-Dusuqi, *Al-'Usrah fi al-Tashri' al-Islami* (al-Dawha, Qatar: Dar al-Thaqafah, 1995), pp. 84-86.

114. Al-Ghandur, *Al-Ahwal al-Shakhsiyah*, pp. 125-26. See Abu-Zahrah, *Al-Milkiyah*, p. 136 and related note 1, p. 154. See also al-Khamlishi, *Al-Ta'liq*, vol. 1, pp. 204-5.

115. See al-Jaziri, *Kitab al-Fiqh*, vol. 4, pp. 51, 56; Muhammad al-Dijwi, *Al-Ahwal al-Shakhsiyah li al-Misriyin al-Muslimin* (Cairo: Dar al-Nashr li al-Jami'aat al-Misriyah, n.d), p. 48; Abu-Zahrah, *Al-Milkiyah*, p. 173; Muhammad Zakariya al-Bardisi, *Al-Ahkam al-Islamiyah fi al Ahwal al-Shaksiyah* (1965), p. 192.

116. Ibn Qudamah, *Al-Mughni*, vol. 7, pp. 374-75; Faraj, *Al-Zawaj*, p. 111. See also al-Dijwi, *Al-Ahwal al-Shakhsiyah li al-Misriyin al-Muslimin*, p. 55; al-Shawkani, *Nayl al-Awtar*, vol. 6, p. 262.

117. Al-Sarakhsi, *Kitab al-Mabsut*, vol. 5, pp. 22-30. See also Ibn Qudamah, *Al-Mughni*, vol. 7, pp. 371-79.

(which sets some of the terms usually set in the Islamic marriage contract). While the Uniform Premarital Agreement Act does not expressly require independent legal counsel for the less empowered spouse, the absence of such counsel may well be considered a factor in determining whether the conditions for the unenforceability of the agreement exist.[118] This position is not very different from that of Abu Hanifah, who validates the marriage, even without the presence of a *wali,* but nevertheless recommends such a presence. His view, however, about the ability of the *wali* to invalidate the marriage if the husband is ineligible goes beyond both the Sunnah of the Prophet and our American law.

### Other Requirements

It is often believed that the *mahr* (the obligatory marital gift that the husband gives his bride) is a *rukn* of the marriage contract or that it is required for the validity of the marriage. In their attempt to protect women and children in marriages where husbands fail to deliver the *mahr,* jurists predominantly have refused to consider the *mahr* a requirement for the validity of the marriage.[119] Instead, they have considered it a senior debt against the husband, and have instructed him to pay it.[120] Where no *mahr* is specified in the marriage contract, the judge simply assigns to the wife a *mahr* that a woman of the bride's qualifications and status would expect.

Since marriages are an important part of the constitution of the community, Islamic law requires Muslims to "publish" the marriage through wedding celebrations and announcements.[121] This requirement not only protects the marrying parties if any question arises in the future about their relationship, but also helps create a healthy social climate that celebrates relations sanctioned by marriage. For similar reasons, Islamic law requires two qualified witnesses at the execution of the marriage contract. It also requires the absence of any temporary or permanent impediment to the marriage.[122] These last two require-

---

118. Gregory, *Understanding Family Law* §4.02[B].

119. See, e.g., Abu Zahrah, *Al-Ahwal al-Shakhsiyah,* pp. 168-73. See also al-Zuhayli, *Al-Fiqh al-Islami,* vol. 9, p. 6521.

120. Al-Zuhayli, *Al-Fiqh al-Islami,* vol. 9, pp. 6570-71.

121. See, e.g., Abu Zahrah, *Al-Ahwal al-Shakhsiyah,* pp. 52-56. See also al-Zuhayli, *Al-Fiqh al-Islami,* vol. 9, pp. 6559-62, 6571, 6618-19; Zirar, *Mawsu'at al-Zawaj,* pp. 290-93; Muhammad Fu'ad Shakir, *Zawaj Batil — al-Misyar, al-'Urfi, al-Sirri, al-Mut'ah* (Egypt: Maktabat Awlad al-Sheikh li al-Turath, 1997), pp. 27-29.

122. Abu Zahrah, *Al-Ahwal al-Shakhsiyah,* pp. 52, 57, 63-105. See also al-Zuhayli, *Al-Fiqh al-Islami,* vol. 9, pp. 6550-51.

ments are discussed by jurists in great detail because they affect the validity of the marriage.[123]

Both Sunni and Shi'i jurists are unanimous in asserting the permanent duration of marriage.[124] Shi'i jurists, however, carved out an exception to the rule, namely, that of *mut'ah* (temporary) marriages. In these marriages, a premarital agreement specifies the duration of the marriage; after that period of time, the marriage expires without need for divorce. Temporary marriages are not common,[125] and Sunni jurists do not recognize the validity of such marriages. Permanent marriages are the entrenched rule even in Shi'i communities, and most Shi'i families refuse to give their daughters away in a temporary marriage.

Temporary marriages were devised to guard warriors from adultery while away from home; thus, they were creatures of necessity. The question is simply one of the legitimacy of carving out this exception to deal with very special circumstances. Temporary marriages were practiced at the time of the Prophet;[126] however, Sunni sources hold that the Prophet flatly prohibited this form of marriage before his death.[127] Shi'i sources disagree.[128] This disagreement constitutes one of the more sensitive areas of difference between the two sects, and is fraught with emotions.

It is important to note that temporary marriages have a measure of protection. They must be based on consent, and the husband must give the wife a *mahr*. If a woman becomes pregnant under this form of marriage, the children are entitled to all the rights and privileges of the children of a permanent marriage. The "temporary" wife is not entitled to maintenance or inheritance, but she does have some rights.[129]

The plight of young Muslim men in the West, where sexual temptations and encounters are overwhelming, has made this issue a modern one. Concerned about the temptations faced by Muslim youth in the United States and Europe, some Sunni jurists in Saudi Arabia and Yemen recently tried to introduce into Sunni jurisprudence and societies some unconventional forms of permanent

123. Al-Zuhayli, *Al-Fiqh al-Islami*, vol. 9, pp. 6525-81.

124. Al-Zuhayli, *Al-Fiqh al-Islami*, vol. 9, p. 6551. See also Group of scholars and intellectuals, *al-Mut'ah wa Mashru'iyatuha fi al-Ilsam* (Beirut: Dar al-Zahra', n.d), pp. 22-23.

125. Zirar, *Mawsu'at al-Zawaj*, pp. 169-74. See also al-Dusuqi, *Al-'Usrah*, pp. 51-55.

126. Al-'Asqalani, *Fath al Bari*, vol. 9, pp. 207-17. See also Ibn Qudamah, *Al-Mughni*, vol. 7, pp. 571-73; Ibn Rushd, *Bidayat al-Mujtahid*, pp. 1036-37.

127. Al-'Asqalani, *Fath al-Bari*, vol. 9, pp. 207-17. See also al-Zuhayli, *Al-Fiqh al-Islami*, vol. 9, pp. 6555-58; Zirar, *Mawsu'at al-Zawaj*, pp. 169-76.

128. 'Izz al-Din Bahr al-Ulum, *Al-Zawaj fi al-Qur'an wa al-Sunnah* (Beirut: Dar al-Zahra', 1978), pp. 269-81. See also *al-Mut'ah wa Mashru'iyatuha fi al-Ilsam*, pp. 27-100.

129. Al-Zuhayli, *Al-Fiqh al-Islami*, vol. 9, p. 6555; *al-Mut'ah wa Mashru'iyatuha fi al-Ilsam*, pp. 32-33. See also Bahr al-Ulum, *Al-Zawaj fi al-Qur'an wa al-Sunnah*, pp. 268-69.

marriage that closely resemble *mut'ah* marriages.[130] One proposal, which is based on the generally correct assumption that young Muslims live with their parents until they marry, suggested waiving the requirement that a newly-wed couple share a residence. The proposal was defended as ncessary to facilitate marriages in situations where there are housing shortages.[131] But in fact, there are no housing shortages in most Western countries. Consequently, Muslim communities around the world became suspicious of this proposal. The form of marriage it advocated was quickly dubbed "*zawaj* (marriage)-friend." The intention was to draw a derogatory analogy between it and Western "boyfriend/girlfriend" relationships. In other words, the community concluded that what was being proposed was a temporary relationship, disguised as a marriage.[132]

Malakah Zirar, a leading Islamic female scholar, has spoken forcefully against such unconventional marriages.[133] She points out that God has given Muslim women specific rights and protections in their marriages, and no scholar should attempt to upset that divine balance.[134] Zirar regards "intention" as a very important requirement in the marriage contract. She argues that if a man enters a marriage with the *intention* of ending it after a specific period of time, then the marriage is invalid.[135] Other Sunni jurists argue that so long as the period is not specified in the marriage contract, the marriage will be deemed valid.

In her opposition to unconventional marriages, Zirar is waging an attack on rich Muslim men who visit economically depressed Muslim countries, marry women there, and, at the end of their visit, leave these women without divorcing them. Although the marriages are not specified as temporary arrangements, they operate in the end as such, but without the protections of a *mut'ah* marriage. In a *mut'ah* marriage, the intention of the man is disclosed from the outset, thus giving the woman a clear choice. Further, the temporary marriage expires at the end of the specified period, and at least the woman will not be left hanging, wondering whether her husband will return or not.

In sum, while there are exceptions both under Shi'i and recent Sunni jurisprudence to facilitate temporary or unconventional marital relations, the basic, common, and entrenched model of marriage for both remains that of a permanent marriage formed through a solemn covenant based on mutual consent.

---

130. Zirar, *Mawsu'at al-Zawaj*, pp. 215-40; Shakir, *Zawaj Batil*, p. 146.

131. This proposal was made a couple of years ago by the Yemeni leader al-Zandani, and it stirred a storm of objections.

132. The issue was the subject of a panel discussion on al-Jazeerah television, summer 2003, in which I participated.

133. Zirar, *Mawsu'at al-Zawaj*, pp. 169-76, esp. 171.

134. Zirar made this statement on the above-referenced television program (see note 132).

135. Zirar, *Mawsu'at al-Zawaj*, esp. pp. 171-74.

## *The* Kitab *Ceremony*

The *Kitab* ceremony usually precedes the wedding by a period of time ranging from minutes to years. The ceremony tends to be a private and solemn affair. In addition to the bride, groom, cleric, parents and immediate family, and close friends, no one else need be present. Other attendees have no specific legal significance, unless they are the two witnesses necessary for the validity of the contract. The father (or someone in his position) is the *wali* whose agreement to the marriage contract is required in most schools of thought (except the Hanafi).[136] In some countries, the father is authorized to sign on behalf of his daughter, with her consent, to shield her from attending a ceremony regarded by some as primarily a "male" event!

The cleric will begin with verses from the Qur'an and then explain the marriage contract to the couple. A well-informed cleric will discuss briefly at this point the covenantal nature of the marriage contract and the Islamic view of marital relations. Then, the cleric will ask the couple about the amount of *mahr* (or other type of *mahr*) they have agreed upon. The *mahr* will be recorded in the marriage contract, unless the couple decides not to divulge it publicly, in which case the contract will refer to the "agreed upon *mahr.*" The cleric will then inquire about any additional stipulated terms, agreed upon by the couple. If there are some, they will be inserted in the marriage contract, so long as they do not contravene its intent.[137] The cleric will then ask each party to express consent to the marriage. Traditionally, a virgin's silence is taken as a sign of acceptance.[138] This is based on a precedent in which the wife of the Prophet, 'A'ishah, pointed out to the Prophet that a virgin in Arabia would be too bashful to express her consent to a marriage offer. The Prophet then said, "Her silence is her acceptance."[139] Jurists, however, made clear that (sad) tears or other signs of distress by a virgin must also be viewed as rejection.[140] It is my view that this rule should not apply to virgins today, especially in the United States, because of the changed nature of our society, and the abuses perpetrated under the cover of this rule.

Ideally (though often not in the United States), the marriage contract will specify the jurisprudential school of thought governing the contract. The par-

136. Al-Ghandur, *Al-Ahwal al-Shakhsiyah*, p. 126; Abu-Zahrah, *Al-Milkiyah*, p. 138; Faraj, *Al-Zawaj*, pp. 134, 136; al-Bardisi, *Al-ahkam al-Islamiyah fi al-Ahwal al-Shaksiyah*, p. 199.

137. Al-'Asqalani, *Fath al-Bari*, pp. 271-75; Abu Zahrah, *Al-Ahwal al-Shakhsiyah*, pp. 156-61; Abu-Zahrah, *Al-Milkiyah*, pp. 235-44.

138. Al-'Asqalani, *Fath al-Bari*, vol. 9, pp. 239-43; Ibn Qudamah, *Al-Mughni*, vol. 7, pp. 384-85; Ibn Rushd, *Bidayat al-Mujtahid*, pp. 942-44.

139. Ibn Rushd, *Bidayat al-Mujtahid*, pp. 942-44.

140. Al-Sarakhsi, *Kitab al-Mabsut*, vol. 5, p. 4.

ties then sign, and the *kitab* comes immediately into effect. Everyone present reads *al-Fatihah* (the first chapter of the Qur'an) and congratulates each other, then departs after some refreshments are served. The *kitab* is a much more somber occasion than the wedding, because it is a religious event.

## The Wedding

The wedding is simply a social affair intended to publicize the marriage in the community and to celebrate it. It is part of the Sunnah of the Prophet, who instructed a groom to celebrate his marriage, even by serving a lamb to his guests.[141] Muslim families, however, have also used this occasion to reflect their social status, as indicated by the size of the party, the guests invited, and the fashions and jewelry exhibited. In some countries, there may be two simultaneous parts to the wedding celebrations, one for men and another for women. The women's celebration tends to be the most exciting, often with singing and dancing that ushers the arrival of the groom, to be joined later by his circumspect bride. The husband would be the only male in this gathering, usually a very uncomfortable position. The partition of the parties by gender is designed to afford the women the opportunity to abandon the formal outer dress and decorum required in public, and celebrate freely. These are also opportunities for mothers to look around for potential spouses for their children.

## Marriage Contracts in the United States

In the United States, Muslims must follow all state law requirements in preparation for marriage. The cleric who oversees the execution of the marriage contract is usually authorized by the state to conduct marriage ceremonies. He would usually have a simple one-page marriage contract specifying the name of the Islamic center he is associated with, the names of the parties and witnesses, as well as the amount of *mahr* involved and any stipulations. He would follow the same procedure described earlier. The *kitab* ceremony is basically the same all over the world because of its religious nature.

Once the parties execute the contract, the marriage springs into existence. After the signing, the cleric files the necessary forms with the state and an official state marriage certificate is then issued. Thus under both Islamic law and state law, it is the date of the execution of the marriage contract, and not the

141. Al-ʿAsqalani, *Fath al-Bari*, vol. 9, pp. 288-89.

wedding, which determines the marital status of the parties. Weddings therefore are viewed, even in the United States, as purely social events.

Marriages in the Muslim world have tended to be highly stable, despite the legal ability of both parties to initiate divorce. This stability is rooted in the centrality of the family in Muslim societies. For this reason, marriages tend to be between whole families and not just two individuals. Thus, at the very first sign of trouble, the extended families step in to resolve potential conflicts. In fact, the Qur'an itself advocates mediation and conflict resolution through the use of one arbitrator or mediator from each of the two families. With the advent of modernity, however, some of these traditions have been broken, and marriages have become increasingly strained.

The situation of American Muslims is a case in point, especially with respect to immigrant Muslims. Most of the immigrants left their extended families behind and have no support system. Furthermore, American society places many pressures on the family unit, including economic and moral ones. As a result of these and other factors, divorces have been rising in the Muslim community, and divorce actions have multiplied in courts.

It is disturbing that in some divorce actions, Muslim husbands have claimed that they did not fully understand the marriage contract, especially with respect to the *mahr* term. Other actions have revealed that the life of the couple, from the beginning, was anything but a reflection of the Qur'anic ideal of "tranquility, affection, and mercy." The picture emerging from these court cases is that marriage at times is not being viewed as seriously as it is supposed to be. This is not unique to American Muslims. It is part of a larger trend which seems to secularize and trivialize marriage by emptying it of its covenantal content *(mithaqan ghalithan)* and by regarding it as a "mere" contract that can be terminated at will. To reverse this trend, the community needs to inform prospective spouses of their rights and obligations and to protect Muslim women and families through education and counseling.

Muslim women have begun audibly expressing their complaints of abuse of authority by both well-intentioned and untrustworthy *walis* who pressure their daughters or other relatives (including sons) into marriage. There have been cases where a prospective spouse did not properly disclose all relevant information about his health, financial situation, or other matters. In other cases the husband claimed he was drawn by fraud into the marriage, and did not understand the document he was signing. In such instances, in the absence of true *ridha*, the marriage is generally voidable by the party whose *ridha* was either lacking or improperly obtained. Realistically, however, once a person is married it is very difficult for him or her to void that marriage. If they were able to do so, most likely they would have avoided the marriage initially. Therefore, it is imperative for Imams executing marriage contracts to ensure the full, informed *ridha* of the prospective spouses.

Such *ridha* can only be based on full disclosure by both parties, adequate opportunity for forming a judgment, and a truly free choice. In the United States, this can be achieved by providing marriage counseling sessions in Islamic centers by Imams and other qualified staff for the prospective spouses. The counseling would provide spouses with the opportunity to disclose information and assess responsibilities of married life, given the circumstances and abilities of each spouse and the common goals they may share. It will also help determine whether *ridha* is likely to develop. This arrangement will help reduce the rising rate of divorce among Muslims in the United States and, just as important, ensure that marriages are based on well-informed *ridha* that is not vitiated by pressure, fraud, deceit, or defect.

Another benefit of premarital counseling is that it could be an effective venue for informing Muslim women of their vast rights within the marriage under Islamic law, and to educate their husbands about these rights as well. As mentioned earlier, Islamic law does not require the woman to perform housework. It also gives the woman the right to keep her finances separate from those of her husband. If the woman plans to benefit from these rights, and the husband plans on a traditional division of labor and a financial union, then the sooner these facts become clear, the better. The counseling period would reveal these differences and help the couple work them out or part ways before any damage is done.

During the counseling process, both parties will develop a better idea about the type of relationship they would like to have in their own marriage. Islamic law provides significant latitude to the parties by allowing them to define their relationship through the use of stipulations in the marriage contract. A primary limitation, however, is that these stipulations do not contradict the intent of the marriage.[142] For example, a prospective wife could insert a stipulation that her husband will be responsible for financing her higher education, or that he will not interfere in her career, but she cannot stipulate that he will not consummate the marriage.[143] A traditional husband who may balk at such permissible stipulations will discover quickly whether his prospective bride shares his view of a married life. Young American Muslim professionals have repeatedly contacted me about the inclusion of various stipulations. Increasingly, it appears, they are agreeing on more egalitarian marriages than those of their parents. Others who prefer traditional marriages are also free to negotiate such marriages. This is part of the freedom of contract in Islam. It is designed to

---

142. Al-'Asqalani, *Fath al-Bari*, vol. 9, pp. 271-75.
143. See, e.g., al-Zuhayli, *Al-Fiqh al-Islami*, vol. 9, pp. 6540-47, esp. pp. 6544-45.

make a marriage strong by ensuring the *ridha* of the parties. The effort at fashioning one's particular life relationship with another can only deepen the commitment to the "solemn covenant" between them.

## Covenant Marriage Laws

It is worthwhile at this juncture to compare Islamic marriage laws with ones more recently proposed in this country to protect marriages from hasty dissolution. Foremost among these laws is Louisiana's Covenant Marriage Law.[144] Under this law, covenant marriage is entered into by heterosexual couples who view marriage as a lifelong relationship and are willing to undergo premarital counseling to help them understand the nature, purposes, and responsibilities of marriage. Counseling would also inform them about the various aspects of the covenant marriage they elect to come under, including the exit conditions. For example, divorce may be obtained by one of the parties only when the other party has totally breached the marriage covenant commitment. Otherwise, a two-year separation period is required. A total breach occurs upon proof of adultery, abuse, certain types of separation, and abandonment of domicile by, or imprisonment of, the other spouse.

Louisiana's Covenant Marriage Law is consistent with Islamic marriage laws insofar as it is a marriage by a heterosexual couple entering a lifelong relationship. Yet, while Islamic marriage is usually intended to be forever (except in *mut'ah* marriages), however, God has permitted Muslims the right to divorce both at will and for cause. Divorce for cause is quite similar to that articulated by the covenant marriage law.[145] It is usually sought by a wronged wife looking to the judge for vindication and reparation.

Divorce at will may seem to contradict the rationale underlying covenant marriage, namely that of preserving marriages by making divorce contingent on good cause. But major Muslim jurists are clear that divorce at will may be exercised only for very good cause (including psychological and emotional cause). Otherwise the divorcing party is rejecting God's blessings for a happy familial life and is accountable to God on the Day of Judgment.[146]

144. La. Rev. Stat. Ann. § 9:272 (2003). Information in this paragraph also comes from § 9:307 of the statute.

145. Compare Ira Mark Ellman, "The Place of Fault in a Modern Divorce Law," *Arizona State Law Journal* 28 (1996): 773 (addressing the relevance of fault in divorce proceedings) with Katherine Shaw Spaht's chapter herein.

146. See, e.g., Abu Zahrah, *Al-Ahwal al-Shakhsiyah*, p. 286; Al-Zuhayli, *Al-Fiqh al-Islami*, vol. 4, p. 296.

In divorce at will, the divorcing party need not divulge the ground for divorce. In this way, the privacy interests of both parties, and sometimes their reputations, are protected. In these circumstances, and where no harm is alleged, the courts usually set up a mediation process to save the marriage from dissolution. The courts leave the final decision to the conscience of the party seeking the divorce. Where the divorce action oppresses one of the parties, the courts attempt to rectify the situation through divorce settlement.

In an attempt to limit the improper use of divorce at will, jurists have attached additional requirements for its validity. For example, the husband may not be angry, drunk, or coerced into his action.[147] It is also strongly preferred that the wife not be in a state of menstruation or recovery from delivery (period of *nafaas*). These preferences are based on a desire to protect the woman from a lengthy waiting period, called *'iddah*, before the divorce becomes final.[148] Further, even if the divorce is proper, the husband has the opportunity for the duration of the waiting period to retract his divorce by simply returning to bed and board.[149] No judicial action is necessary. If, at the end of the waiting period, it turns out that the wife is pregnant, it is preferred that there be no divorce until delivery.[150]

The waiting period in Islamic divorce is much shorter than that of the Louisiana Covenant Marriage Law. Nevertheless, it affords the families an opportunity to intensify their efforts during that period to effect reconciliation. This is one additional indication that the marriage contract is momentous.[151] To the extent that the waiting periods differ between the two systems, the covenant marriage law may be unacceptable because it seems to deny the husband the right to divorce after the passage of the Islamic waiting period. The denial would thus prohibit what God has made permissible, a clear violation of Islamic law (Qur'an 5:87; 66:1). Since, however, the law applies only to those who elect to be covered by it, it could be argued that the husband contractually elected to be bound by a longer period. Since this contractual extension does not violate God's law, then it should be permissible. An analogous example would be that of the husband delegating his right of divorce to

---

147. See, e.g., Abu Zahrah, *Al-Ahwal al-Shakhsiyah*, p. 15; Al-Zuhayli, *Al-Fiqh al-Islami*, vol. 9, pp. 6882-84; al-Dusuqi, *Al-'Usrah*, pp. 233-37.

148. See, e.g., Abu Zahrah, *Al-Ahwal al-Shakhsiyah*, pp. 286-87; al-Zuhayli, *Al-Fiqh al-Islami*, vol. 9, pp. 6922-26, 6950-55.

149. Qur'an 2:228; al-Zuhayli, *Al-Fiqh al-Islami*, vol. 9, pp. 6987-88 and 6991; Abu Zahrah, *Al-Ahwal al-Shakhsiyah*, pp. 312-13; al-Dusuqi, *Al-'Usrah*, pp. 288-89.

150. See, e.g., Muhammad Fakhr al-Din al-Razi, *Tafsir al-Fakhr al-Razi* (1149-1209) (Beirut: Dar al-Fikr, 1985), vol. 30, p. 31.

151. Al-Dusuqi, *Al-'Usrah*, p. 377.

the wife.[152] Many Muslim jurists accept the delegation as valid; others do not. So, the difference in the waiting period will raise an interesting discussion among Muslim jurists.

It is important to recognize the reason behind the shorter waiting period. It is a balancing between two factors: (1) giving time for the spouses to reconcile; and (2) ensuring that no spouse would suffer sexual deprivation through a long waiting period, and hence run the risk of an adulterous relationship. Islamic law provides a great deal of attention to the sexual needs of Muslims, both male and female, as a way of keeping them chaste.[153] It is a well-known fact in Islamic law that a separation of six months is grounds for divorce.[154]

So, while Islamic law limits judicial divorce (as opposed to divorce at will) to cases very similar to those of the Louisiana statute, it is not generally willing to tighten the bond of marriage to an extent that would create unhappiness and oppression for a long period of time. Thus, not only do the waiting periods for divorce differ significantly between the two approaches, but even the forms of divorce are more accommodating under Islamic law. The final decision as to whether a person observed his or her covenant faithfully remains a matter between that person and God. God has informed us about the importance of marriage in Islam, and the gravity of the marriage commitment. But balancing that with the right to privacy and the sexual rights of individuals within a marriage results in both men and women being given a faster divorce than is available under the covenant marriage law. To agree to a law that imposes, except under certain circumstances, greater waiting hardship on an alienated couple is to expose Muslim men and women to unnecessary temptation and loneliness that may indeed affect their chastity. This is as grave a consideration for any Muslim as that of the importance of the marriage contract, and must be balanced with it.

In summary, the Islamic marriage contract is a solemn covenant before God, between a freely consenting man and a freely consenting woman, which is of grave importance. Hence it is most worthy of fulfillment. Consequently, society should assist couples, through counseling, workplace restructuring, and other helpful methods to preserve their families. Islamic law, however, does not force Muslim couples to continue within a marriage that has proven to be irredeemably broken, for God is all-merciful. Counseling informs couples of their duties, but divorce remains in the hands of the couple. The propriety of exercising of this power, however, is primarily a matter between the individual and his or her God.

152. Al-Khamlishi, *Al-Ta'liq*, vol. 1, pp. 348-53; al-Ghandur, *Al-Ahwal al-Shakhsiyah*, p. 349.
153. See, e.g., al-Zuhayli, *Al-Fiqh al-Islami*, vol. 9, p. 6923; al-Dusuqi, *Al-'Usrah*, pp. 377-78.
154. Ibn Qudamah, *Al-Mughni*, vol. 8, pp. 143-44; Abu-Zahrah, *Al-Ahwal al-Shakhsiyah*, pp. 366-67; al-Zuhayli, *Al-Fiqh al-Islami*, vol. 9, pp. 7066-67.

# 8 Marriage, Love, and Sexuality in Islam: An Overview of Genres and Themes

*Richard C. Martin*

*The companionship of women provides relaxation which relieves dis-*
*tress and soothes the heart. It is incumbent upon the pious to acquire*
*such comfort by permissible means.*

Abu Hamid al-Ghazali, *Ihya' 'ulum al-din*

The medieval scholar and intellectual who penned the remark just quoted followed it by another proverb: "The wise man is desirous only of three things:
provisioning himself for a return journey, seeking a livelihood, or [seeking]
pleasure in something not forbidden."[1] Sexual pleasure in the earthly estate of
marriage and amiable relations between a husband and wife were enjoined by
Imams and mentioned in public discourse. The warrant for such concerns
about seemingly private matters was nothing less than Islamic law, which was
and is founded upon the Qur'an. Beyond the law, sex and marriage were specu-
lated on by litterateurs, mystics, theologians, and other writers from the earliest
times. Levity was not absent from such discussions, a matter to which we will
refer again below. Jokes were often made about what to do with difficult or un-
cooperative spouses. Advice was frequently given without legal warrants.

The purpose of this chapter is to acquaint the reader with a sample of Islamic reflections on love and marriage beyond jurisprudence *(fiqh, shari'a)*, to
which modern scholars usually turn when discussing this topic. I have written
this essay, accordingly, from the perspective of cultural studies rather than jurisprudence, although Islamic law and some legal scholars will figure into the

---

1. From Abu Hamid al-Ghazali, *Ihya' 'ulum al-din*, translated by Madelain Farah as *Marriage and Sexuality in Islam: A Translation of al-Ghazali's Book on the Etiquette of Marriage from
the Ihya'* (Salt Lake City: University of Utah Press, 1984), p. 65.

survey of genres and cultural information about marriage in Islam. It is written especially for the non-Islamicist or nonspecialist in Islamic studies. It seeks to introduce those interested in comparative studies to figures like Ahmad ibn Hanbal (d. 855) and Abu Hamid al-Ghazali (d. 1111), whose writings on marriage, or some of them, have survived and are available in scholarly translations. To begin this excursion from Islamic law into the culture and social practice of marriage in Muslim societies, we turn to the main topic of this volume, the theology of covenant.

## Theological Foundations of Covenant in the Abrahamic Traditions

The most basic meaning of covenant in the Abrahamic religions is the notion of a primal agreement between God and humankind to bear responsibility toward each other. The divine-human covenant then becomes a model for institutional and human relations within each tradition. To set the stage for understanding the specific difference of the Islamic notion of covenant, it may be useful to review briefly Jewish and especially Christian teachings on the theology of covenant relationships.

For Jews, the covenant par excellence was established by God with his chosen people, promising salvation in exchange for faithfulness and obedience. Christians hold that a new covenant (testament) was established by Christ. As early as the second century CE, the old covenant was identified as the covenant of works. That original covenant was modified and perfected, Christians held, by the covenant of grace, which grants salvation and beatitude to those (Christians) who enter into this agreement in faith and good works. The notion of marriage as a covenant relationship is based upon the divine-human covenant.

The early church of the Roman and Orthodox traditions, although divergent in theology and practice, commonly based marriage on sacramental authority, established in canon law and administered by ordained clergy.[2] The basic Lutheran revision was to deprive matrimony of sacramental status, yet religious ritual and theological significance remained central to Protestant views of marriage. Luther founded his view on the notion of two kingdoms,

2. On the Orthodox tradition, see the chapter in this volume by Stanley Samuel Harakas. On the Western Christian tradition, especially the Roman Catholic, Lutheran, Calvinist, and Anglican traditions, see John Witte, Jr., *From Sacrament to Contract: Marriage, Religion and Law in the Western Tradition* (Louisville: Westminster John Knox, 1997), and the chapters by Michael Lawler, James Turner Johnson, and Max Stackhouse herein.

218

heavenly and earthly. The proper context of marriage, though blessed by the church, was the earthly estate. It was the genius of John Calvin, John Witte Jr. has shown, to divide the notion of covenant as well. Witte explains it this way:

> In his later years, Calvin used the doctrine of covenant to describe not only the vertical relationships between God and man, but also the horizontal relationships between husband and wife. Just as God draws the elect believer into a covenant relationship with him, Calvin argued, so God draws husband and wife into a covenant relationship with each other. Just as God expects constant faith and good works in our relationship with Him, so God expects connubial faithfulness and sacrificial works in our relationship with our spouses.[3]

Thus, the notion of a divinely established covenant relationship was extended to marriage in the earthly estate of human society at the beginning of the modern period. The Islamic theology of covenant falls broadly into this pattern, with specific differences.

The Qur'an states God's covenant with his creatures in several passages. Qur'an 7:172 is the most often cited in this regard: "And when your Lord brought forth from the Children of Adam [their offspring], from their loins, and made them testify, 'am I not your Lord?' They said 'Truly, we so testify.'" The same *aya* (verse) goes on to state an eschatalogical reason for this pre-eternal covenant: "lest you say on the Day of Resurrection, 'of this we were unaware.'" The eschatological dimension is significant, and we shall return to it later. This "causing humankind to testify" implies the divine-human covenant. Known as *mithaq* in Arabic, it is attested twenty-five times elsewhere in the Qur'an. In this key passage, the eternal agreement and relationship is with the whole of humankind, not with a chosen portion of it to the exclusion of others. Yet, the Qur'an also recognizes the covenant between Allah and Israel: "And when we made a covenant *[mithaq]* with the Children of Israel: Worship none save Allah, and treat parents and kin, orphans and the needy well, and speak well to humankind, rise up for the prayer *[salat]*, and pay the poor offering *[zakat]*. But then, save for a few, you, the averse ones, back-slid" (2:83; cf. 5:12). Sometimes the relation between God and the prophets is called a covenant. The following passage from Qur'an 3:81 appears as a calque on the preter-eternal covenant with Adam, cited above:

> And when Allah made a covenant with the prophets *[al-nabiyyin]*, [he said] "behold the Book and the Wisdom I have brought to you. Then will come to

you a Messenger who will confirm for you what you possess. So believe him and help him." He said, "do you consent to undertake my covenant [or burden, *isr*] [which I lay] upon you?" They said, "we consent." He said, "then so testify, and I will so testify with you."

In one passage (5:14), God's *mithaq* with Christians is mentioned, and like other passages when the divine covenant with Israel is specified (for example, 5:12 and 5:70), the theme of breaking the compact implies eschatological consequences. The Qur'anic concept of *mithaq* is also applied to agreements or compacts of peace between Muslims and non-Muslims (for example, 4:90). This latter reference to a *mithaq* between Muslims and other communities also came to be known as an ʿ*ahd,* a treaty or a covenant between two parties. It belongs to the same semantic field as ʿ*aqd,* "contract," which Azizah al-Hibri has explained in detail in her chapter in this volume.

The main theme of covenant or *mithaq* in the Qur'anic worldview, however, is the eternal covenant between God and his creatures. Specific covenants between God and the Israelites, or God and the Christians, have a synecdochical relationship — a part standing for the whole — to the covenant between God and humankind for all eternity. The eschatological significance of the divine covenant is especially prominent in Islamic thought. Moreover, in Islam, the concept of a chosen people dissolves into a single relationship of faithfulness between God and all of humankind. The covenant is the theological cornerstone of Islam as a universal religion.

What bearing does this notion of covenant have upon marriage in Islam? Standing in the semantic shadow of the divine-human covenant of faithfulness from all eternity, Qur'an 4:21 refers to the *mithaq* that exists between a man and a woman in marriage. The verse occurs in the context of the requirement in a second marriage, after divorcing another woman in order to remarry, that the husband should not take from his first wife the money he had given to her prior to the divorce. Qur'an 4:21 then follows: "How can you take it back when one of you [the husband] has been with the other [the woman], and the [woman] has made an inviolable covenant *[mithaq ghaliz]* with you?" As Azizah al-Hibri has pointed out, marriage in Islam is often regarded in religious legal discourse, *Shariʿa,* as a purely contractual relationship, a characterization she seeks to qualify by pointing to the term *covenant* in this passage as a qualification of the marriage relationship. Al-Hibri shows that although a concept of covenant (ʿ*ahd)* existed in early Islamic legal discussions of marriage, the weight of the discourse is on contractual obligations (ʿ*uqud,* sing. ʿ*aqd).*[4] The present chapter

4. See the chapter by Azizah al-Hibri herein.

will also address the foundations of marriage in sacred law *(Shari'a)* when we turn to the writings of Ahmad ibn Hanbal.

Another corollary of the divine covenant in Islam is that all human beings are by their created nature Muslim (those who testify or submit to the divine will). It is linked ritually and liturgically with the first half of the first Pillar of Islamic practice, the *shahada* or Testimony: that there is no God but Allah (and the second half: that Muhammad is [God's] Messenger). The implied universal Muslim nature of humanity troubled Islamic theologians, known as *mutakal-limun,* more than it did their Christian counterparts in the Middle Ages. We learn this from recorded disputes over the question of whether persons living beyond the pale of Islamic faith, particularly those who lived before Muhammad and the revelation of the Qur'an, were bound by the teachings of Qur'an and Sunna for salvation.[5] Many theologians among the major schools of thought found it difficult, perhaps because of the Qur'anic covenant, to write off those human beings — who did not confess Islam but who led moral lives on other religious or rational grounds — as being excluded from the possibility of eternal salvation. Other implications of the Qur'anic covenant bear more directly upon the theme of this chapter and volume, however, and to these we turn in the next sections of this chapter.

An important difference between Islam and Christianity with respect to marriage is worth noting as we close this introductory section, however. The roles of Jesus and Muhammad as models to be emulated within their respective faith traditions is fundamental: Jesus did not marry; Muhammad, by contrast, had several wives. This difference, we might say, of modeling on the founders was profoundly to affect believers in each tradition, who looked to Jesus and Muhammad for guidance in matters pertaining to marriage. In the case of Jesus, sexual asceticism was emblematic of his physical and spiritual purity. In the early church, some Christians practiced "friendship marriages" (couples living together in community without sexual congress), and celibacy was required of priests in the Roman Catholic tradition. Both priests and nuns take vows of celibacy when taking holy orders or ordination. The classic treatise on *The Imitation of Christ,* attributed to Thomas à Kempis in the fifteenth century, begins with a citation from John 8:12: "He who follows me walks not in Darkness." Thomas then comments: "By these words of Christ, we are advised to imitate His life and habits, if we wish to be truly enlightened and free from all blindness of heart. Let our chief effort, therefore, be to study the life of Jesus Christ."[6] In the chapters

---

5. See A. Kevin Reinhart, *Before Revelation: The Boundaries of Muslim Moral Thought* (Albany: State University of New York Press, 1995).

6. Thomas à Kempis, *The Imitation of Christ,* trans. William Benham, Harvard Classics,

that follow marriage is not mentioned. If Christ was a spiritual model to be imitated in monastic and clerical life where marriage was renounced, Jesus did not serve as a model for ordinary believers who were allowed and even encouraged to marry. How, by comparison, does the figure of the Prophet Muhammad serve as model for his followers with respect to marriage?[7]

## The Example *(Sunna)* of the Prophet

The Sunna or practice of the Prophet Muhammad in all aspects of daily life is, after the Qur'an, the second major source of God's will for his creatures. This is the case as much for the conduct of married life as it is for proper observance of ritual duties. The Sunna is known from the transmitted and recorded sayings (sing., *hadith*) attributed to Muhammad by his closest companions, which reveal what he said, did, or otherwise indicated to be right or wrong. Scores of Hadiths about Muhammad's married life have been preserved in the major collections, known as the *sahih* ("sound"), and many of these bear the name of Muhammad's youngest wife, 'A'isha, as the original transmitter. Many contemporary books, pamphlets, and webpages on marriage in Islam cite such Hadiths. Let us attend to a few of them to get a sense of their importance in determining how Muslims might seek guidance in a life of marital covenant with a spouse.[8]

The most frequently cited collection of Hadiths in modern writing about Islam is that of Abu 'Abdullah Muhammad ibn Isma'il al-Bukhari (d. 870), whose multi-volume work is known simply as "The Sound" *(al-sahih)*.[9] Bukhari's collection organizes the thousands of Hadiths it cites topically, and the ordering of these topics and subtopics is instructive. Many Islamic works of jurisprudence *(fiqh)* follow the same structure. The first topic or "book" *(kitab)* is titled "How the Divine Inspiration Started." Then follows sections on faith *(iman)* and religious knowledge *('ilm)*, and then sections on the condition and

---

vol. 7 (New York: P. F. Collier and Son, 1909), p. 213. I have modernized the English of Benham's translations of Scripture and the *Imitation*.

7. The condition of bodily and spiritual purity *(tahara)* is fundamental to participation in the ritual duties *('ibadat)* of Islam. Lawful sexual relationship with a spouse (known as *nikah*, the usual Arabic translation of *marriage*) and ritual lustrations to achieve purity after sex and before worship are quite normal in Islamic cultural patterns.

8. Where possible, I shall cite the more accessible English translations of Arabic sources for the average reader to consult further.

9. I will cite *The Translation of the Meanings of Sahih al-Bukhari, Arabic-English*, trans. Muhammad Muhsin Khan, 9 vols. (Lahore: Kazi Publications, 1971 or 1972).

practices of purity *(tahara)* and what makes one impure or unable to perform the religious duties. Then, quite logically, follow sections on prayer — the five daily canonical prayers or *salat,* but also many other forms of prayer (which often go unmentioned in textbooks on Islam). Thereafter one finds books on the religious duties, such as pilgrimage and paying the poor due *(zakat).* It is not until the seventh of nine volumes by Bukhari that we find a book on the topic of marriage *(nikah)* and divorce *(talaq),* which, along with inheritance, are major topics in Muslim family law.

The book on marriage comprises 127 chapters, each chapter containing one to several individual Hadiths on a given subtopic. Al-Bukhari begins his book on *nikah* with the observation that marriage is recommended in the Qur'an: "marry women of your choice" (Qur'an 4:3). The very first Hadith dismisses celibacy as a spiritual ideal: three men came to the houses of the wives of the Prophet Muhammad to ask them how the Prophet worshipped Allah. The answers they heard made them feel insufficiently pious, so one vowed to pray all night long henceforth, the second promised to fast throughout the year (presumably dawn to dusk), and the third pledged celibacy forever. Muhammad told them that he feared God more than any of them did, "yet I fast and break my fast, I do sleep and I also marry women. So he who does not follow my tradition *[sunna]* is not [one of my followers]."[10] Bukhari reports further that "Allah's Apostle forbade 'Uthman bin Maz'un to abstain from marrying (and other pleasures), and if he had allowed him [to abstain], we would have gotten ourselves castrated."[11] The meaning of the latter comment seems to be that excessive self-denial is a form of castration, which Islam forbids. But what if a young man with normal healthy sexual appetites is unable to support a wife — biological and economic conditions that are just as common today as they might have been in the time of Muhammad the Prophet, especially in poorer countries such as Egypt? The following Hadith suggests the depth of the dilemma that the emphasis on marriage might create. Would castration be better than falling into sexual sin out of wedlock? Addressing Muhammad, Abu Hurayra reports the following exchange:

> "O Allah's Apostle, I am a young man and I am afraid that I might commit illegal sexual intercourse and I cannot afford to marry." He kept silent, and then I repeated my question once again, but he kept silent. I said the same thing again (for the third time) and he remained silent. Then I repeated my question (for the fourth time), and only then the Prophet, peace be upon

---

10. Bukhari, vol. 7, Book 68 *(Nikah),* ch. 1, pp. 1-2.
11. Bukhari, vol. 7, ch. 8, no. 11, p. 8.

him, said, "O Abu Hurayra! The pen has dried after writing what you are going to confront. So [it does not matter whether you] get yourself castrated or not."[12]

Here again, this time with a touch of irony, the Prophet's advice is against castration, which would not get Abu Hurayra what he wants (a wife) but would get him what he does not want, eschatological punishment.

If marriage is enjoined and castration is strongly discouraged as a way to diminish the desire for sexual relations when no spouse is available, then what alternatives exist for the earnest believer? Bukhari reports a conversation with the Prophet in which the narrator says,

> We used to participate in the holy battles [ghazw, skirmishes against opponents] and we had no [wives]. So we said [to Muhammad], "Shall we get ourselves castrated?" He forbade us that and then allowed us to marry women with a temporary contract, and recited to us: "O you who believe! Make not unlawful the good things which Allah has made lawful for you, but commit no transgression" (Q. 5:87).[13]

This refers to the practice of *mut'a* (lit., "enjoyment") marriages, which in early Islam, under the exigencies of war, for example, were permitted. In the later development of Islamic law, Sunni jurists generally disallowed such temporary marriages for the purpose of sexual enjoyment while Ithna 'Ashari Shi'a have permitted it when certain conditions have been met. In his study of the traditional training of Shi'ite clerics in the context of post-revolutionary Iran, Roy Mottahedeh discusses the practice of mut'a marriages, especially among some students. This calls to mind that Bertrand Russell wrote somewhere that students should be allowed sexual relations without the requirement of marriage when their studies are their paramount duty. Many Iranis, however, see the practice of *mut'a* marriage as, if legally justified, still morally suspect in the modern urban environment of Tehran.[14]

In Chapter 12 of al-Bukhari's collection of Hadiths on marriage, the question is asked: what type of woman should one seek in marriage? Qualities to look for in a future wife strike us as nearly universal in traditional societies, despite the first clause of the following Hadith. Abu Hurayra narrates that "the

12. Bukhari, vol. 7, ch. 8, no. 18, p. 9.

13. Bukhari, vol. 7, ch. 8, no. 13, pp. 8-9.

14. Roy P. Mottahedeh, *The Mantle of the Prophet: Religion and Politics in Iran* (New York: Simon and Schuster, 1985), and Wilfred Madelung, "Shi'i Attitudes Toward Women As Reflected in Fiqh," in *Society and the Sexes in Medieval Islam,* by the Sixth Giorgio Levi della Vida Conference, ed. Afaf Lutfi al-Sayyid Marsot (Malibu, Calif.: Undena, 1979).

Prophet, peace be upon him, said 'the best women are the riders of camels and the righteous among the Quraysh. They are the kindest women to their children in their childhood and the more careful women of the property of their husbands.'[15] This report supports the frequent observation about the marriage covenant in Islam that it is expected of the husband that he provide a living for his wife and family, and it is expected of the wife that she manage the household well and care for the children, especially in their earlier years.

The modern period has witnessed considerable interest by Muslims living in diasporic communities in Europe, the Americas, and elsewhere in guidance in marriage directly from the Sunna of the Prophet. This is particularly true for those Muslims for whom the surrounding social ethos is non-Muslim and secular. Hence, there has been a growing market for books and pamphlets on weddings, marriage, and related topics, such as Islamic names for children. The Internet is another important source for such information, and it is easy to access. These works are generally based on well-attested works on marriage from early and medieval Islam.

We turn now to look at two such classical sources on marriage in Islam, by Ahmad ibn Hanbal (d. 855) and Abu Hamid al-Ghazali (d. 1111), whose writings are still read over a millennium after they lived; happily they exist now in readable, well-annotated translations.

## Ahmad ibn Hanbal (d. 855)

Ahmad ibn Hanbal was the youngest among the patronymic founders of the Sunni and Shi'i legal traditions which were established in Islamic jurisprudence by the tenth century and have survived to this day. His *madhhab* (school of interpretation and application) was the chief expression of Islamic Traditionalism in Sunni Islam. After Ibn Hanbal's demise, the Hanbali *madhhab* formed to comprise mainly a class of scholars known as *muhaddithun* or *ahl al-hadith* (people of Hadith). In the ninth century, some three centuries after the death of the Prophet Muhammad and the Muslim conquests of West Asia and parts of North Africa, competing trends among jurists, theologians, and mystics struggled to establish religious authority on what each argued was fundamental. The Hanafi *madhhab*, for example, named after Abu Hanifa al-Nu'man ibn Thabit (d. 767) advocated a legal method based on the educated opinion *(ra'y)* of the jurist, in support of which precise scriptural, traditional, and other established warrants were adduced. (His understanding of the process of legal reasoning

15. Bukhari, vol. 7, ch. 12, no. 19, pp. 11-12.

was not unlike that of Oliver Wendell Holmes, Jr., some twelve centuries later.) The *mutakallimun* (theologians) of Ibn Hanbal's time largely belonged to a rationalist school known as the Mu'tazilites. They argued that only those Hadiths that made rational sense should be used in legal arguments and in religious interpretation. The Mu'tazilites opposed the tendency among Hanbalis and other traditionalists to test the authenticity of Hadiths solely on the known reliability of the transmitters of each report. Shi'i legal scholars made the Imams descended from 'Ali ibn Abi Talib the fulcrum of legal authority in interpreting the Qur'an and Sunna of the Prophet.

What makes Ibn Hanbal's surviving discourses on marriage especially relevant today is the fact that throughout Islamic history his *madhhab* has inspired reform movements that have had populist appeal and been led by powerful advocates. In his own day he was imprisoned for refusing to subscribe to the Mu'tazilite doctrine that the Qur'an was not the eternal word of God but rather was created on the tongue that recited it and on the paper on which it was written. (The Mu'tazilites had argued that if the Qur'an were eternal, thus co-eternal with God, and not created like all other speech, then God's eternal unity would be compromised.) In the fourteenth century, Ibn Taymiyya led a reform that linked jihad against enemies with purification of religious practice in the wake of the Mongol invasions and the devastation they had caused Muslim society and religious identity. In the eighteenth century, Muhammad ibn 'Abd al-Wahhab became an ardent follower of the Hanbali school. He forged an alliance with Ibn Sa'ud, a local ruler in the province of Nejd in Arabia, to lead a movement of purification and reform against Sufi Islam, popular tribal practices, and other religious innovations. In the twenty-first century, global religious movements, such as al-Qa'ida, are infused with Wahhabi and Hanbali teaching, although few Muslims who identify themselves as Hanbalis or Wahhabis in law and practice accept or support the militant project of al-Qa'ida. For all of these traditionalist reformers, the marriage contract and strict adherence to its terms and provisions were seen as essential to a strong and stable Islamic society.

Ahmad ibn Hanbal applied his traditionalist and populist worldview to a few texts that have survived such devastations as time, vermin, fire, Crusaders, and Mongol invaders. Susan A. Spectorsky has published a translation and critical introduction to discourses by Ahmad ibn Hanbal on marriage and divorce. These appear in three versions by Ibn Hanbal's son, 'Abdallah, and two other scholars of the Hanbali tradition.[16] The context for the textual editions of these

---

16. Susan A. Spectorsky, *Chapters on Marriage and Divorce: Responses of Ibn Hanbal and Ibn Rahwayh* (Austin: University of Texas Press, 1993).

and other scholarly discourses of the period are responses to questions addressed to noted jurists on specific topics. The following passage from the collection by ʿAbdallab ibn Ahmad ibn Hanbal gives a flavor of this genre:

> ʿAbd Allah said, "I heard my father say, about a man who married a woman without a *wali* [male relative] in the presence only of witnesses, 'That is not valid' *[la yajuzu]*."
>
> Someone said to my father while I was listening, "Does the governor *[amir]* or the judge *[qadi]* have the most right to give [a woman] in marriage?"
>
> He said, "the judge, because he is in charge of sexual relations and legal judgments."[17]

This was the question and answer format of early Islamic scholarship in law, theology, and all the religious sciences. Many texts like the one just quoted bear the direct stamp of oral discussions recorded by a disciple. By the tenth century, the *risala* (written questions) and responses by leading scholars in the major urban centers like Baghdad, Damascus, and Basra led to longer treatises with more developed arguments. The brief passage quoted above involves two different questions and two rather terse answers, with little or no argument. Nonetheless, Ibn Hanbal's discourses enunciate more or less the scope of the legal questions about marriage and divorce in the ninth century.

The nature of the marriage contract is not well attested in the three Ibn Hanbal texts translated by Spectorsky, but in one of them, the compilation by Abu Dawud al-Sijistani (d. 888), the author reports: "'I heard Ahmad [ibn Hanbal] asked what the minimum prerequisites were for a marriage contract.' He said, 'A suitor, someone to give the bride in marriage, and two witnesses.'"[18] In ideal circumstances the woman's father gives his daughter in marriage after obtaining her consent. The younger the bride-to-be is, the greater is the father's authority to determine the contract. In the absence of the father, a guardian or *wali* represents the girl or woman. Ibn Hanbal opposes the suitor acting as *wali*, as in the case where a non-eligible male has charge of a young girl he wishes to marry. In that case, Ibn Hanbal prefers that another guardian be appointed. Ibn Hanbal also expressly opposes the practice of temporary marriage *(mutʿa)* mentioned above. Another question put to Ibn Hanbal was whether or not *coitus interruptus* was permissible. He replies that it requires the permission of a wife who is a free woman, but not of a female slave. This is one of the indica-

---

17. Spectorsky, *Chapters on Marriage and Divorce*, p. 91.
18. Spectorsky, *Chapters on Marriage and Divorce*, p. 62.

tions that birth control was practiced in early Islam, but not without explicit agreement.

In Islam, divorce is considered an integral aspect of the legal understanding of marriage, even though the Qur'an requires arbitration between the spouses if dissolution is threatened, and a Hadith states that divorce is in God's eyes the most detested of permitted human acts. The term for divorce or repudiation is *talaq,* and the rules for a *talaq al-sunna* (permitted divorce) were discussed by Ibn Hanbal. Divorce by triple repudiation — divorce by the husband stating three times, "I divorce you" — was well established by the ninth century. The treatises by Ibn Hanbal and his followers indicate that the question of the *intention* of the husband at the time of the repudiation was under dispute as to whether intention to divorce was not only necessary but also sufficient to effect a legal divorce. The texts also take up the question of whether or not a single stated repudiation, if the intention is nonetheless to divorce one's wife, can be considered legally sufficient. The question suggests the possibility that a first and even a second "I divorce you" could act as a threat and not necessarily be intended as a final attempt to rid oneself of one's spouse. Ibn Hanbal also offered judgments on whether other angry remarks made to a spouse might serve as the *talaq* repudiation. He mentions such angry statements as "I have no wife" and "I make you a gift to your family." These linguistic variations work only on certain conditions, for example, in the latter statement, only if the family will accept the woman back. In general, although his treatment of divorce and other topics is not systematic, Ibn Hanbal is fairly consistent in his view that men should be held accountable for their statements of declaration to divorce, which is in keeping with his requirement of morally upright behavior in matters of sex and marriage.[19]

Taken as a whole, these texts on marriage by Ibn Hanbal and his followers offer scholars doing comparative studies on sex, marriage, and divorce rich material on the cultural practices of Muslims in early medieval Islamic societies. Significant are the very questions asked and the exceptions that spring up once a standard answer is provided. They also indicate the mindset and reasoning of one of Islam's most morally resolute jurists and theologians.

But what about Ibn Hanbal's more personal thoughts on marriage? Our next classical author on marriage, Abu Hamid al-Ghazali, gives us a hint of Ibn Hanbal's character in this regard. He writes that a traditionalist contemporary of Ibn Hanbal named Bishr ibn al-Harith (d. ca. 840) is reported to have said, "Ahmad b. Hanbal was preferred over me on three accounts: for seeking what is lawful for himself and others, while I seek it for myself only; for his ability to get

19. Spectorsky, *Chapters on Marriage and Divorce,* pp. 31-32.

married in contrast to my inability; and for being appointed an Imam for the common people."[20] Ghazali also passes on the report that Ibn Hanbal "[re]married the second day following the death of the mother of his son, ʿAbdullah, and said, 'I detest spending the night as a celibate.'" Ghazali contrasts this positively with other known jurists and public personalities who for one reason or another refrained from marriage and thus, he points out, from following the Prophet's Sunna.[21] In another passage Ghazali reports that Ibn Hanbal declared he "preferred a one-eyed [woman] over her sister who was beautiful. For he asked: 'who is better behaved of the two?' He was told: 'The one-eyed.' He replied: 'Give her to me in marriage.'" Ghazali goes on to comment: "Such is the constant endeavor of one who does not seek [mere] sensual pleasures. If someone cannot secure his faith without a source of pleasure, then let him seek beauty, because enjoyment of what is lawful strengthens faith."[22]

## Abu Hamid Al-Ghazali

Marriage in Islam, along with worshipping God in seclusion, is among the highest virtues of God's servants. On this the learned scholars of Islam, or *ulema,* were agreed, according to the great medieval jurist and theologian Abu Hamid al-Ghazali (d. 1111). They differed only as to which virtue should be held in higher esteem, the relationship of marriage or the act of worship. Some of the ulema qualified the requirement of marriage by arguing that in uncertain social and economic times, when supporting a spouse and family is not guaranteed, it is better to abstain from marriage. Not all scholars agreed with such cautions, however. "The truth about [marriage]," Ghazali tells us, "cannot be revealed except by first presenting what has been transmitted in the *akhbar* [reports] and *athar* [traces of texts] regarding encouragement and discouragement of marriage, and by explaining its benefits and shortcomings, thereby elucidating the virtues or disadvantages of marriage as pertains to everyone who has or has not been spared its calamities." With this rather candid acknowledgement that the institution has its challenges and human casualties, Imam Ghazali introduces an investigation of our topic that is all the more remarkable because it is expressed by a leading Muslim jurist in the Middle Ages in a decidedly nonjuristic work.[23] Before turning to a review of this unique work, it may

20. Farah, *Marriage and Sexuality in Islam,* p. 51.
21. Farah, *Marriage and Sexuality in Islam,* p. 51.
22. Farah, *Marriage and Sexuality in Islam,* p. 88.
23. Farah, *Marriage and Sexuality in Islam,* p. 47.

be useful to describe the turbulent life and complicated intellectual journey of al-Ghazali.

Abu Hamid Muhammad ibn Muhammad al-Ghazali al-Tusi was born in the central Asian province of Khurasan in the city of Tus in 1058. He and his brother Ahmad, also a famous scholar, were orphaned in their youth, but were able in the context of Islamic social moral responsibility for the homeless, such as widows and orphans, to receive a strong early education in Tus. After the usual training in Qur'an, Hadith, and the other religious sciences, Abu Hamid studied the theology of the orthodox Sunni Ash'arite school in Naysabur with the most illustrious scholar of that school at the time, the Imam al-Haramayn al-Juwayni. Like Saint Augustine six centuries earlier, Ghazali wrote a "Confessions" of sorts, titled *Deliverance from Error*.[24] In it we learn of his intellectual flirtations with skepticism and other worldviews competing with monotheism in his day, including the Peripatetic school of philosophy. Many of his critiques of philosophy and theology have survived and are hailed as among the greatest intellectual literary achievements in medieval Islam.

Al-Ghazali was called to a professorship in the newly opened *madrasa* or law college in Baghdad by its patron and founder, the famed vizier Nizam al-Mulk, in 1091. Some four years later he underwent a severe mental crisis and, after seeing to the care of his family, left his post and Baghdad, apparently to steep himself in the secrets and practices of Sufism. Those years in mystical training and seclusion are not well documented in his autobiography or in any other source. But when he reemerged in Baghdad he had worked out an Islamic medieval synthesis of sorts that placed Islamic mysticism at the center of his religious faith, which no longer suffered doubts, and his intellectual worldview, which was still informed by a broad knowledge of philosophy and religious theological systems. His later works written after his return to Baghdad and to public life investigate Islamic legal and theological questions from a viewpoint informed by Sufism. The work here under consideration, whose title is translated as *The Revivification of the Religious Sciences,* has a substantial section on "The Etiquette of Marriage."

Ghazali's book on "The Etiquette of Marriage" divides its subject matter into three chapters. An overview makes it clear that this text departs radically from juristic texts, like that of Ahmad ibn Hanbal discussed above. Chapter one discusses the advantages and disadvantages of marriage, and draws some conclusions. Chapter two deals with the marriage contract, but in a broader

24. *Al-Munqidh min al-dalal,* translated by W. Montgomery Watt as *The Faith and Practice of al-Ghazali* (Chicago: Kazi, 1982 [1951]).

discussion of behavioral etiquette in marriage, the requisite qualities of character in a woman and a man, and the qualities conducive to a happy marriage. Chapter three, titled "The Etiquette of Cohabitation," in two parts, explores the obligations and rights of the husband and rules of preferred conduct for the woman. As such the text reads much more like the *belles lettres* genre of *al-mahasin wal-masawi*, "the merits and faults" of places, persons, ethnic and social groups, and the like, and, in this case, of the social relationship of marriage.

Ghazali opens his discussion of the advantages and disadvantages of marriage by observing that the ulema up to his time had been divided on the question of whether choosing marriage or foregoing marriage in favor of seclusion for the worship of God is preferable. In general, marriage is preferred by jurists, as we have already seen, but Ghazali says that some scholars contemporary with his own time believed that such a preference is compromised by the fear that the character of women is no longer assured.

Ghazali mentions five advantages to marriage. The first of these is *procreation,* which is regarded as the prime reason for which marriage was instituted. The second is *satisfaction of sexual desire,* which means "fortification against the devil, curbing lust, warding off the excesses of desire, averting the eye, and safeguarding relief."[25] Here Ghazali pleads for a balance of earthly desire and desire for the hereafter; managing the former through marriage enhances the possibility of the latter. The third advantage is *companionship:* "comfort and relaxation for the soul through companionship; seeing and dallying comfort the heart and strengthen it for the performance of the obligatory rituals."[26] Again we see overtones of the theme with which we opened this chapter — the theology of covenant. They recur in the brief discussion of Sufism: that earthly love and desire are but a dim reminder of divine love and desire for the Beloved. In this regard, Ghazali quotes a report in which the Prophet Muhammad said, "I complained to [the Angel Gabriel] of my inability to have coitus, and he suggested that [I eat] *harisah* [a spicy dish]." "If this be true," Ghazali goes on to comment, "it can be interpreted only as a preparation for relaxation and cannot be interpreted to imply warding off desire; for it is rather a kindling of desire, and whoever is deprived of sexual desire is denied most of this intimacy."[27] The fourth advantage, *ordering the household,* means specifically that the male head of the household, through marriage, becomes free of the household duties of cooking, cleaning, and the like, in order

25. Farah, *Marriage and Sexuality in Islam,* p. 59.
26. Farah, *Marriage and Sexuality in Islam,* p. 65.
27. Farah, *Marriage and Sexuality in Islam,* pp. 65-66.

to earn a living for the household and to study religion. Again, citing the Prophet: "Let each among you have a grateful heart, a tongue which invokes [the name of God], and a faithful, virtuous wife who assists you toward the hereafter."[28] The fifth advantage, *disciplining the self*, pertains to the virtue of helping and giving freely from what one earns to others, specifically in the first instance to one's spouse and offspring.

Al-Ghazali, the social critic, also steps back from his role as jurist and guardian of Islamic religious norms to speculate on the disadvantages of marriage. In so doing he cites other Muslim scholars up to his time, thus indicating that not every writer thought marriage a good and beneficial thing. Among the disadvantages, the most serious, as he sees it, is the *inability to seek lawful gain*, which is contingent on the times in which he lived. He means that in the unstable social and political environment of Baghdad in the eleventh century, the desire for the good life and the need for a domestic life safe from harsher elements are naturally compelling. A husband is tempted to blameworthy pursuits in order to satisfy the whims and desires of his family, whereas a bachelor is free from such demands that may drag him down and away from piety and religion.[29] A second disadvantage of marriage is mainly an economic one — the difficulty in upholding the rights and responsibilities one assumes toward wives and children. Ghazali says, "It has been related that one who deserts his family is like a runaway slave in that his prayer and his fasting are not acceptable until he returns to them."[30] The third and related disadvantage of marriage, according to al-Ghazali, is "that the wife and the offspring could distract [the husband] from Almighty God, luring him to pursue the world and indulge in providing a comfortable life for his children through gathering wealth and hording it for them. . . ."[31] Throughout the discussion of advantages and disadvantages of marriage is the recognition that sexual desire is the basis for marriage, but it is related and subordinate to the sublime desire of humans for God. Meeting one's obligations to God as well as to one's spouse and family is seen as not easy, especially when the society and political order are unstable, but just as emphatic is Ghazali's belief that husbands must perform their marital obligations, even if doing so threatens to detract them partially from their devotion to God. The duties of the wife are also discussed at length in this text. We note, however, a lesser concern on Ghazali's part for a woman's ability to pursue a life of piety within the clamor of the extended household she manages.

28. Farah, *Marriage and Sexuality in Islam*, p. 67.
29. Farah, *Marriage and Sexuality in Islam*, p. 71.
30. Farah, *Marriage and Sexuality in Islam*, p. 72.
31. Farah, *Marriage and Sexuality in Islam*, p. 73.

In the end, Ghazali concludes that, all in all, it is better to marry than not, but that each person approaching marriage should judge for himself which is the best for him, based on his circumstances. In making this point he mentions the comparison that we also made earlier of the difference between Jesus and Muhammad with respect to marriage.

> Should you ask, "Why did Jesus abstain from marriage in spite of its virtue? And if it is preferable to free oneself for the worship of God, why then did our prophet take on numerous wives?" Know ye, then, that it is preferable to combine the two [i.e., devotion to a spouse and family and to God] in the case of one who is able, whose desire is strong, and whose ambition is high, because no preoccupation can distract him from God.[32]

In other words, Ghazali seems to say that both Jesus and Muhammad are models worthy of emulation, but the higher virtue is the Sunna of the Prophet, which combined a life devoted to God with model behavior as husband and father.

In this section we have already left the discourse of law and the canons of normative behavior for broader social opinion on the advantages and disadvantages of marriage. In the remainder of this essay I move to still other cultural reflections on love, marriage, and sexuality that formed the cultural context in which marriage existed as a social and religious institution.

## Themes of Sexuality and Love in Islamic Culture

*Nikah,* as most writers on marriage in Islam remind us, literally means to have sexual intercourse. The mutual benefits and responsibilities of marriage include physical and psychological experiences of love and sexuality that reverberate throughout other cultural forms and institutions, as al-Ghazali has just reminded us. Who else besides jurists and theologians like Ghazali reflected on the topic of marriage?

Islam arose in seventh-century Arabia in an oral culture in which poetry and oratory were highly valued and cultivated. Poets especially pursued the topoi of the lover and the beloved. We may take as the most classic example the Arabic ode or *qasida* poems, a mainstay of pre-Islamic cultural production and valued highly in Islamic times as well. More generally, the human relationship of love, both physical and spiritual, was also a celebrated theme of the beloved

---

32. Farah, *Marriage and Sexuality in Islam*, p. 76.

in the *qasida* poetry of pre- and early-Islamic poets. H. A. R. Gibb described the conventional opening theme of the *qasida*, known as the *nasib*, in the following manner:

> In the opening lines the poet is supposed to be traveling on a camel with one or two companions. The road leads him to the [site] of a former encampment of his own or a friendly tribe, the remains of which are still visible. He beseeches his companions to halt for a moment, and sorrowfully recalls how, many years ago, he spent here the happiest days of his life with his beloved.[33]

The poignancy of this remembrance of love is often emphasized in the final lines of the opening love theme, when the poet recalls being separated from his beloved as her tribe moved out to find greener pastures, and the poet-lover moves on in his journey with his companions. The following *nasib* from the *qasida* known as the *Mu'allaqa* by the famous poet Imru' al-Qays carries something of the power of emotion in the opening lines, even in translation:

> Stay! Let us weep, while memory tries to trace
> The long-lost fair one's sand-grit dwelling place
> Though the rude winds have swept the sandy plain
> Still some traces of that spot remain.
> My comrades reined their coursers by my side,
> And "Yield not, yield not to despair," they cried.
> (Tears were my sole reply; yet what avail
> Tears shed on sands, or sighs upon the gale?)[34]

More scandalous oftentimes were sentiments of love expressed in the genre known as the *ghazal*, which abandoned the artifices and overwrought conventions of the *qasida* for more melodic expression. A chivalrous theme appears in the following passage from a *ghazal* by the Umayyad Age poet 'Umar ibn Abi Rabi'a (d. 720), who was several times exiled for his audacious lyrical expressions of passion:

> Ah for the throes of a heart sorely wounded!
> Ah for the eyes that have smit me with madness!

33. H. A. R. Gibb, *Arabic Literature: An Introduction* (London: Oxford University Press, 1963), p. 15.

34. Quoted in Gibb, *Arabic Literature*, p. 16, from the translation by William Alexander Clouston, *Arabian Poetry, for English Readers* (Glasgow: [McLaren and Son, printers], 1881), p. 373.

Gently she moved in the calmness of beauty.
Moved as the bough to the light breeze of morning.
Dazzled my eyes as they gazed, till before me
All was a mist and confusion of figures.
Ne're had I sought her, and ne're had she sought me;
Fated the hour, and the love, and the meeting.[35]

The mythical romance cycle of Majnun and Layla is one of the most pervasive and popular of themes in Islamic literature, poetry, and song. It dates back
at least to the seventh century, and its theme has attracted hundreds of imita-
tors throughout the centuries. The most popular and imitated was the Persian
poem by the famous Nizami (ca. 1141-1180). Scholars believe that Majnun was
none other than the seventh-century poet and contemporary of the Prophet
Muhammad, Qays ibn Mulawwah. The romance of Majnun and Layla appears
in virtually all Islamic languages, including Arabic, Persian, Kurdish, Pashto,
Turkish, and Urdu. According to one tradition of the Majnun/Layla cycle, the
two fated lovers spent their youth together in an idyllic pastoral setting tending
their flocks; according to another tradition, the protagonists (called Qays and
Layla in this version) meet as young adults by chance and fall madly in love.
When he asks for Layla's hand in marriage, Qays learns that her father has already pledged her to another. In his substantive survey of Islamic literature on
Majnun and Layla, J. A. Haywood describes the effect on the distraught lover
(*majnun* in Arabic means crazed, insane, literally possessed by *jinn*):

> Gripped by the most violent anguish, Kays loses his reason and sets out to
> wander half-naked, refusing nourishment and living among wild animals.
> His father takes him on a pilgrimage to make him forget Layla, but his mad-
> ness only intensifies. He does, however, have moments of lucidity when he
> talks of his lady-love and composes verses which he recites to those curious
> people who come to see him. Until his death, he encounters Layla on only
> one further occasion.[36]

The theme of Majnun and Layla, lover and beloved, is found in the mystical writings of Sufi poets as well. Among the best known in both the Islamic
world and the West is Jalal al-Din al-Rumi (d. 1273). His spiritual teacher and
catalyst for the divine ecstasy in his well-known mystical poetry was Shams al-

---

35. Quoted in Gibb, *Arabic Literature*, p. 44, from the translation by W. G. Palgrave, "The
Poet 'Omar," in *Essays on Eastern Questions* (London, 1872).

36. J. A. Haywood, "Madjnun Layla," in *Encyclopaedia of Islam*, second ed., ed. J. van Let et
al. (Leiden: E. J. Brill, 1997), 5:1103b.

Din al-Tabrizi (d. 1248). As with mystics in other religious traditions, Sufis used the allegory of human love — even erotic love, especially the feeling the lover has toward the beloved — to express the divine/human encounter. Shams al-Din warns that God can be seen only with the vision of the lover; those who look upon God with the vision of knowledge (that is, the ulema, theologians, and philosophers) will not see him.

We see from this brief survey of themes of ecstatic love and longing of the lover for the beloved that the social institution of marriage in Islam was surrounded by a popular cultural tradition of the power of love in human life. Beyond these poetic and mystical themes, what place did love and marriage have in the sociology of knowledge in classical Islam?

Marriage was also a topic of discussion in the scholarly field of ethics and appropriate social manners, known as *akhlaq* (lit. "innate dispositions"). Ethics in the medieval Islamic universe of discourse was derived from an amalgam of sources that included not only the Qur'an and the traditions or Hadith of the Prophet, but also the pre-Islamic Arabian tradition (for example, tribal Sunna or practice based on usage and custom), as well as elements of both Hellenistic and Persian thinking about proper moral conduct. The ethics of hospitality and loyalty to one's kin as well as manliness and courage were part of this taxonomy of proper conduct. In the urbanizing ethos of Islam during the first four centuries, there was added to this cultivation of innate dispositions the educated possession of *adab*, which came to mean "the high quality of soul, good upbringing, urbanity and courtesy."[37] If contact with other cultures widened the range of ideas that made a person witty and urbane, *'ilm* or knowledge of the religious sciences and disciplines, such as Qur'an, Hadith, law, theology, and Arabic linguistics, were essential to the cultivation of Islamic *akhlaq*. In a chapter on "Ethics and Life in the World," in his marvelous new book *Following Muhammad*, Carl Ernst points out that the Islamic notion of *akhlaq* "is actually a good parallel to both the Greek notion of ethics and the Roman concepts of mores (from which we derive the term 'morality'). In all three cases, we are dealing with a plural noun having to do with customs and correct modes of behavior."[38] One such text of the *akhlaq* genre, the *Niche for Lamps* by al-Khatib al-Tabrizi (d. 1337), divides the discussion of proper conduct into twenty-five chapter-topics. The discussion of proper conduct in marriage falls right in the middle. It is preceded by eleven chapters on religious practices, beginning with faith, religious knowledge, and purity, and in-

37. Francesco Gabrieli, "Adab," in *Encyclopaedia of Islam*, second ed., 1:175.
38. Carl W. Ernst, *Following Muhammad: Rethinking Islam in the Contemporary World* (Chapel Hill, N.C.: University of North Carolina Press, 2003), p. 109.

cluding the Five Pillars. The discussion of marriage falls in a larger middle section on social relations, which includes commerce, freed slaves, and punishments. Clothing, food, dreams, manners, and rebellion are among the topics that round out the discussion of proper conduct in Islamic society in this genre.[39]

## Conclusion

The foregoing survey of traditional Islamic texts on love, marriage, and sexuality makes clear that these were rich topics, not only among jurists and theologians but for litterateurs, poets, mystics, and moralists — and no doubt such topics were also quite popular among ordinary Muslims as well. The most basic meaning of the human estate of marriage, as in the eternal divine covenant of God with humankind, is mutual obligation for the benefit, protection, and pleasure of each party. Nonetheless, the marriage contract, enacted according to the requirements of the Shariʿa, is, like the divine/human contract, not strictly among equals. The law sees the relationship primarily from the point of view of the rights and obligations of the male spouse parallel to God's superior position in the divine covenant, although it is not silent on the rights of women when a marriage is contested at the moment of divorce. Rereadings of the classic texts of Scripture and tradition for a more balanced view of the human covenant of marriage, such as the one proposed by Professor al-Hibri in this volume, are finding greater expression in recent decades. The role of Jesus as celibate founder of Christianity and the role of Muhammad as prophet who was also a husband and father indicate important differences between these two great religious traditions whose histories have been so deeply entwined.

Contemporary non-Muslim views of the treatment of women in Islam, so often critical and censorious, are justified in some respects. Many Muslims advance some of the same criticisms. What we learn from this broader review of literature on love, marriage, and sexuality in Islam is the following. From the earliest decades of Islam, hundreds if not thousands of jurists like Ahmad ibn Hanbal and scholars like al-Ghazali reflected carefully on the privileges and responsibilities of men and women in love, in marriage, and in sexual union, in the context of the societies and times in which they lived. We have witnessed in the writings of these two jurist-intellectuals a concern for fairness and shared, if not equal, responsibility in the marital partnership. Many scholars construed the marriage relationship in relation to their understanding of the relation of

39. Ernst, *Following Muhammad*, pp. 111-12.

the human to the divine. And they felt they understood better their relationship to God from the powerful intimacies of a man and woman in a covenant relationship. Those changes in thinking about marriage and Muslim family law that are now occurring in the globalizing societies of postmodern Islam and cyber-Islam seem profound to scholarly observers. Yet, al-Ghazali's eleventh-century Baghdad was vastly more cosmopolitan and socially diverse than Ibn Hanbal's ninth-century Baghdad. Populist reforms bring new orthodoxies, and in the more successful cases they may be more attuned to the social and political realities of their age. We presume, then, that within the vast array of classical literature on marriage, whose surface this essay has barely scratched, are renewable ideas that will inform twenty-first-century Muslim understandings of sexuality, love, and marriage.

## 9  The Modern American Covenant Marriage Movement: Its Origins and Its Future

*Katherine Shaw Spaht*

## What Is Covenant Marriage?

Covenant evokes a rich heritage both in the law, as a special form of contract with specific formalities and greater binding force, and in religion, as an unbreakable and perpetual agreement between the Creator and humankind. The word *covenant* added as an adjective preceding *marriage* carries with it that rich heritage from these dual sources to imbue and renew our understanding of a very old, yet indispensable, social institution. Max Stackhouse describes covenant's effect this way:

> The sociotheological idea of covenant is so rich with ethical content that it gives moral meaning to all it touches. . . . [A] covenant shifts the terms of . . . relationships. It is not cut casually, for it entails not only celebration and sacrifice but also the incorporation of new shared duties and rights that nourish life with other meanings, and thus a sense that these duties and rights are based on an enduring law and purpose as established by a higher authority.[1]

As used in this article, *covenant marriage* refers to a legally enforceable, statutory form of marriage, which is optional and which affords a stronger commitment from both spouses to their marriage. A covenant marriage statute ordinarily is composed of three unique components. The first component is mandatory premarital counseling that stresses the seriousness of marriage and the expectation that the couple's marriage will be lifelong. The second component is a Declaration of Intent, with a legally binding agreement that, if difficulties arise during the marriage, the spouses will make all "reasonable efforts to

1. Max L. Stackhouse, *Covenant and Commitments: Faith, Family, and Economic Life* (Louisville: Westminster John Knox, 1997).

preserve the marriage, including marriage counseling." The third component provides limited grounds for divorce (which vary in each of the three states that have adopted a covenant marriage statute), making termination of the marriage depend on either misconduct by a spouse which society collectively condemns, or a lengthy waiting period of two years living separate and apart.[2]

## Genesis of the Idea of Covenant Marriage in Louisiana and Passage of the Legislation

Two parallel events in the law of Louisiana played a role in motivating the desirability of recognizing legally and then remedying the suffering of the children of divorce. The first was the repeal of legal protection against a parent's unjust disinheritance of his children regardless of their age.[3] Not surprisingly, the unjust disinheritance of the deceased's children most often involved children of a former marriage alienated from the deceased by virtue of a divorce from the other parent. Second, the passage of a more liberal divorce law without the bill's original financial disincentives in effect promoted rather than deterred divorce, a story as old as California's no-fault divorce law. To a lesser extent but still a motivating factor, a more liberal divorce law meant an "innocent" spouse under a more restrictive divorce law founded upon *fault* of the other spouse lost negotiating leverage. Although both events culminated in legislation passed during the 1990s, the seeds of their success were planted in 1981, the peak year for divorces in the United States.

In 1981 a Louisiana state senator introduced legislation to amend the Louisiana Constitution; the amendment would have eliminated entirely the institution of forced heirship. During the same period, the Marriage/Persons Committee of the Louisiana State Law Institute began meeting almost monthly to recommend legislative revision of the Louisiana law regulating the family. These two ostensibly unrelated occurrences culminated in legislation and state

2. Katherine Shaw Spaht, "Louisiana's Covenant Marriage: Social Analysis and Legal Implications," *Louisiana Law Review* 59 (1998): 63, 74-75.

3. An amendment to the Louisiana Constitution in 1995 eliminated protection against the Legislature's reducing the scope of forced heirship legislation to protect only children under the age of twenty-four and those who, regardless of their age, are permanently incapable of caring for their persons or administering their estates. See La. Const., Art. XII, V, and La. Civ. Code Art. 1493. See also Katherine Shaw Spaht, "Forced Heirship Changes: The Regrettable 'Revolution' Completed," *Louisiana Law Review* 57 (1996): 55-146; Cynthia Samuel, "Letter from Louisiana: An Obituary for Forced Heirship and A Birth Announcement for Covenant Marriage," *Tulane European and Civil Law Forum* 12 (1998): 1-12.

constitutional change in the fall of 1995. This focused attention on the problem underlying the repeal of forced heirship: divorce and the resulting suffering for untold numbers of American children. By 1996 the social science evidence supporting the thesis of the suffering of children of divorce was quickly accumulating, and could no longer be ignored by policy-makers.

1996 was a watershed year. A state legislator from Michigan, Representative Jesse Dahlman, introduced a package of legislation that would have modified that state's unilateral no-fault divorce law by denying a no-fault divorce to a spouse if the other spouse objected.[4] Her efforts garnered widespread national media attention that sparked publicity for and examination of the then current social science data. That national publicity, as it turned out, planted a new but variant seed in Louisiana, this time in the form of covenant marriage legislation.

In 1996 a first-term Louisiana representative named Tony Perkins expressed interest in divorce law reform. After exploring various reform alternatives, including the proposal advanced in Michigan, Representative Perkins decided to author "covenant marriage" legislation, an idea borrowed, refined, and adapted from a bill introduced in Florida in 1990 by then Representative Daniel Webster. It was not, however, the only divorce reform bill introduced in Louisiana in 1997. Senator Max Jordan introduced a bill that would have prohibited divorce for couples with children below the age of twenty-four absent proof of *fault* grounds for divorce. The strategy of introducing two different bills reforming divorce law in the two chambers of the Louisiana Legislature was to determine which of the two approaches would be the more popular. There was no expectation among the participants that either would pass in 1997. After all, the two pieces of legislation that served as catalysts for covenant marriage legislation — one that virtually repealed forced heirship and the other that made no-fault divorce quicker — required many years of unsuccessful legislative efforts and attendant lobbying. The strategy adopted for divorce reform, however, had the ultimate effect of enhancing the chance that the "covenant marriage" bill would pass.

In fact, the Louisiana Senate bill was the first of the two bills heard in committee. Not surprisingly, in the Senate Committee on Judiciary A there was staunch opposition from the two lawyers on the committee. Nonetheless, the opponents yielded to permit the reporting of the bill to the floor of the Senate without recommendation. At the same time, Representative Perkins had recruited twenty-seven co-sponsors of the covenant marriage legislation, enough of whom were members of the House committee that would review the bill to

4. That Michigan legislator, Rep. Jesse Dalman, introduced Mich. H.B. No. 5217, 89th Legis., Reg. Sess. (Mich. 1997); S. File No. 2935.

assure passage by the committee. On the same night that the House Committee on Civil Law and Procedure heard the covenant marriage bill, the Senate debated its own bill on the floor of the Senate. It was the last bill considered by the Senate that evening before adjournment. The Senate bill was defeated handily, with only twelve of the thirty-nine senators voting for the bill. With overwhelming support of the members of the House committee and proponents of the measure, however, the covenant marriage bill passed in the House. The only opposition to the covenant marriage bill present at the committee hearing came from a representative of the American Civil Liberties Union (ACLU), who argued that the legislation represented an unconstitutional failure to separate church and state.

Ultimately, the recorded roll call vote of senators on the Senate bill would serve as a blueprint for obtaining the necessary votes of Senate committee members for the covenant marriage bill. After the covenant marriage bill passed the floor of the House of Representatives by a vote of 91-8, the bill was assigned to the same committee — the Committee on Judiciary A — which had earlier heard the Senate bill. With the bill's passage by a lopsided vote in the House of Representatives, the two largest state newspapers, the *Times-Picayune* in New Orleans and *The Advocate* in Baton Rouge, weighed in and urged defeat of the covenant marriage bill. A week before the hearing on the covenant marriage bill in the Senate committee, Judith Wallerstein announced the results of her landmark twenty-five-year study of the children of divorce. The results of that widely publicized and anticipated study were not reassuring about the resiliency of children after their parents' divorce. The Senate committee hearing on the covenant marriage bill proved to be the most difficult step in the legislative process, requiring strategic compromises and additions to the bill, which were necessary to secure a majority vote recommending the bill's passage. Once again, during the Senate committee hearing, the only testimony against the bill came from the ACLU, but at this hearing the objection to the bill was different. According to the ACLU female lawyer, a covenant marriage could serve to "trap" a wife who is the victim of domestic abuse in a dangerous marriage. On the Senate floor Representative Perkins accepted an amendment to the covenant marriage legislation that included physical and sexual abuse of the spouse or child of the parties as immediate grounds for divorce. That addition to the grounds for divorce represented the first time in Louisiana legal history that such conduct constituted grounds for an immediate divorce. It remains grounds for an immediate divorce in Louisiana, but only in a covenant marriage. The covenant marriage bill as amended passed the Senate 28-9.

The legislation, however, still produced its share of drama. Rather than concur in the Senate amendments, Representative Perkins asked the House to reject the amendments and send the bill to a joint Conference Committee. The House complied with his request. At 4:00 PM on the last day of the legislative session, which was to adjourn at 6:00 PM, the bill in the form of a report from the conference committee passed both the House of Representatives and the Senate. Governor Mike Foster promised Representative Perkins that he would sign the bill. With the Governor's signature, Louisiana became the first state to enact legislation offering its married citizens the option to bind themselves to a stronger legal commitment than current universal "no-fault" divorce law permitted. Passage of the legislation ignited not only widespread national interest in and discussion of marriage and divorce, but also a re-commitment of religious leaders and denominations, especially Christian ones, to concern for lifelong marriage and the harm caused by divorce.

This idea of an optional form of marriage was admittedly unexceptional. As early as 1945, French law professor Léon Mazeaud proposed an indissoluble marriage option with the ringing declaration, "let each choose! . . . No one can protest, for each remains free to bind himself up to death or only up to divorce. . . ."[5] His historical description recognized divorce as "[b]orn from the fight led against the church. . . ." Over the past ten years in this country there have been similar suggestions that varied from an indissoluble marriage option identical to that proposed by Mazeaud, to a vaguer proposed "super-vows," to more options than covenant marriage legislation allows, options that invite couples to custom-design the content of their marriage contract.[6] All of these proposals bear in common recognition of the political realities involved in solving "the divorce problem."

## How Covenant Marriage Works

Covenant marriage attempts to lessen the problem of divorce by strengthening the institution of marriage. John Witte explains the logic well:

> The Western tradition has learned, through centuries of experience, to balance the norms of marital formation, maintenance, and dissolution. . . . The

5. Henri Mazeaud et al., *Leçons de Droit Civil: La Famille,* ed. Laurent Levenuer, seventh ed. (Paris, 1995), bk. 1, vol. 3, no. 1415, part II, pp. 654-55.

6. Christopher Wolfe, "The Marriage of Your Choice," *First Things* (February 1995): 37-41; Amitai Etzioni, "How to Make Marriage Matter," *Time* (September 1993): 76. See also *Opportuning Virtue: Lessons to Be Learned from Louisiana's Covenant Marriage Law: A Communitarian Report,* ed. Amitai Etzioni and Peter Rubin (1997); Eric Rasmussen and Jeffery Evans Stake, "Lifting the Veil of Ignorance: Personalizing the Marriage Contract," *Indiana Law Journal* 73 (1998): 453-503.

> lesson in this is that rules governing marriage formation and dissolution must be comparable in their stringency. . . . Loose formation rules demand loose dissolution rules, as we see today. To fix "the modern problem of divorce" will require reforms of rules at both ends of the marital process.[7]

There are, as was noted, three components to covenant marriages: mandatory premarital counseling, the declaration of intent, and limited grounds for divorce.

### Premarital Counseling

A couple interested in covenant marriage must first arrange for premarital counseling. Although the counseling is mandatory, the statute simply requires that a priest, minister, or rabbi — or the secular alternative, a professional marriage counselor — perform the counseling. Similarly, the statute requires only that the counseling focus on the seriousness of marriage, the intention that marriage be lifelong, and the legal obligation of covenant spouses to take all reasonable steps to preserve their marriage if marital difficulties arise.[8] The counselor then attests on a special form that the counseling took place. Some denominations, such as Catholicism, historically have had structured and extensive premarital programs which require a few months to complete; such programs qualify as fulfillment of the mandatory premarital counseling required for a covenant marriage.

If a couple belongs to a denomination without such programs, they may not be informed of the covenant marriage option until arriving at the Clerk of Court's office to obtain the marriage license. Because a marriage license is valid in Louisiana for only thirty days, most couples wait until a week or less before the scheduled ceremony to appear and apply for the license. A 2001 statute requires that the Clerk of Court deliver a pamphlet prepared by the Attorney General, which explains the availability of the option of a covenant marriage and what the law requires for entering into such a marriage, to every couple who applies for a marriage license.[9] Even if, however, the couple is fortunate and does receive a copy of the pamphlet (which often does not happen due to the widespread failure by the Clerks' staff to properly implement the statute), it may be too late to complete the mandatory premarital counseling.

7. John Witte Jr., *From Sacrament to Contract: Marriage, Religion and Law in the Western Tradition* (Louisville: Westminster John Knox, 1997), pp. 217-18.

8. La. R.S. 9:237 (2001).

9. La. R.S. 9:237 A, C (2001).

In a Gallup poll commissioned by the team of social scientists studying Louisiana's covenant marriage legislation, the premarital counseling component garnered the support of 81 percent of respondents who believed that it was very or somewhat important, compared to 19 percent who believed that it was not very or not at all important.[10] Nevertheless, and more surprisingly, Christian denominations have not embraced, universally or enthusiastically, the option of covenant marriage. At first there were objections from the Catholic church about requiring the religious counselor to inform the couple of the grounds for divorce; curative legislation in 1999 solved this problem by removing that requirement from the content of the counseling. Nonetheless, the Catholic pre-Cana sessions with engaged couples still do not inform the participants of the covenant marriage option. Leaders of other denominations, such as the Methodist and the Episcopalian, object, respectively, to adding a new tier of marriage that would have the effect of denigrating other marriages of lower legal commitment and to a return of the "bad old days" of fault-based, more-difficult-to-obtain divorce. Only a few Christian churches in Louisiana require their members who marry to contract a covenant marriage. Jewish leaders in Louisiana have informally, and without public statement, rejected embracing covenant marriage.

## Declaration of Intent: Content of the Special Contract

As a second step in the process of entering into a covenant marriage, the couple signs a document entitled the Declaration of Intent that contains a "special" contract superimposed upon the ordinary marriage relationship, obligating covenant couples to disclose to each other information that might affect the decision to marry. The Declaration also contains a promise to take reasonable steps to preserve the marriage, if marital difficulties arise; those steps may include marital counseling or other remedies. The counseling requirement is a legal obligation that is enforceable as any other contractual obligation of the same nature — through damages, pecuniary and nonpecuniary, rather than specific performance.[11] In the same Gallup poll described above, it was this commitment, cast in the form of a legal obligation undertaken in advance to try to preserve the marriage, that proved the most popular: "92.3% of respon-

10. Katherine Shaw Spaht, "What's Become of Louisiana's Covenant Marriage through the Eyes of Social Scientists," *Loyola Law Review* 47 (2001): 709, 713-17.

11. For a comprehensive discussion of this obligation and its enforceability, see Spaht, "Louisiana's Covenant Marriage," pp. 103-5.

dents believed that the couple agreeing in advance to seek counseling if marital difficulties arise during the marriage was very or somewhat important, whereas 7.7% believed that it was not very or not at all important."[12]

## Restricted Grounds for Divorce

The most distinctive feature of a covenant marriage, restricted grounds for divorce, proved to be its least popular component; nonetheless, among those Louisiana citizens polled, two-thirds (65.7 percent) supported restricted grounds for divorce. Grounds for divorce in a covenant marriage consist of four causes in the nature of *fault* — adultery, conviction of a felony, abandonment for one year, and physical or sexual abuse of a spouse or a child of either of the parties.[13] Absent proof of such fault, parties must live separate and apart for two years, significantly longer than the six months required for a divorce in standard contract marriages in Louisiana. By restoring fault grounds for divorce and adding a significantly longer waiting period for a no-fault divorce, covenant marriage legislation emphasizes the importance to society of marriage and its duration. Unless there is grave misconduct by a spouse that makes the common life intolerable, either spouse must wait two years to obtain a divorce. Specifying the misconduct that provides grounds for divorce implicitly defines the appropriate behavior for spouses in marriage through objective, societal norms currently missing from the law of most states. Furthermore, the significantly longer waiting period of living separate and apart for covenant couples, combined with the legal obligation to take reasonable steps to preserve their marriage, offer the real and distinct possibility that the marriage can be saved. The two-year period affords sufficient time for counseling or the pursuit of other reasonable steps to be successful.

The total number of newly married couples entering into covenant marriage in Louisiana remains exceedingly small: 2 or 3 percent. A partial explanation for the small number of such couples includes the failure of the staff of Clerks' offices to implement the legislation as envisioned by the sponsors of covenant marriage and the more fundamental failure of religious denominations to encourage or insist that their congregants participate. Those who do contract a covenant marriage have a different profile from standard married

12. Spaht, "What's Become of Louisiana's Covenant Marriage," p. 714.
13. La. R.S. 9:307 A, B (1997). Paragraph B makes a provision for separation from bed and board in a covenant marriage for all the grounds for divorce that are listed in A and an additional ground — habitual intemperance or cruel treatment (physical or mental) that renders the life together insupportable.

couples, the result of self-selection effects. According to a five-year social science study of 250 covenant couples and 200 standard married couples, covenant couples "received more pre-marital counseling, were more religious and more conservative; whereas, standard married couples were more likely to have cohabited, experienced more marital conflict, talked less before marriage about important issues that can cause marital problems, received less approval of their spouse from their parents, were more likely to have been previously married and were more likely to have given birth to or fathered a child previously and to bring a child into the marriage."[14]

Interestingly, the study also found that "[w]omen are the leading force in a decision to get a covenant marriage. . . . [I]n the case of couples who elect covenant marriages, the woman is more often the leader. And with the couples who elect standard marriages, not surprisingly, [the leader] is usually the man."[15] The most obvious explanation for women leading in the choice of a covenant marriage is that women, particularly women with a vested interest in childbearing, apparently feel the need for the protection of stronger divorce laws. Covenant couples are more educated, both wives and husbands, and hold more traditional attitudes than do standard married couples.[16] Furthermore, covenant couples have a forceful conviction that their choice is important and believe that their covenant marriage makes a statement to a society in which marriage is under siege about the value of marriage.

## The Exodus and Adaptation of Louisiana's Covenant Marriage: The Cases of Arizona and Arkansas

Arizona adopted covenant marriage legislation in 1998,[17] less than a year after Louisiana's statute became effective. In 2001, Arkansas followed by adopting a covenant marriage statute[18] that bears an even closer resemblance to Louisiana's statute than does the covenant marriage legislation of Arizona. All three statutes contain the familiar three components of mandatory premarital counseling, a legally binding agreement to take reasonable steps to preserve the marriage, and restrictive grounds for divorce. No doubt the success enjoyed by cov-

---

14. Spaht, "What's Become of Louisiana's Covenant Marriage," p. 722.

15. Spaht, "What's Become of Louisiana's Covenant Marriage," p. 721.

16. Laura A. Sanchez et al., "Social and Demographic Factors Associated with Couples' Choice between Covenant and Standard Marriage in Louisiana" (draft presented at the annual meeting of the Southern Sociological Society in Atlanta, Ga., May 2002).

17. Ariz. Stats. §§ 25-901-04 (1998).

18. Ark. Stats. §§ 9-11-801-08 (2001).

enant marriage as a divorce reform effort is attributable to its optional character. The rest of the story, however, is that covenant marriage legislation has been introduced in many other states, but in each instance failed to pass. Often covenant marriage legislation failed to pass despite its optional character because of the composition of the committee to which the bill was referred or actions by the chair of such committees. Most often covenant marriage legislation failed because the legislative committees consisted of a majority of lawyers, or their chairs were practicing lawyers who exercised their many prerogatives to defeat or delay the legislation. Such was the experience of covenant marriage proponents in Oklahoma, Texas, and Oregon.

The provisions of both the Arkansas and Louisiana statutes that enumerate the grounds for divorce in a covenant marriage are more restrictive than those provisions contained in the Arizona statute. The greater permissiveness of the Arizona statute is not surprising considering the results of a Gallup poll in Arizona that surveyed its citizens' attitudes about divorce reform and covenant marriage legislation in particular. Illustrative of the more liberal attitude toward divorce found in the poll, the Arizona statute permits a covenant spouse to seek a divorce for physical or sexual abuse of a relative of either spouse permanently living in the matrimonial domicile, rather than limiting the grounds for divorce to physical or sexual abuse of a spouse or a child of the parties. In addition, Arizona covenant marriage law permits a spouse to seek a divorce for either domestic violence or emotional abuse as well as for the habitual abuse of alcohol or drugs. In the most significant departure from covenant marriage statutes in Louisiana and Arkansas, the Arizona legislation provides that the state can render a divorce in a covenant marriage upon proof of mutual consent to the divorce by both husband and wife.[19] Significantly, however, the Arizona covenant marriage statute does preclude unilateral no-fault divorce, which constitutes a serious and significant restriction on the availability and ease of divorce.

Benefiting from Louisiana's experience, the proponents of covenant marriage legislation in Arkansas, including Governor Mike Huckabee, solicited the cooperation of the civil servants charged with implementation of the legislation. The Arkansas covenant marriage statute is even more restrictive in two respects than the Louisiana statute: abandonment for one year is not grounds for divorce in an Arkansas covenant marriage, and two years rather than one year must elapse after a legal separation before a covenant spouse can seek a divorce in Arkansas.[20] Governor Huckabee, an ordained Southern Baptist minister and

19. Ariz. Stats. §§ 13-3601 (1998).
20. See Ark. Stats. §§ 9-11-808 (2001). In addition, if there are minor children of the marriage at the time of the judgment of separation and filing of divorce, the parties must wait an

the most important proponent of covenant marriage in Arkansas, also sought to promote the covenant marriage choice among Christian denominations in his state. The Governor has actively sought to secure a requirement that couples who marry in a Southern Baptist church in Arkansas do so in accordance with the covenant marriage statute. Louisiana has not enjoyed such official endorsement of covenant marriage by its governor, Mike Foster. It will be interesting to contrast the popularity of covenant marriage in Louisiana with that in Arkansas over the next few years to determine if official endorsement by a highly placed governmental official increases the number of couples exercising their option under their respective covenant marriage statutes.

## Why Is Covenant Marriage Legislation Important and Worth Promoting?

The most obvious answer to this question is that covenant marriage legislation has thus far been the *only* successful divorce reform effort.[21] Other, less obvious, answers focus on the current state of American culture, the moral confusion of our citizens, the failure to understand and appreciate the public character and purposes of marriage, the divisions that exist within our citizenry on salient issues, and disagreements about the most effective means to accomplish restoration of marriage as a protected, secure, and privileged sanctuary for adults and children.[22]

With a sober understanding of the difficulty in reversing a cultural trend that developed over a two-hundred-year period, indefatigable proponents of covenant marriage legislation view its long-term potential to move the culture in a better direction as both encouraging and hopeful. Covenant marriage reform begins with a couple, the equivalent of a grass roots movement, and encourages that couple to participate in a social movement focused on the lauda-

---

additional six months to seek a divorce (unless the grounds for the separation consist of physical or sexual abuse of the child). Compare La. R.S. 9:307 A (1997); Ark. Stats. §§ 9-11-808 (2001). Arizona does not extend the waiting period on the basis of the existence of minor children of the marriage. See Ariz. Stats. §§ 25-903 (1998).

21. This question and the answers draw extensively from Katherine Shaw Spaht, "Why Covenant Marriage May Prove Effective As a Response to the Culture of Divorce," in *Revitalizing the Institution of Marriage for the Twenty-First Century: An Agenda for Strengthening Marriage,* ed. Alan Hawkins, Lynn D. Wardle, and David Orgon Coolidge (Westport, Conn.: Praeger, 2002), 59-67.

22. See Bridget Maher, "Why Marriage Should Be Privileged in Public Policy," *Insight* no. 254 (Washington, D.C.: Family Research Council, April 16, 2003).

tory goal of strengthening the institution of marriage principally for the sake of children. This attitude is in fact reflected in the results of data collected by Steven Nock's research team: "Covenant couples have a forceful conviction about the importance of their choice that, of course, standard couples do not share; covenant couples believe that they are making a powerful social statement about marriage as an institution."[23] Even among the small percentage of standard married couples who had heard of covenant marriage and discussed the option, the team "found evidence that some of those currently in standard marriages, *particularly women,* had preferred covenant marriage, but perhaps faced barriers."[24]

### 1. Covenant marriage emphasizes strengthening marriage, not only preventing divorce.

Covenant marriage legislation, unlike other divorce reform efforts, addresses each phase of the marrying process: before, during, and at the end. By requiring premarital education that emphasizes the seriousness of marriage and the understanding that marriage is lifelong, the law ensures that the bride and groom discuss and resolve issues not necessarily confronted without premarital counseling. Good premarital education, with effective tools such as premarital inventories, encourages some ill-equipped couples to postpone marriage or to reconsider their decision to marry. For other couples premarital education highlights areas of disagreement and explores possible conflict resolution techniques, which can prove invaluable over the duration of a marriage. Difficulties inevitably arise in a marriage, and the legal obligation to take reasonable steps to preserve their marriage ensures that the covenant spouses' initial commitment to their marriage will continue over its duration. Covenant marriage legislation assumes that every marriage will experience its challenges and difficulties and provides in advance a legal commitment to take reasonable steps to preserve the marriage.

At the end of the mandatory premarital counseling, which includes an explanation that the couple is legally obligated to try to preserve the marriage if marital difficulties arise, prospective covenant spouses must execute a legal document that contains their agreement to enter into a covenant marriage and all that this commitment entails; the document is signed by each party and the signatures are then notarized. The statute envisions that the couple will have read the official pamphlet that explains the differences between standard and

---

23. Katherine Shaw Spaht, "Revolution and Counter Revolution: The Future of Marriage in the Law," *Loyola Law Review* 49 (2003): 1-78.

24. Sanchez, "Social and Demographic Factors Associated with Couples' Choice."

covenant marriages because the affidavit of the couple attests to having done so. Solemnity accompanies the ritual of executing the Declaration of Intent, which the couple files with the affidavit and the attestation of the counselor that he or she performed premarital counseling for the couple. A covenant couple begins marriage with an attitude averse to divorce, reflected in the contents of the Declaration of Intent. This attitude toward divorce, research suggests, may serve to ensure greater marital quality and thus fewer marital difficulties.[25]

In fact, recent data from the study of 250 covenant couples launched in 1998 confirms the earlier findings. The everyday pattern of a covenant marriage reveals that covenant couples "are far more likely to choose communication strategies that do not revolve around attacking or belittling their partner."[26] Covenant spouses are less likely "to respond to conflict with sarcasm or hostility, two communication strategies that . . . are particularly strongly associated with poor marriage outcomes." As expected, covenant couples are more likely to participate in premarital classes and "address a greater number and broader range of issues in these classes. . . ." Two years after covenant couples married, they "described their overall marital quality as better than did their standard counterparts." From the standpoint of commitment, covenant couples were more committed to their marriages two years after the ceremony than at the time of their marriage; whereas their standard marriage counterparts had changed little in their level of commitment. With the growing centrality of marriage for covenant couples, they experienced "higher levels of commitment . . . , higher levels of agreement between partners . . . , fewer worries about having children . . . and *greater sharing of housework.*" It is not too early in light of this most recent data collected by the researchers to conclude that covenant marriages are better marriages. Steven Nock, a professor of sociology at the University of Virginia and director of the research study, opines, "internally, the [covenant] marriages are *vastly better,* and covenant couples agree about who does what, the fairness of things, etc., much more than standard couples."

Professor Nock considers these couples as participants in a "new" form of marriage "that preserves the traditional, conventional and religious aspects of the traditional institution, but also resolves the various inequities often associ-

---

25. Paul R. Amato and Stacy J. Rogers, "Do Attitudes toward Divorce Affect Marital Quality?" *Journal of Family Issues* 20 (January 1999): 70. "Although most Americans continue to value marriage, the belief that an unrewarding marriage should be jettisoned may lead some people to invest less time and energy in their marriages and make fewer attempts to resolve marital disagreements. In other words, a weak commitment to the general norm of life-long marriage may ultimately undermine people's commitments to particular relationships" (p. 70).

26. Spaht, "Revolution and Counter Revolution," 52-54.

ated with gender in modern marriages."[27] In his opinion, "a central theme that discriminates between the two types of unions [is] *sanctification of marriage*."[28] Sanctification of the marriage reflects the view of covenant couples that

> the marriage warrants consideration apart from the individualistic concerns of either partner. In regard to some matters covenant couples appear to defer to the interests of their marriage even when the individual concerns of the partners may appear to conflict. *And this orientation to married life . . . helps resolve the customary problems faced by newly married couples in regard to fairness and equity.*

The covenant couple's model of marriage is an "institutional view of marriage: [t]his view of marriage elevates the normative (expected) model of marriage to prominence in the relationship." The two sources of this sanctified view of marriage are "the centrality accorded religion by the couple [and] beliefs about the life of marriage independent[ ] of the individual," as if the marriage itself was a party to the couple's relationship. The data collected from covenant couples who are participants in the study supports an old idea: "Two individuals do not make a strong marriage. Rather it takes the presence of a set of guiding principles around which these two individuals orient their behaviors and thinking."

## 2. Covenant marriage legislation combines components appealing to political conservatives and liberals.

A strategic combination of concepts attractive to both conservatives and liberals makes covenant marriage legislation more appealing than other forms of divorce reform. Thoughtful conservatives and liberals deeply concerned about marriage and the undesirable consequences of the divorce culture can find in covenant marriage legislation some component to support. For conservatives the restrictive grounds for divorce in the nature of fault on the part of a spouse reintroduce objective fault, signaling that state law will once again willingly and confidently judge marital behavior by a common, objective moral code. For liberals, the components of marital education and counseling made mandatory by the legislation offer the possibility of educating citizens to make better choices rather than imposing upon couples a particular outcome. In fact, the entire regime of covenant marriage is based upon choice, which in other contexts is readily embraced by liberal policy-makers.

27. Steven L. Nock, e-mail sent to author, 16 September 2002.
28. Steven L. Nock, Laura Sanchez, and James D. Wright, "Intimate Equity: The Early Years of Covenant and Standard Marriages" (draft presented at the annual meeting of the Population Association of America, Minneapolis, Minn., May 2003), 6.

**3. Covenant marriage invites religion back into the public square to assist in serving a public whose need is to preserve marriages.**

The provisions of a covenant marriage statute that impose premarital counseling as a prerequisite to marriage permit the celebrant of a marriage to provide the required counseling. The invitation extended by the state through the legislation offers a religious cleric, most of whom are committed to lifelong marriage, the opportunity to counsel a couple about the value of permanent marriage. When difficulties arise, as inevitably they will, and the covenant couple is obligated to take steps to preserve their marriage, the hope is that the couple will return to the same counselor, or his equivalent, to obtain assistance in overcoming those difficulties. Religious authorities are particularly well equipped to offer intensive one-on-one counseling for couples; they speak with moral authority yet with compassionate concern for the couple and their families, all of whom are affected if the marriage ends.

Although it is appropriate for religious officials to be suspicious of governmental intrusion, covenant marriage legislation merely invites religion's assistance, as evidenced in the minimal content of premarital counseling specified in the statute. Rather than banishing religion from the public square, covenant marriage legislation invites religion back into public life to offer a service that religion is uniquely qualified to perform — preserving marriages. Increasingly, policy-makers recognize that only the moral authority of religion can effectively solve the most stubborn of our country's social problems, and they deliberately seek faith-based organizations with which government can partner. Restoration of a public and religious partnership for solving one of our country's most intractable problems, sustaining marriages, offers the hope of a more secure future for our children.

**4. Covenant marriage seeks to persuade, not coerce, citizens to elect a stronger commitment to marriage that sublimates to some extent the autonomous self.**

The continuous, decades-long assault on traditional moral values has imposed enormous costs. The results of this assault that encouraged cultural revolutions — such as the sexual revolution — reveal a society of hardened, cynical victims, and this is especially true of women. Reflective of the same pursuit of the autonomous self and consistent with the new "therapeutic" society, no-fault divorce encapsulated in legal language a process of the disintegration of marriage that was no one's fault. These views, informed and fueled by the cultural revolutions, and combined with the uniquely American language of *rights,* support the conclusion that divorce for no good reason is one more individual entitlement.

Referred to on one occasion as a cultural "sleeping giant,"[29] covenant marriage legislation depends upon the effort of individual couples to change the culture; covenant marriage requires a form of evangelizing traditional marriage. Individual Americans need to be convinced of the value of keeping one's promises, of persevering through difficult times, of personal sacrifice for a transcendental cause (that is, their marriage), and of a duty to one's children, a duty to assume the role of adult by providing a stable, warm, and loving home environment. Children deserve to be children, sheltered and protected from adult concerns and discontent. Covenant married couples in Louisiana are participating in this evangelization: the quality of their marriages confirms the rewards of living a married life that reflects the timeless virtues of duty, perseverance, and self-sacrifice.

## 5. Covenant marriage offers traditional communities a refuge from the broader postmodern culture.

Until the dominant culture in America changes, covenant marriage legislation permits those who subscribe to a traditional set of values to create an alternative legal structure for family life that social science research supports as the ideal. The legislation "allows a minority to live their desired lives without forcing a change in lifestyle on the majority."[30] According to Christopher Wolfe, the liberal ideal of autonomy is incompatible with the substantive moral ideal of marital fidelity "embraced by certain traditional communities that from one perspective are 'within' the American community and from another perspective are not."[31] One might rephrase Wolfe's description of such individuals to say that they are "in the world" but not "of the world." This predicament applies to people of deep religious faith or, as Gertrude Himmelfarb observes, to an entirely "dissident culture" which includes "those of little or no religious faith" but who abide by traditional values and are unembarrassed by the language of morality.[32]

Covenant marriage legislation offers the dissident culture the opportunity to live as a traditional community under a stricter moral code reinforced by law, within the larger dominant culture that is subject only to minimal moral constraints. Covenant marriage legislation offers the opportunity to demonstrate a

29. Joe Loconte, "I'll Stand Bayou," *Policy Review* 89 (May/June, 1998): 30, 32-33.

30. Jeffery Evans Stake, "Paternalism in the Law of Marriage," *Indiana Law Journal* 74 (1999): 801, 807.

31. Wolfe, "Marriage of Your Choice," pp. 37-41.

32. Gertrude Himmelfarb, "The Panglosses of the Right Are Wrong," *The Wall Street Journal*, 4 February 1999, A22. She is also the author of *One Nation, Two Cultures* (New York: Knopf, 1999).

"better way" to lay the foundation for the reconstruction of strong and stable families.

**6. Covenant marriage offers the promise of surviving migratory divorce.**
No divorce reform effort can accomplish its goals if one spouse can simply cross state lines and, by establishing a new domicile, seek relief in another state with more liberal divorce laws. Because of the unique characteristics of a covenant marriage, a court in the state with more liberal divorce laws may be compelled to reexamine the 1942 United States Supreme Court opinion in *Williams v. North Carolina I.*[33] In that decision, the United States Supreme Court erroneously melded together the distinct issues of judicial and legislative jurisdiction, which were otherwise clearly considered separately in cases requiring the application of conflict of laws principles.

If a court in the more liberal state where the plaintiff spouse seeking a divorce is newly domiciled was compelled to separate the issue of jurisdiction to render a divorce from the issue of what divorce law should apply (choice of law), general choice of law rules would favor the application of the covenant marriage law of the plaintiff's former domicile. Two reasons emerge for that favoritism: (1) the fact that the distinguishing characteristic of a covenant marriage is the parties' voluntary agreement after counseling, which is expressed in an additional contract containing an express choice of (for example) Louisiana law; and (2) the fact that the covenant marriage law does not eliminate, but simply delays, the availability of a unilateral no-fault divorce.

Covenant marriage offers the potential for reversing judicial social engineering, which as early as 1942 reduced divorce laws in the states to the "lowest common denominator." The barriers and obstacles to divorce erected by North Carolina for the protection of its citizenry crumbled in obeisance to the Supreme Court's dictate that North Carolina must give full faith and credit to a judgment of divorce rendered in Nevada, a state with a more liberal divorce law.

## Responses to the Most Common Criticisms of Covenant Marriage

While arguing that covenant marriage is a failure because of the extremely low number of couples choosing the option, the same critics insist that couples should not be permitted to choose the option. In a recent liberal publication,

33. *Williams v. North Carolina*, 317 U.S. 287 (1942).

one author refers to conservatives' "silly" ideas, like covenant marriage, that no one wants. If no one wants the option of covenant marriage, how does its existence, authorized by legislation, threaten its opponents? There is absolutely no evidence in Louisiana's experience that either parents or ministers will *force* a couple to choose a covenant marriage. Even if a particular church requires marrying couples to contract a covenant marriage, that requirement does not prevent a resisting couple from marrying. There are only a few such churches in Louisiana, and ample opportunity exists to marry in another church or to marry with a secular authority as celebrant.

Why would the legislative option frighten opponents of covenant marriage? After all, covenant marriage consists of a voluntary choice and, based upon both empirical and anecdotal evidence, no one *forces* a couple to adopt covenant marriage. How can the opponents even frame an argument if the legislation offers a *choice?* A number of objections have been tried.

## 1. Women will be trapped in abusive marriages.

The history as well as the content of covenant marriage legislation in Louisiana belies the motive of binding women to an abusive husband. Covenant marriage makes available, for the first time in the history of Louisiana law, immediate divorce on grounds of physical or sexual abuse. There is no waiting period and no cooling-off period. Theoretically, depending upon how quickly litigation progresses in a particular court, an abused spouse can obtain a divorce much more quickly in a covenant marriage than in a standard marriage, which requires the abused spouse to live separate and apart from the abuser for six months before filing for divorce.

It is also easy to rebut the argument that covenant marriage will place victims of spousal abuse at risk because pre-divorce counseling is required. The statute requires only "reasonable steps to preserve the marriage, including marital counseling." Emphasis should be upon *reasonable.* As I have written elsewhere, in most cases of domestic violence where the spouse has been a victim, joint counseling would not be reasonable. No obligation to preserve the covenant marriage assumed by the victim of violence requires her to risk her life.[34] There have reportedly been cases in which effective joint counseling of spouses, coupled with family protection for the victim, has resulted in reconciliation, but that evidence is merely anecdotal.

34. Spaht, "Louisiana's Covenant Marriage: Social Analysis," p. 101. "Reasonable steps to preserve the marriage could include her individual counseling through a battered women's program and a separated intervention with the batterer who also submits to additional therapy." Legislation passed in 2004 (adds La. R.S. 9:307 C) exempts such victims from the counseling requirement.

The assumption made by the opponents of covenant marriage that women will remain trapped in abusive marriages raises the issue of how many such marriages exist. The persistence of such arguments in opposition to divorce reform creates the impression that domestic violence in marriage is widespread. A recent study entitled *Does Divorce Make People Happy? Findings from a Study of Unhappy Marriages* reported that

> [s]taying married did not typically trap unhappy spouses in violent relationships. Eighty-six percent of unhappily married adults (including 77 percent of unhappy spouses who later divorced or separated) reported no violence in their relationship. Ninety-three percent of unhappy spouses who avoided divorce reported no violence in their marriage five years later.[35]

These data about the small minority of divorces that occur because of violence confirmed earlier findings by Paul Amato and Alan Booth that "a majority of divorces involving children now dissolve not angry, violent marriages but relatively low-conflict marriages."[36] Another study concluded "that only 20 percent of children who experienced divorce had parents who *argued* frequently while married (compared to seven percent of children whose parents stayed married)."[37]

Studies that differentiate among relationships — such as "partner" from "ex-partner" and "husband" from "ex-husband" — make it clear that the safest place for a child and his mother is in the home with her husband who is also the child's biological or adoptive father. In a report compiling the results of three such studies that differentiated a child's risk of physical or sexual abuse based upon family structure, the researchers found that in all of the following situations the rate of abuse is much higher than for a child living with his biological parents who are married: "*The rate of abuse is 14 times higher* if the child is living with a biological mother who lives alone. . . . *The rate of abuse is 20 times higher* if the child is living with biological parents who are not married but are cohabiting. *The rate of abuse is 33 times higher* if the child is living with a mother

35. Linda J. Waite et al., *Does Divorce Make People Happy? Findings from a Study of Unhappy Marriages* (New York: Institute for American Values, 2002), 4.

36. Alan Booth and Paul R. Amato, "Parental Predivorce Relations and Offspring Postdivorce Well-Being," *Journal of Marriage and the Family* 63 (2001): 197-212. In an earlier book entitled *A Generation at Risk: Growing Up in an Era of Family Upheaval* (Cambridge, Mass.: Harvard University Press, 1997), the two authors postulated that as many as two-thirds of divorces in marriages with children occurred for "soft" reasons, such as "we grew apart."

37. Donna Ruane Morrison and Mary Jo Coiro, "Parental Conflict and Marital Disruption: Do Children Benefit When High-Conflict Marriages Are Dissolved?" *Journal of Marriage and the Family* 61 (1999): 626-37.

who is cohabiting with another man."[38] In fact, individuals active in opposing domestic violence often also oppose marriage. Those advocates will remain unconvinced because they actually believe that marriage itself traps women.

## 2. Restoring fault of a spouse as grounds for divorce reintroduces acrimony and perjury in divorce.

Nothing has reduced the acrimony and bitterness of divorce. Currently, those emotions surface in disputes over child custody and in debates over what state law should provide with respect to child custody. Shifting the acrimony from the divorce proceeding itself to the incidental matter of child custody in no way lessens the bitterness engendered by divorce, nor does it control vengeful actions of the parents directed at each other. By concentrating the vitriol on child custody disputes, no-fault divorce law fails in its most vital function and in its original intention, namely, protecting the innocent children from the consequences of their parents' resentments. Increasingly, lawyers observe that a parent will use suspected sexual abuse in an attempt to deny to the other parent, often the parent whose conduct resulted in the divorce or who initiated the divorce, joint custody, or visitation with the child. Is relegating the emotional loss and accompanying bitterness of divorce to child custody disputes an improvement in the law? A legal system that permits a proceeding between two spouses in which they can air and resolve those emotions has to be superior to one that shifts the expression of those emotions to the issue of the custody of the children.

The widely perceived problem of perjured testimony prior to the enactment of no-fault divorce laws constituted a failure of the lawyers and judges in their responsibility to seek truth. In Louisiana there were never widespread assertions that such perjury existed. The Louisiana judiciary developed ancillary rules to prevent perjured testimony concerning a spouse's fault in a divorce proceeding. For example, the judiciary in an adultery case refused to permit testimony of the accused spouse or his or her paramour on the ground that to do so would essentially permit divorce by mutual consent. Even the testimony of private detectives who gathered evidence of clandestine meetings of the spouse and his or her paramour produced skepticism. After all, detectives received money to produce the evidence of adultery that existed and thus could be tempted to manufacture the evidence necessary or to give false testimony about what they observed. In other words, there were, and still are, legal mechanisms that could reduce, if not eliminate, perjured testimony.

38. Patrick F. Fagan and Dorothy B. Hanks, "The Child Abuse Crisis: The Disintegration of Marriage, Family, and the American Community," *Backgrounder*, no. 115 (1997): 10.

A less obvious consequence of no-fault divorce is that elimination of legal fault denied bargaining advantage to an innocent spouse. The innocent spouse who desired to preserve her marriage could no longer refuse to seek a divorce in an attempt to reconcile with the other spouse. Under a unilateral no-fault divorce law, the other spouse can simply file his own petition for divorce for irreconcilable differences. A lawyer from Indiana stated the result of such no-fault divorce laws eloquently: "Our non-fault . . . system gives all the leverage to the most unreasonable party," including the party who may have been guilty of grievous fault.[39] Even if the innocent spouse was unsuccessful in persuading the spouse at fault to reconcile, she could refuse to file a petition of divorce, which she alone had the exclusive right to do, until he agreed to provide an acceptable financial settlement for her and for the children. That same lawyer from Indiana expresses this idea as follows: "Under the old system, at least the dumped spouse[s] could, unless themselves guilty of . . . fault, obtain reasonable provision for themselves and the children by simply refusing to grant a divorce until a fair settlement was negotiated." Today this leverage would translate into the ability to obtain from the spouse guilty of fault financial concessions, including an obligation to provide for the child's college expenses, which in most states parents are not legally obligated to provide.

Use of *guilt* in the context of describing the spouse at fault was purposeful. Fault grounds for legal separation or divorce communicated societal norms of acceptable behavior for spouses within marriage. Certain conduct listed in the form of grounds for divorce communicated society's expectations, as law almost always does, in the form of objective norms. To be habitually intemperate; to be cruel, either physically or emotionally, to the other spouse; to have sexual intercourse with another person not your spouse — all this was deemed unacceptable behavior. This behavior was so violative of social norms that the offended spouse could seek legal relief from his or her obligation to remain married to the defendant. Even though in every other respect law signaled the intense interest of society in the duration and stability of marriage, there was social consensus about the limits to maintaining a particular marriage, a marriage where the harm inflicted on a spouse exceeded the benefit society gained by its continuation.

### 3. Extending the waiting period for obtaining a no-fault divorce just prolongs the fighting and has no effect in preserving marriages.

In the most recent research about the vacillating rhythm of happiness in marriage, the data reveal that the passage of time can heal what one spouse, or far

---

39. Brent Welke, Letter to Indiana Judiciary Committee Chairman, March 2, 1999.

less often both spouses, believe is an unhappy marriage.[40] Nonetheless, many Americans believe that divorce is the sole cure for an unhappy marriage.

The findings of a research team, in response to the question, "Does divorce typically make adults happier than staying in an unhappy marriage?" include the following: (1) "Unhappily married adults who divorced or separated were no happier, on average, than unhappily married adults who stayed married." (2) "Divorce did not reduce symptoms of depression for unhappily married adults, or raise their self-esteem, or increase their sense of mastery, on average, compared to unhappy spouses who stayed married." (3) "The vast majority of divorces (74%) happened to adults who had been happily married five years previously." (4) "Unhappy marriages were less common than unhappy spouses." (5) "Staying married did not typically trap unhappy spouses in violent relationships." (6) "Two out of three unhappily married adults who avoided divorce or separation ended up happily married five years later." (7) "Many currently happily married spouses have had extended periods of marital unhappiness, often for quite serious reasons, including alcoholism, infidelity, verbal abuse, emotional neglect, depression, illness and work reversals."

Considering such empirical findings, would it not be sensible to slow down the divorce process? If divorce does not necessarily produce happiness and over a five-year period an unhappy marriage can become happy, should not the law consider lengthening the waiting period even with the retention of no-fault divorce? Covenant marriage legislation extends the waiting period by one-and-a-half years, in combination with the legal obligation to take reasonable steps, including counseling, *to preserve* the marriage. What if a more general divorce law reform combined a lengthy waiting period with the couple's duty to seek marriage counseling?

Another interesting finding reported in the same study suggests the need for further refinement of the reform proposal: "Spouses who turned their marriages around seldom reported that counseling played a key role." In evaluating why, the authors report that

> When husbands behaved badly, *value-neutral* counseling was not reported by any spouse to be helpful. Instead wives in these marriages appeared to seek outside help from others to pressure the husband to change his behavior. Men displayed a strong preference for religious counselors over secular counselors, in part because they believed these counselors would not encourage divorce.[41]

---

40. Waite et al., *Does Divorce Make People Happy?* 4-5.
41. Waite et al., *Does Divorce Make People Happy?* 6.

Rated as the most popular component of covenant marriage according to the Gallup survey, the counseling or other reasonable step covenant couples are obligated to try must be directed to *preserving* the marriage. Not all forms of counseling are equal.

**4. Restricting divorce for covenant couples is useless because a spouse can sue in a state with more liberal divorce laws.**
An advantage of covenant marriage over other divorce reform efforts is that covenant marriage potentially could survive the migratory divorce phenomenon. A covenant marriage is a special contract superimposed upon the ordinary marriage contract. It thus creates the possibility that *Williams v. North Carolina* could be reexamined. If traditional conflict of laws analysis is applied to a divorce instituted by a covenant spouse in another state with more liberal divorce laws, the court should distinguish between judicial and legislative jurisdiction. At the same time that the court sustains the analysis of the United States Supreme Court that the court has jurisdiction to render a divorce judgment if the spouse is a domiciliary, it could also apply the Louisiana law of covenant marriage in determining whether the spouse was entitled to a divorce. If the court recognized a distinction in the two inquiries, then the court could apply traditional conflict of laws analysis about which state's divorce law applies. Louisiana's covenant marriage Declaration of Intent contains a choice of law clause in which the spouses to a covenant marriage agree to be bound by the Louisiana law of covenant marriage. Considering the usual deference of courts to choice of law clauses in other contracts, the covenant marriage might well survive the migration of one spouse to another state.

**5. Divorce reform is against the interests of the legal profession.**
Lawyers often oppose divorce reform because reform is a threat to their economic livelihood. No-fault divorce permitted family law attorneys to make money on the volume of divorces they handled and to satisfy their clients, at least parties who desire divorce. Because there is no defense to a no-fault divorce other than reconciliation, the lawyer simply completes the blank portions of a uniform pleading (petition) and files it. The lawyer need not prove facts entitling the petitioner to a divorce, which involves time-consuming discovery and the use of possibly salacious material to prove fault grounds for divorce. Without a defense to the action for divorce, the lawyer can concentrate on the more lucrative and satisfying litigation, litigation that divides the property accumulated by the couple. Unlike the former fault system of divorce there is little possibility that the client will fail to obtain the divorce judgment, so the lawyer may begin work immediately on the incidental matters dependent upon the

judgment itself. Work on those incidental matters, except for child custody, ordinarily concerns money and requires hours of legal analysis for which the attorney may charge the client. In addition, the content of the law that classifies property acquired during marriage, for example, is far more intellectually engaging and interesting than having to build a case for divorce on the basis of the behavior of the client's spouse.

In a small book detailing the legal profession's responsibility for no-fault divorce in California, Judy Parejko helps the reader understand how lawyers cleverly reshaped no-fault divorce legislation to eliminate the conciliation components in the bill that was introduced. She also describes the legal profession's contribution to the interpretation of *irreconcilable differences* as simply one spouse's desire to divorce. Her book *Stolen Vows* makes a valuable contribution by exposing the motivations of lawyers in opposing divorce reform, whether in the form of lawyers who serve on legislative committees to which such bills are referred, or of the profession as a whole which sees its livelihood threatened by reform efforts. In the words of Indiana lawyer Brent Welke, writing to the chairs of the Indiana Judiciary Committee, "Please be advised that, speaking as a lawyer, I am unalterably opposed to any change in our divorce act. Our divorce act has greatly increased divorces, crime, bankruptcy and juvenile caseloads. Any change in our no-fault system would be a financial disaster for the bar and for me personally, as these type of cases comprise a majority of my practice."[42]

**6. Louisiana's low covenant marriage rate shows that covenant marriage is failing to have an impact on the divorce rate, much less the culture.**
Clearly, the Louisiana covenant marriage option, as demonstrated by the percentage of newly married couples choosing it, faces obstacles. Despite a theology that unequivocally endorses marriage as permanent, Christian denominations have failed or refused to encourage, much less require, persons marrying in their houses of worship to adopt the state law option closer to their biblical teachings. Less surprisingly, the staff of the state bureaucracy charged with providing information on the option to Louisiana citizens have subverted the effort by simply refusing to do so and by openly discouraging the choice because of the additional work involved. The latter obstacle has been well documented as a part of the social science study underway comparing covenant and standard married couples.[43] The results of this study should prove extremely useful in the broader context of understanding and remedying obstacles to similar changes in public policy. Other obstacles include lack of cultural and commu-

42. Welke, letter.
43. Spaht, "What's Become of Louisiana's Covenant Marriage."

nity support for a couple's selection of covenant marriage and the individual American's self-absorption and aversion to commitment. It is counter-cultural to foreclose one's options in advance by making a permanent commitment to a relationship that might "just stop working" for you. Americans have increasingly become commitment averse.

So, with what appear to be insurmountable obstacles — personal, cultural, and religious — is covenant marriage legislation worth the effort? Are the only marriages being saved those marriages least likely to end by divorce? On the contrary. Louisiana's covenant marriage legislation sparked an expanded national conversation on fragmented family and marriage structures. The conversation focused national attention on the consequences of divorce for the children and adults affected. The release of social science research on family structure no longer involves quiet publication in professional journals and, thereafter, published critiques of the study's design or conclusions. Instead, the release of new social science data on the subject prompts press conferences, as well as media appearances and commentary by the study's author(s) and critics. For the first time, many average Americans discuss the latest study data and argue about the implications for our communities and country. Divorce is no longer viewed as a benign experience for all of the parties involved.

Moreover, the laboratory of covenant marriage tests three different "tools" for preserving marriages — premarital counseling, pre-divorce counseling, and a more difficult and time-consuming divorce process that relies on "fault" and longer waiting periods. At the end of the experiment, the data may hold a treasure trove of valuable insights as to which of these components proves valuable in ensuring a person's commitment to his marriage. The laboratory has already yielded information of value, such as the leadership role of women in covenant marriage. Their leadership role affirms the view that women in particular desire a stronger commitment in marriage for their own security and that of their children. A stronger commitment with barriers to an easy divorce permits a wife who becomes a mother to invest in her children and family at the expense of investing in her career. The laboratory results also suggest that restoring an ideal of marriage as a stronger, more binding commitment adds the feature of transcendence and the "sanctification" of the marriage. The marriage itself becomes a third party to the relationship between husband and wife, to which one or both spouses may defer. This reverence for marriage as an institution results, according to the study data, in a qualitatively better marriage — less conflict, better communication, and greater gender equity in performing household tasks.

Covenant marriage legislation, which permits a couple the choice of a more binding marital commitment, offers a relatively cost-free experiment in what can improve the quality and longevity of a marriage. That experiment, still in progress, is already revealing an extraordinary amount of information that can prove useful to federal and state policy-makers. The same information may also be useful to different religious traditions by confirming the moral wisdom and revelations of their traditions and by giving them confidence in the value of restoring a spiritual dimension to the institution of marriage.

# 10 What Does Covenant Mean for Relationships?

*Margaret F. Brinig and Steven L. Nock*

Over the past several years, both of us have thought substantially about covenant.[1] The concept of covenant comes to us originally from religious sources, so we pay explicit attention here to what the Bible and organized religion have to say about it. We have also drawn from our own disciplines of law, economics, and sociology as they explain or stem from the initial concepts.

Though used rarely in law, the term *covenant* is beginning to appear when applied to marital relationships. Those who have at least heard of the covenant marriage options in Louisiana[2] (and, presumably, Arizona[3] and Arkansas[4]) tend to fall into two camps: those who are strongly in favor and those who are strenuously opposed. More than 50 percent of the Louisiana adults surveyed in a Gallup poll[5] had never heard of the concept. Some county clerks advise

1. Steven L. Nock is the Principal Investigator of National Science Foundation Grants #SBR-9803736, #SES-9819156, and private foundation support recently awarded to study the implementation, development, and measurable outcomes of covenant marriage in Louisiana. Margaret Brinig is a consultant to the project.

2. La. Civ. Code art. 9, §§ 102 *et seq.* (2005).

3. Ariz. Rev. Stat. § 25-901 (1998).

4. Ark. Stat. §§ 9-141-201 (2005).

5. Gallup Organization surveyed a random sample of 540 Louisiana citizens by phone between July and September of 1998. Only 43.1 percent indicated they'd heard of covenant marriage, and only 35 percent were aware that the legislation had been enacted. When asked whether covenant marriage was a good idea or not, of those who had heard of covenant marriage, about 25 percent said it was really too soon to tell; among the remainder, 81 percent said that it was a "good idea" or a "very good idea." Likewise, 56 percent of respondents would have a favorable or very favorable reaction to their own child choosing a covenant marriage. See Alan Hawkins, Steven Nock, Julia Wilson, Laura Sanchez, and James Wright, "Attitudes about Covenant Marriage and Divorce: Policy Implications from a Three-State Comparison," *Family Relations* 51 (2002): 166-75.

against it, or fail to pass out the statutorily required brochures because they feel it is silly or too time-consuming. Not surprisingly, couples marrying after the Louisiana legislation took effect have largely opted for "standard marriage," though the number finding covenant marriage attractive has increased from about 1 percent in the first six months to approximately 2 percent thereafter.[6] Most of the considerable media attention has concentrated on the rules for divorce, though the intent of the proponents is to change the nature of marriage.

As the assessments of the Louisiana experiment continue, the concept of covenant itself deserves attention. The idea of covenant has been around at least since biblical times. It figures in the early common law of contracts as the "promise under seal," but is perhaps better known today as the "covenant not to compete" in employment[7] and as the "restrictive covenant" in land sales.[8] Even the nonlawyer associates formality with the word, and perhaps some feeling of being bound to do something. In this chapter we reexamine covenant, emphasizing its applications to the family.[9] We draw on ideas from sociology, law, economics, religion, and feminist thought in looking at what makes a covenant relationship, as opposed to what does not. In the end, we conclude that covenant departs in significant ways from secular, legal contracts.

## The Features of Covenant

A covenant involves at least three interrelated concepts: (1) unconditional love; (2) permanence (even extending beyond the lives of the promising parties themselves); and (3) involvement (or witness) of God, or, at minimum, the larger community. In some ways, these natural law concepts are reflected in law. For example, parties legally cannot change the essential content of their marital or parental responsibilities once they have entered into the relationship.[10] On

6. Steven L. Nock, Laura Sanchez, Julia C. Wilson and James D. Wright, "Covenant Marriage Turns Five Years Old," *Michigan Journal of Gender and Law* 10 (2003): 169-88.

7. Catherine L. Fisk, "Removing the 'Fuel of Interest' from the 'Fire of Genius': Law and the Employee-Inventor, 1830-1930," *University of Chicago Law Review* 65 (1998): 1127-98.

8. Leland B. Ware, "Invisible Walls: An Examination of the Legal Strategy of the Restrictive Covenant Cases," *Washington University Law Quarterly* 67 (1989): 737-72; Donald W. Hansford, "Comment: Injunction Remedy for Breach of Restrictive Covenants: An Economic Analysis," *Mercer Law Review* 45 (1993): 543-58.

9. A related paper by a religion professor is William Johnson Everett, "Contract and Covenant in Human Community," *Emory Law Journal* 36 (1987): 557. Many of the ideas in this section of the chapter first appeared in Margaret F. Brinig and Steven L. Nock, "Covenant and Contract," *Regent University Law Review* 12 (2000): 9-26.

10. See, e.g., *In re Higgason's Marriage*, 516 P.2d 289 (Cal. 1973) (spousal support during

the other hand, parties to a covenant are *beyond* law in certain respects (though law may attempt to be imperialistic).[11] If law tries to change or redefine relationships such as that linking parent and child, by saying formal parental obligations end when the child reaches majority, it contradicts the essential nature of the bond.[12] If law says that a marriage is cleanly broken when the parties divorce, it flies in the face of the unhappiness of many concerned as well as the teachings of the church.[13] While the law may define formal, secular obligations in these ways, it does not alter the fundamental, enduring nature of those obligations accepted as part of covenant.

As covenant relationships develop, they show distinct patterns of call, response, promise, and sign. Biblical examples of covenant illustrate these clearly, as in the familiar Old Testament story of Noah and the flood (Gen. 6–8). Noah was called (7:1) because of his righteousness to build the ark to God's specifications and to enter the ark with his family and the animals. He obeyed. The promises God made were that he would send no more devastating floods (8:21; 9:15), that he would keep regular seasons (8:22), that he would give to people animals as well as plants for food (9:3), and that he would make humans fruitful (9:1, 7). In this account, we see the clear development of the four

---

marriage); *Kujawinski v. Kujawinski*, 376 N.E.2d 1382 (Ill. 1978) (support of college-aged child following divorce); *Buchanan v. Buchanan*, 170 Va. 458, 197 S.E. 426 (1938) (support of child after divorce); *Huckaby v. Huckaby*, 393 N.E.2d 1256 (Ill. 1979) (same); *Pappas v. Pappas*, 75 N.W.2d 264 (Iowa 1956) (same).

11. Margaret F. Brinig, *From Contract to Covenant: Beyond the Law and Economics of the Family* (Cambridge, Mass.: Harvard University Press, 2000).

12. For historical developments in the religious treatment of marriage, see generally John Witte Jr., *From Sacrament to Contract: Marriage, Religion, and Law in the Western Tradition* (Louisville: Westminster John Knox, 1997); John Witte Jr., "The Goods and Goals of Marriage," *Notre Dame Law Review* 76 (2001): 1019.

13. The Catechism of the Catholic Church (New York: Doubleday, 1995) points out that "The consent by which the spouses mutually give and receive one another is sealed by God himself. From their covenant arises 'an institution confirmed by the divine law, . . . even in the eyes of society.' The covenant between the spouses is integrated into God's covenant with man: 'Authentic love is caught up into divine love'" (p. 456, no. 1639). We also read there that "Thus *the marriage bond* has been established by God himself in such a way that a marriage concluded and consummated between baptized persons can never be dissolved. This bond, which results from the free human act of the spouses and their consummation of the marriage, is a reality, henceforth irrevocable, and gives rise to a covenant guaranteed by God's fidelity" (p. 457, no. 1640). Compare those statements with the statement on divorce by the United Methodist Church: "When a married couple is estranged beyond reconciliation, even after thoughtful consideration and counsel, divorce is a regrettable alternative in the midst of brokenness. . . . Although divorce publicly declares that a marriage no longer exists, other covenantal relationships resulting from the marriage remain, such as the nurture and support of children and extended family ties" (*The Book of Discipline of the United Methodist Church* [Nashville, Tenn., 2000], ¶161D).

points just raised. Noah was called from being a farmer and herder first to building, then equipping, and finally waiting in the ark. He responded by doing what God commanded, and he was eventually promised God's continued patience and faithfulness. The symbol or sign of this covenant is the rainbow (9:14), which reminds God and man of God's promise to refrain from again sending a flood.

Biblical covenant relationships promote interdependence and stability, and the institution of marriage should thus promote covenant ideas; the evidence we will present indicates that covenant marriage seems to do so.

Keep in mind that, unlike contracts, covenants need not extend only to husband and wife, but also may involve parents and children — even without the child's ability to consent.

Adam's story (Gen. 2–3) is in many ways like that of the typical parent-child relationship: the God of Genesis created Adam without Adam's promise or even knowledge, and, after literally giving him the world, God unilaterally imposed the condition of obedience upon him. God was to walk in the Garden of Eden (keeping Adam company), and he gave Adam all green plants to eat and the beasts to name. Genesis reports later that God created Eve as a helpmate fitting for Adam. Presumably, Adam at this point had eternal life, for it was only in his disobeying the warning not to eat of the fruit of the tree of knowledge of good and evil that he became subject to death (Gen. 3:19, 22-24). When Adam became disobedient, God did not turn away, but instead expelled him from the Garden so that he would not be able to eat of the tree of life. Adam then had to till the soil, and Eve had to experience pain in childbearing; even so, it was from their seed that God promised the Savior would come (Gen. 3:15).

### Unconditional Love

The story of Hosea illustrates both how unconditional love works in the family and how the Bible analogizes unconditional family love to the love God has for mankind and especially for his people. Unconditional love strikes against the heart of contract law. In the Bible story, the prophet Hosea was told by God to marry a woman of loose reputation and easy virtue. Although she had a series of lovers both before and after their marriage, Hosea continued to love her, and though he was angry at her unfaithfulness he always took her back (Hos. 1:2–3:5). He did not desert the promises he made. Hosea's wife is, of course, the allegorical counterpart to Israel, which time and again was unfaithful to the covenants made by Yahweh with Abraham, Isaac, and Jacob. A contract-based world allows a breach of promise so that one party may engage in a better opportunity.[14] This is called the concept of efficient breach.[15] Contract also implies a need to pay some attention to balances between contracting parties. It is clear from the Christian Bible that if God kept such a balance, without the redeeming work of Christ we would always fall short (Rom. 3:23; 2 Cor. 3:4-6, 12-14).

In stable, covenant-based families, couples do not keep precise track of who owes what to whom. Couples who *do not keep* precise track of who owes what to whom have more stable marriages. For example, in the 1987 to 1988 National Survey of Families and Households,[16] couples were asked how much time they and their spouse spent each week on various household tasks. The spouses were questioned as well, and the responses were found to be highly consistent. The second wave of the study tracked the same people five years later, in 1992 to 1994. Some of the couples had divorced or separated during those five years; others remained intact. Those who thought the division of labor in the household and in the labor market was "just about fair" were more likely to divorce or separate than those who thought the division of work and household tasks were unfair to the other person.[17]

In contrast, a Virginia divorce case involves a wife who thought a contract-like tit-for-tat exchange was necessary. She testified that after the first several years of marriage she felt that a psychological wall was being erected between her and her husband.[18] Each time he did something that wronged her, another brick was added to the wall, so that finally she could not communicate with him at all.

Similarly, both of us have known couples who kept track of how many arguments they had, how many chores each did, or how often they engaged in sexual intercourse. Such keeping track, or expecting loving gestures to be returned, flies in the face of a covenant relationship. We may say covenant relationships are characterized by duty or responsibility[19] rather than by "inherently dynamic emotional states."[20]

14. Margaret F. Brinig, "Status, Contract and Covenant," *Cornell Law Review* 79 (1994): 1573, 1586.

15. Ian MacNeil, "Efficient Breach of Contract: Circles in the Sky," *Virginia Law Review* 68 (1983): 47.

16. James Sweet, Larry Bumpass, and Vaughn Call, "The Design and Content of the National Survey of Families and Households," NSFH Working Paper (Madison, Wisconsin, 1988).

17. Steven L. Nock and Margaret F. Brinig, "Weak Men and Disorderly Women: Divorce and the Division of Labor," in *The Law and Economics of Marriage and Divorce*, ed. Antony W. Dnes and Robert Rowthorn (Cambridge: Cambridge University Press, 2002), p. 85.

18. *Sprott v. Sprott*, 233 Va. 238, 255 S.E.2d 881 (1987).

19. Mary Ann Glendon, *The New Family and the New Property* (Toronto: Butterworths, 1981), pp. 121-30.

20. Milton C. Regan Jr., *Alone Together: Law and the Meaning of Marriage* (New York: Oxford University Press, 1999), p. 67.

There is biological evidence suggesting a difference between contract and covenant-like relationships as well. Helen Fisher[21] reports that two different hormones (or pheromones) are given off during relationships. During the initial stage of the relationship, the hormones create sexual passion and total concern with the other. After several years, these hormones fade and are replaced by a different sort, the kind that characterizes affection rather than passion. Another way of looking at the phenomenon is to note that contracts frequently involve short-term relationships or even instantaneous exchanges (more like the passion).[22] Covenants, because they are designed to be permanent, assume that the balances will be righted eventually — that things will be "a wash" or that imbalance does not matter.[23] (This is more like the affectionate relationships Fisher describes.) Participants in covenants are thus more altruistic than are participants in contracts.

Keeping score of who does what and who owes whom appears to produce less satisfactory unions, while extensive dependencies are central to producing good marriages.[24] In other words, married people appear to thrive when they depend on one another yet do not keep score. Sociologists and economists have investigated factors that foster *commitment* in marriage. Such research seeks to determine why some individuals are more likely than others to remain in a marriage. Commitment is typically understood as the perceived costs of ending the marriage. If an individual envisions no costs whatsoever of ending his or her marriage, then we may say such a person has no commitment to the union. Some economic theory argues that dependency is a primary factor in producing commitment.[25] As couples negotiate the demands of married life, they come to depend on one another more and more. The routine demands of household labor, for instance, require a complex arrangement for shopping, cleaning, caring for children, keeping the checkbook, and many other things. As

21. Helen E. Fisher, "The Four Year Itch," *Natural History* 96 (1987): 22-33.

22. Anthony Kronman, "Contract Law and the State of Nature," *Journal of Law, Economics and Organization* 1 (1985): 5-32.

23. Hosea 6:5-6: "What shall I do with you, O Ephraim? What shall I do with you, O Judah? Your love is like a morning cloud, like the dew that goes early away." In contrast, see G. K. Chesterton, *What's Wrong with the World* (New York: Dodd, Mead, and Company, 1910): "The child must depend on the most imperfect mother; the mother may be devoted to the most unworthy children; in such relations legal revenges are vain. . . . The essential element is not so much duration as security. Two people must be tied together in order to do themselves justice; for twenty minutes at a dance or for twenty years in a marriage."

24. Steven L. Nock, "Commitment and Dependency in Marriage," *Journal of Marriage and Family* 57 (1995): 503-14.

25. Gary S. Becker, *A Treatise on the Family* (Cambridge, Mass.: Harvard University Press, 1991), chap. 2.

couples settle into routines, they become increasingly interdependent. There are also very objective bases for dependency. Most wives earn less than their husbands and, therefore, may be presumed to be dependent on their spouses' earnings.[26]

Research shows that objective dependencies do foster commitment. When partners depend on one another for income or social status, there is greater commitment to the marriage. Objective dependencies of that sort are much less important than spousal *obligation,* however. In an analysis of the National Survey of Families and Households, Nock showed that the strongest predictor of individual commitment to a marriage is the imagined consequences of separation *for the spouse.*[27] After removing the effects of objective types of dependencies (that is, income, education, occupational status, and children), the belief that separation would negatively affect one's husband or wife was significantly more important for individual commitment to a marriage than anything else. The imagined consequences of divorce for one's partner may be taken as a crude measure of an individual's sense of his or her marital obligations or the enduring nature of them. Both husbands and wives who believe their partners depend on them are much more committed to their marriages. Such research suggests that marriages founded on extensive dependencies are stronger. It also suggests that married couples who envision mutual, long-term, and enduring obligations to each other have stronger marriages.

### Permanence

The biblical story of David and Jonathan (1 Sam. 18–20) is one of the many that could be selected to show the permanence of covenant relationships,[28] a concept closely related to the unconditional love discussed above. Jonathan made a covenant with David because, the Bible reports, he "loved David as his own soul" (20:17). David said that if he had any guilt involving Jonathan's father Saul, Jonathan should slay David himself. Jonathan asked God to be witness that he would disclose faithfully whether Saul would do David harm or not, and later Jonathan blessed David and asked him not to cut off his loyalty from his house forever: "When the LORD cuts off every one of the enemies of David

26. Amy L. Wax, "Bargaining in the Shadow of the Market: Is There a Future for Egalitarian Marriage?" *Virginia Law Review* 84 (1997): 509-672; Katherine T. Silbaugh, "Marriage Contracts and the Family Economy," *Northwestern University Law Review* 93 (1998): 65-144.

27. Nock, "Commitment and Dependency."

28. Permanence is a theme amply developed by Witte, "The Goods and Goals of Marriage," pp. 1045-1047.

from the face of the earth, let not the name of Jonathan be cut off from the house of David. . . . And as for the matter about which you and I have spoken, behold, the LORD is between you and me for ever" (1 Sam. 20:15, 23). According to the Bible, God's covenant is thus an everlasting covenant.

The Hebrews repeatedly broke God's law, given to Moses in the form of the Ten Commandments, not just in the time of Moses but also in the succeeding generations. According to Saint Paul, this written covenant did not replace the essential one God had made from the beginning, one that was finally fulfilled in Christ.[29]

In the same way, various human rules and regulations (and even the law of the parties signified by their personal contract) cannot change the essential nature of the parent-child or husband-wife relationship. If we have a law requiring us to support aged parents,[30] this does not supplant our *moral* need to do so[31]

---

29. Jeremiah 31:31-34:

> Behold, the days are coming, says the LORD, when I will make a new covenant with the house of Israel and the house of Judah, not like the covenant which I made with their fathers when I took them by the hand to bring them out of the land of Egypt, my covenant which they broke, though I was their husband, says the LORD. But this is the covenant which I will make with the house of Israel after those days, says the LORD: I will put my law within them, and I will write it upon their hearts, and I will be their God, and they shall be my people. And no longer shall each man teach his neighbor and each his brother, saying, "Know the LORD," for they shall all know me, from the least of them to the greatest, says the LORD; for I will forgive their iniquity and I will remember their sin no more. . . .

The distinction between law and covenant also forms part of the background for the question put to Jesus by the Sadducees in Luke 20:27-36. A woman had married a series of men after their brothers died, according to the laws of Moses. If the marriage promises were forever, how could she be faithful to all of them in heaven? Jesus replied, of course, that in the world of men, there are marriages by the law of man. In heaven, the laws of man are no more.

See also Jeremiah 32:38-41: "And they shall be my people, and I will be their God. I will give them one heart and one way, that they may fear me for ever, for their own good and the good of their children after them. I will make with them an everlasting covenant, that I will not turn away from doing good to them; and I will put the fear of me in their hearts, that they may not turn from me. I will rejoice in doing them good, and I will plant them in this land in faithfulness, with all my heart and all my soul."

30. For example, Va. Code § 20-61 (2000) provides for misdemeanor punishment for any person deserting or willfully neglecting or refusing to pay support of an adult child or aged parent who is handicapped or otherwise incapacitated when the child or parent is in necessitous circumstances.

31. Compare 2 Corinthians 3:4-6, 12-14, proclaiming that "Such is the confidence that we have through Christ toward God. Not that we are sufficient of ourselves to claim anything as coming from us; our sufficiency is from God, who has qualified us to be ministers of a new cov-

even beyond the poverty level,[32] for such services "are presumably rendered in obedience to natural promptings of love and affection, loyalty, and filial duty, rather than upon an expectation of compensation."[33] To take another example, our marriage vows to love one another are stronger than those the state makes against assault,[34] or marital rape,[35] or even the divorce grounds of cruelty.[36] Laws against child abuse cannot replace our duty as parents to fulfill our children's trust as well as to educate and properly raise them.[37] The covenant is thus like the "deeper magic" that C. S. Lewis writes of in *The Lion, the Witch and the Wardrobe*:

> "It means," said Aslan, "that though the Witch knew the Deep Magic [of blood sacrifice for sin], there is a magic deeper still which she did not know. Her knowledge goes back only to the dawn of Time. But if she could have looked a little further Back, into the stillness and the darkness before Time dawned, she would have read there a different incantation. She would have known that when a willing victim who had committed no treachery was killed in a traitor's stead, the Table would crack and Death itself would start working backwards."[38]

### Involvement of God As Witness

Many of the biblical descriptions of covenants involving God as witness are horizontal; that is, they involve covenants between people instead of promises made exclusively between man and God. With these horizontal covenants, often between leaders or between kings and their people, God was called upon to serve as a witness. Then, if one of the parties was not present at the making of the promise or the promise needed to be executed sometime in the future, God

---

enant, not in a written code but in the Spirit; for the written code kills, but the Spirit gives life. . . ."

32. *Mitchell-Powers Hardware Co. Eaton,* 171 Va. 255, 263, 198 S.E.2d 496, 500 (1938) states that the obligor "must do more than relieve pangs of hunger, provide shelter and furnish only enough clothes to cover the nakedness of the parent."

33. *Jacobs v. Church,* 36 Va. Cir. 277 (Spotsylvania Co. 1995).

34. *Counts v. Counts,* 221 Va. 151, 266 S.E.2d 895 (1980); Va. Code § 18.2-57.

35. *Weishaupt v. Commonwealth,* 227 Va. 389, 315 S.E.2d 847 (1984); Va. Code §§ 18.2-61 (2005).

36. Va. Code Ann. §§ 20-91(6) (2005).

37. Margaret F. Brinig, "Finite Horizons? The American Family," *International Journal of Children's Rights* 2 (1994): 293-315.

38. C. S. Lewis, *The Lion, the Witch and the Wardrobe* (New York: Macmillan, 1950), pp. 159-60.

(or a stone or a pillar, standing for God) was a reminder that the covenant was permanent.

A commercial contract, by contrast, is typically a spot contract, with expectations of immediate or nearly immediate performance.[39] Covenants, or especially important contracts like wills[40] or deeds,[41] require other (disinterested) witnesses to be involved since everyone knows that both parties to the promise may not be around at the critical time. Many of the biblical covenants of this type involved kingship or the Levitic priesthood.

The story of Jacob (Gen. 30–31)[42] is a good example to use since again it involves families. Jacob, whose youth and even birth involved some rather shady doings at his brother's expense (25:19-34; 27:1–28:1), also had a stormy relationship with his father-in-law, Laban. When the covenant between the two men was made (31:43-55), Jacob got his kinsmen to help him set up a pile of stones. The two promised mutual non-aggression, and Laban got Jacob to swear that he would not mistreat his wives (Laban's daughters) nor their children. Jacob left with the two wives, their considerable households, and a large fortune in disputed goats. This act shows the actual cleaving of Rachel and Leah to their husband after leaving their father (cf. 2:24),[43] as well as that God is to act as witness to the men's promises. Laban said to Jacob, "See this heap [literally, a "witness heap"] and the pillar, which I have set between you and me. This heap is a witness, and the pillar is a witness, that I will not pass over this heap to you, and you will not pass over this heap and this pillar to me, for harm. The God of Abraham and the God of Nahor, the God of their father, judge between us" (31:52-53).

Secular explanations for the importance of God's witness have been advanced by sociologists for over a century. French sociologist Émile Durkheim[44] argued that religion influences behavior because individuals experience social norms *as divine*. In trying to understand the influence of religion on the family, it is tempting to focus on individuals' religious beliefs or values. But Durkheim argued that another element is also important, perhaps more so.

The idea of a purely private religion is unthinkable, as is the idea of a

---

39. Kronman, "Contract Law and the State of Nature," p. 59.

40. Va. Code Ann. § 64.1-49 (2005) (requisites for validity).

41. Va. Code Ann. §§ 55-48, 55-106 (2005) (acknowledgement of deed).

42. A beautiful fictional parallel is Katherine Paterson, *Jacob Have I Loved* (New York: Crowell, 1980).

43. This "cleaving" is what Judith Wallerstein and Sandra Blakeslee assert makes up the first important step in successful marriages. *The Good Marriage: How and Why Love Lasts* (Boston: Houghton Mifflin, 1995).

44. Émile Durkheim, *The Elementary Forms of the Religious Life* (New York: Free Press, 1965).

purely private language. Religion is also a social institution. A person's private faith is not a religion until it is held by others.[45] A community of believers is a social reality. It is not necessarily a group of persons such as a congregation, but those who share a religious faith are bound together in a fundamentally social relationship. They all conform, to some degree, to the rules, norms, moral values, and beliefs *of fellow believers.* Durkheim argued that the ability of religious beliefs to direct behaviors is inherently social. The social pressure to conform to group norms, he argued, is experienced as a divine power — something not springing from the group, but arising outside it.

Although individuals may form covenants with God (we do this today in our vocations or "callings"), the making of covenants usually involves the witness of others.

## Implications of Covenant for Modern Relationships

Marriage, but not cohabitation, involves a covenant. Marriage is much more permanent than is cohabitation,[46] and more apt to be characterized by unconditional love.[47] Almost by definition, the marriage ceremony involves at least the witness of the community,[48] and frequently the witness and blessing of God.[49] Covenant marriage, to the extent that it is more likely to be permanent than "traditional marriage" because of more pre- and post-marital counseling[50] and because the "transaction costs" of divorce are higher,[51] is even more likely to reflect the kinds of covenants discussed earlier.

45. For example, see *Welsh v. United States,* 348 U.S. 333 (1970) (conscientious objector could not refuse service on the basis of his "merely personal moral code"); *Johnson v. Prince William County Board of Educ.,* 241 Va. 383, 404 S.E.2d 209 (1991) (bona fides of religious belief for home schooling not met when opposition to school attendance came from a "merely personal moral code").

46. Lynne M. Casper and Suzanne M. Bianchi, *Continuity and Change in the American Family* (Thousand Oaks, Calif.: Sage, 2002).

47. Nock, "Commitment and Dependency."

48. See, e.g., W. Va. Code Ann. § 48-2-404 (2005) ("We are gathered here, in the presence of these witnesses, to join together this man and this woman in matrimony"). There can be no secret common law marriage, for the "holding out" to the general public is one of the most important ingredients. See, e.g., *In re Estate of Dallman,* 228 N.W. 2d 187, 190 (Iowa 1977); *Ex Parte Threet,* 160 Tex. 482, 333 S.E.2d 361, 364 (1960).

49. Brinig, "Status, Contract, and Covenant," p. 1599.

50. Katherine Shaw Spaht, "For the Sake of the Children: Recapturing the Meaning of Marriage," *Notre Dame Law Review* 73 (1998): 1547, 1567-69.

51. Margaret F. Brinig and F. H. Buckley, "No-Fault Laws and At-Fault People," *International Review of Law and Economics* 18 (1998): 325-40.

Parent-child covenants illustrate some of the problems occasioned when law tries arbitrarily to cut off relationships at a given time.[52] Because the parent-child relationship is a permanent one, the idea that children suddenly reach independence from parents at age eighteen is unrealistic, and perhaps undermines the earlier relationship. The fact that contemporary adults feel that they ought to be financially and often physically independent even when they become very old[53] also contradicts the idea of covenant.[54]

No-fault divorce, to the extent that it pretends that a "clean break" can occur between spouses of long standing,[55] particularly those who are parents,[56] also contradicts the characteristics of covenant. This suggests that rules of joint custody[57] or of custody shared to the extent it was before the parties separated[58] may better promote the substantial and unconditional loving that should take place between parent and child.

Covenant is a concept that takes us beyond contract. Indeed, the idea that marriages (or society, for that matter) could be organized around contracts, solely, is flawed. In every contract there are actually two: one is the contract we make with another person, but the other is the hidden contract we all make among ourselves to obey the rules of the first contract.[59] Behind the idea of contracts, in other words, is the more fundamental idea of trust that contracts will be honored. While contracts presume rational self-interest and seek to promote and protect it, trust is inherently nonrational. Covenant is more like trust than contract. Alternatively, covenant is faith not based on rationality.

We introduced our topic with a notion of three things required of covenantal relationship, which we consider again here in the modern context as permanence, unconditional love, and community. An alternative way of think-

---

52. Margaret F. Brinig, "The Family Franchise: Elderly Parents and Adult Siblings," *Utah Law Review* (1996): 393-428, at 421.

53. John H. Langbein, "The Twentieth-Century Revolution in Family Wealth Transmission," *Michigan Law Review* 86 (1988): 722-51.

54. Brinig, "Status, Contract, and Covenant."

55. Margaret F. Brinig, "Property Distribution Physics: The Talisman of Time and Middle Class Law," *Family Law Quarterly* 31 (1997): 93-118; Jana B. Singer, "Divorce Reform and Gender Justice," *North Carolina Law Review* 67 (1987): 1103-22, at 1017-21.

56. Brinig and Buckley, "No-Fault Laws," pp. 419-20.

57. Margaret F. Brinig and F. H. Buckley, "Joint Custody: Bonding and Monitoring Theories," *Indiana Law Journal* 73 (1998): 393-427.

58. American Law Institute, *Principles of the Law of Family Dissolution*, § 2.09 (2002); John S. Murray, "Improving Parent-Child Relationships within the Divorced Family: A Call for Legal Reform," *University of Michigan Journal of Law Reform* 19 (1986): 563-600.

59. Thus the principled objection to "efficient breach" is that as a society we lose respect for this hidden contract. MacNeil, "Efficient Breach of Contract."

ing about the need for permanence looks at what happens if we know that a relationship is not permanent, and in fact is about to terminate very soon. Economists refer to decision-making when the actor knows the end is in sight as "the last period problem."[60] Even if the decision-maker has behaved in a cooperative way previously, in the last period he or she has every incentive to take advantage of the situation and try to cheat the other. In fact, this will lead to the "unraveling" of any cooperative deals made since the other actor will also know of the likely defection and will take precautions.[61]

A commercial contractual example of the last period problem is the case of *Bak-A-Lum Corp. of America v. Alcoa Bldg. Prods., Inc.*[62] A distributor had served for some years as the exclusive distributor of ALCOA's goods. Eventually ALCOA arranged with others to sell its products in the same geographic area, but did not tell the distributor, who meanwhile expanded its warehouse and spent significant sums advertising ALCOA's goods. When the distributor sued, the manufacturer explained its behavior as follows:

> The men at [ALCOA] in charge of sales thought a period of secrecy ending with a sudden announcement to Mr. Diamond [plaintiff Bak-A-Lum's president] of the accomplished fact of new distributors would avoid any risk of cooling plaintiff's interest in selling ALCOA products during the several months before the new distributors were named and made ready to go.

The legal result in Bak-A-Lum was that ALCOA had to pay for what the distributor would have profited over a long enough period of time to enable it to wind down the investments made in reliance on the continuation of the contract. Courts are thus aware of the temptation to take advantage in a self-serving way once a definite end of the relationship is in sight.

Similarly, we see that marriage, unlike more fleeting relationships, features unconditional giving rather than a series of reciprocal gift-givings.[63] The many things spouses do for each other cannot simply be regulated as a series of contracts because so much of the giving is unconditional. Thus, permanence and unconditional love go hand-in-hand.

60. Henry N. Butler, "The Contractual Theory of the Corporation," *George Mason University Law Review* 11, no. 4 (1989): 99; Mitu Gulati, "When Corporate Managers Fear a Good Thing Is Coming to an End: The Case of Interim Nondisclosure," *UCLA Law Review* 46 (1999): 675-756, at 713-16.

61. Richard A. Posner, *Aging and Old Age* (Chicago: University of Chicago Press, 1995), pp. 58-61.

62. 351 A.2d 349 (N.J. 1976).

63. Allen Parkman, "The Importance of Gifts in Marriage," *Economic Inquiry* 42 (2004): 483-95.

Finally, marriage is unique because it involves the presence of and partnership with God or at least with the larger community. Marriage is not simply contract or sexual connection without more. The involvement of people in a community of others who share common beliefs and values, and who regularly celebrate them in unchanging fashion, helps to infuse customary behaviors with a sense of awe and sacredness. This is the function of ritual.

Ritual gives us a sense of being able to relax in what is counted on, as Antoine de St. Exupery, speaking through the fox, explains in *The Little Prince*.[64] It is important for the fox to set a regular hour of meeting with the Prince so the fox can look forward to it and prepare in joyful expectation. Such regularity works for unhappy events as well: if we know that a certain evil is coming, we can "rest up" to meet it. Thus the fox, knowing human schedules, gets a regular "day off" from the hunters, who go drinking every Thursday.

The relationships among the faithful come to be experienced as divine as a result of *rituals*. Durkheim noted[65] that every religious tradition is based on scrupulous adherence to conventional rituals. Religion may be thought of as an institution that divides the world into two spheres, the sacred and the profane. The profane is understandable and ordinary. The sacred is mysterious. Rituals serve to connect the sacred with the profane. By reciting prayers, singing verses, kneeling, bowing, fasting, or feasting according to strict rules, individuals collectively *experience the profane as sacred*. Most individuals will say or sing things out loud in collective prayer or song that they probably would not say in conversation. Something about the ritual makes it possible to say such things. According to Durkheim, something about the ritual transforms the profane into the sacred. And that something is the presence of other people doing exactly the same things.

The religiously faithful conform to standards of conduct held out as worthy by those of their faith, and Durkheim argued that such conformity springs from shared or collective religious conviction. Individuals do not experience such conformity as secular or social. The Ten Commandments are not understood or experienced as social norms. But the sanctions for disobeying them are completely social, whether individuals believe that rewards or punishments will follow in this or in another life. In short, the influence of religion according to Durkheim may be thought to reside in personal values, but such values exist in a social environment. It is only the witness of others that creates the experience of the divine. Religious conformity, that is, is a form of social control.

---

64. Antoine de St. Exupery, *The Little Prince,* trans. Katherine Woods (New York: Reynal and Hitchcock, 1943), p. 68.

65. Durkheim, *Elementary Forms of Religious Life.*

## Public vs. Private Reality

Public secular law cannot, even in principle, enforce the personal commitment embodied in a marriage covenant. Nor should it ever be expected to. The former East Germany had a statute (§10 FGB) that mandated that housework was an equal responsibility of husbands and wives.[66] Although this legislation might seem admirable to advocates of equality for women, and although it promoted a higher level of women's employment than did its West German counterpart[67] which allowed for negotiation of household management within each family, it did so at a significant cost to the family. Though in 1988 more than twice as many married women were employed in East Germany, crude divorce rates for 1989 were approximately 50 percent higher behind the Iron Curtain.[68]

Even when couples attempt to share the workload in regard to household and child-care tasks, the balance achieved matters primarily because of how it is experienced and perceived. Some have proposed that the "solution" to the unequal organization of household responsibilities lies in equality like that of the German legislative experiment — achieving equal (or proportionate) shares of responsibility for tasks and responsibilities.[69] We stress, however, that equality is not the same thing as equity. The latter refers to the perceived fairness or justice in a particular circumstance. Research has shown that perceived fairness (that is, perceived equity) is considerably more important in predicting and explaining divorce than is equality (or deviations from it).[70]

On the other hand, recent empirical work[71] tends to show that privately negotiated arrangements, even if not strictly "equal" or "fair," have salutary effects on marital stability. This research investigates the consequences of the actual arrangements selected by husbands and wives in the late 1980s. The data from the National Survey of Families and Households[72] show that one spouse doing a larger share of so-called women's work endangers marriages, regardless

---

66. Margaret F. Brinig, "Equality and Sharing: Views of Household across the Iron Curtain," *European Journal of Law and Economics* 7 (1999): 55-63.

67. Civil Code, BGB § 1356(1).

68. William J. Goode, *World Changes in Divorce Patterns* (New Haven: Yale University Press, 1993), pp. 27, 129.

69. See, for example, Linda C. McClain, "The Domain of Civil Virtue in a Good Society: Families, Schools, and Sex Equality," *Fordham Law Review* 69 (2001): 1617-66.

70. Nock and Brinig, "Weak Men and Disorderly Women"; Liana C. Sayer and Suzanne M. Bianchi, "Women's Economic Independence and the Probability of Divorce: A Review and Reexamination," *Journal of Family Issues* 21 (2000): 906-43.

71. Nock and Brinig, "Weak Men and Disorderly Women."

72. Sweet, Bumpass, and Call, "Design and Content."

of which spouse does it. Greater involvement in traditionally female housework by either partner is associated with higher chances of divorce or separation. However, and more relevant for this project, the consequences of the time that husbands and wives spend in various tasks is strongly conditioned by perceptions of fairness. The most stable relationships were those in which husbands correctly perceived that their wives were doing more hours of paid and unpaid work, and agreed with their wives that the arrangement was "unfair to her."

Autonomy thus works much better than state mandate, but occasionally couples deviate too far. When the state makes particularly bad guesses, shadow institutions will take over. For example, limits on (legislative) divorce in the eighteenth century led to shadow institutions like informal marriage after one party just deserted the other.[73] Divorce reform, though it does affect the permanence of marriage, is likely to work the same way. Though a number of states have entertained proposals for mutual consent divorce or limiting "no-fault" divorce when there are minor children, none has passed.[74] In fact, even the modern covenant marriage legislation may be somewhat hampered by spouses just leaving the jurisdiction when they want to exit the marriage more quickly than their original choice would permit.[75] We therefore prefer an emphasis on custody reform[76] or on changing the nature of marriage.

A recent paper by Nock, Sanchez, Wilson, and Wright[77] suggests that covenant marriage in Louisiana may in fact be changing the essential nature of marriage. Covenant marriage couples are different from those who select standard marriage from the very beginning. Covenant couples have marginally higher levels of completed education, are more politically conservative, are more religious, are more likely to seek and receive marriage counseling, have more support (in terms of approval of the marriage, and for help and assistance). Covenant couples are less likely to have cohabited before marriage. They are also more likely to rely on more pro-social forms of communication and conflict resolution (that is, they are less likely to engage in destructive or hostile forms

73. Richard Chused, *Private Acts in Public Places: A Social History of Divorce in the Formative Era of American Family Laws* (Philadelphia: University of Pennsylvania Press, 1994).

74. For updates, consult www.divorcereform.org/legislation.

75. F. H. Buckley and Larry E. Ribstein, "Calling a Truce in the Marriage Wars," *University of Illinois Law Review* (2001): 561-610; American Law Institute, *Principles*, §7.08.

76. Margaret F. Brinig and Douglas W. Allen, "These Boots Are Made for Walking: Why Most Divorce Filers are Women," *American Law and Economics Review* 2 (2000): 126-68; American Law Institute, *Principles*, §2.09. West Virginia adopted the ALI custody reform proposal in 2000.

77. Steven L. Nock, Laura Sanchez, Julia C. Wilson, and James D. Wright, "Intimate Equity: The Early Years of Covenant and Standard Marriages." Presented at the Annual Meeting of the Population Association of America, Minneapolis, 2003.

of conflict resolution such as avoidance, sarcasm, or hostility). At the time they marry, however, covenant couples have very similar incomes and labor force involvements to those of standard marriage couples.

Nock, Sanchez, Wilson, and Wright found that by the end of the second year of marriage, covenant couples were different (had changed) on a number of different indices. They describe the difference as *institutionalization of the marriage*. Covenant couples describe their marriages as involving three parties: the husband, the wife, and the marriage itself. For covenant couples, the marriage warrants consideration apart from the individualistic concerns of either partner. In regard to some matters, covenant couples appear to defer to the interests of their marriage even when the individual concerns of the partners may appear to conflict. And this orientation to married life arguably helps resolve the customary problems faced by newly married couples in regard to fairness and equity. First, covenant couples endorse traditional marital vows with strong personal commitments (marriage for life, the central role of children in marriage, the role marriage plays in producing a complete individual, and so on) far more often and more strongly than do standard marriage couples. Covenant wives are more traditional with respect to gender ideals, and they have marriages that are seemingly more equitable.

This greater commitment to marriage as an institution and a way of life is why the family incomes of covenant couples grows faster than those of couples in standard marriages in the first two years of marriage. It also explains why covenant couples show greater satisfaction with the marriage and with other areas such as the sharing of household tasks and child care.[78]

## How Communities Aid Marriage and Marriage Aids Communities

### *Sources of Information about Relationships*

Our social networks educate us about our relationships. There is obviously a continuum between the proverbial locker-room conversation about sexual exploits and the (one hopes) more useful things parents teach children about dispute resolution, childbearing and childrearing, and simple manners. Much of this education goes on before we begin grown-up relationships, but parents remain sources of support and guidance long after we become adults. Grandparents and others in the wider community also provide cultural guidelines within which to pursue relationships as well as gain experience about lasting relation-

78. Nock et al., "Intimate Equity."

ships. This type of help is particularly evident in African-American and first-generation American communities. Sometimes such information-passing is more formalized. In some religious traditions and for those electing covenant marriage in Arizona, Arkansas, and Louisiana, couples must attend marriage preparation classes. Generally speaking, this more formalized community involvement is designed to continue during marriage as well.

## Investment

Historically, many families seeking to immigrate to this country have sent a potential high earner along first to establish a foothold and then pay for the others' passage. Such investments by families can also be made by the wider community. In the business and corporate world, much has been made of the ability of new Asian immigrants to the United States to pool assets and earnings to establish funds from which all members can draw. Observers have credited much of the success of the small businesses run by first-generation Asian-Americans to such cooperative financial support (along, of course, with the tremendous industry of the individuals involved).[79]

## Insurance

As Elizabeth and Robert Scott have written,[80] marriage often serves an insurance function. If a marriage contains two potential labor force participants, one can work if the other becomes unemployed or unemployable. Historically, couples often had many children to ensure that at least some could support their parents in old age or carry on the family name, and to do the varied necessary tasks around the homestead.[81] In day-to-day life, many parents rely on their spouse's availability to do chauffeuring and other child-care work if a child gets ill or there is a "snow day." One of Brinig's Indian-American students has told her that the wedding ring she wears, which is not a straight but a wavy circlet in the Hindu tradition, signifies each spouse's duty not only to weather hard times but to help pull the other back to a more central path.

79. Eric A. Posner, "The Regulation of Groups: The Influence of Legal and Nonlegal Sanctions on Collective Action," *University of Chicago Law Review* 63 (1996): 133-98.

80. Elizabeth S. Scott and Robert E. Scott, "Marriage As Relational Contract," *Virginia Law Review* 84 (1998): 1225-1334.

81. See Glenda Riley, *The Female Frontier: A Comparative View of Women on the Prairie and the Plains* (Lawrence: University Press of Kansas, 1988).

## *Dispute Resolution and "Venting"*

When we have had a rough day at the job, whether outside or inside the home, our families, and particularly our spouses, provide helpful ears for our venting. Social science support for the importance of this function is quite extensive. In fact, a paper by Chalandra Bryant and Rand Conger[82] both reviews the literature and establishes a new point: even in marriages of more than fourteen years, relationship-specific support significantly predicted more stable and successful marriages, while friends in common and general personal support did not.

Families are often the best settings to resolve disputes, especially when the wider support group is brought in. The Native American community began the Navajo Peacemaker Court in 1982 because the civil state courts were contrary to Navajo tradition of having the perpetrator and the victim directly "talk out" the problem, with help from family and clans. For example, in domestic violence situations, the Peacemaker Court would restore the victim to her former self — called her state of *hozhó*. The perpetrator, with the assistance of his family and clan, does the restoring.[83]

## *Conventions, Behavior-Channeling, and Union-Building*

Spouses, families, and the wider community are useful in establishing morals, or, more broadly, culture. Culture in this sense includes such mundane decisions as whether and in what way to celebrate one's anniversary, Valentine's Day, or Father's Day. More important, conventions and behavior-channeling include expectations about the duration of marriage; what justifies leaving or divorcing one's spouse; what kind of conduct is acceptable, what cruel. Empirical research shows, for example, that the percentage of divorced people living in the state where a person lived when sixteen years old predicts the age at which that person will marry and even how much education a woman will receive. A higher percentage of divorces predicts an older age at first marriage as well as fewer completed years of school.[84] We know, for example, that in places where

---

82. Chalandra M. Bryant and Rand D. Conger, "Marital Success and Domains of Social Support in Long-Term Relationships: Does the Influence of Network Members Ever End?" *Journal of Marriage & Family* (1999): 437-50.

83. James W. Zion, Elsie V. Zion, and Hozho Sokee, "Stay Together Nicely: Domestic Violence under Navajo Common Law," *Arizona State Law Journal* 25 (1991): 407-26.

84. John H. Johnson and Christopher J. Mazingo, "The Economic Consequences of Unilateral Divorce for Children," University of Illinois, Dept. of Economics, Working Paper 00-1122, SSRN abstract = 236227.

there is a culture of single parenting and/or divorce, more divorces occur, even holding other explanatory variables constant.[85]

## The Central Place of Religion in Relationships

Many of the earlier observations suggest a linkage between the wider community involvement and religion. Obviously, religious authorities can marry people (and in some countries this is exclusively true). Marriages "in" a religion can subject couples to a set of ecclesiastical rules as well as secular ones. Certainly there are strong marriages that are not part of a religious tradition. Moreover, if Catholics and fundamentalist Protestants, for example, divorce at about the same rate as does the general public, is it strong religious tradition or personal adherence that is important in maintaining marital stability?[86]

Most studies find that the stated religious preference at the time of marriage has very little effect on marital stability. Two Methodists marrying, holding other things constant, will divorce about as often as two Catholics, two Jews, or two atheists. A study by the George Barna research group found that born-again Christians are slightly more likely to divorce than the average American (with rates of 27 as opposed to 23 percent of a group of more than three thousand randomly selected adults). A more recent Associated Press article[87] published statistics showing that the so-called Bible Belt states had higher divorce rates than the national average. This higher divorce rate may be caused by both economics as well as religion. Since those with lower incomes and unstable employment have higher divorce rates, one would expect more divorce in poorer regions of the country (the Bible Belt especially). Although this piece noted that Protestants seem to divorce more often than Catholics, the gap seems to be decreasing;[88] still, remarriage for Catholics happens less frequently.[89]

85. Brinig and Allen, "These Boots"; Margaret F. Brinig and F. H. Buckley, "The Price of Virtue," *Public Choice* 98 (1999): 111-29.

86. Myra Beckstrom, "Pollster's Data Tell Churches How Their Believers Behave," *Commercial Appeal* (Aug. 17, 1996): 16A.

87. Associated Press, "Bible Belt States Struggling with Divorce," *Iowa City Press-Citizen* (Nov. 13, 1999): 7A.

88. William Sander, "Catholicism and Marriage in the United States," *Demography* 30 (1993): 373; Bob Mims, "Stats Show Mormons Buck Secularization," *The Salt Lake Tribune* (March 6, 1999): C1.

89. Barbara F. Wilson and Sally C. Clarke, "Remarriages: A Demographic Profile," *Journal of Family Issues* 13 (1992): 123-41.

Religious intensity seems more important than affiliation, however, so that difference in religious observance and the importance of God in one's life do affect couples' ability to stay together over the period in question.[90] Vaughn Call and Tim Heaton found that when both spouses attend religious services regularly, the couple has the lowest risk of divorce, while a difference in church attendance between couples increased the risk of divorce. They posit that church attendance "can either provide a common forum for a couple's religious orientation and family commitment or become a conflict for couples who do not share the same levels of personal dedication." They note that joint participation in church gives a family a sense of purpose and similar values that increase family commitment and social integration. Like other studies, the Call and Heaton study found that all significant religious *affiliation* (though not strength of religious belief and/or behavior) influences disappear once the authors controlled for demographic differences. Call and Heaton's findings showed the negative effects in cases where the spouses differed in church activities, because "joint socialization in religious teachings that support family values and stability affirm the importance of marriage and family," and "joint participation in friendship networks provides a greater potential for interaction with friends in a context that generally supports positive communication between spouses."[91]

Another reason religious homogeneity may be important is that it increases attachment to the community in which the couple lives. Spitze and South found that home ownership increased marital stability and that living in a large metropolitan area (whether in a suburb or central city) decreased it.[92] In earlier work, Buckley and Brinig found that divorce rates from 1979 to 1991 were higher both in metropolitan areas[93] and in "frontier" states.[94]

## The Rationale for Community Involvement

Does the community become involved to strengthen marriages (advancing the individual goals of the couple), or is the relationship more circular than that — one where marriages also strengthen the community? Some historical context

90. Vaughn Call and Tim B. Heaton, "Religious Influence on Marital Stability," *Journal for the Scientific Study of Religion* 36 (1997): 382-92.

91. Call and Heaton, "Religious Influence on Marital Stability," p. 291.

92. Scott J. South and Glenna Spitze, "Determinants of Divorce over the Marital Life Course," *American Sociological Review* 51 (1986): 583-90.

93. Brinig and Buckley, "No-Fault Laws," p. 335.

94. Brinig and Buckley, "No-Fault Laws," p. 337 and Table 5.

will be useful here, too, since marriages historically were so integral to the passing on of land and creation of wealth.[95]

Is community involvement and participation necessary for a strong marriage? Sociological evidence suggests that frequent contact with support mechanisms, family and community, does help marriages. Covenant marriage provides traditions after the marriage ceremony itself that encourage such participation, but we can see how the modern emphasis on autonomy and mobility work against involvement except when the married ask for it.

Children somehow turn marriages into communities.[96] Many studies have noted that the divorce rate falls when the family includes children born during the marriage.[97] The interesting question for this chapter is why that occurs. The obvious reasons include a sense of responsibility,[98] inculcation of altruism,[99] investment,[100] or joy in creation.[101] Perhaps a more subtle reason is that children teach us to give unconditionally and to think of others first. Their presence ensures a more permanent relationship between the adults involved (since parenting will go on after divorce, even if marital relations do not).[102] Hence, two of the three conditions we ascribe to the covenantal nature of families are present even without outside involvement.

## Comparisons between Covenantal and Contract-Like Relationships

Two legal doctrines limit the concept of marital communities and have their source in other family law values: autonomy and pluralism. Parental auton-

95. Glendon, *The New Family;* Langbein, "The Twentieth-Century Revolution."

96. Teresa Stanton Collett, "Marriage, Family and the Positive Law," *Notre Dame Journal of Law, Ethics and Public Policy* 10 (1996): 467-84. See also the discussion of Witte, "The Goods and Goals," pp. 1023-24, noting that "Children . . . are a bond between the parents."

97. For citations, see Linda J. Waite, Gus W. Haggstrom, and David E. Kanouse, "The Consequences of Parenthood for the Marital Stability of Young Adults," *American Sociological Review* 50 (1985): 850.

98. Glendon, *The New Family;* Elizabeth S. Scott, "Rational Decisionmaking about Marriage and Divorce," *Virginia Law Review* 76 (1990): 9.

99. Brinig and Buckley, "No-Fault Laws."

100. Andrew Cherlin, "The Effect of Children on Marital Dissolution," *Demography* 14 (1977): 265-72.

101. Anthony T. Padovano, "Marriage: The Most Noble of Human Achievements," *Catholic World* 238 (May 1, 1995): 140.

102. June R. Carbone, *From Partners to Parents: The Second Revolution in Family Law* (New York: Columbia University Press, 2000).

omy is now constitutionally protected by *Troxel v. Glanville*[103] (as a liberty interest) and will operate to keep third parties (including the state) from interfering in ongoing family relationships.[104] This liberty interest closely parallels the limitations set by the First Amendment separation of church and state.[105]

The other limitation on culturally bound community is pluralism. Sometimes laws designed to fit the covenantal relationships of most simply will not do for groups with cultural differences. For example, when we began comparing kinship care to transracial adoption, data limitations (the small number of black children adopted by white parents) in our sample moved us instead to compare foster care with adoption, for all children and for black children and black parents who care for them. During the time frame for the study, the National Longitudinal Study of Adolescent Health, done at the Carolina Population Center at the University of North Carolina,[106] many of the black children who were in foster care were being cared for by kin (as is the case nationally). For these children, then, the comparison was between kinship care and adoption (by black parents, related or not). What we have found empirically is that *foster* care does not compare favorably with adoption for any children, regardless of race. Adopted children, regardless of race, perform about as well as children remaining with biological families. But foster children do worse on both internal (depression and morbidity) and external (substance abuse, juvenile de-

103. 530 US. 57 (2000).

104. Margaret F. Brinig, "*Troxel* and the Limits of Community," *Rutgers Law Journal* 32 (2001): 733-82.

105. For example, consider the famous Supreme Court case of *Wisconsin v. Yoder*, 406 U.S. 205, 222 (1972), allowing Amish parents the right to keep their children from attending the otherwise compulsory last two years of public school; and the case of *Kilgrow v. Kilgrow*, 107 So. 2d 885 (Ala. 1958), in which a court refused to intervene in an ongoing dispute over parochial versus public school education in an otherwise intact marriage.

106. Richard Udry and Peter Bearman, The National Survey of Adolescent Health, from the Carolina Population Center, UNC 1994-95. The description, found on their website, reads as follows: "Add Health is a school-based study of the health-related behaviors of adolescents in grades 7-12. It has been designed to explore the causes of these behaviors, with an emphasis on the influence of social context. That is, Add Health postulates that families, friends, schools and communities play roles in the lives of adolescents that may encourage healthy choices of activities or may lead to unhealthy, self-destructive behaviors. Data to support or refute this theory were collected in surveys of students, parents, and school administrators." The Add Health study was funded by the National Institute of Child Health and Human Development (NICHD) and seventeen other federal agencies. Fieldwork was conducted by the National Opinion Research Center of the University of Chicago. A description of the research design can be found at http://www.cpc.unc.edu/projects/addhealth/resdesign/index.htm. The URL for the study is http://www.cpc.unc.edu/projects/addhealth/datasets.html.

linquency, and morbidity) measures. The differences are statistically significant and the coefficients are large.[107]

We also discovered, to our surprise, that *kinship* care has different consequences for children of different racial (or cultural) groups. For African-American children, kinship care cannot be statistically distinguished from living with a birth family or being adopted. Not surprisingly, it is African-Americans who claim a long tradition of reliance on extended families in times of crisis. The children were identified as living in kinship care if they were not living with a parent but indicated that either their aunt or their grandmother took the place of their mother. Children who mentioned no biological, foster, or adopted parent were asked if anyone in the household acted in that role. Grandparents and aunts were the overwhelming choices in such circumstances. We designated all 472 such situations as "kinship care." We had no way of knowing whether the living situation was formalized through a guardianship designation or through payments to the kin caregivers through the foster care system. We know, however, that the adolescents we identified as living with kin did not describe their relationships primarily as "foster care" or "guardianship."

For other racial (or cultural) groups, kinship care effects resemble those of foster care, a much less cheerful picture. These children, depending on their race, were more depressed, more likely to be delinquent, more likely to use alcohol, tobacco, and marijuana, and more likely to fear early death or being killed than children living with birth or adoptive parents.

Community matters when we talk about relationships; remember how God's institution of the rainbow after the flood in Genesis 8 helped God and humankind to remember his promise. The power of custom, convention, ritual, and social norms cannot easily be replaced by individual bargains or personal commitments. We are now able to demonstrate this point convincingly by comparing two seemingly similar intimate unions: marriages and informal (cohabiting) relationships.

What is wrong with informal relationships? Many legal scholars presume nothing is amiss. For example, the American Law Institute's Chapter 6 domestic partnership[108] only comes into play at the end of the relationship. It is designed to function in relationships that are "exchange" in nature (most often affecting heterosexual cohabitants but also affecting same-sex partners or partners in void marriages) and to discount those who do not want marriage-like relationships (as is true for some same-sex couples).

---

107. Margaret F. Brinig and Steven L. Nock, "How Much Does Legal Status Matter? Adoptions by Kin Caregivers," *Family Law Quarterly* 36 (2002): 449-74.

108. American Law Institute, *Principles.*

The cohabiting relationship itself is qualitatively different from marriage.[109] In the United States, at least, social class, measured by educational and economic standing, does much to determine those who cohabit rather than marry. Among women nineteen to forty-four years old, nearly 60 percent of high-school drop-outs cohabited compared to under 37 percent for college-educated women. Couples who cohabit express less interdependence than typical married couples.[110] The positive health effects seen for married couples — especially men, though women, too — are not as pronounced.[111] Sex is reportedly not as good.[112] Fathers are less likely to stay involved with their children, or to support them.[113]

Recent research by Shelly Lundberg and Elaina Rose[114] suggests that, although men respond with more work and higher wages at the birth of a child, they do so significantly more in response to births of sons than to births of daughters. The authors state, "Our results are consistent with a model in which the gender composition of a couple's offspring affects the returns to marriage." From a positive perspective, we can argue that the institution of marriage augments bonding with wives and daughters that comes naturally to fathers of sons. From a pessimistic viewpoint, father absence because of the breakup of a cohabiting couple may have the unintended effect of further disadvantaging girls as compared to boys. They found no difference of an effect of child gender on the labor market outcomes of mothers.

While we suspect that many of the undesirable features we have detailed

---

109. Larry L. Bumpass and Hsien-Hen Lu, "Trends in Cohabitation and Implications for Children's Family Contexts in the United States," *Population Studies* 54 (2000): 29, 32; Pamela J. Smock and Sanjiv Gupta, "Cohabitation in Contemporary North America," in *Just Living Together: Implications of Cohabitation on Families, Children and Social Policy,* ed. Alan Booth and Ann C. Crouter (Mahwah, N.J.: Erlbaum, 2002), pp. 53, 61-62.

110. This set of effects is hard to sort out. Do couples cohabit because they are precisely the sort who are less likely to be dependent upon one another, or does causation work the other way?

111. Amy Mehraban Picata, "Health Consequences of Marriage on the Retirement Years," *Journal of Family Issues* 21 (2000): 559; Susan L. Brown, "Child Well-Being in Cohabiting Families," in *Just Living Together,* ed. Booth and Crouter, p. 173; Susan Brown and Alan Booth, "Cohabitation Versus Marriage: A Comparison of Relationship Quality," *Journal of Marriage and Family* 58 (1996): 668-78.

112. Linda J. Waite and Kara Joyner, "Emotional Satisfaction and Physical Pleasure in Sexual Unions: Time Horizon, Sexual Behavior, and Sexual Exclusivity," *Journal of Marriage and Family* 63 (2001): 247.

113. Wendy D. Manning, "The Implications of Cohabitation for Children's Well-Being," in *Just Living Together,* ed. Booth and Crouter, pp. 121, 143.

114. Shelly Lundberg and Elaina Rose, "The Effects of Sons and Daughters on Men's Labor Supply and Wages," *Review of Economics and Statistics* 84 (2002): 251-68.

above come from cohabitation itself, we know that proving this hypothesis will be difficult. To begin with, studies in the United States simply have not collected the right data.[115] Empirically, causation is difficult to tease out.[116] For example, did a couple cohabit (and then divorce) because they were less dependent on each other, or did they become less interdependent over time because they were cohabiting (or both)? Or did the cohabitation produce some other effects that led to unhappiness, but in a case where divorce would have been practical only if the couple were not dependent?

Why might marriage work when *not* preceded by cohabitation? There are a number of reasons. It might be that the novelty of a couple's new life together outweighs the strain of adjustment to marriage. Thus the honeymoon was a time set apart to explore each other sexually but also to begin the process of adjusting to living with a new person. In various accounts of newlyweds, we hear of them setting up their new things and feeling as though they are "playing house."

Marriage, unlike cohabitation, also signifies commitment to discard in some ways one's individuality for a new identity and responsibilities.[117] At this point each spouse views the other as someone whose well-being must always be taken into account. Further (and obviously circular in a discussion of why mar-

---

115. Other questions that we would like answered in addition to those currently on the National Survey of Families and Households include the following:

> If you answered yes to whether you cohabited with your spouse prior to marriage, for how long? Were you already engaged when you moved in together? Did you anticipate you'd be marrying even though you had made no formal pledge? How long did you live together prior to marriage? What made you decide to get married? When did you decide to marry? Which of you first proposed getting married? Did you cohabit because you were unsure whether you wanted to marry? Have you ever cohabited with someone other than your spouse? Why did your relationship end? Did you decide that you'd found out too many things about the other person, or about your relationship, to make a marriage work? Did you simply tire of each other? Did you receive any financial settlement from that other relationship? How did your relationship change when you got married?

116. Larry L. Bumpass and James A. Sweet, "National Estimates of Cohabitation," *Demography* 26 (1989): 615-25; Neil G. Bennett et al., "Commitment and the Modern Union: Assessing the Link between Premarital Cohabitation and Subsequent Marital Stability," *American Sociological Review* 54 (1988): 127-38; William G. Axinn and Arland Thornton, "The Transformation in the Meaning of Marriage," in *The Ties That Bind*, ed. Linda J. Waite (New York: Aldine de Gruyter, 2000), pp. 147, 161; Bumpass and Lu, "Trends in Cohabitation," p. 8; Smock and Gupta, "Cohabitation in Contemporary North America," pp. 59-60 (reviewing other studies).

117. Nock, "Commitment and Dependency in Marriage"; Steven L. Nock, *Marriage in Men's Lives* (New York: Oxford University Press, 1999).

riage should be given legal protection), the marriage, in this respect like a corporation, becomes a legal entity, an identity.

From a sociological perspective, cohabitation is not a social status, while marriage is. Once a couple is married, parents, friends, and employers treat them differently. That difference may be a problem for couples who cohabit first, but it will not be for those who directly enter marriage.

If relationships are envisioned developmentally, we may expect that early experiences inform and influence subsequent ones. The evidence from the United States suggests that the early experiences of cohabitation may establish relationship trajectories that conflict with the expectations of legal marriage. The most obvious way in which American cohabitation might do this is by fostering greater individuality or independence while discouraging commitment. American cohabitors, in fact, are more independent, more egalitarian in who does what in the household, and less committed to conventional systems of beliefs about lifelong marriage. Marriage, on the other hand, is well defined in American culture and law,[118] and the elements that constitute American marriages (pledge of lifetime commitment, dependency, childbearing, and so on) differ notably from the typical patterns observed among cohabiting couples.

Most heterosexual cohabiting couples fall into one of two groups. One set of couples may be on their way to marriage,[119] in which case the abolition of heartbalm actions[120] by legislatures and common law suggests a public policy to treat them differently from married persons. Another set of couples affirmatively wishes to reject marriage.[121] As Canadian academic Nicholas Bala writes, "The motivations for living together outside of marriage are complex, but these relationships frequently arise because one party (often the man) is unwilling to make the commitment of marriage and does not want to undertake the legal obligations of marriage."[122] The Comments to the American Law Institute's Principles of the Law of Family Dissolution[123] note that Chapter 6 on domestic partnerships "diminishes the effectiveness of that strategy" of avoiding responsibility. To the extent that the goal of other chapters involving property distri-

---

118. Nock, "Commitment and Dependency in Marriage"; Nock, *Marriage in Men's Lives*.

119. Bumpass and Sweet, "National Estimates of Cohabitation," p. 615.

120. For a review, see Margaret F. Brinig, "Rings and Promises," *Journal of Law, Economics, and Organization* 6 (1990): 203-15. The heartbalm actions typically involving engaged couples were breach of marriage promise and seduction. For a recent case discussion, see *Miller v. Ratner*, 688 A.2d 976 (Md. Ct. App. 1997).

121. Nicholas Bala, "Review of From Contract to Covenant," *Été* (summer 2001): 140-42; Comment to American Law Institute, *Principles*, §6.02, at 14.

122. Bala, "Review," 1.

123. American Law Institute, *Principles*.

bution and "compensatory payments" is to encourage specialization between spouses and investment in the family,[124] applying the same principles to dissolving domestic partnerships flies in the face of reality: cohabiting couples are less specialized than married couples, are less interdependent, and have far more embedded equality goals.[125]

On the other hand, married couples are in a relationship designed to feature permanence, which encourages unconditional love. Here we have a family: people who are committed to each other over the very long-term horizon, and who are giving to each other without an expectation of immediate return (or perhaps any return). In Steven Nock's terminology,[126] they are living in the past and future, in a world of debts and futures, rather than the present. At this point, society (the community, meaning the religious community, the state, and even extended families) will act to support the family.[127] There will be laws promoting families,[128] giving constitutional rights (as in *Troxel v. Granville*),[129] and protecting the entity from outside assault.[130] There will be benefits that flow from being in such a family[131] and obligations that "are the threads from which intimacy is woven."[132] The members of the family live in covenant.

Cohabiting partners thus have less commitment to each other than do married spouses[133] and are more likely to think in terms of short-term rather than long-term consequences. In fact, cohabitation is usually an exchange relationship, which produces less satisfaction[134] than one taking an "internal stance"[135]

---

124. Ira M. Ellman, "The Theory of Alimony," *California Law Review* 77 (1989): 1-82; June Carbone and Margaret F. Brinig, "Rethinking Marriage: Feminist Ideology, Economic Change, and Divorce Reform," *Tulane Law Review* 65 (1991): 953-1010; Jana B. Singer, "Alimony and Efficiency: The Gendered Costs and Benefits of the Economic Justification for Alimony," *Georgetown Law Journal* 82 (1994): 2423-42; Elisabeth M. Landes, "The Economics of Alimony," *Journal of Legal Studies* 7 (1978): 35-63.

125. Nock, "Commitment and Dependency in Marriage," p. 508.

126. Steven L. Nock, "Turn-Taking As Rational Behavior," *Social Science Research* 27 (1998): 235, 239-41.

127. Brinig, "*Troxel* and the Limits of Community."

128. Patricia A. Cain, "Imagine There's No Marriage," *Quinnipiac Law Review* 16 (1997): 27.

129. 530 U.S. 57 (2000).

130. For example, consider the household exemption from bankruptcy and the "family estate" or tenancy by the entireties that shields marital property from creditors.

131. Vermont Civil Union Legislation, 2000 Vermont Laws. P.A. 91 (H. 847), § 1204(c).

132. Nock, "Turn-Taking As Rational Behavior," p. 243.

133. Nock, *Marriage in Men's Lives*, p. 13.

134. Gary L. Hansen, "Moral Reasoning and the Marital Exchange Relationship," *Journal of Social Psychology* 131 (1991): 71-81.

135. Regan, *Alone Together,* p. 24.

central to a meaningful interpersonal relationship. In marriage, a relationship centered upon short-run gains signals instability.[136]

In this chapter, we have traced the idea of covenant from the religious ideal to its modern secular counterpart. We have shown its essential characteristics and why covenant relationships are more likely to be successful than contract-governed or less formal alternatives. We do not suggest that the state require couples to enter into status relationships like marriage. In most situations, however, society ought to prefer and privilege them by setting up conditions where the marriage (or other covenant relationship) is most likely to work.

136. Margaret F. Brinig, "The Influence of *Marvin v. Marvin* on Housework during Marriage," *Notre Dame Law Review* 76 (2001): 1311, 1336-49.

## 11  The American "Covenant Marriage" in the Conflict of Laws

*Peter Hay*

### The Problem Defined: The Extra-State Effects of Covenant Marriage Standards

The "covenant marriage," enacted in Louisiana, Arizona, and Arkansas[1] and introduced in twenty-seven other state legislatures,[2] is a reaction to the evolution of American family law, especially divorce law, over the past quarter century. This chapter explores the extent to which limitations inherent in a covenant marriage are likely to be given effect in noncovenant states and in foreign nations. While beyond the immediate scope of the essay, some of the issues raised also hold implications for other current trends in family law, particularly registered partnerships and same-sex marriages.

In the United States, family law, including divorce law, is state law. Federal law governs the recognition of judgments generally[3] and, as a result of more recent legislation, questions of jurisdiction and recognition of judgments pertaining to child custody and support. Federal statutory and treaty law also govern the civil and criminal consequences of child abduction by the noncustodial

---

1. Louisiana (1997): La. R.S. 9:272 *et seq.* (2003); Arizona: Ariz. R.S. 25-901 *et seq.*; Arkansas: Ark. Code § 9-11-801 *et seq.*

2. Alabama, California, Colorado, Georgia, Indiana, Iowa, Kansas, Maine, Maryland, Michigan, Minnesota, Mississippi, Missouri, Nebraska, New Jersey, New Mexico, Ohio, Oklahoma, Oregon, South Carolina, Tennessee, Texas, Utah, Virginia, Washington, West Virginia, Wisconsin. As of March 2004, all bills had either failed in the states' senates or a senate committee, or further action was postponed indefinitely, or the matter was withdrawn from schedule.

3. U.S. Constitution art. IV, § 1 (requiring states to give "Full Faith and Credit" to judgments of sister states); E. Scoles, P. Hay, P. Borchers, and S. Symeonides, *Conflict of Laws*, fourth ed. (St. Paul, Minn.: Thomson/West, 2004), § 15.8.

parent or another party. But *substantive* family law is state law. This includes marriage: the prerequisites for contracting it (age, degrees of sanguinity, need for formality),[4] the conditions for its dissolution (grounds for divorce, waiting periods), and post-marital duties (support for children and the ex-spouse) and rights (custody) of the parties.

Different societies and different ages have varied greatly in their approaches to marriage[5] and its dissolution. In Western culture, classical Roman law took a very permissive view of dissolution of marriage.[6] Modern Islamic re-

---

4. A few states still permit the "common law marriage," which does not require compliance with formalities. Even states that do not permit such marriages will recognize valid out-of-state common law marriages. For the latter, see, e.g., Cal. Fam. Code § 308.

5. Traditionally, marriage is the formal union, sanctioned by church and state or the state alone, of a man and a woman. More recently, same-sex couples can contract marriage-like civil unions in a number of jurisdictions (e.g., in Denmark, Finland, France, Germany, Hungary, Iceland, the Netherlands, Norway, Portugal, and Sweden; in the United States in California and Vermont; in Canada in Quebec, British Columbia, and Nova Scotia). These unions are intended to give the parties rights and security, as well as obligations, but they are not identical with marriage. The merger of the two institutions — by making marriage available to both heterosexual and same-sex partners — is the most recent development: Netherlands and Belgian legislation, the 2003 decision of the Supreme Court of Ontario, and generally all-Canadian proposals are examples. For the Netherlands, see Johannes Wasmuth, "Eheschließung unter Gleichgeschlechtlichen in den Niederlanden und deutscher ordre public," in *Liber Amicorum Gerhard Kegel*, ed. Hilmar Krüger and Heinz-Peter Mansel (Munich, 2002), p. 237; for Canada generally, see Jo-Anne Pickel, "Judicial Analysis Frozen in Time: *EGALE Canada Inc. v. Canada* (Attorney General)," *Saskatchewan Law Review* 65 (2002): 243-68; for Ontario, see *Halpern v. Toronto* (*City*), 172 O.A.C. 276 (2003) (Ca.) (holding that the common-law definition of marriage offends the equality rights of same-sex couples under s. 15[1] of the Canadian Charter of Rights and Freedoms and ordering the granting of marriage licenses to such couples). On July 17, 2003, the Canadian federal government published a draft bill that would define marriage as "the lawful union of two persons to the exclusion of others." The Government of Canada has asked the Supreme Court of Canada whether the Parliament of Canada has the exclusive legislative authority to enact such a law, and whether the draft is consistent with the Canadian Charter of Rights and Freedoms. For the text of the current draft bill, see http://www.canada.justice.gc.ca/en/news/fs/2004/doc_31110.html. In the United States, the Massachusetts Supreme Judicial Court held that the denial of the right to marry to same-sex couples violated the state's constitution: *Goodrich et al. v. Dep't of Pub. Health et al.*, 798 N.E.2d 941 (2003). Same-sex marriage thus became available in Massachusetts in May 2004. The discussion that follows focuses on the traditional heterosexual marriage that "covenant marriage" legislation seeks to strengthen. In principle, however, much of what is said in connection with party stipulations and undertakings would apply equally in the context of civilly sanctioned same-sex unions or marriages.

6. "In classical law any marriage . . . can be dissolved by agreement of the spouses or by notice given by one of them. Agreements which attempt to exclude or to limit divorce are void, nor is it possible to stipulate for a penalty to be paid in case of divorce." Fritz Schulz, *Classical Roman Law* (Oxford: Clarendon, 1951), p. 132; see also pp. 134-35.

ligious law also readily accommodates dissolution.[7] When civil law became codified in nineteenth-century Europe, family law established strict precondi- tions for divorce.[8] These have now given way to some form of divorce without fault (for instance, because of the breakdown of the marriage) in all European countries.[9]

Until the 1970s, American divorce law was predominantly fault-oriented;[10]

7. In March 2002, a wife from India received a *talaq* or divorce electronically (via e-mail) from her Pakistani husband. Shortly thereafter, she remarried. See Nadhi T. Rathi, *Divorce by Email,* at http://www.rediff.com/netguide/2002/apr/08sadia.htm (April 8, 2002). According to an Australian newspaper, Muslim men in Kuala Lumpur may use text messages on mobile phones to divorce their wives. "Mobile Phone Divorce," *Daily Telegraph* (Sydney) (July 29, 2003): 22, available at 2003 WL 60840477.

8. Under the original French Code Civil, only fault was a ground, restricted to adultery and violent and repeatedly abusive behavior. In 1945, serious offense or neglect of marital duties so as to make continued marital community intolerable were added. Since 1976, the law is as fol- lows: fault (as before); alternatively: (1) breakdown of the marriage and living separately for six years (unilateral application by one spouse), Code Civil [C. Civ.] arts. 237-39 (Fr.); or (2) con- sensual divorce: both agree or one proposes and the other accepts. The second option is not available during the first six months of marriage. After application and conference with the judge, there is a three-month waiting period until divorce is granted. The parties must submit a draft agreement that provides for the consequences of dissolution. C. Civ. arts. 230-32. Germany also followed the fault principle. The original version of the Civil Code (effective January 1, 1900) included, among other grounds, adultery, bigamy, attempted homicide, abandonment, and the breakdown of the marriage if caused by a grave neglect of marital duties or immoral be- havior. The 1938 Ehegesetz ("Marriage Act"), separating the divorce rules from the Civil Code, added the breakdown of the marriage and living separately for three years. The court, however, had discretion to deny the divorce if the plaintiff was responsible for the breakdown. Effective July 1, 1977, the divorce rules were (re)incorporated into the Civil Code, now based on the sole ground of the breakdown of the marriage. Bürgerliches Gesetzbuch [BGB] §§ 1564-76 (F.R.G.). There is an irrebuttable presumption for the breakdown if both parties have lived separately for a year and both consent, otherwise if they have lived separately for three years. BGB § 1566. In the former German Democratic Republic, the breakdown principle had been introduced as early as 1965 and was in force until reunification in 1990. The jurisdictional rules in force in the European Union (except Denmark, which opted out) also provide for waiting periods: Council Regulation (EC) No. 2201/2003 Concerning Jurisdiction and Enforcement of Judgments in Mat- rimonial Matters and in Matters of Parental Responsibility Art. 3(1)(a), [2003] Official Journal L 338/1.

9. No-fault divorces are available in, for example, Austria, Bulgaria, the Czech Republic, Denmark, England, Finland, France, Germany, Greece, Hungary, Ireland, Italy, the Netherlands, Norway, Poland, Portugal, Russia, Scotland, Spain, and Sweden. See Katharina Boele-Woelki et al., eds., *European Family Law in Action,* vol. 1 (Antwerp: Intersentia, 2003), pp. 71-98.

10. For example, until 1967, adultery was the only ground for divorce in New York. N.Y. Dom. Rel. Law § 170 (Supp. 1967); see Michael L. McCarthy, "Retroactive Application of New Grounds for Divorce under § 170 Domestic Relations Law," *Buffalo Law Review* 17 (1968): 902-13. This encouraged spouses to seek a divorce out of state; see note 14 below. On the general subject

when it was not, long waiting periods guarded against a state's becoming a divorce haven.[11] Since then state law has turned from fault-based divorce to no-fault divorce.[12] Waiting periods differ widely, however.[13] In addition, some states recognize virtually instant consensual foreign-country divorces, while others do not.[14] Nevertheless, in the United States a divorce granted by a court of a sister-state with sufficient jurisdiction,[15] or judicially recognized by such a state,[16] is entitled to recognition in all other states, including in the original state of celebration. If expense is no consideration, the parties — or even only one of them, seeking an *ex parte* divorce — therefore can obtain a valid divorce in the state with the "easiest" requirements.

States that have promulgated covenant marriage statutes are resisting this trend toward easy divorce. They have done so by seeking to retain more traditional, stricter standards applicable to all, or by giving those wishing to marry the alternative to opt out of easy dissolution and to bind themselves even more fundamentally — to do more than enter into the *status* of marriage, but to *covenant* to keep it that way except for well-defined reasons and in observance of particular procedures.[17]

"Covenant" has both religious and secular law connotations. It expresses commitment, devotion, perhaps acknowledgment of divine command, but it is also reminiscent of contract — the undertaking to do or not to do something. The dichotomy between the religious and the civil aspects of marriage has been more apparent in Continental law than in the United States. In Europe, mar-

---

see also Homer H. Clark Jr., *The Law of Domestic Relations in the United States,* second ed. (St. Paul, Minn.: West, 1988), § 13.6.

11. See *Sosna v. Iowa,* 419 U.S. 393, 95 S. Ct. 553 (1975).

12. McCarthy, "Retroactive Application," p. 902; Lawrence M. Friedman, "Rights of Passage: Divorce Law in Historical Perspective," *Oregon Law Review* 63 (1984): 649, 667.

13. Nevada: 6 weeks, Nev. Rev. Stat. § 125.020; Iowa: 1 year, Iowa Code § 598.6; Nebraska: 1 year, Neb. Rev. Stat. § 42-349.

14. See, for example, *Rosenstiel v. Rosenstiel,* 209 N.E.2d 709 (N.Y. 1965). For discussion of "easy" Haitian and Dominican Republic divorces and their recognition, see Scoles, Hay, Borchers, Symeonides, *Conflict of Laws,* §§ 15.20-15.22.

15. Scoles, Hay, Borchers, Symeonides, *Conflict of Laws,* §§ 15.6-15.14.

16. For such "domestication" of migratory divorces, see Scoles, Hay, Borchers, Symeonides, *Conflict of Laws,* § 15.14.

17. "As evidence mounts of the social destruction in the wake of surging divorce rates and currently surging cohabitation rates, action is required to restore and protect the institution of marriage — the foundation upon which the family is built." Katherine S. Spaht and Symeon C. Symeonides, "Covenant Marriage and the Law of Conflicts of Laws," *Creighton Law Review* 32 (1999): 1085, 1091. This statement echoes concerns of earlier times: "It is this unlimited and illimitable freedom of divorce [in Roman law] which seemed so highly objectionable to modern moralists and lawyers and so obviously a sign of Roman decadence." Schulz, *Roman Law,* p. 132.

riage generally requires a civil ceremony; a religious one is optional.[18] Each ceremony has its own prerequisites (for example, the publication of banns).[19] In the United States, the civil and religious aspects merge when the marriage ceremony is performed by religious authority.[20] "Marriage" is easy, and so is divorce in a no-fault state. Hence the option, offered by the Louisiana legislation, to enter into something intended to be more lasting, more secure, less vulnerable: the *covenant marriage*.[21]

Louisiana's version of covenant marriage includes the following features that distinguish such a marriage from the traditional form: (1) mandatory premarital counseling to impress the seriousness of marriage upon the couple; (2) the signing of a "Declaration of Intent" by which the couple promises to take all reasonable efforts to preserve the marriage and which stipulates for the application of Louisiana law; and (3) specified fault-based grounds for divorce as well as no-fault divorce, the latter conditioned, however, on a longer period of separation (two years). With respect to dissolution — although not with respect to formation — a covenant marriage is remarkably similar to contemporary substantive European divorce law. They are both a combination of fault grounds and a no-fault possibility, with no-fault divorce made more difficult.

When parties have contracted a covenant marriage in a covenant marriage state and one of them later seeks its dissolution there, he or she will be held to the standards applicable to such marriages. But what if one of the parties changes his or her domicile (which is one of the traditional bases for divorce jurisdiction) to a traditional, noncovenant state (Forum State No. 2 = F-2) and there seeks a divorce: will the new state of domicile recognize the first state's

18. See, for example, BGB § 1310(1). On the "secularization" of family law and the spread of European secular notions to other parts of the world, see Max Rheinstein, "The Law of Family and Succession," in *Civil Law in the Modern World*, ed. A. N. Yiannopoulos (Baton Rouge: Louisiana State University Press, 1965), pp. 27-57.

19. France: posting of marriage banns at town hall required no less than ten working days before the date of marriage. Italy: If one of the parties is an Italian citizen or resident, the marriage announcement has to be posted for two consecutive Sundays at the city hall. This kind of prerequisite also exists in North America: *Ontario Family Act,* R.S.O. 1990, ch. M.3, § 27(2) (Can.) (stating that marriage may not take place until five days after publication of banns).

20. In several predominantly Catholic countries, civil law and authority will recognize religious marriages but still require civil registration. This is true, for instance, in Spain with respect to Catholic and Protestant marriages. See Agreement with the Holy See of 3 January 1975, VI(1-2); Law 24/1992, Nov. 10, 1992, 7(1). Stricter requirements apply to the recognition of Jewish ceremonies: Law 25/1992, Nov. 10, 1992, Annex, 7(1),(3),(4). All of the foregoing reprinted in *Spanish Legislation on Religious Affairs*, ed. Alberto de la Hera and Rosa María Martínez de Codes (Madrid: Ministeria de Justicia, Centro de Publicaciones, 1998), pp. 54, 79, 92.

21. See generally Katherine S. Spaht, "Louisiana's Covenant Marriage: Social Analysis and Legal Implications," *Louisiana Law Review* 59 (1998): 63-130, and her chapter herein.

(Forum State No. 1 = F-1) conditions for dissolution? Put differently: Can covenant marriage legislation effectively ensure observance of its stricter standards nationwide?

What if, second, the parties, or one of them, are foreign nationals and one of them seeks a divorce abroad: will the result depend on whether the petitioner is a national of F-2 (here, the foreign country where the divorce is sought) or of the American covenant state, on the nationality of the respondent, and/or on the present or previous domicile of one or both of the parties?

## U.S. Interstate Recognition of Covenant Marriage Standards upon Divorce

### A Second State's Divorce Jurisdiction

The stricter standards of the covenant marriage state are at issue when divorce is sought in a noncovenant state. As an initial matter, the second state's court (F-2) must have jurisdiction — personal and subject matter jurisdiction — in order to entertain the action. If it does, what law does it apply? The next subsection of this chapter addresses this second question: as will be seen, in American law, jurisdiction and applicable law merge.

In the 1942 case of *Williams v. North Carolina*, the United States Supreme Court held that the petitioner's domicile was a sufficient basis for the assertion of divorce jurisdiction.[22] It did not hold that domicile was required or was the only basis for jurisdiction; that question was not before it.[23] For a divorce with both parties before the court, whether by appearance or as a result of the court's personal jurisdiction over the respondent, the jurisdictional issue becomes *res judicata* for purposes of a collateral proceeding.[24] Domicile as a basis for divorce jurisdiction is therefore relevant only when the petitioner sought the divorce *ex parte*, and it was granted upon respondent's default. In these circumstances, another forum (F-1 or yet another state, F-3) may question F-2's jurisdiction for lack of petitioner's domicile there.[25]

---

22. *Williams v. North Carolina*, 317 U.S. 287, 298, 63 S. Ct. 207, 213 (1942). This conclusion with respect to divorce jurisdiction has old historical roots. In *Pennoyer v. Neff*, 95 U.S. 714, 722 (1877), the Court recognized, in dictum, the right of "every State . . . to determine the civil status and capabilities of all its inhabitants."

23. For detailed discussion, see Scoles, Hay, Borchers, Symeonides, *Conflict of Laws*, § 15.6 *et seq.*

24. *Sherrer v. Sherrer*, 334 U.S. 343, 348-49, 68 S. Ct. 1087, 1089-90 (1948).

25. See *Williams v. North Carolina (II)*, 325 U.S. 226, 65 S. Ct. 1092 (1945). But, "[s]ince an

The F-2 court must not only have personal jurisdiction over the domiciliary party; it must also have subject matter jurisdiction over the case. It must have power to grant a divorce, to dissolve a marriage. It is upon this latter ground, lack of subject matter jurisdiction, that a recent Connecticut court declined to entertain a petition for the dissolution of a Vermont civil union.[26] Vermont, in response to a Vermont Supreme Court decision holding Vermont's marriage laws unconstitutional when they denied marriage to same-sex couples, had chosen to establish the legal form of a civil union for such couples.[27] By not extending its marriage laws to same-sex couples, the Connecticut court reasoned, Vermont obviously treated a civil union as something *other than* marriage. Connecticut, however, only conferred power upon its courts to dissolve marriages, not other types of unions, unknown to Connecticut law. The Connecticut court thus lacked subject matter jurisdiction in the case.

It is most unlikely that this reasoning would extend to covenant marriages. Covenant marriages, after all, are intended as *marriages,* between heterosexuals, by the state of their creation. Apart from the almost universal choice-of-law rule that a marriage valid where celebrated will be recognized as valid elsewhere, an attempt to differentiate between F-2's type of marriage and the marital status conferred by F-1 would probably be unconstitutional.[28]

It thus seems quite clear that, for interstate purposes, the second court would have personal jurisdiction if the petitioner is domiciled there or both parties are before it, whether domiciled there in fact or not. It would also unquestionably have subject matter jurisdiction.

---

appeal to the Full Faith and Credit Clause raises questions under the Constitution . . . , the proper criteria for ascertaining domicile [jurisdiction of the first court], should these be in dispute, become matters for federal determination." 325 U.S. at 231 n.7, 65.

26. *Rosengarten v. Downes,* 802 A.2d 170 (Conn. App. Ct. 2002), *appeal granted,* 806 A.2d 1066 (Conn. 2002).

27. Vt. Stat. T.15 § 1201 *et seq.; Baker v. State,* 744 A.2d 864 (Vt. 1999). For civil unions or registered partnerships elsewhere, see also note 5 above. With the adoption and amendment of Domestic Partnership legislation by California, Cal. Fam. Code § 297 *et seq.,* the same issues now arise in relation to such California partnerships.

28. Compare *Hughes v. Fetter,* 341 U.S. 609, 71 S. Ct. 980 (1951) with *Wells v. Simonds Abrasive Co.,* 345 U.S. 514, 73 S. Ct. 856 (1953).

300

## Applicable Law

### 1. Current Law: Lex Fori

The emphasis on domicile as a jurisdictional requirement in the older case law[29] at once assumed and justified the application of local substantive law (the *lex fori*) to the divorce petition. Because of the assumption, a close connection to the forum was required for it to be entitled to exercise jurisdiction. Otherwise, the forum would be interfering impermissibly with the societal interests of the actual domicile, the home state. It is in part on this ground that the appellate court in *Alton v. Alton*[30] agreed that the trial court lacked jurisdiction to grant the divorce that both parties wanted. The close connection brought the status before the court, as it were. The status, like a thing — a *res* — now had a location, and, as a matter of traditional choice of law, local law, the law of the local forum (the *lex fori* as the *lex rei sitae*), applies to local "things." In these circumstances, an F-2 (divorcing) court does not ask whether the petitioner could have obtained a divorce in the state where the marriage was celebrated or even in which it was lived until the breakup. Its concern is only with its jurisdiction and the rules of its own substantive law. Applied to covenant marriages this means that, without more, covenant-state standards for divorce have no effect on the F-2 decision.

### 2. Choice of Law Alternatives

**a. The Choice-of-Law Clause in the Marriage Contract (Party Autonomy)**
In general, all legal systems seek to apply a closely connected law, a home law, to status questions. They differ in how they define that — as the law of the parties' nationality, their domicile, or their marital residence. American courts opt for domicile and, by combining the choice-of-law question with the jurisdictional inquiry, thereby come to the *lex fori*. Other legal systems separate these questions. If, under such an approach, the applicable law does not follow from the exercise of jurisdiction, the obvious question arises whether the parties may stipulate it themselves. In a Louisiana covenant marriage, the parties stipulate the application of Louisiana law in their "Declaration of Intent."

Parties are generally free to choose the law applicable to their contracts. A choice-of-law clause (in itself a contract) need not even relate to a contractual

---

29. See Scoles, Hay, Borchers, Symeonides, *Conflict of Laws,* § 15.4, for a review of the older cases.

30. *Alton v. Alton,* 207 F.2d 667 (3rd Cir. 1953).

obligation but, especially in Europe, may concern claims in tort and marital property rights. Increasingly, and contrary to earlier practice, the chosen law need not have a particular relationship to the claim or the parties.[31] Limitations exist everywhere, however. They are designed to protect public interests (for instance, currency regulations) and — particularly important in the present context — the "weaker party." Modern codifications thus limit party autonomy in consumer and employment contracts, and courts guard against unfair terms or conditions on the basis of fundamental values that may be grounded in notions of due process and public policy. Whether any such considerations militate against acceptance of a party stipulation away from the otherwise applicable *lex fori* and in favor of the *lex celebrationis* in the present context will be explored further later in this chapter, after review of other choice-of-law approaches.

### b. Full Faith and Credit to the *Lex Celebrationis?*

The U.S. Constitution requires states to give "full faith and credit" to the judgments, records, and "public acts" of other states of the union.[32] Statutes are public acts. Must F-2 therefore honor F-1's covenant marriage statute, quite apart from the spouses' choice of it, including the statute's limitations on divorce?

Some older decisions did require the forum to apply the statutory law of another state.[33] The last decision to do so, however, may also be explained on other grounds.[34] In modern times, the issue has arisen in the context of worker compensation statutes: may a second state (the state of employment, of the injury, or home state of the injured employee) grant an additional or different recovery than permitted under the law under which the claimant has already received an award? The answer has been uniformly "yes," at first because recognition might offend F-2's public policy,[35] later because F-2 should not be forced always to apply another state's law and never its own,[36] and finally because F-2 — virtually — can do what it wants to.[37]

---

31. See UCC § 1-301; Convention on the Law Applicable to Contractual Obligations [Rome Convention], art. 3, 1980 O.J. L 266/1 (in force among member states of the European Union). Even if a connection were required, the choice of the law of celebration (Louisiana in the example) would satisfy the requirement.

32. Scoles, Hay, Borchers, Symeonides, *Conflict of Laws,* § 15.8.

33. For a review of the case law, see Scoles, Hay, Borchers, Symeonides, *Conflict of Laws,* §§ 3.24-3.25, 3.30.

34. Scoles, Hay, Borchers, Symeonides, *Conflict of Laws,* § 3.25 n. 18, concerning *Order of United Commercial Travelers of Am. v. Wolfe,* 331 U.S. 586, 67 S. Ct. 1355 (1947).

35. *Bradford Elec. Light Co. v. Clapper,* 286 U.S. 145, 160, 52 S. Ct. 571, 576 (1932).

36. *Pacific Employers Insur. Co. v. Indus. Accident Comm'n,* 306 U.S. 493, 501, 59 S. Ct. 629, 632 (1939).

37. *Carroll v. Lanza,* 349 U.S. 408, 413-14, 75 S. Ct. 804, 807-8 (1955).

The last statement overstates the point. The forum cannot apply forum law — or any other law — just because it wants to do so. The 1981 United States Supreme Court decision in *Allstate Ins. Co. v. Hague*[38] teaches that the forum must have a "significant contact," or contacts that are significant in aggregation, before it may apply its law. This limitation derives from the Due Process Clause of the Fourteenth Amendment. The defendant should not be subject to forum law with which he or she and the case have no connection. But if the forum does have the requisite contact so that due process is satisfied, the Full Faith and Credit Clause is no longer a bar to the application of the *lex fori.*

In the case of a petition for the dissolution of a convenant marriage celebrated in F-1, the second forum (F-2) does have the requisite contact: the very facts that entitle it to exercise *jurisdiction* — domicile (or other close connection) of the petitioner in the case of an *ex parte* divorce, or the presence and participation of both parties (bilateral divorce) — are contacts permitting the choice of its own F-2 law (the *lex fori*) as the *applicable law.* Application of the law of F-1 where the marriage was celebrated *(lex celebrationis)* would be a matter of choice, not of constitutional requirement.

### c. The Choice of "Home Law" in Family Matters

In the case of *Alton v. Alton,* the appellate court affirmed the trial court's denial of relief for lack of jurisdiction. The parties did not have the requisite contact with the Virgin Islands forum and application of forum law would therefore undermine the societal concerns of their home state. Application of forum law was assumed as a given. Judge Hastie, in dissent, thought that the concerns of the home state could be safeguarded by application of its law in circumstances when the forum's own connection is too slight. This thought anticipated by many years what the decision in *Allstate* today requires in other contexts. That this is still not the rule in divorce results from two circumstances: in an uncontested bilateral divorce, jurisdiction and the substantive result are not open to collateral attack; in an *ex parte* divorce, the jurisdictional facts furnish the required nexus that justifies the application of local law.

It is in the case of a *contested* bilateral divorce where Judge Hastie's thoughts, in combination with the rule of the *Allstate* decision, could have currency, especially in the context of covenant marriages. This assumes, however, that the divorce petition is brought in a wholly unconnected forum. That is unlikely to be the case. The petitioner will bring the action in the state of his or her new home, furnishing domicile as a jurisdictional fact additional to the partici-

---

38. 449 U.S. 302, 101 S. Ct. 633 (1981); *Phillips Petroleum Co. v. Shutts,* 472 U.S. 797, 105 S. Ct. 2965 (1985).

pation of the other spouse and, with it, the freedom for the forum to apply its own law. This is not to say that, whenever different divorce laws may be applicable (as now with the emergence of covenant marriage legislation), the forum *should* apply its law and ignore the other. Judge Hastie's dissent suggests that there are policy reasons to defer to "home law."

European law has long taken a much more differentiated approach to choice of law for marriage dissolution and has separated that inquiry from the assertion of jurisdiction. With "nationality" as the principal personal connecting factor in older European conflicts law (in contrast to the common law's use of domicile),[39] the law of the parties' common nationality was thought to have the greatest concern and express the most relevant societal interests, and it was believed that the forum should safeguard these even though it had jurisdiction. Alternative references, such as the parties' last common habitual residence, apply when there is no common nationality. The European approach to divorce is thus not basically *lex fori*–oriented, but rather reflects Judge Hastie's concerns. American case law, however, continues to adhere to its traditional approach.

### d. Generalizing the Choice-of-Law Principles of the Restatement Second?

American conflicts law — mainly for contracts and torts — has departed from the rule-orientation of the older law. It seeks to apply the law that is appropriate for the case, the parties, even for a particular issue *(dépeçage)*. While several approaches have been suggested and applied, the Restatement (Second) of Conflict of Laws (1971) represents perhaps the overarching statement. In the absence of a valid choice of law by the parties, it calls for the application, in contract and tort, of the law of the "most significant relationship" to the parties or the issue.[40] It has been suggested that the Restatement approach become the standard for choice of law in divorce and that its application would lead to deference to the law of the covenant marriage state as the most significantly related

39. See, for example, for France, Henri Batiffol and Paul Lagarde, *Droit international privé,* 2 vols., seventh ed. (Paris: Librairie générale de droit et de jurisprudence, 1981-83), 2:79; for Germany, German Conflicts Statute art. 17(1), 1st sentence, in combination with German Conflicts Statute art. 14(1); for Italy, Art. 31 Conflicts Statute.

40. The principal provisions are Restatement (Second) of Conflicts of Laws § 145 (torts) and § 188 (contracts) (1971). Sections 145(2) and 188(2), which list a number of contacts to be considered, incorporate by reference the general principles of § 6. Sections 145(2) and 188(2) also provide that the contacts listed (and others that may be relevant, for the list is non-exclusive) should be evaluated according to their "relative" importance to the issue. No further guidance is provided. In addition to the general provision of § 145, the significant relationship test is also invoked for particular tort issues. See Restatement (Second) of Conflicts of Laws §§ 156-73 (1971).

or the state whose policies would be most undermined by non-application of its law.[41]

The Restatement Second test is wider than both Judge Hastie's suggestion and the rules of European law. Judge Hastie had focused on "home law." In the context of the case before him, "home law" was the law of the state from which the parties came (where they were last domiciled) and which would be evaded by application of the Virgin Islands' *lex fori*. The European rules, not formulated with regard to a concrete case, come closer to the Restatement's goal — identification of the most significantly related legal system. The Restatement Second, however, is wider still. It contains no presumptions, and the general principles of its Section 6 accommodate a number of orientations, including a forum bias.

The Restatement's pervasive focus on individual issues *(dépeçage)* is unlikely to work in the covenant marriage context. For example, should a court defer to the covenant marriage state's law for some issues (such as grounds for divorce), but not for others (such as length of a waiting period)? It is difficult to see, even if *dépeçage* were not practiced (because impracticable), how the Restatement Second approach would lead — as a rule, rather than only exceptionally (which would not be much help) — to the law of the covenant marriage state, rather than to local law or the law of a third state (not a covenant marriage state), such as the state of the last common domicile. Even if, objectively, much may be said in favor of the covenant marriage state — as the *lex celebrationis* and because of the parties' choice of its law and mutual undertakings of best efforts — the principles of Section 6, as mentioned, permit a forum bias. As subsection (f), below, will address in additional detail, it seems more likely than not that the forum will opt for local law, given the petitioner's close connection to it.

### e. Change of Characterization from Family Law to Contract: Impairment of Contract?

The previous subsections explored alternatives to the application of the *lex fori* from the perspective of choice of law in family law. In a covenant marriage, however, the traditional notion of "contracting marriage" has a meaning beyond entering the *status* of marriage, with the content and consequences determined by law. It is also, perhaps predominantly, a *contract*, of special solemnity,

41. Spaht and Symeonides, "Covenant Marriage," p. 1113. This suggestion echoes the "comparative impairment" approach to choice of law which, with Professor Symeonides as principal draftsman, became part of Louisiana's conflicts codification and now has been adopted in Oregon as well. La. Civ. Code art. 3537 (2003); Or. Rev. Stat. § 81.130 (2003).

in which — it is said[42] — the undertaking to use best efforts toward the mainte-nance of the marriage is to represent a legal obligation. The express choice of a validating law (namely, the law of the covenant marriage state) underlines the parties' commitment.

If the question at issue — giving effect to the parameters of a covenant marriage in another state — thus presents questions of contract law as much as of family law, would the application of the *lex fori* by F-2, overriding these pa-rameters, be an unconstitutional impairment of contract? The answer, quite clearly, must be "no." A sizeable jurisprudence permits the forum to disregard contractual limitations, valid where made, when contacts to the forum give it a regulatory interest.[43] It is generally thought that the parties may not, by con-tract, modify the nature of the marital status, and the Louisiana rule to the con-trary is considered an exception even there. The contacts to the forum that give it jurisdiction also give it a regulatory interest in the marriage that is now before it. Limitations contracted by the parties and valid elsewhere do not diminish the forum's freedom to apply its own law.

It is free, but it does not have to apply the *lex fori*. Characterizing the limi-tations as contract issues, immediately and quite directly again implicates the Restatement's choice-of-law rules. Perhaps these contract issues are more sig-nificantly related to the state where the obligations were undertaken and were to be performed, than to the forum. But even so, what is the result? By seeking dissolution in F-2 without observing the contractual limitations, the petitioner may be in breach (if the applicable law is indeed that of the covenant state, F-1): the ordinary contract remedy would be money damages (under F-1, possibly also under F-2 law), but not enforcement. Unlike in arbitration, no law requires a court's dismissal of, or abstention in, a case so that the agreed method of set-tlement can run its course. Absent such a requirement, a court *may*, of course, dismiss for other reasons — for instance, because a forum-selection clause chooses a different court, or for reasons of *forum non conveniens*, or because it is unable to give a remedy.[44]

The first of these reasons for dismissal (a forum-selection clause) may re-quire a reading of the choice-of-law clause as incorporating a choice of forum. But this is not American law. The last of the reasons for dismissal (the lack of a remedy) has a parallel in the existence of equitable relief when the relief at law is inadequate, and money damages for the breach of undertakings in the cove-

---

42. See Spaht and Symeonides, "Covenant Marriage," p. 1093.

43. See Scoles, Hay, Borchers, Symeonides, *Conflict of Laws*, §§ 3.26-3.29, with references to case law.

44. See, in the older law, *Slater v. Mexican Nat'l R. Co.*, 194 U.S. 120, 24 S. Ct. 581 (1904).

nant may indeed be inadequate: proceeding with the divorce leaves the respondent with an empty contract claim. Of the three reasons for dismissal, only the first (an implied choice of forum) would effectuate the (original) intent of both parties. The other two represent a court-closing, as far as the petitioner is concerned. All three of the procedural aspects will be the subject of subsection (g) below. For present purposes suffice it to conclude that, while a court may wish to give effect to the contractual undertakings of the parties in some form, its application of local law would not be a forbidden impairment of contract.

## f. The Choice-of-Law Alternatives Evaluated

As discussed earlier, the parties are generally free to choose the applicable law. Limitations on this freedom protect the weaker party, such as in consumer transactions. These limitations are grounded in considerations of public policy. In family law, parties generally cannot, by contract, redefine marriage or the consequences of its possible breakdown. It follows that what they cannot do by express stipulation, they also cannot do by means of a choice-of-law clause. The second court, if it has the requisite contact with the party or parties, will make its own choice of law. The case with a choice-of-law clause thus does not differ, for these purposes, from one without one. Ignoring the parties' choice of law or their express stipulation does not impair their contract, inasmuch as they could not make a contract in this regard. Nor does the Full Faith and Credit Clause command application of the *lex celebrationis*.

In these circumstances, the second forum has traditionally applied local law to decide a petition for dissolution. It bears additional discussion whether a state that has embraced the Restatement Second is likely, in the context of covenant marriages, to depart from the traditional rule or to adhere to it (as the Restatement's forum-orientation in Section 6(2)(b) would also permit).

In an *ex parte* divorce, the petitioner will be a local domiciliary. Equal treatment with other local domiciliaries may require application of local law. Even if a distinction based on the place of marriage formation is constitutionally permissible, public policy considerations favor helping a locally domiciled petitioner. Even legal systems that do not apply local law as a matter of course, but apply the law of the parties' common nationality or last habitual residence, will make an exception in favor of their own nationals: local law applies if it would permit divorce when the foreign law would not. The same result may be expected in an American forum for which "domicile" takes on the same meaning as the relevant connecting factor as "nationality" does in the civil law.[45] The answer may be different if an *ex parte* divorce can be granted on jurisdictional

45. See note 39 above.

grounds less than domicile or habitual residence: the petitioner would no longer be suing "at home." Additionally, *Allstate Ins. Co. v. Hague* would then require a determination whether the quality of forum contacts permits the application of its law.

If the divorce is bilateral, *uncontested,* and the parties perhaps not even domiciled in the forum, the forum does not have the same reason to be protective of them: it *could* engage in Restatement Second analysis and apply "home law." But why should it deny a divorce to parties who consensually want it (and, by not suing at home but in the forum, may even be said to have made an implied choice of law), when it would grant an *ex parte* divorce (above) with one party *not* consenting (at least not expressly)? If the parties do not want "home law" protection, F-2 would be most unlikely, it seems, to effectuate the (now abstract) societal interests of F-1.

In a *contested* bilateral divorce, there obviously is no room to assume an implied choice of forum law. However, and in contrast to an uncontested, consensual divorce, jurisdiction will be part of the contest. If the petitioner satisfies the jurisdictional requirement, the case then does not differ from the *ex parte* divorce discussed above: forum law will be protective of his or her interests. It is only in the case that a nonresident petitioner brings the action at the respondent's domicile (in a noncovenant state)[46] that the forum's protective policies may not apply. The petitioner cannot claim them, and the respondent does not want them but instead invokes the policies of the covenant state's law. In this case, the forum has the sufficient nexus to permit it to apply forum law, but arguably might choose not to do so in order to protect, in Restatement language, the respondent's "justified expectations." Concern for the uniform administration and exercise of its divorce jurisdiction, however, may still lead the forum to apply the *lex fori.*

Finally, the nonresident petitioner may seek a contested bilateral divorce against an equally nonresident respondent. In this constellation, both jurisdiction and the applicable law are in issue. Depending on whether domicile is or is not required,[47] respondent may or may not succeed with a motion to dismiss the case. If the case goes forward, the lack of a genuine nexus to the forum may now indeed preclude the application of forum law. This may be the chosen (covenant-state) law or the law of another, closely connected state (for example, that of the last common domicile).

The impairment-of-contract suggestion similarly will not lead to the en-

---

46. If the respondent is still domiciled in the covenant state, the *lex-fori* approach of current law would result in the application of its law.

47. See Scoles, Hay, Borchers, Symeonides, *Conflict of Laws,* § 3-36.

forcement of the standards of a covenant marriage state. In Louisiana, the contractual limitation assumed by the parties is seen as an exception to their general inability to affect matrimonial law by contract.[48] The public policy arguments outlined above also support F-2's refusal to recognize such an exception with respect to its own law. Even if, contrary to the development of F-2 law, recognition were generally due to the public acts of F-1, public policy would overcome it.

What remains is (at best) a contract that is valid where made, unenforceable in F-2 with respect to counseling requirements and waiting periods, and possibly breached with respect to the "best effort" part: The last might support an action for breach. But what relief could be sought? Injunctive relief is not available for the public policy reasons stated. Thus only damages may be possible. But compensatory damages will be hard to prove and anything else (pain and suffering, punitive damages) would support enforcement and will therefore not be granted.

### g. Changing the Applicable Law through Changing Courts

Unless the approach to choice of law in divorce were to change substantially, the American forum court will apply local law. If the forum state is not a covenant marriage state, the only way to have covenant marriage law apply then lies in a change of courts. As mentioned above in subsection (e), a change of courts could occur if the parties have chosen a court in a state with covenant marriage, and the forum honors the choice, or if the forum court were to dismiss for lack of an appropriate remedy or for reasons of *forum non conveniens*, whereby the latter two obviously overlap.

The parties may have made an express selection of a forum for future disputes. Covenant marriage legislation concerning the "Declaration of Intent" does not require this, and it is not very likely that the parties will augment the standard document. The question must then be whether, from all the circumstances, it should be concluded that they have made an implied forum selection.

In England, the choice of English law may encompass a choice of forum.[49] This is generally not the case in the United States.[50] The choice of the forum is

---

48. Spaht and Symeonides, "Covenant Marriage," p. 1090 n. 22.

49. See Order 11, rule 1(1)(d)(iii) of the Supreme Court of Judicature of England providing for jurisdiction over a nonresident defendant for claims arising out of a contract which was to be "governed by English law." For an application, see *Egon Oldendruff v. Liberia Corporations*, 1996 Lloyd's Rep. 380 (QB Div., Commercial Court, 1995).

50. Compare *Burger King Corp. v. Rudzewicz*, 471 U.S. 462, 482, 105 S. Ct. 2174, 2187 (1985): "Although [a choice-of-law] provision standing alone would be insufficient to confer jurisdic-

separate from that of the applicable law and, while both may occur as a result of implied intent, such intent must appear clearly from the circumstances.[51] In the present case, there may be argument either way. On the one hand, parties who live in the covenant state and sign a choice-of-law clause in its favor may have assumed that any dispute would be resolved there. On the other hand, it may be stretching this to suppose that parties, who have never addressed the question expressly, intend to bind themselves to return to the covenant state to seek a divorce regardless of where, years after marrying, they may now find themselves. Additionally, the choice-of-law clause extends not only to questions relating to dissolution but also to the obligation to make all efforts to preserve the marriage. The latter is plainly compatible with jurisdiction elsewhere.

But probably none of this matters. The second forum, it was seen, exercises divorce jurisdiction and applies its own law because of the close nexus the petitioner has to it (usually domicile). Concern for the local petitioner will not be undone by sending him or her to a forum where he or she no longer wants to be. Hence, even if the parties initially made an implied choice of the covenant state as the future forum, it is unlikely that that choice will force the petitioner, who, admittedly, breaches that undertaking, to sue there.

## International Recognition of Covenant Marriage Standards

Previous discussion assumed that the spouses, after contracting a covenant marriage, later find themselves in one or two other states and one of them there seeks the dissolution of the marriage. The conclusion reached was that such a state would apply its own law and, if different, not honor the restrictions of the covenant marriage state. What if the issue arises abroad? The following addresses the question from the limited perspective of some Western European legal systems.

---

tion, we believe that, when combined with the 20-year interdependent relationship Rudzewicz established with Burger King's Miami headquarters, it reinforced his deliberate affiliation with the forum State and the reasonable foreseeability of possible litigation there."

51. Compare Russell J. Weintraub, *Commentary on the Conflict of Laws,* fourth ed. (New York: Foundation, 2001), p. 445, n. 22. In the European Community, a forum selection must be "in writing or evidenced in writing," or be "in a form that accords with the practices of the parties" or accords with international usage. Council Regulation No. 44/2001, 2001 Official Journal L 12/1, art. 23. Additionally, jurisdiction lies in the courts of the stipulated performance of the contract. Council Regulation No. 44/2001, 2001 Official Journal L 12/1, art. 5. The legislation on jurisdiction in matrimonial matters does not provide for a forum selection by the parties at all.

## Jurisdiction

In the European Union, except Denmark, divorce jurisdiction is governed by European Community Regulation No. 1347/2000.[52] According to Art. 3(1)(a), a court has jurisdiction when both spouses are habitually resident in the state, when they had their last common habitual residence in the state and one of them still does, or if the respondent is habitually resident there. In these circumstances, both parties or at least the respondent have a nexus to the forum. What if the application is *ex parte* and the respondent does not have such a nexus? In these cases, jurisdiction may be based on petitioner's "habitual residence," which, for these purposes, is defined as twelve-months residence before filing or six-months residence when the applicant is also a national of the state.[53] These rules thus require a nexus (habitual residence of one or both spouses) to the forum. Since the court will examine its jurisdiction *ex officio*, jurisdiction cannot be conferred consensually by mere appearance of the spouses. In this respect, the rules are stricter than in the United States. Indeed, the durational residence requirement in the case of the *ex parte* divorce (especially if sought by a nonnational) may be stricter than the American domicile standard. In one other respect, however, the rules are potentially troublesome: If no court in the European Union has jurisdiction under these rules, national law determines jurisdiction and, if it provides for jurisdiction over a nonresident, nonnational respondent, any national of a member state, habitually resident in that or another member state, may avail himself or herself of that jurisdictional basis.

## Applicable Law

### General Rule: Home Law

Unlike American law, European legal systems do not only look for a nexus to the parties for the assertion of jurisdiction but also seek to apply a law that has a nexus to the marriage. In traditional European conflicts law, it is the law of the parties' common nationality, at the time the divorce application is made, that applies,[54] even if one of them is now habitually resident in the forum state.

52. See Council Regulation No. 2201/2003.

53. In the case of Ireland and the United Kingdom, nationality is replaced by "domicile," as defined by Irish and English law, respectively. Council Regulation art. 3(2).

54. See, for example, for Austria: § 20, in combination with § 18 Austrian Conflicts Statute; France: Code Civ. art. 310; Germany: German Conflicts Statute art. 17 in combination with art.

Since there is no national "American" law of divorce, the reference must be particularized further. A U.S. citizen is also a citizen of the state in which he or she "resides." The applicable law is the law of the common state "citizenship." This may be the state where the covenant marriage was contracted — and its standards therefore are applicable — or a U.S. state to which the parties had moved subsequently. In the latter case, the new state's law would apply, quite possibly not incorporating covenant state standards. If only one spouse had moved, covenant state standards might still apply as the law of the spouses' last *common* citizenship, as provided by most of the laws.

Once *both* parties have acquired a common habitual residence in the European forum state, European systems differ. Some — for instance, the Austrian, German, and Italian — still apply home law, whatever that may be in the case of Americans as just discussed, if one of the parties is still subject to it. In contrast, French and Swiss law limit the application of home law to the cases stated. Hence, if both parties are now habitually resident in the forum, the *lex fori* applies.[55] Systems other than the French and Swiss will also ultimately reach forum law, for instance, when there is neither a present common connection to the law of common nationality or habitual residence nor at least maintenance of such by one of the parties.[56]

Covenant state standards thus may find application in European dissolution proceedings, but this would only occur as long as the nexus to the covenant state continues for both, or at least for one, of the parties.

## Exception: Forum Law As the Result of "Hidden" Renvoi

*Renvoi* describes the practice of considering the applicable foreign law's conflicts rules and, if these should refer back to the forum or onward to a third legal system, to follow that reference. For example: The forum (A), where administration of an estate is pending, refers to the law of the decedent's nationality at death (B), the latter to his or her domicile at death (C). Of course, it is also possible that B or C in the example refer back to A. The question for A is whether to follow B's refer-

---

14; Italy: art. 31 (1), Law No. 218 of May 31, 1995, revising Conflicts Statute; Spain: art. 107, Law No. 18/1990 of Dec. 17, 1990, amending the Código Civil on matters concerning nationality; Switzerland: art. 61, second para., IPRG.

55. France: Code Civ. art. 310; Switzerland: art. 61, para. 1 in combination with para. 2, IPRG.

56. See, for example, for Germany, German Conflicts Statute art. 14 German; P. Hay, Internationales Privatrecht no. 188, 189, 195 (second ed. 2002). See also, for Switzerland, A. Heini, M. Keller, K. Siehr, F. Vischer, P. Voelken, et al., *Kommentar zum Bundesgesetz über das internationale Privatrecht (IPRG)*, Anno. 7 to Art. 61 (1993).

ence to C, or, as in the second example, back to itself. American courts generally do not engage in *renvoi* and would apply B substantive law in the example.[57] Many European courts would consider B's conflicts rule and apply C law.

In circumstances when a European court would look to the American home law of the parties to a divorce proceeding before it, as discussed above, it might consult the American state's conflicts rules for the law applicable to divorce. It would find none: the *lex fori* applies whenever the American court has jurisdiction. To put it differently, the conflicts rule is contained in the jurisdictional rule: whoever has jurisdiction applies local law; if a European court has jurisdiction, American courts would assume that the European court would apply its own law. It is a case, not of an express, but of a "hidden *renvoi*" (hidden in the jurisdictional rule).[58]

"Hidden" *renvoi* is accepted doctrine in Austria, Germany, and Switzerland.[59] A reference to American home law (for example, the law of a covenant state) would result in the application of the *lex fori*. In countries that do not use "hidden" *renvoi*, covenant state law or the law of a successor "home" state would apply.

The inquiry shows that the European court might apply one of three different laws: the covenant state's, that of a subsequent home state (another covenant state's, a noncovenant state's, its own), or its own as a result of "hidden" *renvoi*. As a practical matter, it may make little difference at present whether European or covenant state substantive law is applied. Both require a nexus to the forum for jurisdiction for *ex parte* divorce, both provide for fault-based divorce, and both — for no-fault divorce — often provide for waiting periods of similar length. Application of European law, however, would disregard any impediments that might flow from the parties' "Declaration of Intent." Differ-

---

57. See generally Scoles, Hay, Borchers, Symeonides, *Conflict of Laws*, §§ 3.13-3.14. As the next sentence in the text shows, in European practice A, B, and C reach the same result, while in American practice A's approach does not bring about such uniformity. Occasional American decisions now engage in *renvoi*, but without calling it such: they see in B's conflicts rule an expression of disinterest to have B law applied which, if that rule refers back to A, then permits the application of forum law. See, for example, *Am. Motorists Ins. Co. v. ARTRA Group, Inc.*, 338 Md. 560, 659 A.2d 1295 (1995).

58. See Peter Hay, "Die Anwendung US-amerikanischer jurisdiction-Regeln als Verweisungsnorm bei Scheidung von in Deutschland wohnhaften Amerikanern," *IPRax* (1988): 265.

59. Austria: Decision of the OGH [Supreme Court] of Nov. 8, 2001, *Österreichische Juristenzeitung* 57 (2002): 265; Decision of the OGH of May 14, 1992, *Zeitschrift für Rechtsvergleichung* (1993): 164, with annotation by H. Hoyer at p. 165; Fritz Schwind, *Internationales Privatrecht* no. 111 (Vienna, 1998). Germany: Gerhard Kegel and Klaus Schurig, *Internationales Privatrecht: Ein Studienbuch*, ninth ed. (Munich, 2004), pp. 411-13; Christian von Bar and Peter Mankowski, *Internationales Privatrecht*, second ed. (Munich, 2003), 1:687, n. 898.

ences may be more significant when a European home-law reference is to the law of an American noncovenant state with lesser requirements for divorce, or when potentially applicable European law becomes more liberal in the future, as part of the overall rethinking in Europe of the law relating to marriage, other forms of partnership, and their respective dissolution.

## Other Issues

### The Contract to Use Best Efforts

In the "Declaration of Intent," the parties to a covenant marriage undertake to use best efforts to uphold the marriage, an undertaking said to be meant as an actionable contractual obligation. Will this undertaking be an impediment to dissolution, in the sense of calling for dismissal of an application for failure first to have explored all avenues for maintaining the marriage?

In the covenant state itself, there may be argument for an affirmative answer, perhaps not so much as a matter of contract law but as a definition of the subject matter jurisdiction of that state's courts.[60] In other courts — in noncovenant states or abroad — the answer must be found in contract law, since the covenant state cannot circumscribe their jurisdiction.

In American noncovenant courts, dismissal would specifically enforce the contractual obligation. But specific performance is not a remedy for this kind of highly personal obligation. The drafters of the legislation themselves see damages as the remedy for breach,[61] even though they do not explain how such damages would be quantified. Perhaps more important, it is difficult to see how, in the United States, a state could deny access to divorce jurisdiction to one group of residents and not to others on the basis of the fact that the marriage was contracted out of state and there subject to impediments to its dissolution.

Foreign legal systems that apply home law will make exceptions when home law precludes dissolution. Mere difficulty, however, is not enough; "there is no basic civil right to divorce."[62] Moreover, European contract law, contrary

60. For a parallel, see the first New York *get* statute, which withheld the granting of a civil divorce until impediments to remarriage (including "religious restraints," such as the issuance of a *get*) had been removed. New York, Domestic Relations Law § 253 (McKinney 1986). For discussion, see Michael Broyde, *Marriage, Divorce and the Abandoned Wife in Jewish Law* (New York: Ktav, 2001), p. 35 *et seq.*, and his chapter herein.

61. Spaht, "Louisiana's Covenant Marriage Statute," p. 103.

62. See Staudinger/v.Bar/Mankowski, Kommentar zum EGBGB, Art. 17, no. 106 (thirteenth ed. 1996), with references to German case law.

to the common law, does not regard the remedy of specific performance as extraordinary. Nonetheless, the action would not be dismissed. To do so would unacceptably allow foreign law to define local subject matter jurisdiction or treat the contract as an implied choice-of-court clause, a reading rejected earlier. Again the remedy will be damages. Their award raises its own conflict-of-laws questions and problems; they will not be pursued further here.

### Consequences of Dissolution

The dissolution of a marriage raises questions regarding its consequences for other aspects of the relations of the parties, particularly marital property, child custody, and support. To the extent that these require judicial resolution, this will ordinarily occur at the time of dissolution in a bilateral divorce. Subsequent changes (in child custody and support) as well as the initial determination in an *ex parte* divorce raise separate questions of jurisdiction and applicable law.[63] Covenant marriage legislation does not purport to cover, and the parties' "Declaration of Intent" does not address, the incidents of marriage and the consequences of dissolution. Existing law remains unaffected.

## Conclusion

In the United States, the law of the state where the marriage was celebrated (the *lex celebrationis*) ordinarily governs the validity of the marriage; the law of the state where the action is brought (the *lex fori*) governs divorce. As to divorce, judicial jurisdiction and applicable law converge. In a covenant state, an out-of-state covenant-state marriage will be judged by covenant-state standards but not because the forum adopts the out-of-state standards; rather, this will be done because these standards are now also local law. Covenant marriage standards then become applicable much in the same way that a "uniform" law applies as local law — not as a function of the law of conflict of laws.

If someone seeks to dissolve a covenant marriage in a noncovenant state, the stringency or permissiveness of the latter's substantive law will determine the prerequisites for divorce. The same is generally true abroad. While, in contrast to the United States, many foreign legal systems do apply home law as a matter of conflicts law (and would thus respect covenant-state restrictions

---

63. For discussion in the American (mainly) interstate setting, see Scoles, Hay, Borchers, Symeonides, *Conflict of Laws*, § 15.27 *et seq.*

when American sister states would not!), this reference to home law is quite limited. "Hidden *renvoi*," where it is accepted doctrine, leads to forum law. In other countries, forum law takes over as the ties to the home law become looser, or as a nexus to the forum (such as habitual residence of the parties) in fact now makes the latter the home.

Covenant marriage legislation seeks to counteract permissiveness and to redefine the bonds of marriage in more traditional terms. Opposite trends in Europe and elsewhere seek to redefine the legal nature of relationships and to revisit the preconditions for the dissolution of traditional marriages. The Netherlands has a single form of marriage for heterosexual and same-sex unions by legislation. Massachusetts and Ontario made same-sex marriage possible by judicial decision.[64] A great many European countries provide for registered partnerships for same-sex couples (as do Vermont and, more recently, California with their institution of "civil unions"); except for the name, such partnerships provide the same rights and duties as the traditional marriage.

The divide between these trends — nationally and internationally — and covenant marriage legislation is growing. Despite a traditional home-law orientation in the conflicts law of many civil law countries, a nexus to the forum will often lead to application of that forum's law. The contract aspect of the "Declaration of Intent" in a covenant marriage does not change this conclusion. Party choice does not change forum policy. If this means no enforcement through dismissal, a damage remedy for breach will also not be awarded at a level to function as the indirect equivalent to enforcement. Little then remains.

Accordingly, the legal efficacy of covenant marriages is basically restricted to the state in which they are contracted when the issue arises there. Parallel effects in other states will be the result of parallel legislation, in analogy to uniform laws.

---

64. See note 5. The Ontario decision resulted in a surge of applications for marriage licenses by same-sex couples. "From early June [of 2003] through late February [2004], 1,143 of the 12,046 couples who got married in Toronto were of the same sex. One-fourth of those same-sex couples were from the United States." Dan Chapman, "Gay Union Pioneers Send Ripples South," *The Atlanta Journal-Constitution* (Mar. 4, 2004) (Home ed.): 1A.

# Bibliography

Abbott, Walter M., gen. ed. *The Documents of Vatican II*. Joseph Gallagher, translation ed. London: G. Chapman, 1966.

Abd Al-Halim Abu Shuqqah. *Tahrir al-Mar'ah fi 'Asr al-Risalah*. 6 vols. Kuwait, 1990.

Abu Bakr Muhammad Ibn al-'Arabi. *Ahkaam al-Qur'an*. Beirut, 1987.

Abu Zahrah, Muhammad. *Al-Ahwal al-Shakhsiyah*. Cairo, 1957.

———. *Al-Milkiyah wa Nathariyat al-'Aqd*. Cairo, 1996.

Adams, Abigail. "December 23, 1782." In *The Book of Abigail and John: Selected Letters of the Adams Family*, ed. L. H. Butterfield et al. Cambridge, Mass.: Harvard University Press, 1975.

Ali, A. Yusuf, trans. *The Meaning of the Holy Qur'an*. Eleventh ed. Maryland: Amana Corp., 2004.

Allen, Diogenes. *Love: Christian Romance, Marriage, and Friendship*. Cambridge, Mass.: Cowley, 1987.

Allen, Joseph L. *Love and Conflict: A Covenantal Model of Christian Ethics*. Nashville: Abingdon, 1984.

Amato, Paul R., and Stacey J. Rogers. "Do Attitudes toward Divorce Affect Marital Quality?" *Journal of Family Issues* 20, no. 1 (January 1999): 69-86.

Anderson, F. I., and David Noel Freedman. *Hosea: A New Translation with Introduction and Commentary*. New York: Doubleday, 1980.

Anderson, G. A. *A Time to Mourn, A Time to Dance: The Expression of Grief and Joy in Israelite Religion*. University Park, Pa.: Pennsylvania State University Press, 1991.

Anderson, Katherine, Don S. Browning, and Brian Boyer, eds. *Marriage: Just a Piece of Paper?* Grand Rapids: Eerdmans, 2002.

An-Na'im, Abdullahi, ed. *Islamic Family in a Changing World: A Global Resource Book*. London: Zed Books, 2002.

al-'Asqalani, Ibn Hajar. *Fath al-Bari Sharh Sahih al-Bukhari*. Beirut, 1989.

Axinn, William G., and Arland Thornton. "The Transformation in the Meaning of Marriage." In *The Ties That Bind*, ed. Linda J. Waite. New York: Aldine de Gruyter, 2000.

Backer, Emile de. "Tertullian." In *Pour l'histoire du mot sacramentum*, ed. J. de Ghellinck. Louvain: Spicilegium Sacrum Lovaniensis, 1924.

Balch, David, and Carolyn Osiek. *Families in the New Testament World: Households and House Churches.* Louisville: Westminster John Knox Press, 1997.

al-Ba'li, Abd al-Hamid Mahmoud. *Dhawabit al-'Uqud.* Cairo, 1989.

Baltzer, Klaus. *The Covenant Formulary in Old Testament, Jewish, and Early Christian Writings.* Philadelphia: Fortress, 1971.

Balzell, Digby E. *Puritan Boston and Quaker Philadelphia.* New York: Free Press, 1979.

Barth, Markus. *Ephesians: Translation and Commentary on Chapters Four to Six.* The Anchor Bible. New York: Doubleday, 1974.

al-Baqi, Zaidan 'Abd. *Al-Mar'ah Bayna Al-Din Wa Al-Mujtama'.* Cairo, 1977.

Batiffol, Henri, and Paul Lagarde. *Droit international privé.* 2 vols. Paris: Librairie générale de droit et de jurisprudence, 1981-83.

Baxter, Richard. *The Reformed Liturgy: "Of the Service of Matrimony."* In his *The Practical Works.* 4 vols. London: G. Virtue, 1838.

Becker, Gary S. *A Treatise on the Family.* Cambridge, Mass.: Harvard University Press, 1991.

Beckstrom, Myra. "Pollster's Data Tell Churches How Their Believers Behave." *Commercial Appeal.* Aug. 17, 1996, 16A.

Bell, Catherine. "Ritual Behavior." Ph.D. Dissertation. Berkeley, Calif., 1989.

————. *Ritual Theory, Ritual Practice: Perspectives and Dimensions.* Rev. ed. New York: Oxford University Press, 1995.

Bennett, Neil G., et al. "Commitment and the Modern Union: Assessing the Link between Premarital Cohabitation and Subsequent Marital Stability." *American Sociological Review* 53 (1988): 127-38.

Berger, Brigitte, and Peter L. Berger. *The War over the Family.* New York: Anchor Press/ Doubleday, 1983.

Berger, Peter. *The Capitalist Revolution.* New York: Basic Books, 1986.

Biddle, Perry H., Jr. *A Marriage Manual.* Grand Rapids: Eerdmans, 1994.

Blankenhorn, David. *Fatherless America: Confronting Our Most Urgent Social Problem.* New York: Basic, 1995.

Bleich, David. "Jewish Divorce: Judicial Misconceptions and Possible Means of Civil Enforcement." *Connecticut Law Review* 16 (1984): 201-89.

Booth, Alan, and Ann C. Crouter, eds. *Just Living Together: Implications of Cohabitation on Families, Children, and Social Policy.* Mahwah, N.J.: Erlbaum, 2002.

Booth, Alan, and Paul R. Amato. *A Generation at Risk: Growing Up in an Era of Family Upheaval.* Cambridge, Mass.: Harvard University Press, 1997.

————. "Parental Predivorce Relations and Offspring Postdivorce Well Being." *Journal of Marriage and the Family* 63 (2001): 197-212.

Booty, John. *The Book of Common Prayer 1559.* Charlottesville, Va.: Published for the Folger Shakespeare Library by the University Press of Virginia, 1976.

Bradstreet, Anne. "To My Dear and Loving Husband." In *The American Puritans: Their Prose and Poetry,* ed. Perry Miller. Garden City, N.Y.: Doubleday, 1956.

Breck, John. *The Sacred Gift of Life: Orthodox Christianity and Bioethics.* New York: St. Vladimir's Seminary Press, 2000.

Breitowitz, Irving A. *Between Civil and Religious Law: The Plight of the Agunah in American Society.* Westport, Conn.: Greenwood, 1993.

Brinig, Margaret F. "Equality and Sharing: Views of Household across the Iron Curtain." *European Journal of Law and Economics* 7 (1999): 55-63.

———. "The Family Franchise: Elderly Parents and Adult Siblings." *Utah Law Review* (1996): 393-428.

———. "Finite Horizons? The American Family." *International Journal of Children's Rights* 2 (1994): 293-315.

———. *From Contract to Covenant: Beyond the Law and Economics of the Family.* Cambridge, Mass.: Harvard University Press, 2000.

———. "Property Distribution Physics: The Talisman of Time and Middle Class Law." *Family Law Quarterly* 31 (1997): 93-118.

———. "Rethinking Marriage: Feminist Ideology, Economic Change, and Divorce Reform." *Tulane Law Review* 65 (1991): 953-1010.

———. "Rings and Promises." *Journal of Law, Economics, and Organization* 6 (1990): 203-15.

———. "Status, Contract and Covenant." *Cornell Law Review* 79 (1994): 1573-1602.

———. "Troxel and the Limits of Community." *Rutgers Law Journal* 32 (2001): 733-82.

Brinig, Margaret F., and Douglas W. Allen. "These Boots Are Made for Walking: Why Most Divorce Filers Are Women." *American Law and Economics Review* 2 (2000): 126-68.

Brinig, Margaret F., and Steven L. Nock. "Covenant and Contract." *Regent University Law Review* 12 (2000): 9-26.

———. "How Much Does Legal Status Matter? Adoptions by Kin Caregivers." *Family Law Quarterly* 36 (2002): 449-74.

Brinig, Margaret F., and F. H. Buckley. "Joint Custody: Bonding and Monitoring Theories." *Indiana Law Journal* 73 (1998): 393-427.

———. "No-Fault Laws and At-Fault People." *International Review of Law and Economics* 18, no. 3 (1998): 325-40.

———. "The Price of Virtue." *Public Choice* 98 (1999): 111-29.

Brown, Susan, and Alan Booth. "Cohabitation Versus Marriage: A Comparison of Relationship Quality." *Journal of Marriage and Family* 58 (1996): 668-78.

Browning, Don S. *Marriage and Modernization: How Globalization Threatens Marriage and What to Do about It.* Grand Rapids: Eerdmans, 2003.

Browning, Don. S., et al. *From Culture Wars to Common Ground: Religion and the American Family Debate.* Louisville: Westminster John Knox, 1997.

Broyde, Michael J. "Informing on Others for Violating American Law: A Jewish Law View." *Journal of Halacha and Contemporary Society* 41 (2002): 5-49.

———. *Marriage, Divorce and the Abandoned Wife in Jewish Law: A Conceptual Approach to the Agunah Problems in America.* New York: Ktav, 2001.

———. "The New York State Get [Jewish Divorce] Law." *Tradition: A Journal of Jewish Thought* 29, no. 4 (1995): 3-14.

Broyde, Michael J., and Chaim Malinowitz. "The 1992 New York Get Law: An Exchange." *Tradition: A Journal of Jewish Thought* 31, no. 3 (1997): 23-41.

Broyde, Michael J., and Chaim Malinowitz. "The 1992 New York Get Law: An Exchange III." *Tradition: A Journal of Jewish Thought* 32, no. 1 (1999): 99-100, and 33, no. 1 (1999): 101-9.

Broyde, Michael J., and Jonathan Reiss. "The Ketubah in America: Its Value in Dollars, Its

Significance in Halacha, and Its Enforceability in American Law." *Journal of Halacha and Contemporary Society* 47 (2004): 101-24.

Bryant, Chalandra M., and Rand D. Conger. "Marital Success and Domains of Social Support in Long-Term Relationships: Does the Influence of Network Members Ever End?" *Journal of Marriage and the Family* 61 (1999): 437-50.

Buckley, F. H., and Larry E. Ribstein. "Calling a Truce in the Marriage Wars." *University of Illinois Law Review* (2001): 561-610.

al-Bukhari, Muhammad Ibn Isma'il. *Sahih al-Bukhari.* Beirut, n.d.

Bumiller, Elisabeth. "Why America Has Gay Marriage Jitters." *New York Times Week in Review,* Aug. 10, 2003.

Bumpass, Larry L., and Hsien-Hen Lu. "Trends in Cohabitation and Implications for Children's Family Contexts in the United States." *Population Studies* 54 (2000): 29-41.

Bumpass, Larry L., and James A. Sweet. "National Estimates of Cohabitation." *Demography* 26, no. 4 (1989): 615-25.

Burke, Raymond L. "Vatican Council II and Matrimonial Law." In *Vatican II: Assessment and Perspectives,* ed. René Latourelle. 3 vols. New York: Paulist, 1988-89.

Buss, Martin J. *The Prophetic Words of Hosea: A Morphological Study.* Berlin: Töpelmann, 1969.

Butler, Henry N. "The Contractual Theory of the Corporation." *George Mason University Law Review* 11 (1989): 99-123.

Cahill, Lisa Sowle. *Between the Sexes: Foundations for a Christian Ethics of Sexuality.* Philadelphia: Fortress, 1985.

————. *Sex, Gender, and Christian Ethics.* Cambridge/New York: Cambridge University Press, 1996.

Cain, Patricia A. "Imagine There's No Marriage." *Quinnipiac Law Review* 16 (1997): 27-60.

Call, Vaughn, and Tim B. Heaton. "Religious Influence on Marital Stability." *Journal for the Scientific Study of Religion* 36, no. 3 (1997): 382-92.

Calvin, John. *Institutes of the Christian Religion.* Ed. John T. McNeill. Trans. Ford Lewis Battles. Philadelphia: Westminster, 1960.

Campbell, Colin. *The Romantic Ethic and the Spirit of Modern Consumerism.* Oxford: B. Blackwell, 1987.

Caprile, G., ed. *Concilio Vaticano II.* Roma: Edizioni La Civilta Cattolica, 1969.

Carbone, June R. *From Partners to Parents: The Second Revolution in Family Law.* New York: Columbia University Press, 2000.

Carbone, June, and Margaret F. Brinig. "Rethinking Marriage: Feminist Ideology, Economic Change, and Divorce Reform." *Tulane Law Review* 65 (1991): 953-1010.

Cargill Thompson, W. D. J. *The Political Thought of Martin Luther.* New York: Barnes and Noble, 1984.

Casper, Lynne M., and Suzanne M. Bianchi. *Continuity and Change in the American Family.* Thousand Oaks, Calif.: Sage, 2002.

Chapman, Dan. "Gay Union Pioneers Send Ripples South." *The Atlanta Journal Constitution,* March 4, 2004.

Cherlin, Andrew. "The Effect of Children on Marital Dissolution." *Demography* 14 (1977): 265-72.

Chesterton, G. K. *What's Wrong with the World*. New York: Dodd, Mead, and Company, 1910.

Chrysostom, John. *On Genesis*. In *Drinking from the Hidden Fountain: A Patristic Breviary*. Cistercian Studies Series no. 148. Kalamazoo, Mich.: Cistercian Publications, 1993.

Chused, Richard. *Private Acts in Public Places: A Social History of Divorce in the Formative Era of American Family Laws*. Philadelphia: University of Pennsylvania Press, 1994.

Clark, Homer H., Jr. *The Law of Domestic Relations in the United States*. Second ed. St. Paul, Minn.: West Pub. Co., 1988.

Cleaver, Robert. *A Godlie Forme of Householde Government*. London, 1598.

Clouston, William Alexander. *Arabian Poetry, for English Readers*. Glasgow: [McLaren and Son, printer], 1881.

Cohen, Bernard I., ed. *Puritanism and the Rise of Modern Science*. New Brunswick, N.J.: Rutgers University Press, 1990.

Collett, Teresa Stanton. "Marriage, Family and the Positive Law." *Notre Dame Journal of Law, Ethics and Public Policy* 10 (1996): 467-84.

Colloquium. "Creativity and Responsibility: Covenant, Contract, and the Resolution of Disputes." *Emory Law Journal* 36 (1987): 533-40.

Cott, Nancy F. *Public Vows: A History of Marriage and Nation*. Cambridge: Harvard University Press, 2000.

Delhaye, Philippe. "Dignité du mariage et de la famille." In *L'Église dans le Monde de ce temps*, ed. Yves Congar and Michael Peuchmaurd, vol. 2, pp. 387-453. Paris: Du Cerf, 1967.

Denzinger, Henricus, and Adolphus Schönmetzer. *Enchiridion Symbolorum Definitionum et Declarationum de Rebus Fidei et Morum*. Freiburg: Herder, 1965.

Doms, Herbert. *The Meaning of Marriage*. Trans. George Sayer. London: Sheed and Ward, 1939.

Durkheim, Émile. *The Elementary Forms of the Religious Life*. New York: Free Press, 1966.

Eichrodt, Walter. *Theology of the Old Testament*. Trans. J. A. Baker. 2 vols. Philadelphia: Westminster, 1961, 1967.

Elazar, Daniel J. *Covenant and Commonwealth: From Christian Separation through the Protestant Reformation*. New Brunswick, N.J.: Transaction, 1996.

————. *Covenant and Polity in Biblical Israel: Biblical Foundations and Jewish Expressions*. New Brunswick, N.J.: Transaction, 1995.

Ellman, Ira Mark. "The Place of Fault in a Modern Divorce Law." *Arizona State Law Journal* 28 (1996): 773-838.

————. "The Theory of Alimony." *California Law Review* 77 (1989): 1-82.

Elon, Menachem. *Principles of Jewish Law*. 4 vols. Jerusalem: Keter, 1973.

Epstein, Louis M. *The Jewish Marriage Contract*. New York: Jewish Theological Seminary of America, 1927.

Ernst, Carl W. *Following Muhammad: Rethinking Islam in the Contemporary World*. Chapel Hill, N.C.: University of North Carolina Press, 2003.

Etzioni, Amitai. "How to Make Marriage Matter." *Time,* September 1993, 76.

Evdokimov, P. *The Sacrament of Love: The Nuptial Mystery in the Light of the Orthodox Tradition*. Crestwood, N.Y.: St. Vladimir's Seminary Press, 1985.

Everett, William Johnson. *Blessed Be the Bond: Christian Perspectives on Marriage and Family.* Philadelphia: Fortress, 1985.

————. "Contract and Covenant in Human Community." *Emory Law Journal* 36 (1987): 557-68.

————. *Religion, Federalism, and the Struggle for Public Life: Cases from Germany, India, and America.* New York: Oxford University Press, 1997.

Fagan, Patrick F., and Dorothy B. Hanks. "The Child Abuse Crisis: The Disintegration of Marriage, Family, and the American Community." *Backgrounder* 115 (1997): 1-15.

Falk, Z. W. *Jewish Matrimonial Law in the Middle Ages.* London: Oxford University Press, 1966.

Farah, Madelain. *Marriage and Sexuality in Islam: A Translation of al-Ghazali's Book on the Etiquette of Marriage from the Ihya'.* Salt Lake City: University of Utah Press, 1984.

Faraj, Ahmad. *Al-Zawaj wa Ahkamuhu fi Madhahib ahl al-Sunnah.* Mansourah, Egypt, 1989.

Feldman, David M. *Birth Control in Jewish Law.* New York: New York University Press, 1968.

Fessenden, Tracy, N. Radel, and M. J. Zaborowska. *The Puritan Origins of American Sex.* New York: Routledge, 2001.

Finkelman, Paul. "New York's Get Laws: A Constitutional Analysis." *Columbia Journal of Law and Social Problems* 27 (1993): 55-100.

Fisher, Helen E. "The Four Year Itch." *Natural History* 96 (1987): 22-33.

Fisk, Catherine L., "Removing the 'Fuel of Interest' from the 'Fire of Genius': Law and the Employee-Inventor, 1830-1930." *University of Chicago Law Review* 65 (1998): 1127-98.

Freidman, Mordechai Akiva. *Jewish Marriage in Palestine.* 2 vols. Tel Aviv: Tel Aviv University, 1983.

Friedman, Lawrence M. "Rights of Passage: Divorce Law in Historical Perspective." *Oregon Law Review* 63 (1984): 649-70.

Fuchs, Eric. *Sexual Desire and Love.* Cambridge: J. Clarke, 1983.

Fukuyama, Francis. *Trust: The Social Virtues and the Creation of Prosperity.* New York: Free Press, 1995.

Gabrieli, Francesco. "Adab." In *Encyclopedia of Islam,* ed. J. van Let et al. Second ed. Leiden: E. J. Brill, 1997.

Gagnon, Robert. *The Bible and Homosexual Practice.* Nashville: Abingdon, 2001.

al-Ghandur, Ahmad. *Al-Ahwal al-Shakhsiyah fi al-Tashri' al-Islami.* Kuwait, 1972.

al-Ghazali, Abu Hamid. *'Ihya' 'Ulum al-Deen,* eleventh century, reprint. Egypt: Mustafa Babi al-Halabi Press, 1939.

al-Ghazali, Abu Hamid. *Marriage and Sexuality in Islam: A Translation of al-Ghazali's Book on the Etiquette of Marriage from the Ihya'.* Trans. Madelain Farah. Salt Lake City: University of Utah Press, 1984.

al-Ghazali, Abu Hamid. *The Faith and Practice of al-Ghazali.* Trans. W. Montgomery Watt. Chicago: Kazi, 1982.

Gibb, H. A. R. *Arabic Literature: An Introduction.* London: Oxford University Press, 1963.

Ginzberg, Louis. *The Legends of the Jews.* New York: Jewish Publication Society, 1968.

Glendon, Mary Ann. *The New Family and the New Property.* Toronto: Butterworths, 1981.

Goode, William J. *World Changes in Divorce Patterns.* New Haven: Yale University Press, 1993.

Gouge, William. *Of Domesticall Duties Eight Treatises.* London, 1622.

Green, Joyce H., John V. Long, and Roberta L. Murawski. *Dissolution of Marriage.* Colorado Springs: Shepard's/McGraw-Hill, 1986.

Greenawalt, Kent. "Religious Law and Civil Law: Using Secular Law to Assure Observance of Practices with Religious Significance." *Southern California Law Review* 71 (1998): 781-844.

Greenberg-Kobrin, Michelle. "Civil Enforceability of Religious Prenuptial Agreements." *Columbia Journal of Law and Social Problems* 32 (summer 1999): 359-400.

Gregory, John De Witt, et al. *Understanding Family Law.* New York: Matthew Bender, 1993.

Gulati, Mitu. "When Corporate Managers Fear a Good Thing Is Coming to an End: The Case of Interim Disclosure." *UCLA Law Review* 46 (1999): 675-756.

Hall, Catherine. "The Sweet Delights of Home." In *A History of Private Life,* gen. ed. Michelle Perrot, Philippe Ariés, and Georges Duby. Cambridge, Mass.: Belknap Press of Harvard University Press, 1990.

Hansen, Gary L. "Moral Reasoning and the Marital Exchange Relationship." *Journal of Social Psychology* 131 (1991): 71-81.

Hansford, Donald W. "Comment: Injunction Remedy for Breach of Restrictive Covenants: An Economic Analysis." *Mercer Law Review* 45 (1993): 543-58.

Harakas, Stanley S. "Christian Faith Concerning Creation and Biology." In *La Theologie dans l'Eglise et dans le Monde: Les Études theologiques de Chambésy,* 4. Chambésy, Switzerland: Publications of the Orthodox Center of the Ecumenical Patriarchate, 1984.

―――. *Health and Medicine in the Eastern Orthodox Tradition: Faith, Liturgy, and Wholeness.* New York: Crossroad, 1990. Reprint edition Minneapolis: Light and Life, 1996.

―――. "Religious Question Box." *Hellenic Chronicle* (November 13, 1986): 4.

Häring, Bernhard. *Commentary on the Documents of Vatican II.* Vol. 5. New York: Herder and Herder, 1969.

Harrison, L. E., and S. P. Huntington. *Culture Matters: How Values Shape Human Progress.* New York: Basic, 2000.

Hawkins, Alan, Steven L. Nock, Julia C. Wilson, Laura Sanchez, and James Wright. "Attitudes about Covenant Marriage and Divorce: Policy Implications from a Three-State Comparison." *Family Relations* 51 (2002): 166-75.

Hay, Peter. "Die Anwendung US-amerikanischer jurisdiction-Regeln als Verweisungsnorm bei Scheidung von in Deutschland wohnhaften Amerikanern." *IPRax* (1988): 265.

Haywood, J. A. "Madjnun Layla." In *Encyclopedia of Islam,* ed. J. van Let et al. Second ed. Leiden: E. J. Brill, 1997.

Hera, Alberto de la, and Rosa María Martínez de Codes, ed. *Spanish Legislation on Religious Affairs.* Madrid: Ministeria de Justicia, Centro de Publicationes, 1998.

al-Hibri, Azizah. "Islam, Law and Custom: Redefining Muslim Women's Rights." *American University Journal of International Law and Policy* 12 (1997): 1-44.

―――. "Islamic Constitutionalism and the Concept of Democracy." *Case Western Reserve Journal of International Law* 24 (1992): 1-28.

———. "The Muslim Perspective on the Clergy-Penitent Privilege." *Loyola Los Angeles Law Review* 29 (1996): 1723-32.

Hillers, Delbert R. *Covenant: The History of a Biblical Idea.* Baltimore: Johns Hopkins Press, 1969.

Himmelfarb, Gertrude. "The Panglosses of the Right Are Wrong." *The Wall Street Journal*, 4 February 1999, A22.

Hodkinson, Keith. *Muslim Family Law: A Sourcebook.* London: Croom Helm, 1984.

Holmes, Michael W., ed. *The Apostolic Fathers: Greek Texts and English Translations.* Grand Rapids: Baker Books, 1999.

Howard, George Eliot. *A History of Matrimonial Institutions.* 3 vols. Chicago: University of Chicago Press, 1904.

Hugenberger, Gordon P. *Marriage As a Covenant: A Study of Biblical Law and Ethics Governing Marriage Developed from the Perspective of Malachi.* Leiden: Brill, 1994.

Hunt, L. "The Unstable Boundaries of the French Revolution." In *A History of Private Life*, gen. ed. Michelle Perrot, Philippe Ariés, and Georges Duby. Cambridge, Mass.: Belknap Press of Harvard University Press, 1990.

Hunter, David G., trans. and ed. *Marriage in the Early Church.* Minneapolis: Fortress, 1992.

Ibn al-Arabi, Abu Bakr Muhammad. *Ahkaam al-Qur'an.* Beirut: Dar al-Ma'rifah, 1987.

Ibn Hazm, Abu Muhammad Ali Ibn Sa'ed. *Al-Muhalla bi al-Athar.* Beirut, 1988.

Ibn Rushd, Abu al-Walid Muhammad. *Bidayat al-Mujtahid wa Nihayat al-Muqtasid.* Beirut, 1995.

Ibn Taymiyyah, Taqi al-Din Ahmad. *Majmou'at al-Fatawi.* al-Mansoura, Egypt, 1998.

Jacob, E. *Osee.* Neuchâtel: Delachaux et Niestlé, 1965.

James, E. O. *Christian Myth and Ritual: A Historical Study.* Cleveland: Meridian, 1965.

al-Jaziri, Abd al-Rahaman. *Kitab al-Fiqh 'ala al-Madhahib al-Arba'ah.* Beirut, 1969.

Jedin, Hubert. *A History of the Council of Trent.* Trans. Ernest Graf. St. Louis: Herder, 1958.

Jerome. *Comment in Osee.* In *Patrologiae Cursus Completus, Series Latina*, ed. J. P. Migne. Paris: Vrayet de Surcy, 1845.

Johnson, James T. *A Society Ordained by God: English Puritan Marriage Doctrine in the First Half of the Seventeenth Century.* Nashville: Abingdon, 1970.

Kahan, Linda. "Jewish Divorce and Secular Court: The Promise of *Avitzur.*" *Georgetown Law Journal* 73 (1984): 193-224.

Kempis, Thomas à. *The Imitation of Christ.* Trans. William Benham. New York: P. F. Collier and Son, 1909.

Kent, James. *Commentaries on American Law.* 12th ed. Ed. Oliver Wendell Holmes Jr. 2 vols. Boston: Little, Brown, and Company, 1896.

al-Khamlishi, Ahmed. *Al-Ta'liq 'Ala Qanun al-Ahwal al-Shakhsiyah.* 2 vols. Rabat, 1987.

Khazdan, Alexander. "Byzantine Hagiography and Sex in the Fifth through Twelfth Centuries." Dumbarton Oaks Papers, number 44. Washington, D.C.: Dumbarton Oaks Research Library and Collection, 1990.

Koukoules, Phaidon. *Byzantinon Bios kai Politismos.* Athens: French Institute of Athens, 1951.

Kronman, Anthony. "Contract Law and the State of Nature." *Journal of Law, Economics and Organization* 1 (1985): 5-32.

Kwam, Kristen E., et al., eds. *Eve and Adam: Jewish, Christian, and Muslim Readings on Genesis and Gender.* Bloomington: Indiana University Press, 1999.

Lamm, Norman. "Recent Additions to the Ketubah." *Tradition* 2 (1959): 93-119.

Lampe, G. W. H., ed. *A Patristic Greek Lexicon.* Oxford: Clarendon, 1961.

Landes, David. *The Wealth and Poverty of Nations.* New York: W. W. Norton, 1998.

Landes, Elizabeth M. "The Economics of Alimony." *Journal of Legal Studies* 7 (1978): 35-63.

Langbein, John H. "The Twentieth-Century Revolution in Family Wealth Transmission." *Michigan Law Review* 86 (1988): 722-51.

Langford, Andy. *Christian Weddings: Resources to Make Your Ceremony Unique.* Nashville: Abingdon, 1995.

Lawler, Michael G. "Faith, Contract, and Sacrament in Christian Marriage: A Theological Approach." *Theological Studies* 52 (1991): 725-29.

———. *Family: American and Christian.* Chicago: Loyola, 1998.

———. *Marriage and the Catholic Church: Disputed Questions.* Collegeville, Minn.: Liturgical Press, 2002.

———. *Symbol and Sacrament: A Contemporary Sacramental Theology.* Omaha: Creighton University Press, 1995.

Levin, Leo, and Meyer Kramer. *New Provisions in the Ketubah: A Legal Opinion.* New York: Yeshiva University Press, 1955.

Lewis, C. S. *The Lion, the Witch and the Wardrobe.* New York: Macmillan, 1950.

Lieberman, Saul. *Tosefta Kifshuta: Nashim.* New York: Jewish Theological Seminary of America, 1973.

Locke, John. *Two Treatises of Government.* Ed. Peter Laslett. Cambridge: Cambridge University Press, 1960.

Loconte, Joe. "I'll Stand Bayou." *Policy Review* 89 (May/June 1998): 30-34.

Lundberg, Shelly, and Elaina Rose. "The Effects of Sons and Daughters on Men's Labor Supply and Wages." *Review of Economics and Statistics* 84 (2002): 251-68.

Luther, Martin. *Luther's Works.* Ed. Jaroslav Pelikan et al. St. Louis: Concordia, 1955-1971.

Macedo, Stephen, and Iris Marion Young, eds. *Child, Family, and State.* New York: New York University Press, 2003.

MacNeil, Ian. "Efficient Breach of Contract: Circles in the Sky." *Virginia Law Review* 68 (1983): 947-70.

Madelung, Wilfred. "Shi'i Attitudes Toward Women As Reflected in Fiqh." In *Society and the Sexes in Medieval Islam,* by the Sixth Giorgio Levi della Vida Conference, ed. Afaf Lutfi al-Sayyid Marsot. Malibu, Calif.: Undena, 1979.

Maher, Bridget. "Why Marriage Should Be Privileged in Public Policy." *Insight* no. 254. Washington, D.C.: Family Research Council, April 16, 2003.

Mason, Mary Ann, Arlene Skolnick, and Stephen D. Sugarman. *All Our Families: New Policies for a New Century: A Report of the Berkeley Family Forum.* New York: Oxford University Press, 1998.

Mazeaud, Henri, et al. *Leçons de Droit Civil: La Famille.* Ed. Laurent Levenuer. Seventh ed. Paris, 1995.

McCarthy, Michael L. "Retroactive Application of New Grounds for Divorce Under § 170 Domestic Relations Law." *Buffalo Law Review* 17 (1968): 902-13.

McClain, Linda C. "The Domain of Civil Virtue in a Good Society: Families, Schools, and Sex Equality." *Fordham Law Review* 69 (2001): 1617-66.

McCurdy, William E. "Divorce — A Suggested Approach with Particular Reference to Dissolution for Living Separate and Apart." *Vanderbilt Law Review* 9 (1956): 685-708.

Meilaender, Gilbert. *The Limits of Love: Some Theological Explorations.* University Park, Pa.: Pennsylvania State University Press, 1987.

Meiselman, Moshe. *Jewish Woman in Jewish Law.* New York: Ktav, 1978.

Melanchthon, Philip. *Apology of the Augsburg Confession.* In *The Book of Concord,* ed. Theodore G. Tappert. Philadelphia: Fortress, 1959.

Meyendorff, John. "Christian Marriage in Byzantium: The Canonical and Liturgical Tradition." Dumbarton Oaks Papers, number 44. Washington, D.C.: Dumbarton Oaks Research Library and Collection, 1990.

———. *Marriage: An Orthodox Perspective.* New York: St. Vladimir's Seminary Press, 1984.

Miller, Perry. *The New England Mind: The Seventeenth Century.* Boston: Beacon, 1961.

Milton, John. *The Doctrine and Discipline of Divorce* and *Tetrachordon.* In *The Complete Prose Works of John Milton,* gen. ed. Don M. Wolfe. Volume 2, ed. Ernest Sirluck. New Haven/London, 1959.

Molin, Jean-Baptiste, and Protais Mutembe. *Le rituel du mariage en France du XIIe au XVIe siècle.* Paris: Beauchesne, 1974.

Moraites, Demetrios. "Gamos." In *Threskeutike kai Hthike Egkuklopaideia,* ed. A. Martinos. Athens: Matinos Publications, 1964.

Moran, William. "The Ancient Near Eastern Background of the Love of God in Deuteronomy." *Catholic Biblical Quarterly* 25 (1963): 77-87.

Morgan, Edmund S. *The Puritan Family: Religion and Domestic Relations in Seventeenth-Century New England.* Rev. ed. New York: Harper and Row, 1966.

Morrison, Donna Ruane, and Mary Jo Coiro. "Parental Conflict and Marital Disruption: Do Children Benefit When High-Conflict Marriages Are Dissolved?" *Journal of Marriage and the Family* 61 (1999): 626-37.

Mottahedeh, Roy P. *The Mantle of the Prophet: Religion and Politics in Iran.* New York: Simon and Schuster, 1985.

Muhammad Jawad Maghniyah. *Al-Fiqh ʿala al-Madhahib al-Khamsah.* Sixth ed. Beirut, 1969.

Muhammad Rashid Rida. *Huquq Al-Nisa' Fi Al-Islam.* Repr. ed. Beirut, 1975.

Murray, John S. "Improving Parent-Child Relationships within the Divorced Family: A Call for Legal Reform." *University of Michigan Journal of Law Reform* 19 (1986): 563-600.

Nadel, Edward S. "A Bad Marriage: Jewish Divorce and the First Amendment." *Cardozo Women's Law Journal* 2 (1995): 131-72.

Nichols, James Hastings. *Democracy and the Churches.* Philadelphia: Westminster, 1946.

Nichols, Joel A. "Louisiana's Covenant Marriage Law: A First Step Toward a More Robust Pluralism in Marriage and Divorce Law." *Emory Law Journal* 47 (1998): 929-1001.

Nock, Steven L. "Turn-Taking As Rational Behavior." *Social Science Research* 27 (1998): 235-44.

Nock, Steven L., and Margaret F. Brinig. "Weak Men and Disorderly Women: Divorce and the Division of Labor." In *The Law and Economics of Marriage and Divorce,* ed. Antony W. Dnes and Robert Rowthorn. Cambridge: Cambridge University Press, 2002.

Nock, Steven L., Laura Sanchez, and James D. Wright. "Intimate Equity: The Early Years of Covenant and Standard Marriages." Draft presented at the annual meeting of the Population Association of America, Minneapolis, Minn., May 2003.

Nock, Steven L., Laura Sanchez, Julia Wilson, and James D. Wright. "Commitment and Dependency in Marriage." *Journal of Marriage and the Family* 57 (1995): 503-14.

———. "Covenant Marriage Turns Five Years Old." *Michigan Journal of Gender and Law* 10 (2003): 169-88.

Novak, David. *Covenantal Rights: A Study in Jewish Political Theory.* Princeton, N.J.: Princeton University Press, 2000.

———. *Halakhah in a Theological Dimension.* Chico, Calif.: Scholars Press, 1985.

———. *The Image of the Non-Jew in Judaism.* New York: Edward Mellen, 1983.

———. *Jewish Social Ethics.* New York: Oxford University Press, 1992.

———. "The Marital Status of Jews Married under Non-Jewish Auspices." *Jewish Law Association Studies* I, ed. B. S. Jackson. Chico, Calif.: Scholars Press, 1985.

———. *Natural Law in Judaism.* Cambridge: Cambridge University Press, 1998.

Omar Rida Kahalah. *A'lam al-Nisa' fi 'Alamay al-Arab wa al-Islam.* 5 vols. Beirut, 1977.

Padovano, Anthony T. "Marriage: The Most Noble of Human Achievements." *Catholic World* 238 (May 1, 1995): 140.

Palmer, Paul F. "Christian Marriage: Contract or Covenant." *Theological Studies* 33 (1972): 617-65.

Parker Society, eds. *The Two Liturgies.* Cambridge: Printed at the University Press, 1844.

Parkman, Allen. "The Importance of Gifts in Marriage." *Economic Inquiry* 42 (2004): 483-95.

Perkins, William. *Christian Oeconomie.* Vol. 3 of William Perkins' *Workes,* 3 vols. Cambridge, 1609.

Picata, Amy Mehraban. "Health Consequences of Marriage for the Retirement Years." *Journal of Family Issues* 21 (2000): 559-86.

Pollard, A. W., and G. R. Redgrave. *A Short-Title Catalogue of Books Printed in England, Scotland, and Ireland, and of English Books Printed Abroad 1475-1640.* London: Bibliographical Society, 1926.

Porter, Muriel. *Sex, Marriage, and the Church: Patterns of Change.* North Blackburn, Australia: Dove, 1996.

Posner, Eric A. "The Regulation of Groups: The Influence of Legal and Nonlegal Sanctions on Collective Action." *University of Chicago Law Review* 63 (1996): 133-98.

Posner, Richard A. *Aging and Old Age.* Chicago: University of Chicago Press, 1995.

Post, Stephen. *Spheres of Love: Toward a New Ethics of the Family.* Dallas: Southern Methodist University Press, 1994.

Pricke, Robert. *The Doctrine of Superioritie, and of Subjection.* London, 1609.

Quaisi, Ghada G. "Religious Marriage Contracts: Judicial Enforcement of Mahar Agreements in American Courts." *Journal of Law and Religion* 15 (2000-2001): 67-82.

al-Qurra Daghi, Ali M. A. *Mabda' al-Ridha fi al-'Uqud.* Beirut, 1985.

Ramsey, Paul. "Human Sexuality in the History of Redemption." In *The Ethics of St. Augustine,* ed. William S. Babcock. Atlanta: Scholars, 1991.

Rasmussen, Eric, and Jeffrey Evans Stake. "Lifting the Veil of Ignorance: Personalizing the Marriage Contract." *Indiana Law Journal* 73 (1998): 453-502.

al-Razi, Muhammad Fakhr al-Din. *Tafsir al-Fakhr al-Razi.* Beirut, 1985.

Regan, Milton C. *Alone Together: Love and the Meaning of Marriage.* New York: Oxford University Press, 1999.

Reinhart, Kevin. *Before Revelation: The Boundaries of Muslim Moral Thought.* Albany: State University of New York Press, 1995.

Reynolds, Philip Lyndon. *Marriage in the Western Church: The Christianization of Marriage during the Patistric and Early Medieval Periods.* Leiden: E. J. Brill, 1994.

Reynolds, Philip Lyndon, and John Witte, Jr., eds. *To Have and to Hold: Marrying and Its Documentation in Western Christendom, 400-1600.* Cambridge/New York: Cambridge University Press, forthcoming 2006.

Rheinstein, Max. "The Law of Family and Succession." In *Civil Law in the Modern World,* ed. A. N. Yiannopoulos. Baton Rouge: Louisiana State University Press, 1965.

Rida, Muhammad Rashid. *Huquq al-Nisa' Fi al-Islam.* Reprint ed. Beirut: al-Maktab al-Islami, 1975.

Riley, Glenda. *The Female Frontier: A Comparative View of Women on the Prairie and the Plains.* Lawrence: University Press of Kansas, 1988.

Ritzer, Korbinian. *Formen, Riten und Religiöses Brauchtum der Eheschliessung in den Christlichen Kirchen des Ersten Jahrtausends.* Münster: Aschendorffsche, 1962.

Roberts, Alexander, and James Donaldson, eds. *The Ante-Nicene Fathers.* 10 vols. Buffalo: Christian Literature Publishing, 1885-96.

Roberts, William P. "The Family As Domestic Church: Contemporary Implications." In *Christian Marriage and Family: Contemporary Theological and Pastoral Perspectives,* ed. Michael G. Lawler and William P. Roberts. Collegeville: Liturgical Press, 1996.

Rogers, W. C. *A Treatise on the Law of Domestic Relations.* Chicago: T. H. Flood, 1899.

Sacks, Jonathan. "Social Contract or Social Covenant." *Policy Review* (July/August, 1996): 54-57.

Samuel, Cynthia. "Letter from Louisiana: An Obituary for Forced Heirship and a Birth Announcement for Covenant Marriage." *Tulane European and Civil Law Forum* 12 (1998): 183-94.

Sanchez, Laura A. "Social and Demographic Factors Associated with Couples' Choice between Covenant and Standard Marriage in Louisiana." Draft presented at the annual meeting of the Southern Sociological Society in Atlanta, Ga., May 2002.

Sander, William. "Catholicism and Marriage in the United States." *Demography* 30 (1993): 373.

al-Sanhuri, Abd a-Razzaq. *Massadir al-Haqq fi al-Fiqh al-Islami.* Beirut, 1953-1954.

al-Sarakhsi, Muhammad bin Ahmad. *Kitab al-Mabsut.* 30 vols. Beirut, 1968.

Sayer, Liana C., and Suzanne M. Bianchi. "Women's Economic Independence and the Probability of Divorce: A Review and Examination." *Journal of Family Issues* 21 (2000): 906-43.

Schaff, Philip, ed. *A Select Library of the Nicene and Post-Nicene Fathers,* first series. 14 vols. New York: Scribners, 1886-89.

Scherman, Nosson, ed. *The Complete Artscroll Siddur.* Rabbinical Council of America Edition. New York: Mesorah Publications, 1995.

Schulz, Fritz. *Classical Roman Law.* Oxford: Clarendon Press, 1951.

Scoles, E., P. Hay, P. Borchers, and S. Symeonides. *Conflict of Laws.* Fourth ed. St. Paul, Minn.: Thomson/West, 2004.

Scott, Elizabeth S., and Robert E. Scott. "Marriage As Relational Contract." *Virginia Law Review* 84 (1998): 1225-1334.

Scott, Patti A. "New York Divorce Law and the Religion Clauses: An Unconstitutional Exorcism of the Jewish Get Laws." *Seton Hall Constitutional Law Journal* 6 (summer 1996): 1117-89.

Searle, Mark, and Kenneth W. Stevenson. *Documents of the Marriage Liturgy.* Collegeville, Minn.: Liturgical Press, 1992.

al-Shawkani, Muhammad Ibn Ali. *Fath al-Qadir.* Beirut: Dar al-Khayr, 1992.

al-Shawkani, Muhammad Ibn Ali Muhammad. *Nayl Al-Awtar.* 9 vols. Beirut, 1973.

Sherwood, Yvonne. *The Prostitute and the Prophet: Hosea's Marriage in Literary Theoretical Perspective.* Sheffield: Sheffield Academic Press, 1996.

al-Sijistani, Abu Dawud Sulayman Ibn al-Ash'ath. *Sunan Abu Dawud.* Beirut, 1969.

Silbaugh, Katherine T. "Marriage Contracts and the Family Economy." *Northwestern University Law Review* 93 (1998): 65-144.

Singer, Jana B. "Alimony and Efficiency: The Gendered Costs and Benefits of the Economic Justification for Alimony." *Georgetown Law Journal* 82 (1994): 2423-42.

———. "Divorce Reform and Gender Justice." *North Carolina Law Review* 67 (1987): 1103-22.

Smidt, Corwin, ed. *Religion As Social Capital: Producing the Common Good.* Waco, Tex.: Baylor University Press, 2003.

Smock, Pamela J., and Sanjiv Gupta. "Cohabitation in Contemporary North America." In *Just Living Together: Implications of Cohabitation on Families, Children, and Social Policy,* ed. Alan Booth and Ann C. Crouter. Mahwah, N.J.: Erlbaum, 2002.

South, Scott J., and Glenna Spitze. "Determinants of Divorce over the Marital Life Course." *American Sociological Review* 51 (1986): 583-90.

Spaht, Katherine Shaw. "For the Sake of the Children: Recapturing the Meaning of Marriage." *Notre Dame Law Review* 73 (1998): 1547-80.

———. "Forced Heirship Changes: The Regrettable 'Revolution' Completed." *Louisiana Law Review* 57 (1996): 55-146.

———. "Louisiana's Covenant Marriage: Social Analysis and Legal Implications." *Louisiana Law Review* 59 (1998): 63-130.

———. "Revolution and Counter Revolution: The Future of Marriage in the Law." *Loyola Law Review* 49 (2003): 1-78.

———. "What's Become of Louisiana's Covenant Marriage through the Eyes of Social Scientists." *Loyola Law Review* 47 (2001): 709-28.

———. "Why Covenant Marriage May Prove Effective As a Response to the Culture of Divorce." In *Revitalizing the Institution of Marriage for the Twenty-First Century: An Agenda for Strengthening Marriage,* ed. Alan Hawkins, Lynn D. Wardle, and David Orgon Coolidge. Westport, Conn.: Praeger, 2002.

Spaht, Katherine Shaw, and Symeon C. Symeonides. "Covenant Marriage and the Law of Conflicts of Laws." *Creighton Law Review* 32 (1999): 1085-1120.

Spectorsky, Susan A. *Chapters on Marriage and Divorce: Responses of Ibn Hanbal and Ibn Rahwayh*. Austin: University of Texas Press, 1993.

Spidlik, Paul, compiler. *Drinking from the Hidden Fountain: A Patristic Breviary*. Trans. Paul Drake. Cistercian Studies Series no. 148. Kalamazoo, Mich.: Cistercian Publications, 1994.

St. Exupery, Antoine de. *The Little Prince*. Trans. Katherine Woods. New York: Reynal and Hitchcock, 1943.

Stackhouse, Max L. *Covenant and Commitments: Faith, Family, and Economic Life*. Louisville: Westminster John Knox, 1997.

———. "The Moral Roots of the Corporation." *Theology and Public Policy* 5, no. 1 (1993): 29-39.

Stackhouse, Max L., and Diane Obenchain, eds. *Christ and the Dominions of Civilization*. Vol. 3 of *God and Globalization*. Harrisburg, Pa.: Trinity Press International, 2002.

Stake, Jeffery Evans. "Paternalism in the Law of Marriage." *Indiana Law Journal* 74 (1999): 801-18.

Stevenson, Kenneth W. *Nuptial Blessing: A Study of Christian Marriage Rites*. New York: Oxford University Press, 1982.

Story, Joseph. *Commentaries on the Conflict of Laws, Foreign and Domestic, in Regard to Contracts, Rights, and Remedies, and Especially in Regard to Marriages, Divorces, Wills, Successions, and Judgments*. Boston: Hilliard, Gray, and Company, 1834.

al-Tabari, Abu Ja'far. *Jami' al-Bayan fi Tafsir al-Qur'an*. 23 vols. Repr. of ninth cent. ed. Beirut, 1978.

Tipton, Steven M., and John Witte, Jr., eds. *Family Transformed: Religion, Values, and Society in American Life*. Washington, D.C.: Georgetown University Press, 2005.

Trembelas, Panagiotes N. *Mikron Euchologion. Tomos A'. Ai Akolouthvai kai Taxeis Mnestron kai Gamou, Euchelaiou, Cheirotonion kai Baptismatos Kata tous en Athenais Kodikas*. Athens, 1950.

Turbanti, Giovanni. *Un Concilio per il Mundo Moderno: La Redazione della Costituzione Pastorale 'Gaudium et Spes' del Vaticano secundo*. Bologna: Il Mulino, 2000.

Van den Eynde, D. *Les définitions des sacrements pendant la première période de la théologie scholastique*. Rome: Antonianum, 1950.

Van Leeuwen, Mary Stewart. "Faith, Feminism, and the Family in an Age of Globalization." In *Religion and the Powers of the Common Life*, ed. Max L. Stackhouse and Peter Paris, vol. 1 of the God and Globalization series. Harrisburg, Pa.: Trinity Press International, 2000.

Van Leeuwen, Mary Stewart, et al. *After Eden: Facing the Challenge of Gender Reconciliation*. Grand Rapids: Eerdmans, 1993.

Vernier, Chester G. *American Family Law*. 5 vols. Stanford, Calif.: Stanford University Press, 1931-1938.

Vogel, Frank E. *Islamic Law and Finance: Religion, Risk, and Return*. The Hague, 1998.

Von Holzhausen, Fr. John, and Fr. Michael Gelsinger, trans., Fr. N. M. Vaporis, ed. *An Orthodox Prayer Book*. Brookline, Mass.: Holy Cross Orthodox Press, 1977.

Vöörbus, A. A. *Celibacy, A Requirement for Admission to Baptism in the Syrian Church*. Stockholm, 1951.

Waite, Linda J., et al. *Does Divorce Make People Happy? Findings from a Study of Unhappy Marriages.* New York: Institute for American Values, 2002.

Wait, Linda J., Gus W. Haggstrom, and David E. Kanouse. "The Consequences of Parenthood for the Marital Stability of Young Adults." *American Sociological Review* 50 (1985): 850.

Waite, Linda J., and Kara Joyner. "Emotional Satisfaction and Physical Pleasure in Sexual Unions: Time Horizon, Sexual Behavior, and Sexual Exclusivity." *Journal of Marriage and Family* 63 (2001): 247-64.

Walker, Williston. *A History of the Christian Church.* Rev. ed. New York: Scribner, 1959.

Wallerstein, Judith, and Sandra Blakeslee. *Second Chances: Men, Women, and Children a Decade After Divorce.* Fifteenth anniversary ed. Boston: Houghton Mifflin, 2004.

Wallerstein, Judith, Julia Lewis, and Sandra Blakeslee. *The Unexpected Legacy of Divorce.* New York: Hyperion, 2000.

Walzer, Michael. *The Revolution of the Saints: A Study in the Origins of Radical Politics.* Cambridge: Harvard University Press, 1965.

Ware, Leland B. "Invisible Walls: An Examination of the Legal Strategy of the Restrictive Covenant Cases." *Washington University Law Quarterly* 67 (1989): 737-72.

Warmflash, Lawrence M. "The New York Approach to Enforcing Religious Marriage Contracts." *Brooklyn Law Review* 50 (1984): 229-54.

Wax, Amy L. "Bargaining in the Shadow of the Market: Is There a Future for Egalitarian Marriage?" *Virginia Law Review* 84 (1997): 509-672.

al-Wazir, Zayd Ibn Ali. *Al-Fardiyah: Bahth fi Azmat al-Fiqh al-Fardi al-Siyasi 'inda al-Muslimin.* Virginia: Yemen Heritage and Research Center, 2000.

Weber, Max. *The Protestant Ethic and the Spirit of Capitalism.* Second Roxbury ed. Trans. Talcott Parsons. Los Angeles: Roxbury, 1998.

Weintraub, Russell J. *Commentary on the Conflict of Laws.* Fourth ed. New York: Foundation, 2001.

Weir, David A. *Early New England: A Covenanted Society.* Grand Rapids: Eerdmans, 2005.

Weiser, Artur, and K. Elliger. *Das Buch der zwölf Kleinen Propheten.* Göttingen: Vandenhoeck and Ruprecht, 1967.

Wesley, John. *The Sunday Service of the Methodists in North America, with Other Occasional Services.* Nashville: Methodist Publishing House, 1792.

Whatley, William. *A Bride-Bush; or, A Wedding Sermon.* London: Imprinted by Felix Kyngston for Thomas Man, 1617.

Whitehead, Barbara Dafoe. *The Divorce Culture.* New York: Alfred A. Knopf, 1997.

Wilcox, Bradford W. *Sacred Vows, Public Purposes: Religion, the Marriage Movement and Marriage Policy.* Washington, D.C.: The Pew Forum on Religion and Public Life, 2002.

Wilson, Barbara F., and Sally C. Clarke. "Remarriages: A Demographic Profile." *Journal of Family Issues* 13 (1992): 123.

Witte, John, Jr. *An Apt and Cheerful Conversation on Marriage.* Atlanta: Emory University, 2001.

———. *From Sacrament to Contract: Marriage, Religion, and Law in the Western Tradition.* Louisville: Westminster John Knox, 1997.

———. "The Goods and Goals of Marriage." In *Marriage, Health, and the Professions,* ed.

John Wall, Don S. Browning, William J. Doherty, and Stephen Post. Grand Rapids: Eerdmans, 2002.

————. *Law and Protestantism: The Legal Teachings of the Lutheran Reformation.* Cambridge: Cambridge University Press, 2002.

————. *Religion and the American Constitutional Experiment: Essential Rights and Liberties.* Second ed. Boulder, Colo.: Westview, 2005.

Witte, John, Jr., and Robert M. Kingdon. *Sex, Marriage, and Family Life in John Calvin's Geneva,* vol. 1: *Courtship, Engagement, and Marriage.* Grand Rapids: Eerdmans, 2005.

Witte, John, Jr., and Richard C. Martin, eds. *Sharing the Book: Religious Perspectives on the Rights and Wrongs of Proselytism.* Maryknoll, N.Y.: Orbis, 1999.

Wolfe, Alan. *Moral Freedom: The Search for Virtue in a World of Choice.* New York: W. W. Norton, 2001.

Wolfe, Christopher. "The Marriage of Your Choice." *First Things* (February 1995): 37-41.

Wolff, Hans W. *Hosea: A Commentary on the Book of the Prophet Hosea.* Philadelphia: Fortress, 1974.

Woodhouse, A. S. P., ed. *Puritanism and Liberty.* Second ed. Chicago: University of Chicago, 1950.

Yates, Wilson. "The Protestant View of Marriage." *Journal of Ecumenical Studies* 22 (1985): 41-54.

Yee, Gale A. *Composition and Tradition in the Book of Hosea: A Redaction Critical Investigation.* Atlanta: Scholars Press, 1987.

al-Zabidi, Muhammad Murtadha. *Taj al-'Arus.* Eighteenth cent. repr. Beirut, n.d.

Zeliger, Gerald. "Should Clergy Endorse 'Living in Sin'?" *USA Today* (July 24, 2003): 13A.

Zion, James W., Elsie V. Zion, and Hozho Sokee. "Stay Together Nicely: Domestic Violence under Navajo Common Law." *Arizona State Law Journal* 25 (1991): 407-26.

Zirar, Malakah Yusuf. *Mawsu'at al-Zawaj wa Al-'Alaqah al-Zawjiyah.* Cairo, 2000.

Zornberg, Lisa. "Beyond the Constitution: Is the New York Get Legislation Good Law?" *Pace Law Review* 15 (1995): 703-84.

al-Zuhayli, Wihbah. *Al-Fiqh al-Islami wa Adillatuhu.* Beirut: Dar al-Fikr al-Mu'asser, 1997.

# Index